Short-term/Working Memory

A Special Issue of
The International Journal of Psychology

Edited by

Ian Neath
Purdue University, West Lafayette, IN, USA

Gordon D.A. Brown
University of Warwick, UK

Marie Poirer and Claudette Fortin
Université Laval, Québec, Canada

LONDON AND NEW YORK

First published 1999 by Psychology Press

Published 2018 by Routledge
2 Park Square, Milton Park, Abingdon, Oxon OX14 4RN
52 Vanderbilt Avenue, New York, NY 10017

First issued in paperback 2018

Routledge is an imprint of the Taylor & Francis Group, an informa business

Copyright © 1999 Taylor & Francis

All rights reserved. No part of this book may be reprinted or reproduced or utilised in any form or by any electronic, mechanical, or other means, now known or hereafter invented, including photocopying and recording, or in any information storage or retrieval system, without permission in writing from the publishers.

Notice:
Product or corporate names may be trademarks or registered trademarks, and are used only for identification and explanation without intent to infringe.

Typeset by J&L Composition Ltd, Filey, North Yorkshire

ISBN 13: 978-1-138-88305-5 (pbk)
ISBN 13: 978-0-86377-653-3 (hbk)

Contents*

Short-term/Working Memory: An Overview — 273
Ian Neath, Gordon D.A. Brown, Marie Poirier, and Claudette Fortin

Item Interference and Time Delays in Working Memory: Immediate Serial Recall — 276
Barbara Anne Dosher

Determinants of Short-term Forgetting: Decay, Retroactive Interference or Proactive Interference? — 285
Georgina Anne Tolan and Gerald Tehan

Comparing Short-term Memory and Memory for Rapidly Presented Visual Stimuli — 293
Veronika Coltheart

Phonological Similarity and Trace Degradation in the Serial Recall Task: When CAT Helps RAT, but not MAN — 301
Anthony B. Fallon, Kim Groves, and Gerald Tehan

Short-term Memory in Time Interval Production — 308
Claudette Fortin

Localizing Localization: The Role of Working Memory in Auditory Localization — 317
Natasha Merat, John A. Groeger, and Deborah J. Withington

Attentional Selectivity in Short-term Memory: Similarity of Process, not Similarity of Content, Determines Disruption — 322
William Macken, Sébastien Tremblay, David Alford, and Dylan Jones

The Effect of Noise on Memory for Spoken Syllables — 328
Aimée M. Surprenant

Semantic Contribution to Immediate Serial Recall Using an Unlimited Set of Items: Evidence for a Multi-level Capacity View of Short-term Memory — 334
Nicole Caza and Sylvie Belleville

Effects of Word Processing and Short-term Memory Deficits on Verbal Learning: Evidence from Aphasia — 339
Nadine Martin and Eleanor M. Saffran

The Influence of Long-term Memory Factors on Immediate Serial Recall: An Item and Order Analysis — 347
Jean Saint-Aubin and Marie Poirier

The Microanalysis of Memory Span and Its Development in Childhood — 353
Nelson Cowan, J. Scott Saults, Lara D. Nugent, and Emily M. Elliott

Measuring Memory Span — 359
John A. Groeger, David Field, and Sean M. Hammond

Working Memory and Spoken Language Comprehension in Young Children — 364
Anne-Marie Adams, Lorna Bourke, and Catherine Willis

Verbal and Spatial Short-term Memory: Two Sources of Developmental Evidence Consistent with Common Underlying Processes — 374
Y.M. Lisa Chuah and Murray T. Maybery

Estimating the Capacity of Phonological Short-term Memory — 378
Susan E. Gathercole and Susan J. Pickering

Phonological Short-term Memory and Foreign Language Learning — 383
Elvira V. Masoura and Susan E. Gathercole

The Development of Memory for Serial Order: A Temporal-contextual Distinctiveness Model — 389
Gordon D.A. Brown, Janet I. Vousden, Teresa McCormack, and Charles Hulme

Coding Position in Short-term Memory *Richard N.A. Henson*	403
Modelling The Disruptive Effects of Irrelevant Speech on Order Information *Ian Neath*	410
Testing the Idea of Distinct Storage Mechanisms in Memory *Donald Laming*	419
Item and Associative Interactions in Short-term Memory: Multiple Memory Systems? *Bennet Murdock*	427
Redintegration and Response Suppression in Serial Recall: A Dynamic Network Model *Stephan Lewandowsky*	434
Redintegration and the Useful Lifetime of the Verbal Memory Representation *Richard Schweickert, Shengbao Chen, and Marie Poirier*	447
The Dimensionality of Memory Strength Between Levels of Both Serial Position and Word Frequency Category *Matthew Duncan*	454
Power Function Forgetting Curves as an Emergent Property of Biologically Plausible Neural Network Models *Sverker Sikström*	460
Subject Index	465

---

* This book is also a special issue of the *International Journal of Psychology* which forms Issues 5 and 6 of Volume 34 (1999). The page numbers run on from Issue 4 of the journal and so will begin on page 273.

Short-term/Working Memory: An Overview

Ian Neath
Purdue University, West Lafayette, IN, USA

Gordon D.A. Brown
University of Warwick, UK

Marie Poirier and Claudette Fortin
Université Laval, Québec, Canada

This special issue of the *International Journal of Psychology* has its origins in the Quebec 98 Conference on Short-Term Memory, held in Quebec City, Canada, in June 1998. Following this conference, participants were invited to submit contributions based on, and expanding upon, their presentations. The enthusiastic response made it possible to collect the exciting selection of papers that you will find here. Because of the finite space available, the editors and reviewers were faced with the difficult problem of selecting only a limited number of the excellent papers that were submitted. The outcome of this process is this special issue, which we believe provides an up-to-date overview of current research on short-term/working memory, including the challenges, controversies, and recent theoretical advances in this field.

The terms "short-term memory" and "working memory" encompass a wide variety of ideas about how people process, retain, and retrieve information. The common thread through all the different conceptions is the study of how people remember over the short term; indeed, a strength of the current issue lies in the diversity of approaches to the study of memory that it encompasses. Many of the papers adopt the working memory framework of Baddeley and his colleagues (Baddeley, 1986; Baddeley & Hitch, 1974, 1994), with some emphasizing the mnemonic aspects of the framework and others focusing on working memory's attentional role. Some use a more traditional notion of short-term memory and others present new models or extend models from other domains to the issue of memory over the short-term. A handful even suggest that models of memory originally designed to explain memory over the long term may also explain short-term memory phenomena. As Crowder (1983, 1989) noted, simply demonstrating memory over the short-term does not necessarily mean that we have a distinct short-term memory system.

The papers are loosely clustered around several themes, beginning with the cause of forgetting. An as yet unresolved debate concerns whether the loss of information over the short-term is due to decay (Peterson & Peterson, 1959; Cowan, Saults, & Nugent, 1997) or interference (Keppel & Underwood, 1962; Neath & Nairne, 1995). Both Dosher (this issue) and Tolan and Humphreys (this issue) examine the role that interference—from a variety of different causes—plays in the loss of information when memory is assessed either immediately or after a short delay. Rehearsal, including its role as a possible means of recoding information and offsetting the deleterious effects of the passage of time, has played a central role in theories of short-term and working memory (Atkinson & Shiffrin, 1968; Glanzer, 1972; Baddeley, 1986). Coltheart (this issue) explores the similarities between the rapid serial visual presentation (RSVP) paradigm, in which rehearsal during presentation is precluded, and more standard immediate serial recall tests. Fallon, Groves, and Tehan (this issue) look at the extent to which phonological coding can still be present even after relatively long periods of distractor activity, explicitly bringing together the notions of coding, decay and rehearsal.

Views of short-term or working memory have long included the role of attention and the distribution of resources to coordinate various tasks (Broadbent, 1958); the second set of papers concentrate on this function. Fortin (this issue) examines the timing capabilities exhibited by people while they are engaged in secondary tasks. Merat, Groeger, and Withington (this issue) use secondary tasks to determine which components of working memory are associated with sound localization. Macken, Tremblay, and Jones (this issue) review the literature on the disruption of memory due to irrelevant sounds and discuss which factors are implicated in this effect. Surprenant (this issue) looks at the effects of irrelevant noise on memory for spoken items, rather than the more commonly used visually-presented materials, and compares capacity and processing explanations.

Although most theorists posit a primary role for phonological processing in short-term/working memory, semantic information can also affect performance over the short term (Shulman, 1972). The next set of papers look at the contributions to short-term memory performance from sources usually associated with long-term memory. Caza and Belleville (this issue) carefully distinguish between lexical and semantic levels of representation and find contributions from both on short-term memory tasks. Martin and Saffran (this issue) demonstrate that long-term memory factors such as imageability and frequency, as well as certain linguistic relationships, can affect learning in aphasic subjects. Saint-Aubin and Poirier (this issue) examine how degraded phonological traces can be reconstructed through the use of long-term knowledge and conclude that the long-term memory factors produce results at odds with most current models of short-term memory.

A hallmark of early research into short-term memory was the magical number 7 ± 2 (Miller, 1956). One example of this apparent limit on performance is memory span, the number of items a person can immediately recall in order. Cowan, Saults, Nugent, and Elliott (this issue) examine why memory span increases as children develop and discuss the theoretical implications of measuring span using non-traditional measures. Groeger and Hammond (this issue) look at relationships between memory span and other tasks, parsing out those aspects of the task that are due to memory and those that rely on other aspects of cognition.

The concept of working memory has played an influential role in shaping how developmental changes in children are characterized, especially with regard to language acquisition (Gathercole & Baddeley, 1993). The next subset of papers looks at some of these developmental changes. Adams, Bourke, and Willis (this issue) examine spoken language comprehension in young children, especially the relationship among the components of working memory and other measures. Chuah and Mayberry (this issue) examine the relationship between verbal and spatial short-term memory performance in children, finding commonalities between the two developmental processes. Gathercole and Pickering (this issue) test phonological short-term memory for both words and nonwords using multiple tasks and discuss the validity of measures of phonological storage capacity. Masoura and Gathercole (this issue) investigate the role of phonological short-term memory in foreign language learning.

The study of how people represent order information is particularly important in the study of short-term/working memory given that measures such as memory span require the production of items in the correct order. The papers in the next cluster use simulation and computational models to examine in detail how item and order errors might be caused. Brown, Vousden, McCormack, and Hulme (this issue) apply a memory model originally designed to account for adult data to serial order data from children. The key mechanism for improvement during development is in representing items in a more temporally distinct fashion. Henson (this issue) develops a new model of how people store and retrieve a sequence of items in order that includes both temporal and positional factors. Neath (this issue) extends Nairne's (1990) feature model to include order information and demonstrates hwo the loss of item information can produce order errors.

Since the late 1950s, much work has been done that focuses on the proposition that short-term memory is separate from long-term memory (Atkinson & Shiffrin, 1968; Waugh & Norman, 1965). Two papers question this idea. Laming (this issue) analyzes single trial free recall data and finds that the quantitative conditions necessary to conclude that short-term memory is separate from long-term memory are not met. Murdock (this issue) demonstrates how TODAM, a model that assumes a single memory system, handles data from both long- and short-term paradigms.

A key issue in short-term/working memory research is redintegration, the process that disambiguates partially retrieved mnemonic information and results in an overt response. Lewandowsky (this issue) develops a dynamic network model of redintegration and response suppression that predicts both the accuracy and error data seen in serial recall and also the temporal dynamics of retrieval. Schweickert, Chen, and Poirier (this issue) also examine redintegration, analyzing data using a relatively simple—but powerful—multinomial processing tree model.

The last two papers return to more general issues and explore common characterizations of the memory process. Duncan (this issue) tests the assumption, common in many situations, that a global assessment of memory strength underlies memory judgements and discusses the extent to which the data support the idea that strength is unidimensional. Sverker (this issue) notes that whereas the typical forgetting curves follow a power function, many connectionist models do not predict this. He then develops a plausible neural network model that can demonstrate the power function forgetting curves commonly observed.

Are there any general conclusions that can be drawn regarding the state of the field? As organizers, one aspect of the conference that we particularly enjoyed, in addition to the pleasant surroundings of Quebec City, was the mixture of perspectives from around the world. It has long been clear in the study of short-term/working memory that different theoretical frameworks have been emphasized by researchers in different countries, although there has always been a healthy degree of cross-fertilization. An encouraging aspect of the papers in the present issue is the methodological eclecticism they employ: Various computational modelling techniques and many new experimental methodologies, including techniques designed to assess the role of proactive and retroactive interference in short-term memory tasks, are in evidence.

The present papers reflect good theoretical progress over the past decade. Recent years hve seen a much greater understanding of the nature of short-term memory tasks, and an increase in the range of sources being considered for effects. Thus many key effects observable in traditional short-term memory tasks are now attributed to retrieval-stage processes such as redintegration, proactive interference from previous trials, and interference or time-based forgetting during output delays in serial recall. A possibly discouraging aspect is that many findings in the short-term/working memory field have turned out to be due to details of the particular methodology employed, rather than reflecting fundamental principles of memory.

However, we can end on an optimistic note. The theoretical sophistication of models of short-term/working memory continues to increase year by year, and there are, for example, encouraging signs of convergence in models of short-term memory for serial order. Furthermore, there is an increasing understanding of the utility of short-term storage, combined with a willingness to look for common principles that may characterize memory storage and retrieval at many different time scales. We are confident that future years will see continued growth and progress of the field.

The collection of papers presented in this introduction is a reflection of the variety of the issues and approaches currently represented in short-term/working memory research. We hope that the reader will find this diversity as exciting and enlightening as we do.

REFERENCES

Atkinson, R.C., & Shiffrin, R.M. (1968). Human memory: A proposed system and its control processes. In K.W. Spence & J.T. Spence (Eds.), *The psychology of learning and motivation* (Vol. 2, pp. 89–195). New York: Academic Press.

Baddeley, A.D. (1986). *Working memory*. New York: Oxford University Pess.

Baddeley, A.D., & Hitch, G.J. (1974). Working memory. In G.H. Bower (Ed.), *The psychology of learning and motivation* (Vol. 8, pp. 47–89). New York: Academic Press.

Baddeley, A.D., & Hitch, G.J. (1994). Developments in the concept of working memory. *Neuropsychology, 8*, 485–493.

Broadbent, D.E. (1958). *Perception and communication*. New York: Pergamon.

Cowan, N., Saults, J.S., & Nugent, L.D. (1997). The role of absolute and relative amounts of time in forgetting within immediate memory: The case of tone-pitch comparisons. *Psychonomic Bulletin & Review, 4*, 393–397.

Crowder, R.G. (1983). The demise of short-term memory. *Acta Psychologica, 50*, 291–323.

Crowder, R.G. (1989). Modularity and dissociations in memory sytems. In H.L. Roediger & F.I.M. Craik (Eds.), *Varieties of memory and consciousness: Essays in honour of Endel Tulving* (pp. 271–294). Hillsdale, NJ: Lawrence Erlbaum Associates Inc.

Gathercole, S.E., & Baddeley, A.D. (1993). *Working memory and language*. Hove, UK: Lawrence Erlbaum Associates Ltd.

Glanzer, M. (1972). Storage mechanisms in recall. In G.H. Bower & J.T. Spence (Eds.), *The psychology of learning and motivation* (Vol. 5, pp. 129–193). New York: Acdemic Press.

Keppel, G., & Underwood, B.J. (1962). Proactive inhibition in short-term retention of single items. *Journal of Verbal Learning and Verbal Behavior, 1*, 153–161.

Miller, G.A. (1956). The magical number seven plus or minus two: Some limits on our capacity for processing information. *Psychological Review, 63*, 81–97.

Nairne, J.S. (1990). A feature model of immediate memory. *Memory & Cognition, 19*, 332–340.

Neath, I., & Nairne, J.S. (1995). Word-length effects in immediate memory: Overwriting trace decay theory. *Psychonomic Bulletin & Review, 2*, 429–441.

Peterson, L.R., & Peterson, M.J. (1959). Short-term retention of individual verbal items. *Journal of Experimental Psychology, 58*, 193–198.

Shulman, H.G. (1972). Semantic confusion errors in short-term memory. *Journal of Verbal Learning and Verbal Behavior, 11*, 221–227.

Waugh, N.C., & Norman, D.A. (1965). Primary memory. *Psychological Review, 72*, 89–104.

Item Interference and Time Delays in Working Memory: Immediate Serial Recall

Barbara Anne Dosher
University of California, Irvine, USA

Limitations on immediate recall span have been related by some to temporal limitations of an articulatory rehearsal loop (Baddeley, 1986), and by others to retroactive interference from subsequent items (Lewandowsky & Murdock, 1989; Neath & Nairne, 1995). In the current study, the number of intervening items and retention delays were partially decoupled by varying presentation rate and materials sets. Recently, memory span effects often attributed to temporal limits in rehearsal were shown to be directly related to the output delays during the act of recall (Dosher & Ma, 1998). A functional model of working memory provides a framework within which to evaluate the relative contributions of item interference and retention delays in the accuracy of recall at each serial position. Output delays during recall and interference from items during study were the primary factors in limiting recall, with small additional effects of time delays during study.

Les limites de l'empan, en rappel immédiat, ont été reliées à une limite temporelle de la boucle articulatoire (Baddeley, 1986) et aussi, à l'interférence rétroactive des items subséquents (Lewandowsky & Murdock, 1989; Neath & Nairne, 1995). Dans la présente étude, le nombre d'items interfèrent et les délais de rétention ont été manipulés en faisant varier le rythme de présentation et les ensembles d'items. Il a été récemment démontré que les effets d'empan mnémonique, souvent attribués aux limites temporelles de l'autorépétition, étaient directement reliés aux délais de production durant le rappel (Dosher & Ma, 1998). Un modèle de mémoire de travail fournit une structure permettant d'évaluer les contributions relatives de l'interférence des items et des délais de rétention dans la précision du rappel à chaque position sérielle. Les délais de production durant le rappel et l'interférence des items durant l'étude sont les principaux facteurs qui limitent le rappel.

INTERFERENCE AND TEMPORAL LIMITS IN WORKING MEMORY

Limits on working memory have been related in different theories either to item interference or to temporal limits. For example, Lewandowsky and Murdock (1989, p. 28), in introducing their model of short-term memory, state that "... relative to interference, [temporal] decay has been shown to be of little importance in forgetting." Similarly, Neath and Nairne (1995, p. 430) comment that "... forgetting ... is ... a particular form of retroactive interference and is not dependent on time per se ..." In contrast, the dominant model of working memory by Baddeley (1986, p. 178) posits a central role for temporal decay: "... the system resembles a tape recorder whose capacity is limited by time rather than by the amount of information or number of events." Models of working memory in general emphasize either item interference or temporal delays as a primary limitation on performance.

This paper provides a quantitative evaluation of the contributions of item interference and temporal delays in limiting memory span. First, the temporal limitations on immediate recall of Baddeley and colleagues (Baddeley, 1986) are recast as retention delays, including delays during recall output (Dosher & Ma, 1998). Second, a joint interference and delay model is evaluated (Dosher, 1999). The functional model relates performance accuracy at each list position to encoding strength, retroactive item interference, and nonspecific interference during delays at either input or output. The current experiment partially decouples items and time by manipulating rate of presentation and stimulus materials.

RECASTING TEMPORAL DELAYS IN RECALL

Limits on immediate memory are related by Baddeley and colleagues (Baddeley, 1986; Baddeley, Lewis, & Vallar, 1984; Baddeley, Thomson, & Buchanan, 1975) to the time to speak a list of items. Working memory span is said to correspond to the number of items that can be spoken in 1.5–2sec, a reflection of a time-limited subvocal rehearsal loop. However, ouput delays during

---

Requests for reprints should be addressed to Barbara Anne Dosher, Department of Cognitive Science, 3151 Social Science Plaza, University of California, Irvine, CA 92697-5100, USA (E-mail: bdosher@uci.edu).
This work was supported by Grant SBR-9396076 (NSF/AFOSR).

© 1999 International Union of Psychological Science

recall itself substantially exceed the hypothesized 2sec temporal limit, often extending to 4-6sec for a span-length list (Dosher, 1999; Dosher & Ma, 1998). Furthermore, output delays during recall have recently been shown to provide an equally good account of limits on span as pronunciation durations (Dosher, 1999; Dosher & Ma, 1998). Based on these findings, the temporal limits on immediate memory are recast not as limits on pronunciation duration, but rather as temporal limits on recall output.

The focus on output limits during recall follows earlier work: Schweickert and Boruff (1986) argued for the application of temporal limits to output delays. Cowan et al. (1992) found that words that take longer to say appearing early in a list reduce memory span, presumably due to increased output delays (see Cowan, 1992; Cowan, Keller, Hulme, Roodenrys, & Rack, 1994; Schweickert, McDaniel, & Riegler, 1994; Stigler, Lee, & Stevenson, 1986; for related work).

Retention delays during recall output are manipulated here by using three materials: digits, discriminable letters, and a matched word set (Dosher & Ma, 1998), which are approximately matched on phonemic discriminability and immediate recognition, yet are recalled at different rates: words more slowly than letters, letters more slowly than digits.

ITEMS VERSUS TIME IN IMMEDIATE RECOGNITION

In an elegant early study, Wickelgren (1970) contrasted the impact of intervening items and time in determining forgetting in immediate recognition. Twelve-item lists were presented at rates of 1, 2, or 4 words per second, and tested immediately. The forgetting functions of log d' versus item or time delay were linear, implying approximately exponential forgetting. However, neither delay measured in items nor delay measured in time accounted simply for Wickelgren's data. When delay was measured in items, the rate of forgetting was fastest for the 1 per second condition, which introduced longer times between study and test. When delay was measured in time, the rate of forgetting was fastest for the 4 per second condition, which introduced more items in a given time delay. Wickelgren concluded that both intervening items and retention interval were important in forgetting in short-term recognition. Unfortunately, recall does not lend itself to these simple tests of recognition. A model test is required.

FUNCTIONAL MODEL OF SHORT-TERM MEMORY

In order to evaluate the importance of items and time in forgetting for immediate serial recall, a functional model of working memory (an extension of Dosher, 1999) was tested. The experiment manipulated the stimulus materials and presentation rate. The data consist of accuracy of recall, Pr_{klmr}, in list position k, list length l, material m, and rate of presentation r. Encoding, forgetting, and successful recall are considered in turn.

Items are encoded during study with a strength (in position), α_{kr}, which depends only on list position k and presentation rate r. Input position effects are often hypothesized (Cohen & Grossberg, 1986; Dosher & Ma, 1998; McElree & Dosher, 1989, 1993; Wickelgren & Norman, 1966, 1971) and generally reflect primacy. In general, encoding strength might also depend on material; however, approximately equal encoding strengths have been previously demonstrated for the three tested materials (Dosher & Ma, 1998).

The focus of the current study is on mechanisms of forgetting. Loss in item strength (forgetting) may be the result of both specific interference from intervening items and nonspecific interference during the retention interval. Specific item interference is counted in the number of intervening items, and nonspecific interference is counted in time. Varying presentation rate manipulates the study component of the retention interval; varying materials manipulates the recall component of the retention interval. The functional model separately considers the items encoded after an item and the number of items recalled before the item. Retention delays are similarly divided into the time following the item during study and the time during recall before the item is produced. If l is the list length and k is the list position of a particular item, $(l-k)$ is the number of items following item k in the presentation phase, $(k-1)$ is the number of items preceding item k in (an accurate) recall, t_s is the time after item k during list presentation (reflecting presentation rate), and t_o is the time from the end of list presentation to the output of the kth item during recall.

Forgetting is assumed to be exponential in these four factors: $e^{-(\beta_{Is}(l-k)+\beta_{Io}(k-1)+\beta_{Ts}t_s+\beta_{To}t_o)}$. The values β_{Is}, β_{Io}, β_{Ts}, and β_{To} are parameters estimated from the data that quantify the relative importance of the four predictors of forgetting. The form $e^{-(\beta_{Ts}t_s+\beta_{To}t_o)}$ simply combines time loss in study and in output. The added factors $e^{-(\beta_{Is}(L-k)+\beta_{Io}(k-1))}$ are equivalent to an increased rate of loss during the encoding or the production of an item. Exponential loss provides a reasonable approximate description of the rapid forgetting over very short delays (e.g. Dosher, 1999; Dosher & Ma, 1998; Lewandowsky & Murdock, 1989; Rubin & Wenzel, 1996; Wickelgren, 1970).

The strength of the item (in position) at the time of its recall determines the accuracy of recall. If memory strength at the time of recall exceeds a threshold τ, then that item is recalled accurately. The strength distributions are assumed to be Gaussian ($\sigma = 1$), so the probability of correct recall is $1 - \Phi(\tau, \mu_{klmr}, \sigma)$, where Φ is the cumulative Gaussian probability associated with threshold τ for the relevant strength distribution, $klmr$. The notions of strength in position and recall threshold are both components of the Lewandowsky and Murdock (1989) model.

To summarize, the mean strength (in position) of an item in a particular serial position is a function of the initial encoding strength, the number of items between encoding and recall, and the amount of time between encoding and production; and strength is associated with a recall accuracy by a threshold function. For serial position k of list length l for material m and presentation rate r, the probability of correct recall is: $1-\Phi(\tau, \mu_{klmr} = \alpha_{kr} \, e^{-(\beta_{Is}(l-k)+\beta_{Io}(k-1)+\beta_{Ts}t_s+\beta_{To}t_o)}, \sigma = 1)$. This functional model of performance provides a quantitative evaluation of the importance of item- and time-related forgetting. The relationship of the functional model to other mechanistic accounts of working or immediate memory (e.g. Lewandowsky & Murdock, 1989; Neath & Nairne, 1995) is considered in the General Discussion.

EXPERIMENT

Method

Participants. Four native-English speakers with normal or corrected-to-normal vision and hearing each participated in 16 sessions of approximately 1 hour.

Stimuli. The three materials sets were: the 10 digits (0–9); a set of 10 discriminable letters from Tetzlaff (1988) (F, H, M, O, P, Q, R, W, X, Z); and a set of 10 words whose phonemic structure was based on the pseudodigits of Sperling, Parish, Pavel, and Desaulnier (1984) (HOW, GEM, KEY, FLU, TALL, SAYS, CUTS, VISIT, LIKE, MAIN). These sets were approximately matched for phonemic discriminability and immediate recognition effects (see Dosher & Ma, 1998).

Design. Each block of trials presented a single material, with four randomly ordered blocks per material per session. Each 12-trial block tested in random order 6 list lengths (4 to 9) at each of 2 presentation rates (0.571 and 0.857sec per item). Participants served in seven sessions of spoken recall, seven sessions of "keyboard" recall, in which the recall response was entered on a keyboard, and two pronunciation time sessions in which a visible list was read quickly aloud. The sample size per subject in each recall condition was 28. The current paper emphasizes the keyboard data.

Procedure. The sequence of events for each trial was as follows. A warning stimulus appeared for 1.0sec, then items of the list appeared in succession for either 0.571 or 0.857sec each. The last item was followed by a brief (0.143sec) mask string (#############), followed by recall. An interval of (1.3 list length + 1.43)sec was allowed for the recall response.

Participants were instructed to recall in the correct order. Keyboard responses were single keystrokes with the index finger of the dominant hand. Individual keys were marked with the digits, letters, and words, each in a separate region of the keyboard. For both keypress and spoken recall, recall ended with a terminator key (any key on the top row, all marked with "TT"). Keyboard recall allows the timing of each response and produces results which are similar to those for spoken recall (Dosher & Ma, 1998; see also Schiano & Watkins, 1981, for a pointing response).

In pronunciation duration (list-reading) sessions, the entire list appeared simultaneously, arrayed from the top to the bottom of the screen. The blocking structure, list lengths, etc. were otherwise identical to those of the recall session. The instructions were to take a breath, and then read the list from top to bottom quickly without pausing. The experimenter pressed a key at the beginning and the end of the reading production (Dosher & Ma, 1998).

Analyses. Only perfect recall was scored correct for span calculations. The proportions of correct responses in each position (correct item in the correct position) were also scored. Average times of response were based on all trials, correct and incorrect, of the correct length. Accurate trials are associated with faster response times and hence response times for correct trials systematically underestimate retention interval. (See Dosher & Ma, 1998, for a more detailed discussion.)

Span values, the list lengths (or output times) corresponding to 50% completely correct recall, were estimated by fitting an inverse cumulative Gaussian function on probability correct, $Pr = 1-\Phi(z|\mu,\sigma)$, where the mean μ is the span. All fits used a modified grid search method (Reed, 1976). The quality of model fits are reported in terms of a goodness of fit adjusted for the number of free parameters,

$$R^2 = \left[\sum_{i=1}^{n}(\hat{y}_i - \bar{y})^2/(N-k)\right]\left[\sum_{i=1}^{n}(y_i - \bar{y})^2/(N-1)\right]^{-1}$$

where the y_i are the observed values, $\hat{y}_i$ are the predicted values, $\bar{y}$ is the mean of the observed values, N is the total number of observations, and k is the number of free parameters in the model.

RESULTS

Span Data

The data on completely correct recall for the three materials parallel earlier observations of Dosher and Ma (1998). Although the materials were approximately matched in discriminability and in immediate recognition, recall accuracy differed for the three materials. For both spoken and keypress recall, the overall accuracy differed substantially with list length and materials, but slightly and nonsystematically for display rate (Fig. 1, Panels A–D). (One of the four participants had a relatively low span and hence zero accuracy and undefined recall times on list length nine and some list length eight conditions. The span data from all four participants are reported, but the figures represent data from the three

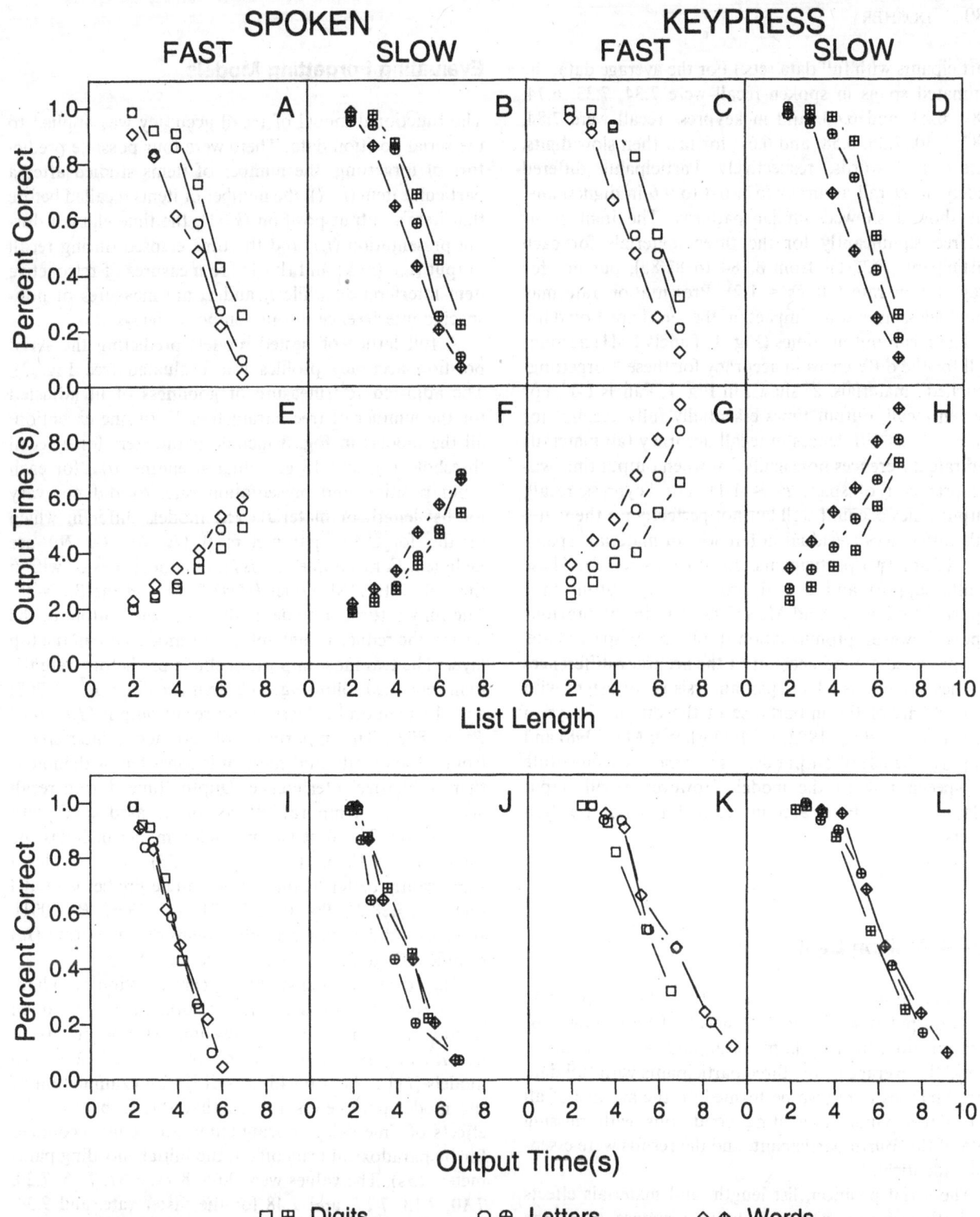

FIG. 1. Span (whole list) data for both spoken and keypress recall. Panels A–D show the percentage of completely correct recall for each of the three materials, separately for the two presentation rates as a function of list length. The item spans are highest for digits, intermediate for letters, and lowest for words. Panels E–H show the corresponding recall output times (times from the beginning of the recall interval to the final terminator key). Panels I–L show the percentage of completely correct recall graphed as a function of the recall output times. Recall output times essentially equate the performance for the three materials.

participants with full data sets.) For the average data, the estimated spans in spoken recall were 7.34, 7.33, 6.74, 6.89, 6.23, and 6.40, and in keypress recall were 7.84, 7.82, 7.30, 7.36, 6.58, and 6.61, for fast then slow digits, letters, and words, respectively. Participants differed widely in overall accuracy (e.g. 6.4 to 9.6 in digit spans) but showed showed similar patterns. The item spans differed significantly for the three materials for each participant [$F(2,31)$s from 8.284 to 87.85], but not for presentation rate (all Fs < 1.2). Presentation rate may nonetheless have some impact on the serial position data.

The recall output times (Fig. 1, Panels E–H) account well for the differences in accuracy for these "forgetting-matched" materials, as shown in Fig. 1, Panels I–L. For spoken recall, output times essentially fully account for the materials differences in recall accuracy (all materials and rate differences nonsignificant when output time was the predictor of span, Fs < 1.1). For keypress recall, output times account well but not perfectly for the materials differences (residual differences in materials spans, $P < .05$ for two participants, all other Fs < 1.2). These results support and extend properties of output time reported by Dosher and Ma (1998). (As in the previous report, however, pronunciation duration, or speech rate, also provided a good account of the accuracy differences for these materials.) This span analysis is consistent with prior claims of the importance of the output delays in recall (Cowan et al., 1992, 1994; Dosher & Ma, 1998) and supports the use of output delays in recall as a substitute for speech rate in the model. However, recall ouput delays alone cannot account fully for serial position effects.

Serial Position Data

Recall accuracy (Fig. 2, Panels A–F) and corresponding recall output times[1] (Fig. 2, Panels G–L) are shown for each position, list length, material, and rate. (The figure shows the average of the three participants with full data sets. Analyses were also performed on the average of all four participants eliminating conditions with missing data of the fourth participant, and the results were essentially identical.)

The serial position, list length, and materials effects on both accuracy and cumulative response times are quite obvious. Presentation rate effects are relatively subtle: The slow presentation rate may produce slightly flatter error profiles and initial recall responses are somewhat later in faster than in slower presentation conditions. Since these data are the subject of explicit modelling, statistical analyses are omitted for brevity.

---

[1] The flattening of the functions at the final list positions of long list lengths almost certainly reflect underestimates of true output delays since correct recall lengths are systematically associated with faster responding at the longest list lengths; this is a flaw in these data.

Evaluating Forgetting Models

The functional model of recall accuracy was applied to the serial position data. There were four possible predictors of forgetting: the number of items studied after a particular item ($l-k$), the number of items recalled before that item's output position ($k-1$), the time elapsed during presentation (t_s), and the time elapsed during recall output (t_o). (l–k) and (k–1) are measures of retroactive item interference, while t_s and t_o are measures of nonspecific interference during temporal delays.

A full lattice of nested models predicting the serial position accuracy profiles was evaluated (see Fig. 3). The adjusted R^2s measure of goodness of fit adjusted for the number of free parameters. With one exception, all the models in Fig. 3 include parameters for a recall threshold (τ), and 18 encoding strengths, α_{kr}, for each input position and presentation rate; αs did not vary for list length or material. The models differ in which of the forgetting parameters β (*Is*, *Io*, *Ts*, *To*) are included. For example, the *IsTsTo* model is nested within the fully saturated model *IsIoTsTo* (by setting $\beta_{Io} = 0$). The fully saturated model is shown at the bottom of the lattice; the reduced single-predictor models are in the top layer. The two most important single predictors were the items encoded following each item (*Is* alone, $R^2 = .768$) and the temporal delays during recall output (*To* alone, $R^2 = .802$). The importance of retroactive interference from subsequently studied items is consistent with models that emphasize interference. Ouptut time during recall accounts for temporal effects often associated with speech rate. The best two-predictor model includes the same two predictors (*IsTo*, $R^2 = .923$), and provides a significantly better fit than either single predictor model [$F(1,212)$ 428.21, $P < .001$; $F(1,212) = 333.67$, $P < .001$]. In no case did adding preceding items during output (*Io*) significantly improve the fit of the model.

Time delays during study (*Ts*) (presentation rate) have a modest impact on the serial position effects. Although adding *Ts* did not substantially improve the quality of fit—R^2s are essentially the same for the *IsTsTo* and *IsTo* models [$F(1,211) = 0.946$, $P > .15$]—an examination of the model parameters reveals that this is because the effects of time delays during study are being accounted for by paradoxical tradeoffs in the initial encoding parameters (αs). The values were 9.65, 8.71, 8.57, 7.75, 7.20, 7.10, 7.13, 7.17, and 7.48 for the faster rate, and 9.34, 8.28, 8.23, 7.69, 7.20, 7.16, 7.01, 7.43, and 7.44 for the slower rate. Thus, in this model fit and in fits excluding *Ts* as a factor in forgetting, the estimated αs for the slower presentation rate conditions are *lower* than those for the faster presentation rate, especially for early input positions where the *Ts* differ most. There is no principled reason for acquisition strength to be worse when study time is longer (presentation rate is slower). Thus, this represents *Ts* contamination of the estimates of initial encoding strength.

The best fitting and most parsimonious model of the serial position data assumed that the initial acquisition

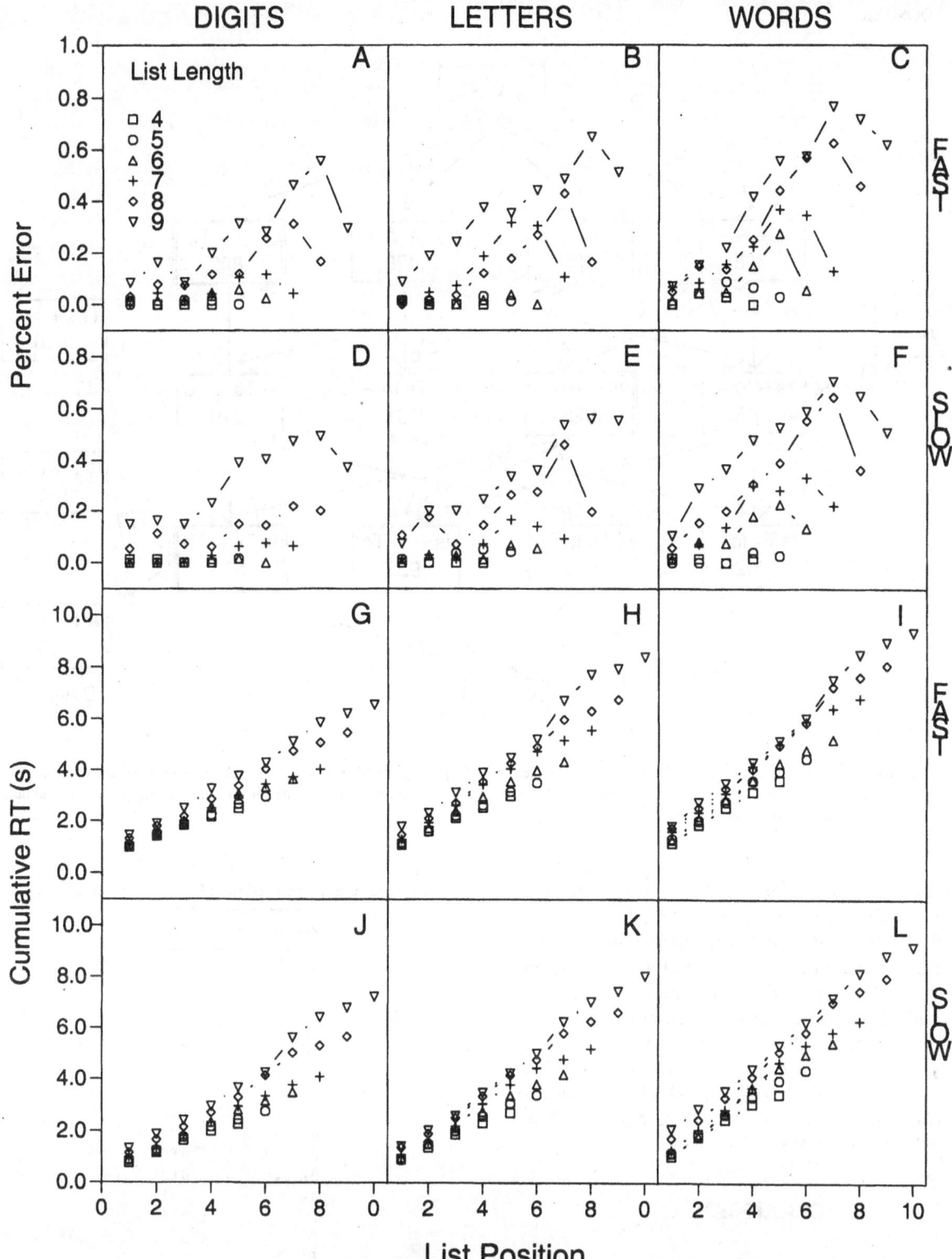

FIG. 2. Serial position data for keypress recall. Panels A–F show the percentage of error data for each serial position, list length, material, and presentation rate condition. Panels G–L show the corresponding cumulative output times during recall, the output time predictor in the functional model.

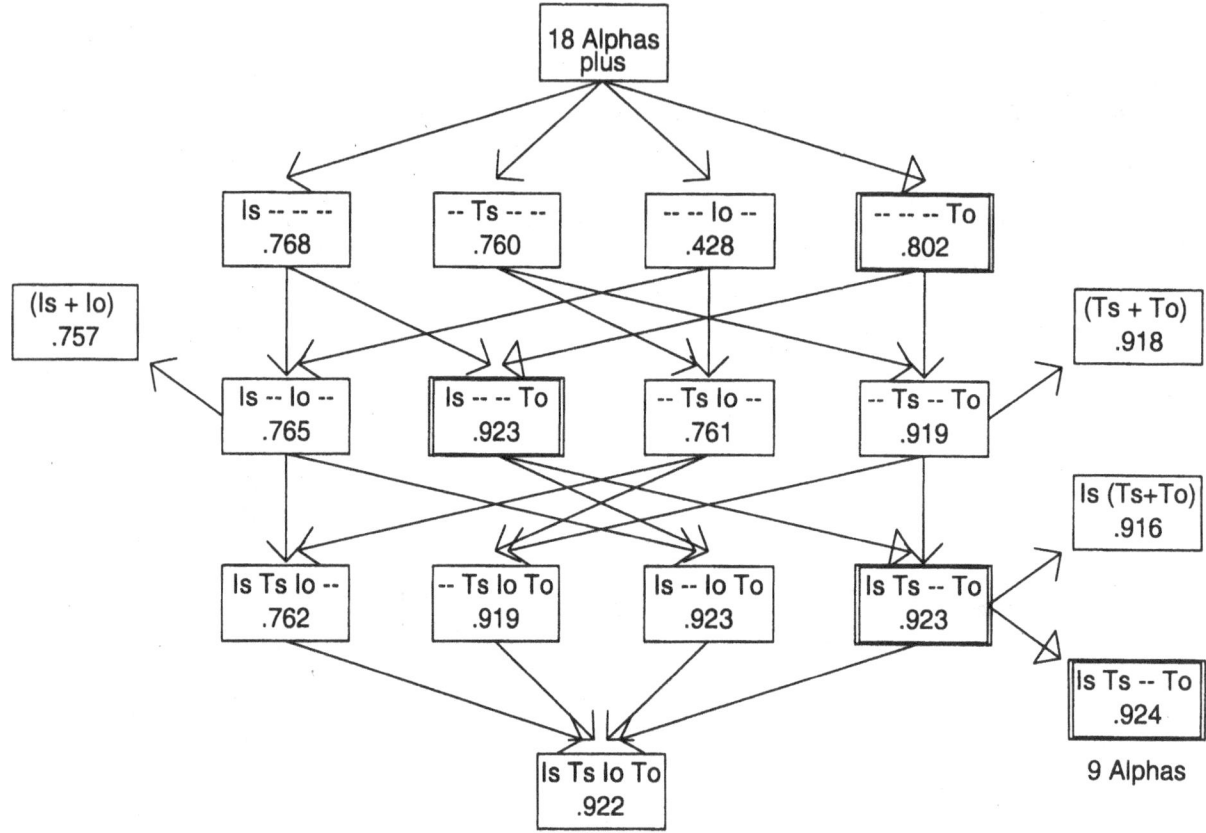

FIG. 3. The lattice of models tested in the evaluation of four predictors of forgetting: βs for the number of subsequent items during study, Is, the number of preceding items during recall, Io, the time following an item in study, Ts, and the output time for an item during recall, To. The numeric values are R^2 for those models. (See text for details.)

parameters were the same for the fast and slow presentation rates. This reduced the number of estimated parameters from 22 (18 αs, τ, and βs for Is, To, Ts) to 13 (9 αs, τ, and βs for Is, To, Ts), while providing almost as good an account of the data in raw r^2, and a slightly higher adjusted R^2 [$F(9,211) = 0.699$, n.s., for the comparison of the 13 and 22 parameter models]. The best estimates of the parameters of this model are shown in Table 1.[2] The primacy pattern exhibited by the αs is typical in similar models of short-term recognition (McElree & Dosher, 1989; Wickelgren, 1970; Wickelgren & Norman, 1966) and recall (Dosher & Ma, 1998).

DISCUSSION

This experiment evaluated the impact of items and time on forgetting in working memory. The number of intervening items was partially decoupled from time delays during recall by manipulations of presentation rate and materials. The analysis of span data (whole list accuracy) extended earlier results (Dosher & Ma, 1998), providing further support for recasting limits usually associated with speech rates (Baddeley, 1986) as instead reflecting output delays during recall.

An analysis of the serial position data using a functional model of recall (Dosher & Ma, 1998) indicated three contributing factors in loss of items (in position) from working memory: Retroactive interference from subsequent items during study and output delays in recall were major factors, while time delays during study were a secondary factor. The finding that both items and

TABLE 1
Parameter Estimates of Best Fitting Forgetting Model

Parameter	Value
α_1	9.44
α_2	8.40
α_3	8.30
α_4	7.62
α_5	7.13
α_6	6.99
α_7	6.90
α_8	7.10
α_9	7.24
β_{Is}	0.059
β_{Ts}	0.021
β_{To}	0.113
τ	3.00
R^2	.924

[2] The slight increase in α in position 9 reflects a list final recency effect not accounted for by the model. If encoding levels for the slower presentation rate were actually higher than for the faster rate, then this model underestimates β_{Ts}.

time during study affect forgetting in short-term memory is consistent with the conclusions from recognition data of Wickelgren (1970). The finding that recall output delays are important is consistent with a number of prior recall studies manipulating materials (e.g. Cowan et al., 1992; Dosher & Ma, 1998; Schweickert et al., 1994).

The functional model does not provide a mechanistic account of working memory. However, the functional model analysis and the effects it reveals may pose constraints on mechanistic models. The importance of retroactive interference models of span is consistent with a number of interference models of span (e.g. Lewandowsky & Murdock, 1989; Nairne, 1990; Neath & Nairne, 1995). (However, the feature model of Neath and Nairne implements retroactive interference only from the successor item, and the Lewandowsky and Murdock model includes retroactive interference throughout both study and recall.) These models do not incorporate delay per se as an important factor in forgetting. The importance of time delays at output is consistent with hypothesized temporal limits on recall (Baddeley, 1986; Schweickert & Boruff, 1986) if one accepts the recasting of speech rate effects as output time effects. Time decay is the key factor in the trace decay model of Brown and Hulme (1995), and may also be consistent with sequenced production network models such as Burgess and Hitch (1992). However, these models do not explicitly incorporate interference factors in recall.

Brown and Hulme (1995) are one exception; they argued that both interference and time delays may produce loss from working memory. Recent attempts to model both study and recall in working memory within a simulated scheduling architecture (Kieras, Meyer, Mueller, & Seymour, 1998) might also accommodate both interference and time delays. Of course, interference models may propose alternative mechanisms to account for the importance of time delays, and temporal limitation models may propose alternative mechanisms to account for the effects attributed to interference. One example of this is the feature model, which introduces the concept of segmented storage to account for speech rate effects on span (Neath & Nairne, 1995).

The importance of serial position data in specifying the functional model suggests that serial position predictions, as well as more traditional predictions about speech rate, suppression, and lexicality effects, may serve a profitable role in testing mechanistic models of working memory. The current experiment and analysis suggest that working memory models may need to incorporate both item interference and time decay (i.e. time-related nonspecific interference), or proxies for them, as limiting factors in immediate memory performance.

REFERENCES

Baddeley, A.D. (1986). *Working memory*. Oxford: Oxford University Press.

Baddeley, A.D., Lewis, V.J., & Vallar, G. (1984). Exploring the articulatory loop. *Quarterly Journal of Experimental Psychology, 36*, 233–252.

Baddeley, A.D., Thomson, N., & Buchanan, M. (1975). Word length and the structure of short-term memory. *Journal of Verbal Learning and Verbal Behavior, 14*, 575–589.

Brown, G.D.A., & Hulme, C. (1995). Modeling item length effects in memory span: No rehearsal needed? *Journal of Memory and Language, 34*, 594–621.

Burgess, N., & Hitch, G.J. (1992). Toward a network model of the articulatory loop. *Journal of Memory and Language, 31*, 429–460.

Cohen, M.A., & Grossberg, S. (1986). Neural dynamics of speech and language coding: Developmental programs, perceptual grouping, and competition for short-term memory. *Human Neurobiology, 5*, 1–22.

Cowan, N. (1992). Verbal memory span and the timing of spoken recall. *Journal of Memory and Language, 31*, 668–684.

Cowan, N., Day, L., Saults, S., Keller, T.A., Johnson, T., & Flores, L. (1992). The role of verbal output time in the effects of word length on immediate memory. *Journal of Memory and Language, 31*, 1–17.

Cowan, N., Keller, T.A., Hulme, C., Roodenrys, S., & Rack, J. (1994). Verbal memory span in children: Speech timing clues to the mechanisms underlying age and word length effects. *Journal of Memory and Language, 33*, 234–250.

Dosher, B. (1999). *Output times in immediate recall: Word length, phonological similarity, and lexicality effects.* Manuscript submitted for publication.

Dosher, B., & Ma, J.J. (1998). Output loss or rehearsal loop? Output time vs. pronunciation time limits in immediate recall for forgetting-matched materials. *Journal of Experimental Psychology: Learning, Memory, and Cognition, 24*, 316–335.

Kieras, D.E., Meyer, D.E., Mueller, S., & Seymour, T. (1998). *Insights into working memory from the perspective of the EPIC architecture for modelling skilled perceptual-motor and cognitive human performance.* University of Michigan Technical Report, Epic. 10. (TR-98/ONR-EPIC-10).

Lewandowsky, S., & Murdock, B.B. (1989). Memory for serial order. *Psychological Review, 96*, 26–57.

McElree, B., & Dosher, B.A. (1989). Serial position and set size in short-term memory: The time course of recognition. *Journal of Experimental Psychology: General, 118*, 346–373.

McElree, B., & Dosher, B. (1993). Serial comparison processes in judgements of order. *Journal of Experimental Psychology: General, 122*, 291–315.

Nairne, J.S. (1990). A feature model of immediate memory. *Memory and Cognition, 18*, 251–269.

Neath, I., & Nairne, J.S. (1995). Word-length effects in immediate memory: Overwriting trace decay theory. *Psychonomic Bulletin and Review, 2*, 429–441.

Reed, A.V. (1976). MODPAC: A modular package of programs for fitting model parameters to data and plotting fitted curves. *Behavior Research Methods and Instrumentation, 8*, 375–377.

Rubin, D.C., & Wenzel, A.E. (1996). One hundred years of forgetting: A quantitative description of retention. *Psychological Review, 103*, 734–760.

Schiano, D.J., & Watkins, M.J. (1981). Speech-like coding of pictures in short-term memory. *Memory and Cognition, 9*, 110–114.

Schweickert, R., & Boruff, B. (1986). Short-term memory capacity: Magic number or magic spell? *Journal of*

Experimental Psychology: Learning, Memory, and Cognition, 12, 419–425.

Schweickert, R., McDaniel, M.A., & Riegler, G. (1994). Effects of generation on immediate memory span and delayed unexpected free recall. *Quarterly Journal of Experimental Psychology: Human Experimental Psychology, 47A*, 781–804.

Sperling, G., Parish, D.H., Pavel, M., & Desaulnier, S. (1984). *Auditory list recall: Phonemic structure, acoustic confusibility, and familiarity.* Paper at the Psychonomics Society, 11th November.

Sperling, G., & Speelman, R.G. (1970). Acoustic similarity and auditory short-term memory: Experiments and a model. In D.A. Norman (Ed.), *Models of human memory* (pp. 152–202). New York: Academic Press.

Stigler, J.W., Lee, S.-Y., & Stevenson, H.W. (1986). Digit memory in Chinese and English: Evidence for a temporally limited store. *Cognition, 23*, 1–20.

Tetzlaff, L. (1988). *Two studies of knowledge structures: Age of acquisition in short-term memory performance and tradeoffs between short-term memory and intelligibility in noise.* Unpublished doctoral dissertation, New York University.

Wickelgren, W. (1970). Time, interference, and rate of presentation in short-term recognition memory for items. *Journal of Mathematical Psychology, 7*, 219–235.

Wickelgren, W.A., & Norman, D.A. (1971). Invariance of forgetting rate with number of repetitions in verbal short-term recognition memory. *Psychonomic Science, 22*, 363–364.

Wickelgren, W.A., & Norman, D.A. (1966). Strength models and serial position in short-term recognition memory. *Journal of Mathematical Psychology, 3*, 316–347.

Determinants of Short-term Forgetting: Decay, Retroactive Interference, or Proactive Interference?

Georgina Anne Tolan and Gerald Tehan
University of Southern Queensland, Toowoomba, Australia

In two experiments short-term forgetting was investigated in a short-term cued recall task designed to examine proactive interference effects. Mixed modality study lists were tested at varying retention intervals using verbal and nonverbal distractor activities. When an interfering foil was read aloud and a target item read silently, strong PI effects were observed for both types of distractor activity. When the target was read aloud and followed by a verbal distractor activity, weak PI effects emerged. However, when a target item was read aloud and nonverbal distractor activity filled the retention interval, performance was immune to the effects of PI for at least 8 seconds. The results indicate that phonological representations of items read aloud still influence performance after 15 seconds of distractor activity.

Dans deux expériences, l'oubli à court terme est examiné dans une tâche de rappel avec indice développée afin d'examiner les effets d'interférence proactive. Des listes de modalité mixtes ont été utilisées à différents intervalles de rétention en utilisant des activités distractives verbales et non verbales. Lorsqu'un distracteur était lu à voix haute et qu'un item cible était lu silencieusement, un effet d'interférence proactive important était observé pour les deux types d'activités de distraction. Lorsque la cible était lue à voie haute et que des activités distrayantes verbales étaient ensuite exécutées, un effet d'interférence proactive plus faible était observé. Néanmoins, lorsqu'un item cible était lu à voix haute et qu'une activité distrayante non verbale était réalisée au cours de l'intervalle de rétention, la performance n'était pas affectée par l'interférence proactive pendant au moins huit secondes. Les résultats indiquent que les représentations phonologiques d'items lus à voix haute influencent encore la performance après quinze secondes de distraction.

Most current models of short-term memory assert that to-be-remembered items are represented in terms of easily degraded phonological representations. However, there is disagreement on how the traces become degraded. Some propose that trace degradation is due to decay brought about by the prevention of rehearsal (Baddeley, 1986; Burgess & Hitch, 1992, 1996), or a switch in attention (Cowan, 1993); others attribute degradation to retroactive interference (RI) from other list items (Nairne, 1990; Tehan & Fallon, 1999; Tehan & Humphreys, 1998). We want to add proactive interference (PI) to the possible causes of short-term forgetting, and by showing how PI effects change as a function of the type of distractor task employed during a filled retention interval, we hope to evaluate the causes of trace degradation.

By manipulating the type of distractor activity in a brief retention interval it is possible to test some of the assumptions about decay versus interference explanations of short-term forgetting. The decay position is quite straightforward. If rehearsal is prevented, then the trace should decay; the type of distractor activity should be immaterial as long as rehearsal is prevented. From the interference perspective both the Feature Model (Nairne, 1990) and the Tehan and Humphreys (1995, 1998) connectionist model predict that there should be occasions where very little forgetting occurs.

In the Feature Model items are represented as sets of modality-dependent and modality-independent features. Forgetting occurs when adjacent list items have common features. Some of the shared features of the first item are overwritten by the latter item, thereby producing a trace that bears only partial resemblance to the original item. One occasion in which interference would be minimized is when an auditory list is followed by a nonauditory distractor task. The modality-dependent features of the list items would not be overwritten or degraded by the distractor activity because the modality-dependent features of the list and distractor items are different to each other. By the same logic, a visually presented list should not be affected by an auditory distractor task, since modality-specific features are again different in each case.

In the Tehan and Humphreys (1995) approach, presentation modality is related to the strength of phonological representations that support recall. They assume that auditory activity produces stronger representations than does visual activity. Thus this model also predicts that when a list is presented auditorially, it will not be much affected by subsequent nonauditory distractor activity. However, in the case of a visual list with auditory

---

Requests for reprints should be addressed to Gerry Tehan, Department of Psychology, University of Southern Queensland, Toowoomba, QLD, Australia 4350.

distraction, the assumption would be that interference would be maximized. The phonological codes for the list items would be relatively weak in the first instance and a strong source of auditory retroactive interference would follow. This prediction is the opposite of that derived from the Feature Model. Since PI effects appear to be sensitive to retention interval effects (Tehan & Humphreys, 1995; Wickens, Moody, & Dow, 1981), we have chosen to employ a PI task to explore these differential predictions.

We have recently developed a short-term cued recall task in which PI can easily be manipulated (Tehan & Humphreys, 1995, 1996, 1998). In this task, participants study a series of trials in which items are presented in blocks of four items, with each trial consisting of either one or two blocks. Each trial has a target item that is an instance of either a taxonomic or rhyme category, and the category label is presented at test as a retrieval cue. The two-block trials are the important trials because it is in these trials that PI is manipulated. In these trials the two blocks are presented under directed forgetting instructions. That is, once participants find out that it is a two-block trial they are to forget the first block and remember the second block because the second block contains the target item. On control trials, all nontarget items in both blocks are unrelated to the target. On interference trials, a foil that is related to the target is embedded among three other to-be-forgotten fillers in the first block and the target is embedded among three unrelated filler items in the second block. Following the presentation of the second block the category cue is presented and subjects are asked to recall the word from the second block that is an instance of that category.

Using this task we have been able to show that when taxonomic categories are used on an immediate test (e.g. *dog* is the foil, *cat* is the target, and *ANIMAL* is the cue), performance is immune to PI. However, when recall is tested after a 2-second filled retention interval, PI effects are observed; target recall is depressed and the foil is often recalled instead of the target.

In explaining these results, Tehan and Humphreys (1995) assumed that items were represented in terms of sets of features. The representation of an item was seen to involve both semantic and phonological features, with the phonological features playing a dominant role in item recall. They assumed that the cue would elicit the representations of the two items in the list, and that while the semantic features of both target and foil would be available, only the target would have active phonological features. Thus on an immediate test, knowing that the target ended in -*at* would make the task of discriminating between *cat* and *dog* relatively easy. On a delayed test they assumed that all phonological features were inactive and the absence of phonological information would make discrimination more difficult.

A corollary of the Tehan and Humphreys (1995) assumption is that if phonological codes could be provided for a nonrhyming foil, then discrimination should again be problematic. Presentation modality is one variable that appears to produce differences in strength of phonological codes with reading aloud producing stronger representations than reading silently. Tehan and Humphreys (Experiment 5) varied the modality of the two blocks such that participants either read the first block silently and then read the second block aloud or vice versa. In the silent aloud condition performance was immune to PI. The assumption was that the phonological representation of the target item in the second block was very strong, with the result that there were no problems in discrimination. However, PI effects were present in the aloud-silent condition. The phonological representation of the read-aloud foil appeared to serve as a strong source of competition to the read-silently target item.

All this research has been based on the premise that phonological representations for visually presented items are weak and rapidly lose their ability to support recall. This assumption seems tenable given that phonological similarity effects and phonological intrusion effects in serial recall are attenuated rapidly with brief periods of distractor activity (Conrad, 1967; Estes, 1973; Tehan & Humphreys, 1995). The cued recall experiments that have used a filled retention interval have always employed silent visual presentation of the study list and required spoken shadowing of the distractor items. That is, the phonological representations of both target and foil are assumed to be quite weak and the shadowing task would provide a strong source of interference. These are likely to be the conditions that produce maximum levels of PI. The patterns of PI may change with mixed modality study lists and alternative forms of distractor activity. For example, given a strong phonological representation of the target, weak representations of the foil and a weak source of retroactive interference, it might be possible to observe immunity to PI on a delayed test. The following experiments explore the relationship between presentation modality, distractor modality, and PI.

EXPERIMENT 1

The Tehan and Humphreys (1995) mixed modality experiment indicated that PI effects were sensitive to the modalities of the first and second block of items. In the current study we use mixed modality study lists but this time include a 2-second retention interval, the same as that used by Tehan and Humphreys. However, the modality of the distractor activity was varied as well. Participants either had to respond aloud verbally or make a manual response that did not involve any verbal output. From the Tehan and Humphreys perspective the assumption made is that the verbal distractor activity will produce more disruption to the phonological representation of the target item than will a nonverbal distractor activity and the PI will be observed. However, it is quite possible that with silent-aloud presentation and a nonverbal distractor activity immunity to PI might be maintained across a 2-second retention interval. From the Nairne perspective, interference effects are likely to be maximized when the modalities of second block and the distractor activity are the same. From the decay perspective, as long as rehearsal is prevented the modality of the distractor should not be an issue.

Method

Participants. Twenty first-year students from the University of Southern Queensland voluntarily participated in this experiment for course credit or a free ticket in a raffle for a cash prize of 200 dollars.

Materials. For the critical items, two instances were sampled from 40 taxonomic categories (McEvoy & Nelson, 1982). The item selected to be an interfering foil was a high dominant instance of the category and the target was a relatively weak member of the category. The filler items were selected from the unused categories from the McEvoy and Nelson norms and from the Shapiro and Palermo (1970) norms, such that there was no overlap between the category membership of filler and critical items.

The experiment consisted of 10 one-block trials and 40 two-block trials. In the standard version of this task, category-specific proactive interference is manipulated in the two-block trials: On an interference trial an interfering foil from the same category as the target item is presented in the first block, and the target appears in the second block. On control or noninterference trials, a target item is presented in the second block with no related item in the first block. In creating the trials for each subject, the target and foil were first randomly assigned to the various experimental conditions. On the 20 interference trials the target and foil were then embedded amongst randomly selected filler items such that two four-item blocks were created. In the case of the 20 control or noninterference trials, the interfering foil was replaced by a filler item, such that the target was the only instance of the category in the list. On the interference trials, foil and target always appeared in the same serial position (on half the trials in position 2 and on the other half in position 3) in their respective blocks. For half the interference and control trials, the word SILENT appeared before the first block and ALOUD appeared before the second block. For the remaining half, the order was reversed. ALOUD appeared before the first block and SILENT appeared before the second block.

All experiments also contain a number of one-block trials that were also tested via immediate cued recall. The order of the filler and experimental trials were randomised for each subject.

Procedure. At the beginning of the experiment subjects were informed that they would be studying a series of one-block and two-block trials, in which each block consisted of four words. It was stressed that at any one point in time they only had to remember the most recent block. Consequently, if the trial was a two-block trial, they were to forget the first block and concentrate on remembering the second block because it would be on this block that they would be tested. They were also told that prior to each block being presented they would receive an instruction about the reading of each item in the block. If the instruction was SILENT they were to read the following four items silently to themselves, but if the instruction was ALOUD they were to read the following four words aloud as they appeared on the screen.

Each trial began with a READY sign displayed on the computer monitor for 2 seconds. The reading instruction was then presented for one second. The block one items were then displayed individually in lower case at a rate of one word per second. The second reading instruction was then presented again for 1 second and then the block two items were presented at a rate of one per second. Following the presentation of the last item in the second block, two two-digit strings were presented for 1 second each. A third of the subjects were asked to read each digit string aloud as it appeared on the screen. This replicates the shadowing procedure that Tehan and Humphreys (1995) used. The remaining two groups were requested to make a magnitude judgement about each digit string as soon as it appeared on the screen. They simply had to indicate if the digit string was greater than 50 or less than 50. The way in which this decision was reported differed for two sets of participants. One set of participants reported their judgements verbally by simply saying "smaller" or "larger"; the second group made no verbal response, instead they hit either the "S" on the keyboard for the smaller judgement or the "L" key when the digit pair was larger than 50. They had 1 second to make a response before the second digit string was presented and the second response had to be made. After the second response had been made, the category cue appeared and subjects had 5 seconds to attempt recall of the instance of that category that had appeared in the second block.

Results

Mean levels of correct recall and errors made, for each condition, are presented in Fig. 1.

Correct Recall. The data were analyzed by a $3 \times 2 \times 2$ mixed factorial analysis of variance, with distractor (3 levels) as the between-subjects factor and modality (2 levels) and interference (2 levels) each as within-subjects factors. An alpha level of .05 was used as a bench mark for statistical significance in this and subsequent analyses. There was a significant main effect for distractor activity, $F(2,57) = 9.90$; $MSe = 57.27$. A Newman-Keuls post hoc test indicated that recall was significantly better in the keyboard distractor condition ($M = 6.55$) than the shadowing ($M = 5.40$) and verbal ($M = 4.90$) distractor conditions, the latter two not differing from each other. Recall was better in the

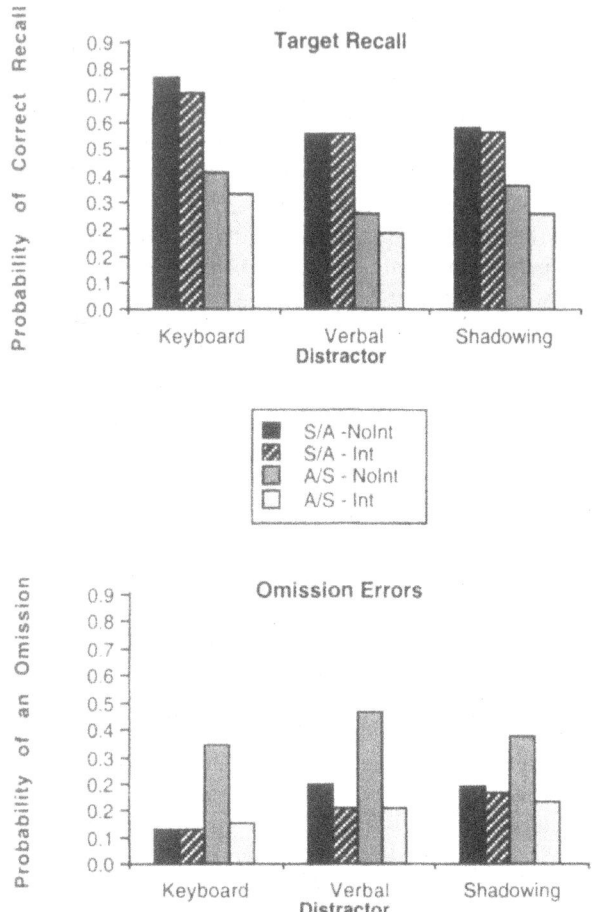

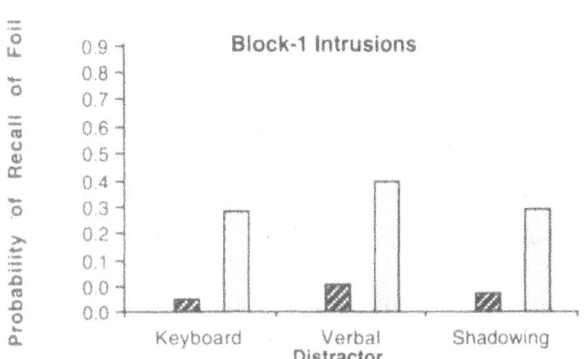

FIG. 1. Mean correct recall, omission errors, and block one intrusions as a function of presentation modality and type of distractor activity in Experiment 1.

silent-aloud condition than in the aloud-silent condition, $F(1,57) = 152.43$; $MSe = 620.82$. PI effects were also present, $F(1,57) = 1.65$; $MSe = 19.27$, but a significant modality by interference interaction was also obtained, $F(1,57) = 4.76$; MSe 6.02. Simple main effects analysis indicated that interference effects were present in the aloud-silent conditions, $F(1,59) = 15.13$, but not in the silent-aloud condition, $F(1,59) = 1.44$. No other interactions were reliable.

Errors. Omission errors and block one intrusions constituted a major source of error, as evidenced in Fig. 1. For omissions, there was a significant main effect for the distractor activity, $F(2,57) = 4.98$; $MSe = 28.39$. A Newman-Keuls analysis showed that significantly fewer omission errors were made after the keyboard distractor activity ($M = 2.16$) than after the shadowing ($M = 3.17$) and verbal ($M = 3.21$) distractor activities, which did not differ from each other. Omissions were more frequent in the aloud-silent condition than in the silent-aloud condition, $F(1,57) = 47.33$; $MSe = 98.82$. Finally, overall there were more omission errors in the noninterference condition than in the interference condition, $F(1,57) = 92.30$; $MSe = 166.67$. A significant modality by interference interaction was evident, $F(1, 57) = 38.30$; $MSe = 98.82$. Main effects analysis indicated that the high frequency of omissions in the noninterference condition was present in the aloud-silent condition, $F(1,59) = 101.8$, but not in the silent-aloud condition, $F(1,59) = 2.37$. No other interactions reached significance.

The block one intrusions, pictured in Fig. 1, were submitted to a 3 × 2 mixed factorial analysis of variance. None of the interactions reached significance; however, the foil was recalled more frequently in the aloud-silent condition than the silent-aloud condition, $F = (1,57) = 159.04$; $MSe = 357.08$. The main effect for the distractor tasks approached statistical significance, $F = (2,57) = 2.70$; $MSe = 8.41$, $P < .076$.

Discussion

There are two aspects to the current results that are of primary interest. The first is that the effects of the distractor activity separate along a verbal/non-verbal dimension rather than a shadowing/magnitude estimation dimension. The equivalence of the shadowing and spoken magnitude response would suggest that the two tasks are equally difficult. However, verbal aspects of the distractor activity are producing more disruption than the keyboard response. One possibility here is that subjects may surreptitiously rehearse while making the manual response. We think that this is unlikely; finding and pressing the S key is probably less automatic than verbally responding "smaller" and given that subjects have only 1 second to process and respond, we do not think that there is sufficient time available to switch attention between rehearsal and distractor tasks.

The interaction of PI effects with presentation modality of the second block is another key aspect of the results. Immunity to PI is observed in the silent-aloud condition; target recall is equivalent in the interference and control conditions and block one intrusions occur relatively infrequently. In the aloud-silent lists target recall is depressed in the interference conditions and block one intrusions represent a major source of error. In other words, strong PI effects are evident. This is exactly the same pattern of performance that Tehan and Humphreys (1995) found on an immediate test.

Consequently, the explanations provided by Tehan and Humphreys seem appropriate in this instance.

The fact that immunity to PI is observed after a 2-second retention interval is something that we have not found before. If the argument presented in this paper is correct then the phonological features of the auditory target item are able to survive 2 seconds of distractor activity. Furthermore, the strength of the block one intrusions would indicate that the phonological representation of the foil in the aloud-silent condition appears to survive for even a longer period of time. Longoni, Richardson, and Aiello (1993) have provided some evidence to suggest that phonological codes may not be as transient as most people think. In the next experiment we looked at forgetting over retention intervals ranging from 1 second to 8 seconds. Again we were interested in the effects of the different distractor activity on PI and modality effects.

EXPERIMENT 2

Method

Participants. Two hundred undergraduates, from introductory psychology units, served as participants. They were given course credit for participating in the experiment. One hundred participants were assigned to the verbal distractor condition and these participants were further divided into groups of 20 participants for each of the 5 retention intervals. The remaining 100 participants engaged in the keyboard distractor condition with groups of 20 participants performing under the 5 different retention intervals.

Materials and Procedure. The number of trials and the formation were exactly the same as those adopted in Experiment 1. In this experiment only two types of distractor activities were employed; the verbal and keyboard versions of the magnitude estimation task. Five retention intervals were used; 1 second, 2 seconds, 3 seconds, 4 seconds, and 8 seconds. For each retention interval the number of digit strings presented after the last item in each trial varied such that participants were making a magnitude estimation judgement once every second, for the respective retention intervals.

Results

The data are summarized in Fig. 2.

Correct Recall. The correct recall scores were subjected to a 2 × 2 × 2 × 5 mixed factorial analysis of variance. The analysis showed a significant effect for retention interval, $F(4,190) = 24.54$; $MSe = 180.44$. The verbal distractor was more disruptive than the keyboard distractor, $F(1,190) = 8.76$; $MSe = 64.41$. There was a highly significant main effect for modality of presentation, $F(1, 190) = 540.61$; $MSe = 1725.78$, and target recall was better in the control trials than the interference trials, $F(1,190) = 161.93$; $MSe = 258.78$. These main effects were moderated by a three-way interaction between distractor, modality, and interference, $F(1, 190) = 5.89$; $MSe = 9.90$. All other significant interactions are incorporated in this three-way interaction. As is evident in Fig. 2, the key finding underlying this interaction is that no reliable differences between the control and interference trials were observed in the silent-aloud condition when a keyboard distractor was required, $F(1, 95) = 1.46$; $MSe = 1.37$. However, PI effects were present in the aloud-silent condition exposed to a verbal distractor activity; $F(1, 95) = 72.58$; $MSe = 1.83$, the aloud-silent condition under keyboard distraction; $F(1, 95) = 75.68$; $MSe = 1.78$, and the silent-aloud condition after verbal distraction $F(1, 95) = 37.00$; $MSe = 1.58$.

Omission Errors. The pattern of omission errors was basically the same as in Experiment 1. Main effects for retention interval, [$F(4,190) = 17.00$; $MSe = 67.26$], presentation modality [$F(1,190) = 104.35$; $MSe = 182.40$], and interference [$F(1,190) = 231.32$; $MSe = 471.24$] were found. There was no main effect for distractor type, $F(1, 190) = 1.38$; $MSe = 5.45$. The interaction between distractor, modality, and interference was significant, $F(4,190) = 4.33$; $MSe = 8.41$. For all comparisons involved, significantly more omissions were made in the control condition than the interference condition but the effects were stronger in the aloud-silent condition; aloud-silent verbal distractor [M control = 4.05, M Interference = 1.30; $F(1,99) = 139.94$], aloud-silent keyboard distractor [M control = 3.81, M Interference = 1.53; $F(1,99) = 87.05$], silent-aloud verbal distractor [M control = 1.90, M Interference = 1.50; $F(1,99) = 7.29$], and silent-aloud keyboard distractor [M control = 1.94, M Interference = 1.18; $F(1,99) = 16.08$].

Block One Intrusions. Analysis of recall of the foil indicated that there were main effects for modality of presentation [$F(1,190) = 529.25$; $MSe = 2.20$], type of distractor activity [$F(1,190) = 9.63$; $MSe = 3.37$], and retention interval [$F(4,190) = 12.49$; $MSe = 3.37$]. The interaction between retention interval and presentation modality was the only significant interaction, $F(4,190) = 4.30$; $MSe = 2.20$. Simple main effects analyses indicated that production of the foil increased with retention interval in the aloud-silent condition, $F(1,198) = 13.55$; $MSe = 1.55$, but remained constant across retention intervals for the silent-aloud conditions, $F(1,198) = 2.44$; $MSe = 4.91$.

Discussion

The results of the experiment are quite straightforward. Again the verbal distractor produces more disruption than the keyboard distractor. As was the case in Experiment 1, there is a relationship between PI effects and presentation modality. In the aloud-silent conditions,

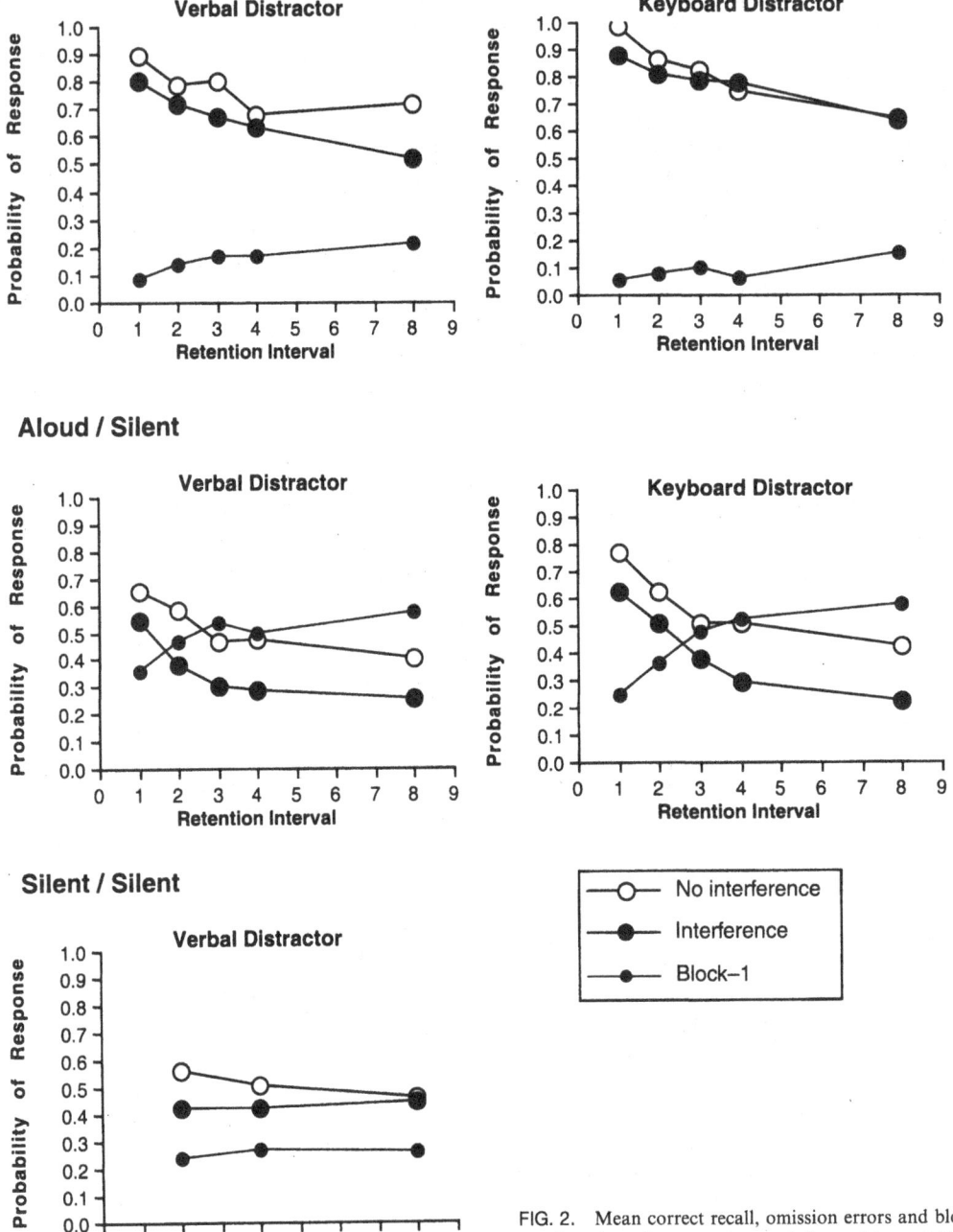

FIG. 2. Mean correct recall, omission errors and block one intrusions as a function of presentation modality and type of distractor activity in Experiment 2.

PI effects are present for both types of distractor activity. In the silent-aloud condition PI effects are present with a verbal distractor, a result that was not observed in Experiment 1. However, immunity to PI is again found with a keyboard distractor, even after 8 seconds of distraction.

If it is true that phonological representations play a key role in determining the presence or absence of PI effects, then the current results speak to the susceptibility of these representations to degradation. In the silent-aloud condition with a nonverbal distractor, target recall remains quite high and there is minimal effect of a visually presented foil. These data suggest that a phonological representation of the target can be held for at least 8 seconds with little degradation. However, with a verbal distractor activity, it would appear that some degradation of the phonological trace is produced. Interference effects are observed across all retention intervals, both in terms of depressed target recall and frequency of block one intrusions.

In some senses, the aloud-silent condition is more interesting. In both the verbal and nonverbal distractor conditions the foil has a large impact upon performance. There are two possible explanations for this: In the first case, Tehan and Humphreys' (1995) initial experiments used mixed modality lists to engender a strong phonological representation of the foil. They found PI effects on an immediate test, just as we find PI effects on a delayed test. They argued that they had been successful in maintaining phonological codes for the foil. Given that the visual distractor activity had little impact on the phonological codes for the target in the current experiment it is possible that the phonological representation of the foil is surviving intact across the different retention intervals. If this is so it would indicate that phonological codes can last for at least 15 to 16 seconds of subsequent activity. The data also suggest that the discrimination between target and foil becomes more difficult at longer retention intervals. Given strong pre-experimental differences between the foil and the target and a strong phonological representation of the foil, recall of the target would become increasingly difficult and recall of the foil would increase as the phonological representation of the target weakens.

The alternative explanation is that the phonological codes have dissipated for both the target and the foil and that the differences we observe are due to the pre-existing differences in category dominance of the target and the foil[1]. If this argument is correct, then performance in the aloud-silent condition should look very similar to performance in a silent-silent condition since in both instances the phonological codes for target and foil no longer support recall. To test for these possibilities a post hoc experiment was conducted using a silent-silent presentation condition with three groups of subjects exposed to either 2, 4 or 8 seconds of verbal distractor activity. The results of these groups are presented in the lowest panel in Fig. 2. Comparing this condition to the aloud-silent condition with verbal distraction, it is clear that performance is reasonably similar in the control conditions, but there are large differences between the interference conditions in terms of target recall and block one intrusions. In other words, the modality of the first block is having an impact upon performance. Hence, it is concluded that the phonological representation of the foil is surviving the distractor activity across all retention intervals when the foil is read aloud.

GENERAL DISCUSSION

The arguments presented in the current paper are based on three assumptions. First, short-term recall is supported by phonological codes. Second, input via audition produces stronger phonological representations than input solely through the visual pathways, and finally,

---

[1] We would like to thank Ian Neath and Jim Nairne for suggesting this possibility.

strong phonological codes are responsible for immunity to PI in short-term recall. In a sense, PI effects have been used as the dependent measure to investigate the effects of modality of presentation and distractor activity in relation to forgetting associated with phonological representations. The results indicate that in mixed modality lists, items that are read aloud appear to have stronger phonological representations than items that are read silently. In the cued recall task, PI effects are either absent or weak when the target is read aloud. On the other hand, PI effects are very strong when the foil is read aloud. The strength of PI effects does not change radically with the type of distractor used or with changes in retention interval.

Several authors, ourselves included, have suggested that phonological codes are relatively transient in that they either decay rapidly (Baddeley, 1986) or are prone to retroactive interference (Nairne, 1990; Tehan & Humphreys, 1995). In the current experiments, phonological codes that are the result of auditory input do not rapidly loose strength with a nonverbal distractor. The effects can be observed after 15 seconds of presentation and distractor activity. This finding is inconsistent with the idea of a rapidly decaying trace.

The absence of strong phonological information is not the sole source of forgetting in these experiments. If one looks at the silent/aloud condition with the keyboard distractor, it is clear that there is very little PI involved. Presumably there is very little degradation of the phonological trace of the target. However, there is forgetting involved in both the interference and control trials, in that absolute levels of target recall deteriorate across retention intervals. There are three possible explanations for this effect. The phonological representations are being degraded by subsequent activity, but only marginally so. The nonverbal distractor activity may not degrade the phonological representations of the target or foil per se, instead it may produce a noisier background for retrieval. Third, the distractor activity may well be incorporated into the list structure such that the target has to be discriminated from an increased number of filler items. Current accounts of such discrimination processes suggest that this is easier to do when the retrieval interval is short rather than long. Whatever the account of the retention interval effects in this and other conditions, forgetting is not likely to be due to the rapid decay of phonological representations.

With verbal distractor activity we see some evidence of increased levels of interference, in that in the no-interference conditions there is an increase in the number of omission errors; in the interference conditions block one intrusions increase in frequency. These findings can again be explained in terms of increased degradation of the phonological trace of the targets, or verbal distractor activity providing a noisier background for retrieval than the nonverbal distractor.

Whereas auditory phonological representations may persist for some time, the same is not true of the representations that are the result of unspoken visual input.

Here there is evidence for the rapid degradation of the phonological trace. In the aloud-silent conditions we see that in the control lists the number of omissions increases dramatically across retention interval as does the number of block one intrusions on the interference trials. These findings indicate that the phonological representations rapidly loose their ability to support recall. As to a cause of the disruption, interference effects are again implicated in this process in that verbal distractor activity produces more disruption than nonverbal distractor activity.

The present research has implications for current theories of short-term memory. Most current theories that address the issue of forgetting assume trace decay as the forgetting mechanism (Baddeley, 1986; Burgess & Hitch, 1996; Schweickert, 1993). The results of the current experiments cast doubt on the forgetting assumptions of these models. Nairne's (1990) feature model and Tehan and Humphreys (1995) explanation of PI assume that forgetting is based upon retroactive interference. Both stress that the modality of the distractor is an important determinant of forgetting such that little degradation occurs if the modality of the distractor is appropriate. There are some differences between the two accounts, however. Tehan and Humphreys make the assumption that auditory distractor activity will produce more disruption than nonverbal distractor activity irrespective of the modality of the study material, and this is what emerges in the two experiments. The results of the aloud-silent condition do pose some problems for the Feature Model. Visual distractors should produce more disruption than auditory distractors. This does not happen; auditory distractors produce more disruption than the visual distractors across all experimental conditions.

This investigation commenced with the observation that very little research had attempted to look at different sources of forgetting. The research presented here is based on the assumption that phonological codes support short-term recall. If this assumption were true then it would appear that auditory presentation leads to stronger phonological representations than visual presentation. This can lead to good memory performance or to strong interference effects depending upon just which items have been strongly activated. If there is a strong phonological representation for a target item then by and large the effects of PI are minimized, and this is particularly true if the strength of the items used as a distractor activity is low. However, if the representations of the distractor items are strong then RI effects are enhanced and PI effects are exacerbated as well. The current results indicate that interference effects are readily observed in short-term cued recall and that if there are any pure decay effects, they are happening at a much slower rate than has previously been observed.

REFERENCES

Baddeley, A.D. (1986). *Working memory.* Oxford: Oxford University Press.

Burgess, N., & Hitch, G.J. (1992). Toward a network model of the articulatory loop. *Journal of Memory and Language, 31,* 429–460.

Burgess, N., & Hitch, G.J. (1996). A connectionist model of STM for serial order. In S.E. Gathercole (Ed.), *Models of short-term memory* (pp. 51–72) Hove, UK: Psychology Press.

Conrad, R. (1967). Interference or decay over short retention intervals. *Journal of Verbal Learning and Verbal Behavior, 6,* 49–54.

Cowan, N. (1993). Activation, attention, and short-term memory. *Memory and Cognition, 21,* 162–167.

Estes, W.K. (1973). Phonological encoding and rehearsal in short-term memory for letter strings. *Journal of Verbal Learning and Verbal Behavior, 12,* 360–372.

Longoni, A.M., Richardson, J.T.E., & Aiello, A. (1993). Articulatory rehearsal and phonological storage in working memory. *Memory and Cognition, 21,* 11–22.

McEvoy, C.L., & Nelson, D.L. (1982). Category name and instance norms for 106 categories of various sizes. *American Journal of Psychology, 95,* 581–634.

Nairne, J.S. (1990). A feature model of immediate memory. *Memory and Cognition, 18,* 251–269.

Schweickert, R. (1993). A multinomial processing tree model for degradation and redintegration in immediate recall. *Memory and Cognition, 21,* 168–175.

Shapiro, S.I., & Palermo, D.S. (1970). Conceptual organization and class membership: Normative data for representatives of 100 categories. *Psychonomic Monograph Supplements, Vol. 3,* No.11 (Whole of No. 43).

Tehan, G., & Fallon, A.B. (1999). A connectionist model of short-term cued recall. In J. Wiles & T. Dartnell (Eds.), *Prospectives in cognitive science* (pp. 221–237). Stamford, CT: Ablex.

Tehan, G., & Humphreys, M.S. (1995). Transient phonological codes and immunity to proactive interference. *Memory and Cognition, 23,* 181–191.

Tehan, G., & Humphreys, M.S. (1996). Cuing effects in short-term recall. *Memory and Cognition, 24,* 719–732.

Tehan, G., & Humphreys, M.S. (1998). Creating proactive interference in immediate recall: Building a dog from a dart, a mop and a fig. *Memory and Cognition, 26,* 477–489.

Wickens, D.D., Moody, M.J., & Dow, R. (1981). The nature of timing of the retrieval process and of interference effects. *Journal of Experimental Psychology: General, 110,* 1–20.

Comparing Short-term Memory and Memory for Rapidly Presented Visual Stimuli

Veronika Coltheart
Macquarie University, Australia

What similarities and differences are there between memory for short lists shown at one item per second and memory for such lists after rapid serial visual presentation (RSVP) at much higher rates—eight items per second? This paper reports that, when pictures are shown at eight per second or one per second, phonological similarity of the picture names reduces recall at the one item per second rate, but not at the eight item per second rate. In contrast, when subjects are shown the written names of the pictures, phonological similarity reduces recall at both rates. It is concluded that phonological coding does not occur for picture lists shown at high rates. The mechanisms underlying memory for pictures and words shown at RSVP and short-term memory rates are considered.

Quelles similarités et quelles différences existe-t-il entre la mémoire de courtes listes présentées au rythme d'un item à la seconde et la mémoire de telles listes lors d'une présentation sérielle visuelle rapide (PSVR) de huit items par seconde? Cet article montre que la similarité phonologique des noms d'images réduit le rappel lorsque ces images sont présentées à un item à la seconde, mais que cette variable n'a pas d'effet à un rythme de présentation de 8 items à la seconde. Par contre, lorsque l'on présente aux participants des noms d'images, la similarité phonologique réduit le rappel aux deux rythmes de présentation. Ces résultats suggèrent que l'encodage phonologique ne s'effectue pas pour des images présentées très rapidement. La discussion porte sur les mécanismes qui sous-tendent la mémoire des images et des mots aux rythmes de présentation étudiés.

This paper reviews and compares research on short-term memory (STM) with memory arising after brief visual presentations, and it reports experiments that contrasted memory for lists of pictures, or their written names, when these lists were shown at high RSVP (rapid serial visual presentation) or standard STM rates of presentation. It is well known that there are limits on people's immediate memory span for short lists of unrelated letters, digits, words, and objects using STM rates of 1 second per item and serial recall.

The limits do not appear to be limits on processes of comprehension as, using serial presentation rates of 10–12 words per second, Forster (1970) demonstrated good recall of sentences, and Potter and Levy (1969) obtained evidence of picture comprehension. Sequences of unrelated pictures or words appear to leave only fleeting memories, but sentences of 12 or more words can be recalled (Potter, 1984; cited in Potter, 1993), and passages can be understood.

Potter (1993, 1999) argued that words and pictures are capable of rapidly activating semantic and conceptual representations, along with scene and sentence parsing processes, in long-term memory. These temporarily active representations can be regarded as a form of very short-term conceptual memory. Potter et al. (1993, 1998) proposed that recall of rapidly presented sentences was not based on surface or phonological codes, but instead involved a reconstruction, or regeneration, of temporarily activated semantic representations. Paraphrased sentence recall by patients with a deficient auditory-verbal short-term memory (Saffran & Marin, 1975) might also reflect regeneration from very short-term conceptual memory.

In contrast, when unrelated word lists are presented at the slower rate of one item per second, research dating from Conrad (1964) and Baddeley (1966) has shown that phonological (speech-based) codes are involved in short-term memory recall. Consequently, theories of memory have included a short-term memory store with a rehearsal process used to retain lists shown at rates of 1–2 items per second (Atkinson & Shiffrin, 1968). Baddeley and Hitch's (1974) theory of short-term working memory consisted of a central executive system served by two slave systems: the visuospatial sketchpad and the articulatory loop (later termed phonological loop by Baddeley, 1986). The phonological loop, which consists of a limited-capacity phonological short-term store and a rehearsal process, is the system used for the recall of

---

Requests for reprints should be addressed to Veronika Coltheart, Psychology Department, Macquarie University, NSW 2109, Australia (Tel: 61-2-9850-8104; Fax: 61-2-9850-9390; E-mail: vcolthea@laurel.ocs.mq.edu.au).

The research reported in this paper was supported by ARC grant awarded to V. Coltheart. The collaboration and assistance of Robyn Langdon, Jo Millar, and Tonia Corner is gratefully acknowledged.

© 1999 International Union of Psychological Science

STM lists. Visually presented items are registered in the phonological short-term store after a process of phonological recoding of written words, or after name retrieval of real or pictured objects.

Some phenomena occur at high rates of visual presentation but not at STM rates of one item per second. First, there is evidence of both visual and conceptual masking (Intraub, 1984). Second, there are information-processing limits not found at STM rates, such as repetition blindness (Kanwisher, 1987). Repetition blindness refers to reduced accuracy when reporting both occurrences of a repeated item, with the second occurrence usually being omitted. Repetition blindness also occurs when items are phonologically identical but differ orthographically (Bavelier & Potter, 1992). Bavelier and Potter proposed that this phonological repetition blindness arises from an early phonological code used in the initial registration of an item in STM (tokenizing), and they found that concurrent irrelevant articulation had no significant effects on RSVP list recall or phonological repetition blindness.

Evidence of phonological coding in STM is provided by the finding that lists of phonologically similar items (letters, words, or pictures with similar names) are recalled less accurately than are lists of dissimilar items (e.g. Baddeley, 1966; Schiano & Watkins, 1981). For visually presented lists, this phonological similarity effect is removed if subjects are required to engage in repetitive, irrelevant articulation (saying "the, the, the, . . ." or "1, 2, 3, 4, 5, 1, 2, 3, 4, 5, . . .") when the list is shown (e.g. Coltheart, 1993; Murray, 1968; Schiano & Watkins, 1981). Baddeley (1986) argued that concurrent articulation disrupts both phonological recoding and rehearsal. The fact that, with auditory presentation, the phonological similarity effect survives concurrent articulation led Baddeley to argue that the locus of the phonological similarity effect is the phonological short-term store and that concurrent articulation prevents access of visual items to this store.

An effect of word length of list items was obtained by Baddeley, Thomson, and Buchanan (1975): Lists of short words are better recalled than are lists of long words, and the word length effect is removed by concurrent articulation (for both visual and auditory lists). Baddeley et al. found a positive correlation between memory performance and speech rate for the list words, and argued that the word length effect is caused by a limited capacity rehearsal loop. The word length effect occurs because fewer long than short words could be rehearsed.

The rehearsal process, formerly termed articulatory rehearsal, was assumed to involve articulatory mechanisms and to occur at overt speech rates (Landauer, 1962). Subsequently, Marshall and Cartwright (1978, 1980) found that inner speech was 15–25% faster than overt speech. Such estimates suggest that rehearsal is unlikely to occur for lists presented at rates of 8–10 items per second.

Short-term memory investigators have used small sets of 8 to 10 items from which lists were repeatedly selected with the item pool visible throughout the task, e.g. Conrad (1964), Baddeley (1966), and subsequent studies using memory span tasks. Researchers using other paradigms in memory, such as reading span, complex span tasks, and RSVP tasks have used new items for every list. The use of repeatedly selected items raises questions about the generality of some of the findings from STM research. Fortunately, it has been shown that both phonological similarity (Coltheart, 1993) and word length (La Pointe & Engle, 1990) reduce recall in STM tasks when completely new words are presented in every list.

PHONOLOGICAL SIMILARITY AND RSVP LIST RECALL

If phonological effects in short-term memory arise from phonological coding and rehearsal processes which can occur only at lower rates of presentation, can these effects be found for lists presented at high rates? Three recent experiments provide evidence of phonological coding when lists were shown at high presentation rates (four, six, and nine words per second) as well as an STM rate of two words per second (Coltheart & Langdon, 1998). Unrepeated list items selected from large word pools were used so that the conditions were comparable with those in RSVP studies using lists of words, pictures, and sentences. Phonological similarity reduced recall even at the high rate of nine words per second. Furthermore, this effect occurred with both serial and free recall instructions. Thus, phonological coding is possible when lists are presented at rates about six to nine times greater than those used in short-term memory research. The effect of phonological similarity decreased as rate of presentation increased, but the size of the effect, at four words per second, was similar to the 14% effect found with the standard one word per second STM rate with new items in each list reported by Coltheart (1993).

The third experiment of Coltheart and Langdon (1998) investigated effects of concurrent irrelevant articulation on recall of lists of phonologically similar and dissimilar words shown at six and nine words per second. Concurrent articulation both reduced recall and eliminated the phonological similarity effect, results observed using short-term memory tasks (e.g. Coltheart, 1993; Murray, 1968). The fact that phonological similarity reduced recall of lists shown at up to nine words per second suggests that the phonological codes established at high rates are not qualitatively different from those generated at STM rates. Furthermore, the detrimental effects of phonological similarity and the effects of concurrent articulation are not simply due to the requirement of correct order in recall as they occurred with free recall.

Recall of lists of words shown at high rates is characterized by frequent omissions. At lower presentation rates, intrusions of unpresented words are more frequent than at high rates. Intrusions were also more common for phonologically similar lists than for dissimilar lists. They sometimes appeared to be combinations of a pair of phonologically similar words and lower rates of presentation are more likely than higher rates to increase the probability of the formation of at least partial memory traces.

Thus, previous experiments (Coltheart & Langdon, 1998) demonstrated phonological similarity (as well as word length effects) with RSVP lists of words new on every trial. Consequently the effects of phonological similarity and word length are not confined to memory paradigms that minimize item encoding and simply require retention of item order, and these effects were observed with free recall instructions and scoring criteria. It is therefore clear that phonological coding has a pervasive role in supporting item recall in memory for visual stimuli shown at very high presentation rates. This indicates a continuity between processes supporting recall at high RSVP rates and those supporting recall at the much lower STM rate. However, semantic, conceptual, and orthographic representations as well as phonological codes may support recall.

RECALL OF RAPIDLY PRESENTED PICTURES

This review has shown that recall of both STM and RSVP word lists is influenced by phonological similarity and by word length. I now consider research in which pictures were presented at high rates. Picture comprehension can occur with sequences of photographs or line drawings shown at rates of 10 pictures per second or higher (Biederman, 1981; Intraub, 1981; Potter & Levy, 1969). Picture comprehension is faster than picture name retrieval, which takes about 250msec longer than reading aloud the picture's written name (Potter & Faulconer, 1975). Moreover, Intraub (1980) found no significant correlation between the time to name a picture and the probability of correct recognition in a memory test. Finally, repetition blindness does not occur for pictures having the same name such as (flying) bat/(baseball) bat (Kanwisher Yin, & Wajciulik, 1999). These results suggest that picture name retrieval is too slow to contribute to the coding of picture lists presented at high rates.

EXPERIMENT 1

It was observed earlier that phonological similarity of names adversely affects recall of short lists of nameable pictures (Schiano & Watkins, 1981), and that this effect was removed by concurrent articulation. Robyn Langdon and I investigated whether picture lists shown at high rates (eight per second) were affected by the phonological similarity of their names. High rates of presentation might not permit retrieval of their names, and hence phonological coding might not be possible.

Method

Twenty-eight undergraduate subjects were presented with lists of five pictures (selected from Snodgrass & Vanderwart, 1984, and a few drawn by R. Langdon) which had similar or dissimilar names. The pictures having a high level of name agreement were selected from a larger set whose names had been elicited in a written task from a sample of undergraduates from the same population. Four vowel sounds (/ae/ /ɑ/ /ʌ/ /ɛ/) were used to create four sets of five lists of five pictures in which all five lists shared their vowel. Thus, each set used a different one of the four vowels. The similar names in a list shared some consonant phonemes as well, e.g. duck, cup, gun, jug, glove. The sets of five pictures having dissimilar names, e.g. phone, leaf, ring, varied in their vowel as well as their consonant sounds (e.g. /u/ /ɪ/ /aɪ/ /ɔ/ /oʊ/ /aʊ/ /eɪ/, etc.). Ten similar and 10 dissimilar pictures were used twice because it was not possible to find 25 similarly named pictures of each of the 4 vowel phonemes used. The 90 similar and 90 dissimilar names were matched on the following properties: mean Celex word frequency (885 and 870; Baayen, Piepenbrock, & van Rijn, 1993), orthographic neighbourhood size (Coltheart et al.'s, 1977, mean N values of 10.5 and 8.8) and length (number of letters: 3.9 and 4.25).

The entire set of pictures was presented twice in a naming task to familiarize subjects with the items and to establish the names given. The mean naming latency for this task was 756msec. The few alternative names given were corrected. The 10 similar and 10 dissimilar lists were then presented at rates of 8 per second and 1 per second. Half the lists at each rate were presented in silent conditions and half while the subject counted from one to five repeatedly. Lists were blocked by rate and articulation condition with order of similar and dissimilar name lists randomized within blocks. Within a block the five similar lists all shared the same vowel phoneme, but between blocks the vowel changed. Assignment of lists to blocks was counterbalanced. Practice lists preceded each block, and illustrated the task conditions for that block. Serial recall was written in booklets in which item positions were indicated by numbered rows.

Results and Discussion

Recall was significantly higher for lists shown at 1 second per picture than for lists shown at eight pictures per second [67% vs. 31% in the silent condition, $F(1, 27) = 209.4$, $P < .0001$]. Concurrent articulation significantly reduced recall [from 49% to 33%, $F(1, 27) = 62.6$, $P < .0001$]. There was a significant three-way interaction between presentation rate, articulation condition, and phonological similarity [$F(1, 27) = 6.01$, $P < .025$]. Pictures with similar names were significantly harder to recall (60%) than those with dissimilar names (75%) *only* in the silent condition when shown at the STM 1-second rate [$F(1, 27) = 45.7$, $P < .0001$]. At the high rate, phonological similarity of picture names did not affect recall ($F < 1$) nor was there any effect of phonological similarity on recall in the concurrent articulation conditions at either high or low rates ($F < 1$ and $F = 1.3$).

Recall of pictures shown at RSVP and STM rates was further examined by a plot of serial position effects in item recall. Typically, recall of short lists visually presented at STM rates displays a modest primacy effect (superior recall of one or two early items) with little or no recency effect. This pattern of recall was observed in the silent condition at the 1-second rate but not at the RSVP rate. As can be seen in Fig. 1, item recall at the RSVP rate exhibited strong primacy and recency effects for the first and last items. The effects of concurrent articulation were predominantly on the recall of early items. Recall of the last item was unaffected, and comparable for pictures shown at both presentation rates.

This experiment showed that phonological similarity of picture names did not affect recall of pictures when the pictures were shown at high rates. We attributed this to the difficulty of retrieving picture names when the pictures were shown at such high rates. However, it is possible that the level of similarity of the names may not have been sufficient to generate an effect at high rates of presentation.

EXPERIMENT 2

Consequently, we conducted a second experiment in which a new set of 28 undergraduate subjects were presented with lists of the written names of the pictures shown at the same rates of 8 per second and 1 per second.

Method

As in the previous experiment, half the lists were presented in silent conditions and half while subjects engaged in concurrent articulation.

Results and Discussion

Recall levels for names were higher than recall for pictures, and higher at the one per second rate than at the eight per second rate (71% and 44% in the silent condition) with the main effect of rate highly significant [$F(1, 27) = 235.1$, $P < .0001$]. Phonological similarity reduced recall at both high and low rates of presentation in the silent condition by 9% and 20% respectively: The main effect of phonological similarity was highly significant [$F(1, 27) = 41.92$, $P < .0001$], as was its interaction with the articulation condition [$F(1, 27) = 16.45$, $P < .0004$]. Concurrent articulation reduced recall, and removed the phonological similarity effect. Thus performance on the picture names shown at high rates in the silent condition displayed a significant phonological similarity effect [$F(1, 27) = 6.11$, $P < .025$], which was even larger than the effects with lists of phonologically similar and dissimilar three-letter words in the experiments reported in Coltheart and Langdon (1998).

Recall as a function of serial position is shown in Fig. 2. The serial position functions in the silent condition were similar to those found for picture lists, with some evidence of a primacy effect for the second item at the RSVP rate. The pattern in the articulation condition was different from that with pictures in that primacy and recency effects were evident, and the last word was better recalled with the RSVP rate than with the STM 1-second rate of presentation.

A comparison of the overall levels of recall for pictures and words shown at eight per second shows substantially lower recall for pictures. This raised the possibility that, for pictures, recall levels were *too low* to permit the detection of phonological similarity effects.

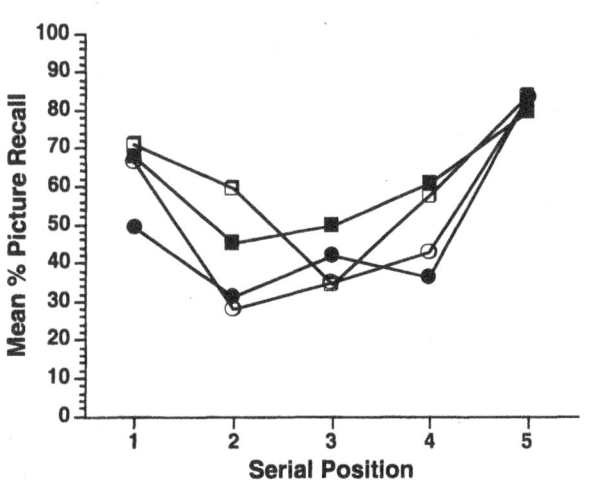

FIG. 1. Mean % pictures recalled for each serial position in silent and articulation conditions.

EXPERIMENT 3

We therefore conducted a further experiment using the same pictures but reducing list length to four items. Twenty-four new undergraduate subjects were presented these lists at rates of eight per second and at one per second. Because the lists were shorter, and all were presented in silent conditions, subjects were presented with more lists in each condition (12) at each rate.

Recall levels were higher for these shorter lists: 45% for lists shown at a rate of eight per second and 90% for lists shown at one per second, and the main effect of rate was highly significant [$F(1, 23) = 1012.1$, $P < .0001$]. The

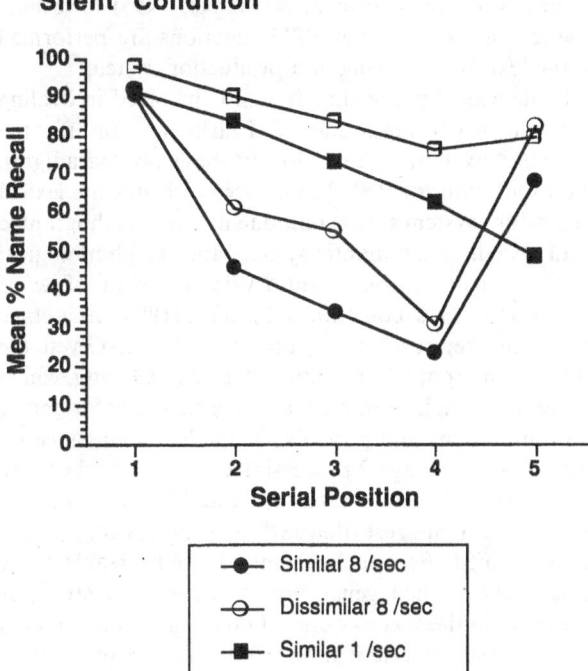

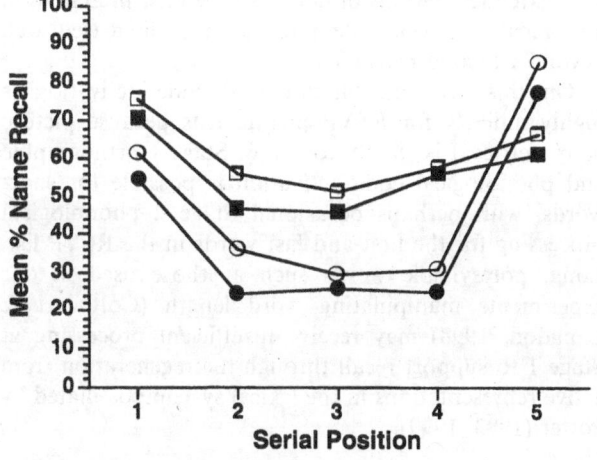

FIG. 2. Mean % picture names recalled for each serial position in silent and articulation conditions.

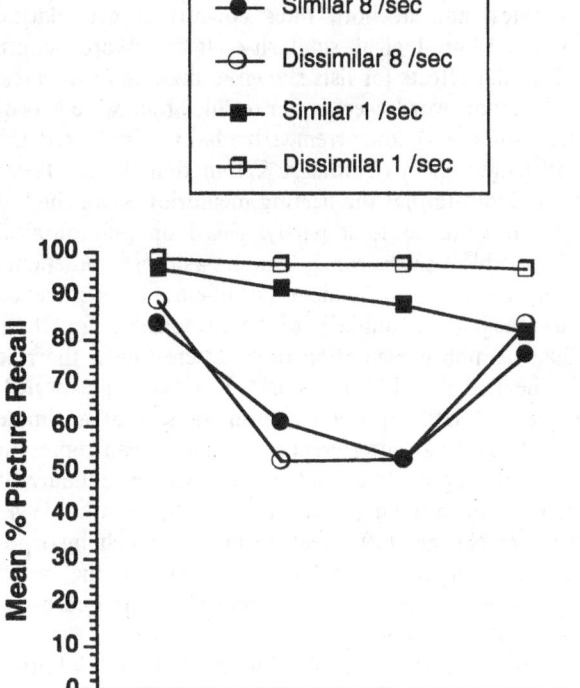

FIG. 3. Mean % pictures recalled for each serial position for lists of four pictures shown at rates of eight per second and one per second.

interaction between rate and phonological similarity yielded [$F(1, 23) = 14.38$, $P < .0009$]. Once again, the phonological similarity effect was significant only at the STM rate of one picture per second with a difference of 12% in recall of pictures with similar and dissimilar names [$F(1, 23) = 42.89$, $P < .0001$]. The serial position functions for these lists are shown in Fig. 3. Item recall at the RSVP rate showed strong primacy and recency effects for the first and last items. Recall of lists presented at the one per second rate was close to 100% correct at all serial positions for dissimilar lists. The inferior recall of pictures with similar names was mainly evident for the third and fourth serial positions.

The results of the experiments on memory for pictures showed no evidence of phonological coding at high presentation rates. This result possibly occurred because the names of list items could not be retrieved in the time available before the next item appears. Consequently, fleeting memories established at high presentation rates of up to 10 items per second may be based on phonological codes, but only if the items' names can be retrieved at those rates. Such retrieval is possible for written words but not for pictures of common objects.

CONCLUSIONS

Our research on short-term memory and RSVP paradigms in which visual information is presented at very high rates of up to 10 words or pictures per second has obtained the following findings. Phonological similarity of list words impairs recall of lists presented at high and low rates, and at both rates concurrent articulation removes phonological similarity effects. Word length had similar effects for lists shown at high and low rates: Lists of short words were better recalled than were lists of long words, and concurrent articulation eliminated the word length effect (Coltheart & Langdon, 1998). These results indicate that the fleeting memories established at high rates are, at least partly, based on phonological coding subject to the same variables as those influencing recall in short-term memory paradigms. It was argued that rehearsal is unlikely to be responsible for these effects at high presentation rates. Interestingly, the role of rehearsal in STM tasks has also been questioned. Brown and Hulme (1995) demonstrated that a simple trace decay or an interference mechanism can represent the word length effect and its removal by concurrent articulation. Similarly, Nairne's (1990; Neath, 1998; Neath & Nairne, 1995) feature model, which incorporates interference mechanisms, represents the word length effect without the requirement of a limited-capacity rehearsal process.

Potter's two-stage model (Chun & Potter, 1995; Potter, 1999) can account for the phonological effects observed at high rates of visual presentation as follows. In the first stage of processing, each stimulus in a sequence is rapidly identified when orthographic, phonological, and conceptual representations in long-term memory are activated. This process of identification can occur at high RSVP rates for written words. This first stage was assumed to generate a representation in conceptual short-term memory, a very fleeting form of memory. The second stage is required for maintenance in short-term memory, and it is a slower, serial process of consolidation which may take up to 400msec per item.

In the case of pictures, visual and semantic representations are rapidly accessed and activated, but name retrieval is a much slower process. Thus, phonological similarity of picture names does not produce repetition blindness (Kanwisher et al., 1999), nor does it reduce list recall when RSVP sequences are presented. RSVP picture recall must rely on other forms of code, visual and/or semantic-conceptual. Kanwisher et al. proposed that object tokens contain viewpoint-invariant object and semantic representations, but not phonological codes. Of course, under the much lower 1-second presentation rates characteristic of STM tasks, picture name retrieval is possible and maintenance of their phonological codes may be less effortful than maintenance of visual features and object representations. STM presentation rates also permit the establishment of inter-item links, which are important for successful retrieval of serial order.

The role of activation of long-term memory lexical and object representations is integral to Potter's (1993, 1999) theoretical account of short-term conceptual memory. Links between short-term memory stores and rehearsal mechanisms and the lexical processing system were unspecified in most theories of STM. However, Monsell (1987) proposed the lexical processing system as the processing system responsible for the functions of the phonological short-term store and rehearsal loop. He suggested that the speech feature buffer and phonological input lexicon constituted the phonological short-term store and that the recycling of phonological output to input representations via activation in the phonological output lexicon served as the rehearsal process. Similar accounts of auditory-verbal STM were offered by neuropsychologists studying memory in patients having STM deficits, e.g. Howard and Franklin (1989), and more recently by Martin and Saffran (1997). The lexical and semantic influences on STM initially reported by Besner and Davelaar (1982) and by Hulme and his colleagues (Hulme, Maughan, & Brown, 1991; Hulme, Roodenrys, Brown, & Mercer, 1995) have likewise led to the view that STM functions are performed by the lexical processing and production system.

If the lexical processing system is involved in dealing both with RSVP input and STM tasks, we can offer the following account of retention in these two paradigms. The rapid input of RSVP sequences activates the lexical processing system's subcomponents: the orthographic input lexicon, the semantic system, and the phonological output lexicon, through automatic processes of word recognition. This constitutes Potter's (1999) first-stage processing, registration in conceptual STM. Given the high rate of input of new items, Stage 2 processing, which is slow and serial, cannot occur, or occurs only for one or two initial items and possibly for the last item, since no item follows it. Stage 2 processing can occur at the more typical STM 1-second rates of input. What is Stage 2 processing? I suggest that Stage 2 processing, which Potter termed the establishment of a rehearsable STM code, is the explicit generation of an ordered string of phonemes in the speech output buffer (the "inner voice") and its subsequent activation of the "inner ear", activation of the speech input buffer and (if the item is a real word) the phonological input lexicon. Note that this entails a single internal utterance, not the multiple utterances of cumulative rehearsal, which perhaps only occur with extended periods of delay between list presentation and recall, or when item duration is increased well beyond 1 second per item.

On this account, phonological code activation is highly unlikely for RSVP picture lists because picture name retrieval is simply too slow. Stage 1 orthographic and phonological code activation is possible for short words, with perhaps occasional Stage 2 phonological processing for the first and last words in the RSVP list. Long, polysyllabic words such as those used in our experiments manipulating word length (Coltheart & Langdon, 1998) may receive insufficient processing at Stage 1 to support recall through the regeneration from active representations in the lexical system postulated by Potter (1993, 1999).

REFERENCES

Atkinson, R.C., & Shiffrin, R.M. (1968). Human memory: A proposed system and its control processes. In K. Spence & J. Spence (Eds.), *The psychology of learning and motivation, Vol. 2* (pp. 89–195). New York: Academic Press.

Baayen, R.H., Piepenbrock, R., & van Rijn, H. (1993). *The CELEX lexical database* (CD-ROM). Philadelphia, PA: Linguistic Data Consortium, University of Pennsylvania.

Baddeley, A.D. (1966). Short-term memory for word sequences as a function of acoustic, semantic and formal similarity. *Quarterly Journal of Experimental Psychology, 18*, 362–365.

Baddeley, A.D. (1986). *Working memory.* Oxford: Oxford University Press.

Baddeley, A.D. (1998). *Is STM just the activated portion of LTM?* Presented at Quebec 98 Conference on short-term memory, Quebec, Canada, 1998.

Baddeley, A.D., & Hitch, G.J. (1974). Working memory. In G.A. Bower (Ed.), *The psychology of learning and motivation, Vol. 8* (pp. 47–49). New York: Academic Press.

Baddeley, A.D., Thomson, N., & Buchanan, M. (1975). Word length and the structure of short-term memory. *Journal of Verbal Learning and Verbal Behavior, 14*, 575–589.

Bavelier, D., & Potter, M.C. (1992). Visual and phonological codes in repetition blindness. *Journal of Experimental Psychology: Human Perception and Performance, 18*, 134–147.

Besner, D., & Davelaar, E. (1982). Basis processes in reading: Two phonological codes. *Canadian Journal of Psychology, 36*, 701–711.

Biederman, I. (1981). On the semantics of a glance at a scene. In M. Kubovy & J.R. Pomerantz (Eds.), *Perceptual organization.* Hillsdale, NJ: Lawrence Erlbaum Associates Inc.

Brown, G.D.A., & Hulme, C. (1995). Modeling item length effects in memory span: No rehearsal needed? *Journal of Memory and Language, 34*, 594–621.

Chun, M.M., & Potter, M.C. (1995). A two-stage model for multiple target detection in rapid serial visual presentation. *Journal of Experimental Psychology: Human Perception and Performance, 21*, 109–127.

Coltheart, V. (1993). Effects of phonological similarity and concurrent irrelevant articulation on STM recall of repeated and novel word lists. *Memory and Cognition, 21*, 539–545.

Coltheart, V., & Langdon, R. (1998). Recall of short word lists presented visually at fast rates: Effects of phonological similarity and word length. *Memory and Cognition, 26*, 330–342.

Conrad, R. (1964). Acoustic confusion in immediate memory. *British Journal of Psychology, 55*, 75–84.

Forster, K.I. (1970). Visual perception of rapidly presented word sequences of varying complexity. *Perception and Psychophysics, 8*, 215–221.

Howard, D., & Franklin, S. (1989). Memory without rehearsal. In T. Shallice & G. Vallar (Eds), *Neuropsychological impairments of short-term memory.* Cambridge: Cambridge University Press.

Hulme, C., Maughan, S., & Brown, G.D.A. (1991). Memory for familiar and unfamiliar words: Evidence for a long-term memory contribution to short-term memory span. *Journal of Memory and Language, 30*, 685–701.

Hulme, C., Roodenrys, S., Brown, G.D.A., & Mercer, R. (1995). The role of long-term memory mechanisms in memory span. *British Journal of Psychology, 86*, 527–536.

Intraub, H. (1980). Presentation rate and the representation of briefly glimpsed pictures in memory. *Journal of Experimental Psychology: Human Learning and Memory, 6*, 1–12.

Intraub, H. (1981). Rapid conceptual identification of sequentially presented pictures. *Journal of Experimental Psychology: Human Perception and Performance, 7*, 604–610.

Intraub, H. (1984). Conceptual masking: The effects of subsequent visual events on memory for pictures. *Journal of Experimental Psychology: Learning, Memory and Cognition, 10*, 115–125.

Kanwisher, N.G. (1987) Repetition blindness: Type recognition without token individuation. *Cognition, 27*, 117–143.

Kanwisher, N.G., & Potter, M.C. (1990). Repetition blindness: Levels of processing. *Journal of Experimental Psychology: Human Perception and Performance, 16*, 30–47.

Kanwisher, N., Yin, C., & Wojciulik, E. (1999). Repetition blindness for pictures: Evidence for the rapid computation of abstract visual descriptions. In V. Coltheart (Ed.), *Fleeting memories: Cognition of brief visual stimuli.* Cambridge, MA: MIT Press.

Landauer, T.K. (1962). Rate of implicit speech. *Perceptual and Motor Skills, 15*, 646.

La Pointe, L.B., & Engle, R.W. (1990). Simple and complex word spans as measures of working memory capacity. *Journal of Experimental Psychology: Learning, Memory and Cognition, 16*, 1118–1133.

Marshall, P.H., & Cartwright, S.A. (1978). Failure to replicate a reported implicit/explicit speech equivalence. *Perceptual and Motor Skills, 46*, 1197–1198.

Marshall, P.H., & Cartwright, S.A. (1980). A final (?) note on implicit/explicit speech equivalence. *Bulletin of the Psychonomic Society, 15*, 409.

Martin, N., & Saffran, E.M. (1997). Language and auditory verbal short-term memory impairments: Evidence for common underlying processes. *Cognitive Neuropsychology, 14*, 641–682.

Monsell, S. (1987). On the relation between lexical input and output pathways for speech. In A. Allport, D. MacKay, W. Prinz, & E. Scheerer (Eds.), *Language perception and production: Relationships between listening, speaking, reading and writing* (pp. 273–311). London: Academic Press.

Murray, D.J. (1968). Articulation and acoustic confusability in short-term memory. *Journal of Experimental Psychology, 78*, 679–684.

Nairne, J.S. (1990). A feature model of immediate memory. *Memory and Cognition, 18*, 251–269.

Neath, I. (1998). *Extending the feature model.* Presented at Quebec 98 Conference on short-term memory, Quebec, Canada, 1998.

Neath, I., & Nairne, J. (1995). Word-length effects in immediate memory: Overwriting trace decay theory. *Psychonomic Bulletin and Review, 2*, 429–441.

Potter, M.C. (1975). Meaning in visual search. *Science, 187*, 965–966.

Potter, M.C. (1976). Short-term conceptual memory for pictures. *Journal of Experimental Psychology: Human Learning, and Memory, 2*, 509–522.

Potter, M.C. (1984). Rapid serial visual presentation (RSVP): A method for studying language processing. In D.E. Kieras & M.A. Just (Eds.), *New methods in reading comprehension research* (pp. 91–118). Hillsdale, NJ: Lawrence Erlbaum Associates Inc.

Potter, M.C. (1993). Very short-term conceptual memory. *Memory and Cognition, 21*, 156–161.

Potter, M.C. (1999). Understanding sentences and scenes: The role of conceptual short term memory. In V. Coltheart (Ed), *Fleeting memories: Cognition of brief visual stimuli.* Cambridge, MA: MIT Press.

Potter, M.C., & Faulconer, B.A. (1975). Time to understand pictures and words. *Nature, 253*, 437–438.

Potter, M.C., & Levy, E.I. (1969). Recognition memory for a rapid sequence of pictures. *Journal of Experimental Psychology, 81*, 10–15.

Potter, M.C., Moryadas, A., Abrams, J., & Noel, A. (1993). Word perception and misperception in context. *Journal of Experimental Psychology: Learning, Memory and Cognition, 19*, 3–22.

Potter, M.C., Stiefbold, D., & Moryadas, A. (1998). Word selection in reading sentences: Preceding versus following contexts. *Journal of Experimental Psychology: Learning, Memory and Cognition, 24*, 68–100.

Saffran, E.M., & Marin, O.S.M. (1975). Immediate memory for word lists and sentences in a patient with a deficient auditory short-term memory. *Brain and Language, 2*, 420–433.

Schiano, D.J., & Watkins, M.J. (1981). Speech-like coding of pictures in short-term memory. *Memory and Cognition, 9*, 110–114.

Snodgrass, J.G., & Vanderwart, M. (1980). A standardized set of 260 pictures: Norms for name agreement, image agreement, familiarity, and visual complexity. *Journal of Experimental Psychology: Human Learning and Memory, 6*, 174–215.

Phonological Similarity and Trace Degradation in the Serial Recall Task: When CAT helps RAT, but not MAN

Anthony B. Fallon and Kim Groves
Northern Territory University, Darwin, Australia

Gerald Tehan
University of Southern Queensland, Toowoomba, Australia

Phonological similarity is observed to affect serial recall detrimentally when correct-in-position scoring is used. Two experiments investigated the role of item and position accuracy scoring of rhyming, similar nonrhyming, and dissimilar lists under immediate recall conditions; articulatory suppression; or a filled delay. In general, rhyme lists produced the best item recall but position accuracy was highest for dissimilar lists. The results are due to a category cueing effect improving item recall for rhyme lists in conjunction with a detrimental effect of phonological similarity on position accuracy.

La similarité phonologique nuit au rappel sériel lorsque l'on considère le nombre de mots rappelés à la bonne position. Dans deux expériences la précision du rappel des items et de leur ordre est évaluée pour des listes qui riment, des listes similaires qui ne riment pas et des listes dissemblables. Ces listes sont utilisées dans une tâche de rappel immédiat, une tâche de rappel avec délai, ou avec suppression articulatoire. De façon générale, les listes contenant des mots qui riment produisent un meilleur rappel des items mais la précision de l'ordre est plus grande pour les listes dissemblables. Ces résultats seraient dus à deux facteurs: 1) l'utilisation d'une indice catégoriel qui améliore le rappel des items pour des listes de mots qui riment et 2) un effet de similarité phonologique qui nuit au rappel de l'ordre des items.

Lists of words that sound similar to one another are harder to remember on an immediate serial recall task than lists of words that contain phonologically dissimilar items (Baddeley, 1966; Conrad & Hull, 1964). Most current models of immediate serial recall (Baddeley, 1986; Brown & Hulme, 1995; Burgess & Hitch, 1992; Nairne, 1990; Schweickert, 1993) assert that serial order is harder to maintain when all items in the list are phonologically similar to one another.

In phonological similarity research, recall has most often been scored in terms of the number of items recalled in correct serial position. However, alternative scoring procedures are available. Item recall is usually scored by counting the number of list items recalled, regardless of the order in which they are recalled (e.g. Crowder, 1979; Watkins, Watkins, & Crowder, 1974). The second procedure scores position accuracy, which can be more complicated. Simply counting the number of transpositions is not acceptable if there are differences in item recall. One solution is to score the number of items recalled in correct position as a proportion of the number of items recalled regardless of position (Poirier & Saint-Aubin, 1995; Saint-Aubin & Poirier, in press; Wickelgren, 1965).

There are important reasons for thinking about immediate serial recall in terms of item and position accuracy scoring. For example, the absence of phonological similarity effects under suppression or a brief retention interval has led a number of authors to suppose that phonemic traces only support recall for a few seconds. After that period, either decay or interference is assumed to reduce the integrity of the trace to levels where it cannot support recall (Baddeley, 1986; Tehan & Humphreys, 1995). If these assumptions are correct, the absence of phonemic representations would be manifest as a null effect of phonological similarity for both the item and accuracy scoring. An alternative way of accounting for the attenuation of similarity effects is to suggest that similarity might have opposite effects on item and accuracy scoring. That is, it is possible that similarity might facilitate item recall but lead to an increase in transposition errors. Thus, under suppression or a delay, the absence of similarity effects could be due to a beneficial effect of similarity at the item level masking a detrimental effect at the accuracy level.

This second scenario might occur if rhyme categories result in a category cuing effect (Crowder, 1979; Huttenlocher & Newcombe, 1976; Poirier & Saint-Aubin, 1995). In both the long-term memory literature (Tulving & Pearlstone, 1966) and short-term memory literature (Huttenlocher & Newcombe, 1976; Poirier &

Requests for reprints should be addressed to Gerry Tehan, Department of Psychology, University of Southern Queensland, Toowoomba, Q. 4350, Australia (E-mail: tehan@usq.edu.au).

© 1999 International Union of Psychological Science

Saint-Aubin, 1995; Saint-Aubin & Poirier, in press), taxonomic category membership acts as an effective retrieval cue to facilitate recall. In the short-term domain this advantage is limited to item recall (Huttenlocher & Newcombe, 1976; Poirier & Saint-Aubin, 1995; Saint-Aubin & Poirier, in press). If taxonomic categories can serve as a retrieval cue, rhyme categories might also improve item recall in phonologically similar lists.

In spite of the fundamental importance of the phonological similarity effect, only six studies have investigated phonological similarity effects at the item level. The results from these studies are equivocal. Sometimes a beneficial effect is observed (Gathercole, Gardiner, & Gregg, 1982; Wickelgren, 1965), sometimes no effect is observed (Poirier & Saint-Aubin, 1996; Watkins et al., 1974); and some studies show a detrimental effect (Coltheart, 1993; Drewnowski, 1980).

The dimension that appears most relevant for discriminating between these studies is the operationalization of phonological similarity. The studies that demonstrated beneficial effects operationalized phonological similarity in terms of items from rhyme categories. Those that demonstrated a detrimental effect operationalized phonological similarity in terms of high phonemic overlap but no category membership (e.g. *can mad cap man cad cat map mat*). The one study (Watkins et al., 1974) that demonstrated a null effect used a mixture of rhyming and nonrhyming items in their similar lists. Given these findings, one might conclude that a beneficial effect of phonological similarity only occurs when rhyming items are used.

In the following studies we investigated item and accuracy scoring of phonological similarity where similarity was operationalized in two distinct ways; either items from rhyme categories or items that had high phonemic overlap but did not come from any single rhyme category. The expectation was that phonological similarity effects would differ for the two types of lists. We expected that there would be differences in item recall between the two types of similar lists and that this would have an impact upon correct-in-position effects. We were not certain about differential order errors but expected both types of similarity to produce transposition errors.

EXPERIMENT 1

Method

Participants. Thirty-six undergraduates from the Northern Territory University volunteered to participate in this experiment. The participants represented a mix of students from a variety of disciplines, tertiary levels, and age groups.

Materials. The materials used in this experiment are those used by Coltheart (1993), plus five additional words. Coltheart's similar materials comprised 50 three-letter-"a" words. These included a limited set of eight final consonants (e.g. *rat, map, tab, fad, can, gag, lax, dam*). Coltheart's similar items can be reorganized into eight rhyme sets (i.e. at, ap, ab, ad, an, ag, ax, am). Because each ending set did not contain six items, five words were added to this pool: *nag, fax, pam, rag,* and *max*. The 50 dissimilar words in Coltheart's set matched the similar words in word frequency.

These two sets were used to create eight dissimilar, eight similar nonrhyming, and eight rhyming six-word lists that were sampled from the appropriate pool without replacement. Thus the words from the similar pool were sampled twice such that each word appeared in one similar and one rhyming list. A requirement of construction of the similar nonrhyming lists was that no items share a final consonant. Similarly, following random sampling, dissimilar items were rearranged across lists so that each list contained the minimum number of words that shared the same start or ending consonant. Essentially, these two sampling constraints were intended to maintain a relatively constant level of similarity and dissimilarity across conditions.

The lists were presented in three blocks of eight trials. The order of the items within each list, the order of the trials within each block, and the order of the blocks within the experiment session were counterbalanced.

Procedure. All subjects were individually tested, and assigned to the between-subject conditions randomly such that 18 participants were assigned to each of the study conditions. Each trial began with a warning tone. Six words were then presented individually in the centre of a computer screen at the rate of one word per second. Immediately following the presentation of the last list item, a row of question marks was displayed as a recall prompt. Strict serial recall instructions were used: Participants were required to write the words in the order they were presented, in columns numbered one to six, and to put a dash if they could not recall an item.

The study conditions for each list differed for the two sets of participants. Half were required to articulate "the" as quickly as possible during presentation of list items. The other half remained silent during item presentation. Everyone attempted to recall the items under silent conditions.

Results

Table 1 summarizes performance for similar nonrhyming, rhyming, and dissimilar trials in silent and suppressed conditions, collapsed across serial position for the three scoring procedures. We used 3×2 mixed-design analyses of variance (ANOVAs) to analyze the three sets of data. In this and all subsequent analyses, an alpha level of .05 was selected, unless specified otherwise.

Correct-in-position performance was better in the silent than the suppression condition, $F(1,34) = 9.21$, $MSe = 0.08$. A main effect of phonological similarity

TABLE 1
Mean Proportions Correct for Rhyming, Similar, and Dissimilar Trials

Scoring Procedure	Similarity		
	Rhyming	Similar	Dissimilar
Silent			
Correct-in-position	0.57	0.45	0.59
Item recall	0.76	0.52	0.65
Recall accuracy	0.71	0.84	0.90
Suppressed			
Correct-in-position	0.38	0.32	0.42
Item recall	0.60	0.39	0.49
Recall accuracy	0.62	0.81	0.84

was also observed, $F(2,68) = 16.02$, $MSe = 0.09$. Post hoc repeated-measures t-tests with sequential Bonferroni adjustments revealed that dissimilar lists were better recalled than the similar nonrhyming lists, $t(35) = 6.37$, but there was no difference between the dissimilar and rhyming lists, $t(34) = 1.33$. Phonological similarity did not interact with the articulatory suppression, $F(2,68) < 1$, $MSe = 0.09$.

For item scoring an item was recalled as correct if it was produced anywhere in the output. Item recall was higher in the silent condition than the suppression condition, $F(1,34) = 10.90$, $MSe = 0.06$. A main effect was also observed for phonological similarity, $F(2,68) = 67.49$, $MSe = 0.01$. Bonferroni adjusted, post hoc comparisons indicated that performance was higher in the rhyming condition than the dissimilar condition, $t(35) = 5.15$. Performance in the dissimilar condition was higher than performance in the similar nonrhyming condition, $t(35) = 6.52$. Phonological similarity did not interact with articulatory suppression, $F(2,68) < 1$, $MSe = 0.01$.

The measure we use to reflect order accuracy involves dividing the correct-in-position score by the item score. This produces the proportion of items in correct position as a function of items correctly recalled; the greater the number of transpositions the lower this proportion will be. Under these scoring conditions, the main effect for suppression was not significant, $F(1,34) = 1.84$, $MSe = 0.05$. A main effect of phonological similarity was observed, $F(2, 68) = 29.91$, $MSe = 0.01$. Bonferroni adjusted comparisons revealed better performance in the dissimilar condition than either the rhyming condition, $t(35) = 7.21$, or the similar nonrhyming condition, $t(35) = 2.34$. In addition, better performance emerged in the similar nonrhyming condition than the rhyming condition, $t(35) = 4.74$. There was no interaction between phonological similarity and articulatory suppression, $F(2,66) < 1$, $MSe = 0.01$.

Discussion

With the correct-in-position scoring under silent conditions we replicate the detrimental effect of phonological similarity with the nonrhyming similar material. However, unlike previous research the phonological similarity effect was not attenuated under suppression for either type of list. We are not sure why this happened, but it may be a function of suppression being a between-subjects variable, rather than a within-subjects variable as it usually is.

With item scoring, recall was best when the items in the list all rhymed. It looks as though membership of a rhyme category can act as a retrieval cue to facilitate item recall. Furthermore, when similar items do not rhyme, similarity has a detrimental effect upon item recall.

Not only are the dissimilar lists well recalled, they are recalled accurately. This is not the case with both types of similar lists where a high number of transposition errors occur. The rhyming items are transposed more often than the nonrhyming similar items. It is not clear whether this is a category effect or due to the fact that there is more phonemic overlap in the representations of the rhyming items than the nonrhyming items. Whatever the explanation, it is the case that the advantage that category membership produces with item information disappears with position accuracy scoring.

In comparing recall of the two similar conditions to that of the dissimilar conditions, we are in a position to evaluate our original proposition that phonological similarity effects under item scoring depend upon the way in which phonological similarity is operationalized. In the current study the comparison between the dissimilar and the similar nonrhyming conditions represent a close replication of Coltheart's experiment. She found that with these materials there was a similarity decrement. We replicate these results. However, when we take the same set of words but reorganize them into their rhyme categories, we find a facilitatory effect of similarity, as have others who have used lists of rhyming items (Gathercole et al., 1982; Wickelgren, 1965). It would seem that we have some evidence to explain the differences in similarity effects that have been observed in prior research.

The absence of phonological similarity effects under silent conditions with the correct-in-position measure for the rhyming lists can be viewed as an item advantage for the rhyming lists being offset by an increased propensity for transpositions. With the nonrhyming similar lists we have a disadvantage for item recall coupled with increases in transpositions, which translates into the phonological similarity decrement. The effects under suppression appear to emerge in much the same way. Both types of similar lists produce transposition errors; rhyming lists have an item advantage, and similar nonrhyming lists do not. Thus, similarity effects in correct-in-position scores appear critically dependent upon item recall. Additionally, these results imply that phonemic influences are still strong under suppression conditions. Consequently, those who have argued that suppression prevents a phonemic trace from being formed (Baddeley, 1986) may well be in error.

Re-analysis of Tehan and Humphreys (1995; Experiment 1)

Tehan and Humphreys (1995) made the same assumption about the effects of a brief, filled retention interval on the phonemic similarity effect. They (Tehan & Humphreys, 1995, Experiment 1) had their subjects study four-item rhyming or dissimilar lists. Recall was tested immediately or after a 2sec retention interval filled with a verbal shadowing task. With the correct-in-position measure they found the usual detrimental effect of phonological similarity on an immediate test, but no difference in recall between rhyming and dissimilar lists on the delayed test. They suggested that the trace became degraded during the 2-second interval such that it no longer supported recall. If this argument is correct, one would expect to find no differences on item or accuracy measures between rhyming and dissimilar lists. However, if the results of Experiment 1 are an indication, it is possible that effects under delayed conditions reflect a trade-off between item and order scoring. In Table 2 we present the original correct-in-position scores and a re-scoring of their data using the item and position accuracy procedures that were used in Experiment 1.

An analysis of item scores indicated no similarity effect on an immediate test, $F(1,19) = 2.02$, $MSe = 0.002$, but on the delayed test, the rhyming words were much better recalled than the dissimilar words, $F(1,19) = 13.84$; $MSe = 0.014$. For the position accuracy measure, dissimilar words were more likely to be recalled in position than rhyming words on both immediate and delayed tests, $F(1,19) = 21.95$; $MSe = 0.005$, and $F(1,19) = 30.26$; $MSe = 0.002$, respectively. In short, our reanalysis of the Tehan and Humphreys (1995) data indicates that their interpretation of the delayed correct-in-position results was incorrect. The attenuation of the phonological similarity effect under delayed testing is the result of a cuing advantage for the rhyming lists in item recall offsetting the deleterious effects of increased transposition errors.

The results of the suppression condition in Experiment 1 and the delayed condition of the Tehan and Humphreys experiments are identical for item and position accuracy scoring. More transpositions are made in the rhyming lists that the dissimilar lists but item recall is better in the rhyming lists than the dissimilar lists. However, in silent conditions, the similarity advantage in item scoring in Experiment 1 is absent in the Tehan and Humphreys experiment. Absolute levels of item recall are higher in the Tehan and Humphreys experiment in which four-word lists were studied, than was the case in Experiment 1 where six-word lists were studied. One possibility is that more forgetting might occur during recall of the long lists than the short lists (Cowan, 1993), such that substantial trace degradation is present for some items in the longer lists. Thus, similarity may facilitate item information with the longer lists in the same way that it does with suppression or a filled retention interval. To bridge the gap between four-word and six-word lists, in the next experiment we use five-word lists.

EXPERIMENT 2

In this experiment we again studied serial recall of dissimilar, rhyming, and similar nonrhyming lists. Recall was tested immediately or after a brief filled retention interval. Experiment 1 (and Tehan and Humphreys) used open word pools to construct the study lists. We wondered what effect a closed word pool might have on item and transposition effects. To this extent, we took Baddeley's (1966) materials that consist of two eight-item word pools: one containing dissimilar items and the other containing nonrhyming similar items. To this we added another eight-item word pool which consisted of eight items from a single rhyme category. Thus all trials in the experiment were constructed from these three word pools. Obviously, with such small word pools, items appeared more than once throughout the experiment. Our expectations were that we would replicate the principle findings of Experiment 1.

Method

Subjects. Forty introductory level students from the University of Southern Queensland participated for course credit. Half the subjects were tested immediately and half were tested after a brief delay.

Materials. Baddeley's (1966) materials were used to construct the dissimilar and nonrhyming similar lists. The word pool for dissimilar lists consisted of the words: *cow day bar few hot pit pen sup*. The nonrhyming similar pool was *can mad cap man cad cat map mat*. The rhyming similar pool was *lip hip tip sip dip zip rip pip*.

For each participant, 33 five-item trials were created by randomly sampling each word pool 11 times. One trial of each type served a practice trial and these three trials represented the first trials that each participant saw. The remaining 30 trials consisted of 10 dissimilar, 10 non-

TABLE 2
Mean Proportions Correct for Rhyming and Dissimilar Trials

Scoring Procedure	Similarity	
	Rhyming	Dissimilar
Immediate		
Correct-in-position	0.69	0.79
Item recall	0.80	0.82
Recall accuracy	0.86	0.97
Delayed		
Correct-in-position	0.32	0.33
Item recall	0.52	0.38
Recall accuracy	0.61	0.86

rhyming similar, and 10 rhyming trials. The order of these trials was randomized for each participant.

Procedure. On each trial the five words in the list were presented at a rate of one word per second. Half the participants were tested immediately after the fifth item in each list. For the remaining participants recall was tested after a 2sec filled retention interval. Following the fifth word in the list, two two-digit numbers were presented at the same rate as the words. Participants were required to read each digit string as it appeared on the computer screen. After the second digit string had been shadowed, recall of the word list was attempted.

Results

The results of the experiment are presented in Table 3 for the three scoring procedures. We used 3×2 ANOVAs to analyze the three dependent measures. For correct-in-position scores there were main effects for similarity, $F(2,72) = 46.76$; $MSe = 0.012$, and retention interval, $F(1,38) = 69.24$; $MSe = 0.035$, and the interaction was significant, $F(2,72) = 3.38$; $MSe = 0.012$. Planned comparisons indicated that on immediate test, dissimilar lists were better recalled than rhyming lists, $F(1,19) = 35.70$; $MSe = 0.009$, and nonrhyming similar lists, $F(1,19) = 58.32$; $MSe = 0.015$. Dissimilar lists were also better recalled than rhyming lists, $F(1,19) = 8.85$; $MSe = 0.011$, and nonrhyming similar lists, $F(1,19) = 22.22$; $MSe = 0.013$, on the delayed test. Furthermore, rhyming lists were better than nonrhyming similar lists on immediate and delayed tests, $F(1,19) = 8.79$; $MSe = 0.014$, and $F(1,19) = 6.51$; $MSe = 0.008$, respectively.

For item recall, there were main effects for similarity, $F(2,72) = 32.51$; $MSe = 0.008$, and retention interval, $F(1,38) = 35.19$; $MSe = 0.034$, and the interaction was significant, $F(2,72) = 5.17$; $MSe = 0.008$. Planned comparisons indicated that on an immediate test, dissimilar lists were better recalled than nonrhyming similar lists, $F(1,19) = 38.77$; $MSe = 0.008$, but there was no difference between dissimilar and rhyming lists, $F(1,19) = 1.98$; $MSe = 0.007$. On the delayed test, dissimilar lists were also better recalled than nonrhyming similar lists, $F(1,19) = 5.76$; $MSe = 0.009$, but rhyming lists were better recalled than dissimilar lists, $F(1,19) = 4.82$; $MSe = 0.012$. Furthermore, rhyming lists were better recalled than similar nonrhyming lists on both an immediate and delayed tests, $F(1,19) = 47.29$; $MSe = 0.006$, and $F(1,19) = 40.07$; $MSe = 0.006$, respectively.

For position accuracy, there were main effects for similarity, $F(2,72) = 38.73$; $MSe = 0.012$, and retention interval, $F(1,38) = 35.04$; $MSe = 0.034$, but the interaction was not significant, $F(2,72) < 1$; $MSe = 0.012$. Planned comparisons indicated that on an immediate test, the proportion of correctly positioned items on dissimilar lists was greater than that for similar lists, $F(1,19) = 48.95$; $MSe = 0.007$, and rhyming lists, $F(1,19) = 63.69$; $MSe = 0.006$. The proportion of correctly positioned items on dissimilar lists was also greater than that for similar lists, $F(1,19) = 13.55$; $MSe = 0.018$, and rhyming lists, $F(1,19) = 31.49$; $MSe = 0.015$, on the delayed test. Furthermore, the proportion of correctly positioned items was equivalent for rhyming and similar lists on immediate and delayed tests, $F(1,19) < 1$; $MSe = 0.015$, and $F(1,19) = 2.94$; $MSe = 0.014$, respectively.

Discussion

It seems that using a closed word pool does not have an overly large impact on patterns of performance, in that we replicate many of the features of Experiment 1. The differences between the dissimilar lists and nonrhyming similar lists are identical for all three scoring procedures. The differences between similar and rhyming lists were also quite similar in that the rhyming lists provided better item information than the similar lists.

There are differences, however, between the dissimilar and rhyming lists across the two experiments. For the correct-in-position measure, detrimental effects of phonological similarity are observed in the immediate condition in this experiment whereas they were not observed in the equivalent condition of Experiment 1. This appears attributable in large part to the fact that rhyming lists produce better item information than dissimilar lists in Experiment 1, whereas with the closed pool in this experiment, item information is equivalent for the two types of lists. The dominance of item information for the rhyming lists in the delayed condition in this experiment is similar to that observed in Experiment 1, where articulatory suppression was used to degrade the trace. Correct positioning of items is better in dissimilar lists than in both types of similar lists and this is true for both retention intervals.

GENERAL DISCUSSION

In the introduction to this paper we indicated that some anomalous similarity effects might be resolved if we were to look at alternative scoring measures. We identified three issues; whether or not using rhyming lists would

TABLE 3
Mean Proportions Correct for Rhyming, Similar Nonrhyming and Dissimilar Trials

	Similarity		
Scoring Procedure	Rhyming	Similar	Dissimilar
Immediate			
Correct-in-position	0.59	0.48	0.78
Item recall	0.82	0.67	0.86
Recall accuracy	0.71	0.71	0.90
Delayed			
Correct-in-position	0.32	0.24	0.42
Item recall	0.66	0.50	0.58
Recall accuracy	0.48	0.48	0.70

provide a cueing advantage over nonrhyming similar lists; whether the presence or absence of similarity effects using item measures that have been reported in other studies could be attributed to a cueing effect; and whether the attenuation of the phonological similarity effect under degraded conditions indicated that phonemic codes no longer supported recall. The results of the current experiments provide fairly unambiguous answers to all three issues.

The results of Experiments 1 and 2 clearly indicate that the way in which phonological similarity is operationalized has a large bearing on performance. Using item measures, rhyming lists produce better recall than the nonrhyming similar lists under all conditions. The clearest explanation for this advantage is in terms of a cueing effect; evidence coming from Experiment 1 where the same set of items was used to construct the similar nonrhyming and rhyming lists. All that varied was the organization of the items within each list. The rhyme ending appears to provide a retrieval cue that enhances item recall. We have indicated elsewhere how retrieval cues might facilitate short-term recall (Tehan & Fallon, 1999) and Nairne and his colleagues have made similar suggestions (Nairne, 1990; Nairne & Kelley, 1999).

The cueing advantage of the rhyming lists is not just limited to comparisons with nonrhyming similar lists. The advantage is also present when comparisons are made between rhyming and dissimilar lists in degraded conditions. When articulatory suppression is required or a filled retention interval is used, rhyming lists produce better item recall than dissimilar lists in both experiments and in the reanalysis of the Tehan and Humphreys' data. On immediate tests where subjects are free to rehearse, similarity effects critically depend upon the item information available for dissimilar lists. In Experiment 1, where we have long lists derived from an open word pool, the cueing advantage for rhyming lists is present. In Experiment 2 and in the Tehan and Humphreys' experiment, there are factors that facilitate item recall of dissimilar lists. In Tehan and Humphreys, the lists are all very short and in Experiment 2 dissimilar words are repeated frequently throughout the experiment. Both these factors appear to promote item availability for dissimilar items to a point where item recall is as good as that for rhyming lists. The results of these experiments clearly suggest that the discrepancies in similarity effects at the item level that were noted in the introduction can be attributed to the way in which similarity is operationalized.

The final point the results speak to involves the role of phonological codes under degraded conditions. Baddeley has argued that the effect of articulatory suppression is to prevent the formation of phonemic traces and Tehan and Humphreys (1995) have argued that a brief retention interval is also sufficient to eliminate these codes. These assumptions would be reflected in the data not only by the absence of a similarity effect in the correct-in-position scores, but also similar absences with item and order scoring. This has not been the case in the current results. As we have seen, phonological similarity continues to affect item and order information effects under degraded conditions. The only conclusion is that phonemic codes still support recall under articulatory suppression or after a brief, filled retention interval. The null effect for correct-in-position scores reflects the opposite influences that rhyme membership has for item recall and serial position accuracy.

REFERENCES

Baddeley, A.D. (1966). Short-term memory for word sequences as a function of acoustic, semantic, or formal similarity. *Quarterly Journal of Experimental Psychology, 18*, 362–365.

Baddeley, A.D. (1986). *Working memory*. London: Oxford University Press.

Brown, G.D.A., & Hulme, C. (1995). Modeling item length effects in memory span: No rehearsal needed? *Journal of Memory and Language, 34*, 594–621.

Burgess, N., & Hitch, G.J. (1992). Toward a network model of the articulatory loop. *Journal of Memory and Language, 31*, 429–460.

Coltheart, V. (1993). Effects of phonological similarity and concurrent irrelevant articulation on short-term-memory recall of repeated and novel word lists. *Memory and Cognition, 4*, 539–545.

Conrad, R., & Hull, A.J. (1964). Information, acoustic confusion and memory span. *British Journal of Psychology, 55*, 429–432.

Cowan, N. (1993). Activation, attention, and short-term memory. *Memory and Cognition, 21*, 162–167.

Crowder, R.G. (1979). Similarity and order in memory. In G.H. Bower (Ed.), *The psychology of learning and motivation: Advances in research and theory, Vol. 13* (pp. 319–353). New York: Academic Press.

Drewnowski, A. (1980). Attributes and priorities in short-term recall: A new model of memory span. *Journal of Experimental Psychology: General, 109*, 208–250.

Gathercole, S.E., Gardiner, J.M., & Gregg, V.H. (1982). Modality and phonological similarity effects in serial recall: Does one's own voice play a role? *Memory and Cognition, 10*, 176–180.

Huttenlocher, J., & Newcombe, N. (1976). Semantic effects on ordered recall. *Journal of Verbal Learning and Verbal Behavior, 15*, 387–399.

Nairne, J.S. (1990). A feature model of immediate memory. *Memory and Cognition, 18*, 251–269.

Nairne, J.S., & Kelley, M.R. (1999). Reversing the phonological similarity effect. *Memory and Cognition, 27*, 45–53.

Poirier, M., & Saint-Aubin, J. (1995). Memory for related and unrelated words: Further evidence on the influence of semantic factors in immediate serial recall. *Quarterly Journal of Experimental Psychology, 48A*, 384–404.

Poirier, M., & Saint-Aubin, J. (1996). Immediate serial recall, word frequency, item identity, and item position. *Canadian Journal of Experimental Psychology, 50*, 408–412.

Saint-Aubin, J., & Poirier, M. (in press). Semantic similarity and immediate serial recall: Is there a detrimental effect on order information? *Canadian Journal of Psychology*.

Schweickert, R. (1993). A multinomial processing tree model for degradation and redintegration in immediate recall. *Memory and Cognition, 21*, 168–175.

Tehan, G., & Fallon, A.B. (1999). A connectionist model of

short-term cued recall. In J. Wiles & T. Dartnell (Eds.), *Prospectives in cognitive science* (pp. 221-237). Stamford, CT: Ablex.

Tehan, G., & Humphreys, M.S. (1995). Transient phonemic codes and immunity to proactive interference. *Memory and Cognition, 23,* 181-191.

Tulving, E., & Pearlstone, Z. (1966). Availability versus accessibility of information in memory for words. *Journal of Verbal Learning and Verbal Behavior, 5,* 381-391.

Watkins, M.J., Watkins, O.C., & Crowder, R.G. (1974). The modality effect in free and serial recall as a function of phonological similarity. *Journal of Verbal Learning and Verbal Behavior, 13,* 430-447.

Wickelgren, W.A. (1965). Short-term memory for phonologically similar lists. *American Journal of Psychology, 78,* 567-574.

Short-term Memory in Time Interval Production

Claudette Fortin
Université Laval, Québec, Canada

This article summarizes results from several studies on the effect of nontemporal processing on concurrent time estimation. These studies use an experimental paradigm that was developed to interpolate various nontemporal tasks in time interval production. Produced intervals were specifically lengthened by increasing the amount of short-term memory processing performed in a concurrent search task. The interference was shown with many short-term memory tasks, using various durations and methods in the temporal task. The effect on temporal production seems to be positively related to the level of difficulty of the short-term memory task. Finally, processing item or order information affects simultaneous time production, whereas its maintenance has no effect. An interference analysis of these phenomena suggests that interruption in time estimation is caused by both temporal and nontemporal tasks simultaneously requiring processing in short-term memory.

Cet article résume les résultats d'études sur l'effet d'un traitement non temporal sur l'estimation temporelle simultanée. Ces études utilisent un paradigme expérimental développé pour insérer différentes tâches non temporelles dans une production d'intervalle temporel. Les intervalles allongent spécifiquement avec l'augmentation de la quantité d'information traitée en mémoire à court terme, lors de l'exécution simultanée d'une tâche non temporelle. L'interférence a été vérifiée avec plusieurs tâches sollicitant la mémoire à court terme, avec différentes durées et méthodes dans la tâche temporelle. L'effet est relié positivement au niveau de difficulté de la tâche de mémoire à court terme. Finalement, le traitement d'information d'item ou d'ordre affecte la production, tandis que le maintien de cette information n'a pas d'effet. Une analyse d'interférence de ces phénomènes suggère qu'une interruption dans l'estimation temporelle est causée par l'utilisation simultanée de la mémoire à court terme dans les tâches temporelles et non temporelles.

Identical time intervals are not necessarily estimated as equal in duration. For example, in one experiment, participants were asked to estimate the duration of a semantic judgement task in which they were to classify words as representing living or nonliving things during a 48-second period. The number of required judgements was varied: 14 in the few-event condition and 28 in the many-event condition. The results showed that the duration in the many-event condition was systematically judged as shorter than the same duration in the few-event condition (Predebon, 1996). These results are consistent with those of a number of studies on the effect of a variety of nontemporal tasks on concurrent time estimation in a prospective paradigm, that is, when the participant knows in advance that the duration will have to be estimated (e.g. Block, 1992; Brown, 1997; Zakay, 1998).

These studies clarify how the conditions in which temporal judgements are performed affect estimated durations. For example, complex interactions between various factors such as the temporal paradigm (prospective versus retrospective), and whether or not overt responses are required, have been shown. These findings are usually interpreted within attentional models of time estimation (e.g. Hicks, Miller, & Kinsbourne, 1976; Thomas & Weaver, 1975), which assume that during a time estimation task, temporal units emitted from an internal source are stored. This accumulation requiring attentional resources, if concurrent processing also requires attention, fewer temporal units will be stored, which results in a relative underestimation of the duration.

Most studies demonstrating a relationship between time estimation and nontemporal processing have used relatively complex nontemporal tasks involving perceptual, cognitive, and motor components, such as card sorting (Hicks et al., 1976), motor tracking (Brown, 1997), or semantic or graphemic classification tasks (e.g. Predebon, 1996), these tasks being executed continuously over moderately long durations (e.g. 20 to 120sec).

In the studies reported here, the interference from nontemporal processing on concurrent time production was analyzed with simple tasks interpolated within discrete time intervals of brief duration. These studies have brought some relevant information concerning four main issues related to this phenomenon. First, within a set of different search tasks, time production has been shown to be affected *specifically* by STM processing. Second, the *generality* of this effect of STM processing on concurrent time estimation has been demonstrated in various conditions. Third, the extent to which STM processing interferes with time estimation was shown to

---

Requests for reprints should be addressed to Claudette Fortin, École de psychologie, Université Laval, Québec (Qc) Canada, G1K 7P4 (Tel: (418) 656–2131(7253); E-mail: Claudette.Fortin@psy.ulaval.ca).

© 1999 International Union of Psychological Science

be related to the level of *difficulty* of the STM task. Fourth, given a certain amount of item or order information to process, *processing* in STM affects concurrent time estimation, while its maintenance has no effect. Before reporting these studies, some common elements concerning the procedures and analyses will be described. Then, the experiments and results related to the four issues will be summarized.

PROCEDURES AND ANALYSES

In these experiments, a temporal production consists of pressing a key twice, the second keypress being executed after a predetermined target duration has elapsed. In general, in the experiments described hereafter, a single target duration is produced throughout the experiment. This performance is generally quite stable, since temporal production is practised during two or three training sessions. These are followed by experimental sessions, in which a nontemporal task is combined with the temporal interval production. The duration of the nontemporal task is estimated in a reaction time control condition. To allow completion of the nontemporal task within the limits of the produced interval and thus induce effective concurrent processing, the duration of nontemporal processing is always shorter than the time estimation duration; the ratio of the mean nontemporal processing duration on the time estimation duration is generally around .25 to .30. There are usually 2 experimental sessions including about 200 experimental trials. The number of participants varies from 7 to 20 in each condition and within-subject designs are generally used. Productions are measured to the nearest millisecond. All the effects reported in the following experiments were statistically significant to at least $P < .05$.

The main dependent variable of interest is the duration of the produced temporal intervals. However, error data in the nontemporal tasks are routinely collected and analyzed, to rule out any interpretation of the differences in temporal performance in terms of speed-accuracy trade-offs. When reaction time control conditions are included, reaction times, as well as error data, are analyzed in these conditions. Different participants are tested in the reaction time and concurrent processing conditions to avoid transfer of strategies from one condition to another. Trials in which there is an error in the nontemporal task are eliminated. Error rates are generally low, around 5% in most of the cases, and they do not exceed 10%.

THE SPECIFIC INTERFERENCE FROM STM PROCESSING ON TIME INTERVAL PRODUCTION

To analyze the specific nature of the interfering operations on time estimation, different search tasks were combined with temporal production of a brief time interval (2 to 4sec) (Fortin, Rousseau, Bourque, & Kirouac, 1993). In four experiments, four different search tasks were combined with temporal production, as shown in Fig. 1. Figure 1a shows a Sternberg's item recognition task interpolated within a time production. After memorizing a set of items, the participant began the temporal production by pressing the middle key of three keys arranged in a row. Then, 500msec after this keypress, a memory probe was presented. When the participant judged that the target interval had elapsed, he/she was instructed to press the left key if the probe belonged to the memory set, the right key if it did not.

In another experiment, a visual search involving some STM processing, but to a lesser extent than in the previous experiment, was combined with a 2-sec time production as illustrated in Fig. 1b. The structure of the trials was similar to that in the first experiment. However, a single item was presented, and the number of items simultaneously presented during the temporal production was varied from one to five. It was assumed

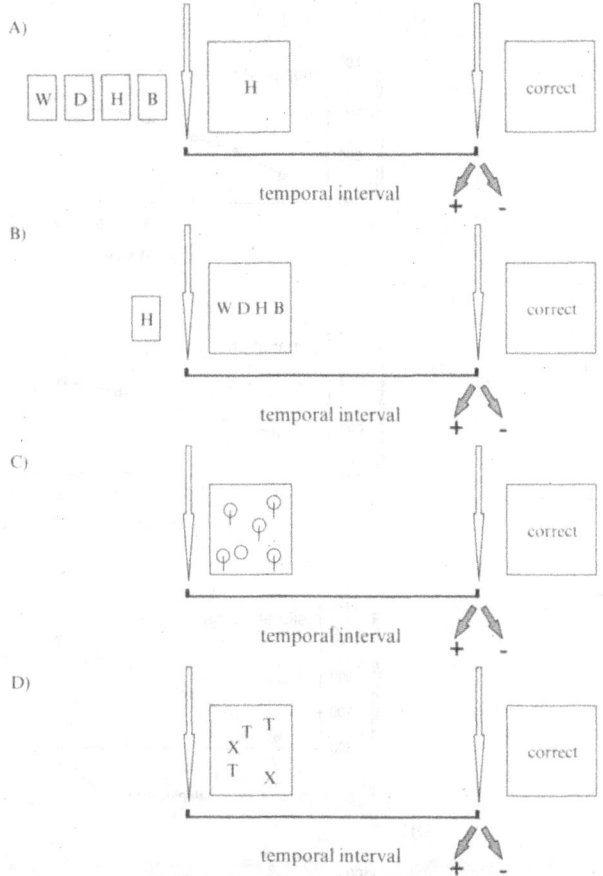

FIG. 1. A) Exp. 1. A memory search is interpolated within a time interval production. The items of the memory set ($N = 1$ to 6) are presented (1sec/item). The interval production begins, and is ended at the end of the subjective target interval by pressing one of two keys depending on the presence or absence of the probe in the set. B) Exp. 2. A single item is presented. The temporal production is ended by pressing on one of two keys depending on the presence or absence of the item in the display ($N = 1$ to 5) presented during the interval. C) Exp. 3. One to twelve visual items are presented during the interval. The response is provided as in the first two experiments. D) Exp. 4. The difference from Exp. 3 concerns the visual stimuli and their number ($N = 1$ to 15).

that the STM processing demands in this experiment were lower than in the first experiment, since there was only one item in memory to which the visually presented elements had to be compared. The memory item varied from trial to trial.

In the third and fourth experiments, visual search tasks borrowed from Treisman's study on visual attention were used (Treisman & Gelade, 1980). In one condition of the third experiment illustrated in Fig. 1c, the absence of a feature was searched for: A circle that was not intersected by a vertical line was searched for among distractors that were circles intersected with lines. A similar task, in terms of attention requirements, was combined with time production, as shown in Fig. 1d. In this experiment, the target, the same throughout the experiment, was a green T to be searched for among brown Ts and green Xs. There is some recent evidence that these visual search tasks do not rely on accumulating information in memory over time, even in the very short-term (Horowitz & Wolfe, 1998). Given the time necessary to complete the visual tasks, the target interval was fixed at 3sec in the third and fourth experiments.

The level of complexity of the nontemporal tasks was varied within experiments by manipulating set size, complexity being defined as the number of operations required to execute the task, while task difficulty refers to the speed or accuracy of performance (e.g. Kantowitz, 1985). The level of difficulty was relatively constant from one nontemporal task to another, since the slopes of reaction time as a function of set size were comparable across experiments, as shown in Fig. 2 (left side). The corresponding functions of temporal productions as a function of set size are shown on the right side of Fig. 2: Mean productions lengthen as a function of set size, but the effect seems dependent on the STM requirements of the nontemporal task. Thus, the higher slope of mean temporal productions as a function of set size is obtained with the strongest STM demands (Exp. 1), and the slope

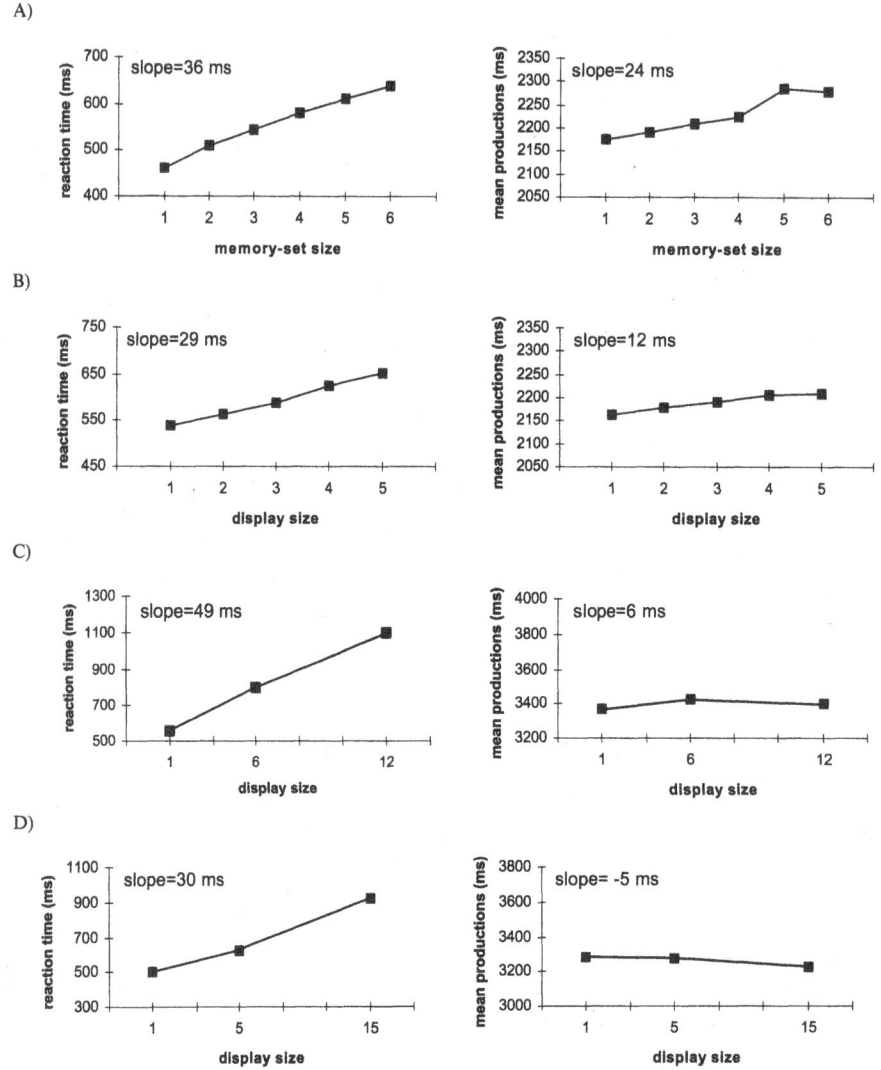

FIG. 2. Reaction times (left) and mean productions (right) as a function of set size in the four experiments illustrated in Fig. 1. In Exp. 1 and 2 (A and B), the target interval is 2sec. Because of the time needed to complete the nontemporal tasks in Exp. 3 and 4 (C and D), the target interval was set at 3sec.

is weaker when they are reduced (Exp. 2). Whereas in these two experiments mean productions varied with set size in the search task, the effect disappeared with search tasks that did not require STM processing (Exp. 3 and 4). These results show a clear dissociation between the level of difficulty of the search task and the effect of varying its complexity on concurrent temporal production. In fact, the effect seems related to the amount of STM processing required in the search task.

These results were interpreted by referring to psychophysical models of time estimation, which assume that temporal estimation requires some accumulation of temporal information emitted from an internal source (e.g. Gibbon, Church, & Meck, 1984). In the practice trials, a criterion of the number of pulses emitted from the pacemaker corresponding to the target interval is developed in reference memory. In the experimental trials, a first keypress would initiate the accumulation process, which would proceed until a criterion corresponding to the target interval is reached. The lengthening of temporal intervals with increasing set size, when concurrent STM processing is required, suggests that this processing interrupts the accumulation process. The interruption increasing the time needed to reach the criterion and the duration of the interruption being positively related to the amount of STM processing required in the search task, the lengthening would be proportional to set size, as observed in Experiments 1 and 2. Moreover, it appears that the total interruption duration is shorter than the nontemporal processing duration: The slopes of temporal production as a function of set size are always weaker than the reaction time slopes. This could be taken as evidence that some processes involved in the search (e.g. perceptual processes) may be performed in parallel with time estimation. Finally, it must be noted that the intercepts of time production functions are always higher than the value of the target duration, which suggests that interrupting time estimation may involve some additional cost unrelated to the nature of the nontemporal task executed during the interruption.

GENERALITY: INTERFERENCE FROM STM PROCESSING ON VARIOUS TIME ESTIMATION AND STM TASKS

Effect on Encoding and Reproducing Temporal Intervals

The interval production task involves two distinct temporal estimation phases: a first phase in which the target interval is encoded, and a second phase in which the interval is produced. In a temporal reproduction task, a different target inverval is presented on each trial. In the reproduction phase, the just-encoded interval is reproduced. Two main characteristics distinguish this temporal task from the time production task that was used in the experiments previously described. First, reproduction is performed without any training. Second, instead of producing the long-term stored representation of a time interval, participants reproduce a just-encoded interval, which minimizes the contribution of long-term memory to the temporal task.

To test the generality of the phenomenon, a STM search task was interpolated within the two phases of a temporal reproduction task (Fortin & Rousseau, 1998). In a first experiment, memory search was performed during the reproduction phase, whereas it was embedded in the encoding phase in a second experiment. In this experiment, the response to the memory search was given by beginning the temporal reproduction with one of two keys (see Fig. 3b).

Interruptions in time estimation should produce different results in the two conditions illustrated in Fig. 3a and 3b. Thus, interrupting the accumulation of temporal information during the reproduction phase should lengthen the reproduced interval. However, if the interruption takes place during the encoding of the to-be-reproduced interval, the amount of information accumulated during the encoding phase should be reduced, so that the perceived duration would shorten. Hence, in this condition, temporal reproductions should shorten as a function of the amount of concurrent STM processing executed during the encoding phase.

In these experiments, the same three target intervals, 1600msec, 2000msec, and 2400msec, were used in each of the two conditions illustrated in Fig. 3a and 3b. The STM demands were manipulated with set size as in previous experiments. In Fig. 3c, mean reproductions as a function of set size are shown, averaged over the three target durations, when STM processing was executed in the reproduction phase. The results are similar to those obtained with a production method, confirming that the effect of STM processing was not dependent on the specific conditions defined in a production paradigm.

The results, when STM processing was required during the encoding phase, are presented in Fig. 3d. Mean reproductions decreased with increasing set size, which supported the hypothesis of STM control in the accumulation process of temporal information. During the encoding of the interval to be reproduced, temporal information would be accumulated to define the criterion number of pulses used to reproduce the target duration. If some concurrent processing interrupts the accumulation process, less temporal information will be accumulated during the interval duration, so that its perceived duration will be shorter. The duration of the interruption being positively related to the amount of nontemporal processing, the perceived duration will shorten with increasing set size.

This negative relationship is analogous to the usual shortening of a perceived duration as a function of the difficulty of a nontemporal task performed during this duration in a prospective time estimation paradigm (e.g. Block, 1992; Macar, Grondin, & Casini, 1994). In these experiments, the nontemporal task is performed during the encoding of the duration to be estimated, which

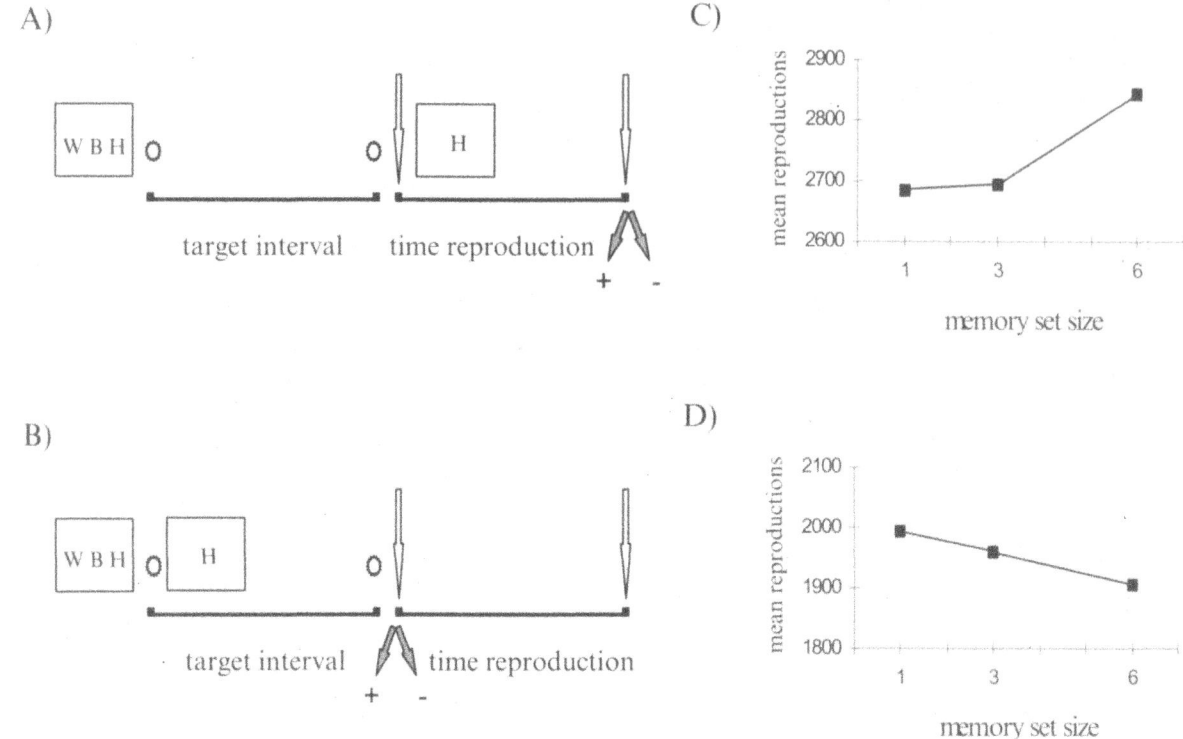

FIG. 3. Trials (left) and mean reproductions (in milliseconds) (right) when the search is performed in the reproduction (A and C) or encoding phase (B and D) of a reproduction task.

produces an underestimation of the total duration. However, when the nontemporal task takes place during an interval production, as in the experiments previously described, the result will be a lengthening of the temporal production as a function of the amount of interfering processing, which in fact reflects a similar loss of temporal information during the time estimation process. Similarly, in the experiments illustrated in Fig. 3, reproductions are generally longer than the target durations when the nontemporal task is performed during the temporal reproduction, whereas they tend to be shorter than the same target durations when it takes place during the encoding of the to-be-reproduced interval. In both cases, these deviations from target intervals may reflect some loss of temporal information related to the concurrent processing situation.

Effect on Different Durations, with Various STM and Temporal Tasks

The interference between STM and temporal processing has proved to be a robust phenomenon, observed with many nontemporal and temporal tasks, and with estimation of various durations. Thus, Sternberg's item recognition task was again combined, as illustrated in Fig. 3a, with reproductions of intervals varying around 2, 4, and 6sec. The effect of set size was significant at all three central durations (Fortin & Couture, 1997). The same item recognition task also affected a continuous production task similar to a standard tapping task (Fortin, Duchet, & Rousseau, 1996). These data show that the effect of a nontemporal task of a given duration, in this case item recognition, is not critically dependent on the use of a specific duration in the time estimation task, or of some time estimation method.

Visuospatial and phonological processing both affected time intervals simultaneously produced in proportion to the amount of processing required in the nontemporal tasks (Fortin & Breton, 1995). In one of these experiments, two polygons were presented on a screen, one polygon being either identical or a mirror version of the other one. The task was, as in classical mental rotation experiments, to decide whether the two stimuli were identical or different. The amount of processing was manipulated by varying the angular disparity between the stimuli. In a reaction time control condition, reaction time was a function of the angular disparity between the stimuli, showing the usual triangular function observed in "same" trials, that is, when the stimuli are identical. The reaction time function, in the "different" trials, was much less systematically related to angular disparity, a result often obtained in mental rotation research (this is why the "different" trial data are often omitted in reports of mental rotation experiments), and which is usually attributed to the use of nonrotational strategies on some proportion of the trials (e.g. Sheppard & Metzler, 1988).

When this mental rotation task was interpolated in a 4sec time interval production, temporal intervals were more systematically related to angular disparity *in the* "same" than in the "different" condition, an effect that was confirmed by a significant interaction between angular disparity and the same/different condition. Furthermore, even if it took longer to execute the nontemporal task in the "different" condition, the mean reaction time being significantly longer in the "different" that in the "same" condition, there was no difference in mean temporal productions between these two conditions. Actually, although the effect was not significant, the opposite trend was observed in the concurrent processing condition: For most values of angular disparity, productions were shorter in the "different" than in the "same" condition. These results suggest that mental rotation interferes with time estimation, whereas the use of nonrotational strategies on some proportion of trials attenuates the effect of angular disparity, even if these strategies are more time consuming than the processes taking place in the "same" condition.

In this study, phonological processing also interfered with time production in an experiment where rhyme judgements were carried out on visually presented stimuli (words and syllables). These results are interesting not only because they confirm the interfering effect of STM processing on time estimation with tasks of a different nature, but also because they showed that this interference could be observed with a task that involves minimal STM load.

DIFFICULTY OF STM PROCESSING AND CONCURRENT TIME PRODUCTION

The dissociation observed between the level of difficulty of search tasks and their effect on concurrent time estimation (cf. Fig. 2) was surprising, considering the relationship between the difficulty of a nontemporal task and its perceived duration, which is frequently observed in time estimation research. Therefore, we hypothesized that within a STM task, varying the level of difficulty could make the interference on concurrent time estimation vary. An experiment was run in which two memory search tasks were combined with time production: the first one was an item recognition task and the second was an item recognition task in which the temporal position of the probe had to be identified in addition to probe recognition (Fortin & Massé, 1999). The results in a reaction time control condition confirmed that the second condition was more difficult than the first: The slope of reaction time as a function of the number of items in the memory set was higher in the item identification + temporal order condition than when only item identification was required. When combined with temporal production, mean temporal intervals also showed a significant interaction of the search condition with set size. In this case, the effect of varying the search task complexity was clearly related to the level of difficulty of the search. These results supported the idea of a relationship between nontemporal task difficulty and its perceived duration that is generally assumed in attentional models of time estimation.

PROCESSING AND MAINTENANCE OF INFORMATION IN STM AND TIME PRODUCTION

Some of the tasks affecting time estimation involved a minimal memory load. This was the case, for example, for the rhyme judgement task, and for the visual search task described in Fig. 1b. In that situation, a single item was memorized, and the elements among which it had to be detected were present during the whole interval duration. In this condition of minimal and constant memory load, productions varied proportionally with set size (cf. Fig. 2b), suggesting that the interference was unrelated to the memory load itself. A memory load is defined here as a set of items to retain for a given retention interval, as used in concurrent processing situations to estimate attentional demands of reaction time tasks (e.g. Logan, 1979).

To test if temporal productions would vary with the memory load when no active STM processing is required, an experiment was run in which memory search was again combined with time production, but with a slight modification to the experimental task: The trial was identical to that illustrated in Fig. 1a, except that the probe was presented immediately after the end of the temporal production (Fortin & Breton, 1995). Therefore, the elements of the memory set had to be maintained in memory during the production, but processing and response related to probe identification were performed after the time interval. In this situation, the function of temporal intervals as a function of memory load (1–6) was flat. These data showed that with an identical load in a memory task, processing item information interfered with time estimation (cf. Fig. 2a), whereas maintaining this information did not.

This dissociation observed between the effects of processing and maintenance of information was also observed with temporal order information (Fortin & Champagne, 1998). In the experiment illustrated in Fig. 4, the memory items were presented successively. The probe was always present in the memory set, so that no decision on the probe presence or absence had to be taken in this experiment. In the "probe-during" condition illustrated in Fig. 4a, a probe and a digit were presented during the temporal production, and the interval was ended by pressing one of two keys to indicate whether the digit represented or did not represent the correct temporal position of the probe in the set. In the "probe-after" condition (Fig. 4b), the probe and digit were presented after the end of the time production. The results, presented in Fig. 4c, show that as with item information, processing temporal order affected concurrent time estimation, whereas maintenance of this information did not.

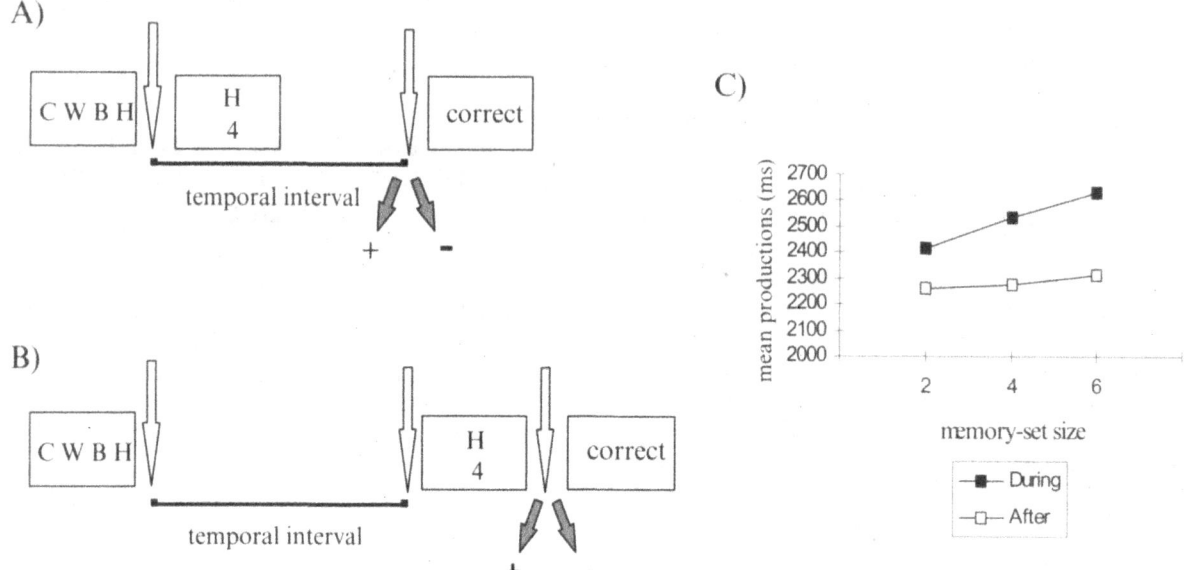

FIG. 4. Experimental trials (left) and results (right) in the "probe-during" (A) and the "probe-after" (B) conditions. Two, four, or six items are successively presented. A member of the memory set was presented with a digit, either during or after the temporal production. The participant had to decide whether the digit indicated or did not indicate the correct temporal position of the probe in the memory set. The response was provided by pressing one of two keys at the end of the subjective target interval in the "probe-during" condition, or by pressing one of two keys after the end of the temporal interval production in the "probe-after" condition.

CONCLUSION

Taken together, the results of these studies support the hypothesis of STM control on time estimation. This hypothesis was formulated within models of time estimation which assume that temporal production proceeds through an accumulation of temporal units emitted from an internal source, a pacemaker, until a criterion number of pulses corresponding to the target duration is reached (e.g. Gibbon et al., 1984). Within this framework, it was suggested that the accumulation process is under the control of an attentional gate or switch enabling accumulation of temporal information when attention is allocated to time estimation (Meck, 1984; Rousseau, Picard, & Pitre, 1984). The STM control hypothesis suggested that the attentional gate enabling the accumulation, or part of the accumulation process itself, could be under STM control (Fortin et al., 1993). The results of the experiments presented here suggest that at some point, STM processing interrupts the accumulation process so that when the interruption takes place during a temporal interval production, more time would be necessary to reach a criterion number of pulses corresponding to the target interval, thus lengthening the produced interval.

Results from the studies presented here allow some inferences concerning the interruption mechanics to be made. STM processing has the property of interrupting the accumulation process, and the duration of the interruption is systematically related to the duration of STM processing, whether this duration is manipulated by varying the STM task complexity or difficulty. The interruption may proceed following a preemptive rule of timesharing between two tasks requiring common resources (Schweickert & Boggs, 1984), although timesharing that would proceed through a series of shifts from one task to another would produce the same pattern of results.

Although the total interruption duration can be manipulated with the amount of information to process, it seems that the effect is not due to the load itself, but instead to the duration of STM processing related to the load. Thus, although it might have been hypothesized that processing temporal order information would be particularly disruptive to a concurrent temporal estimation task, considering the temporal nature of both performances, this appeared not to be the case. The effect of processing order information happened to be similar to that of processing item information, and again, essentially related to the duration of STM processing.

In these experiments, the effect seemed to be related to information processing, and not to maintenance of an equivalent amount of information. For example, the operations that affected the temporal performance could be, in the preceding experiments, mental comparison of the probe to the memory set items, and comparison of phonological or visuospatial representations. Varying the number of items to rehearse, within the range of memory span, had no effect on concurrent time production. This does not imply, of course, that increasing memory load beyond memory span capacity would have no effect.

The duration of the interruption would not correspond to the total duration of nontemporal processing: In the concurrent processing conditions, the slopes are consistently weaker than in the reaction time conditions.

This suggests that some operations involved in the nontemporal tasks may be performed in parallel with time estimation. Some of these operations may be related to perceptual processing, since a manipulation of the amount of visual processing had no effect on concurrent time production (cf. Fig. 2c and 2d). Furthermore, in a temporal production task, temporal information is internally generated and its processing does not involve any perception of external stimuli, so that interference from perceptual processing on this performance is less likely to occur. This observation might also be related to some passive processing conditions in time estimation research, in which visual information is presented during a temporal estimation, without having to produce a response concerning this information. This condition was shown not to affect concurrent time estimation (e.g. Predebon, 1996). In our experiments, processing of visually presented information was required additionally, and even in these conditions, no effect of varying task complexity was observed on time production.

When a nontemporal task is combined with temporal production or reproduction, the intercept of the mean time interval function is always longer than the target duration (cf. right side of Fig. 2, Figs. 3c and 4c). This lengthening seems to be due to the mere presence of a nontemporal task, independently of the load that this task involves, and is actually also observed in the absence of any effect of the nontemporal task complexity (cf. Figs. 2c and 2d). This suggests that executing a nontemporal task causes some loss of temporal information in the accumulation process, which could be attributed to attentional requirements related to shifting from one task to another, or simply to interrupting time estimation (Fortin & Massé, 1998).

It has been suggested that both attention and STM could be involved in time estimation (Fortin et al., 1993; Meck, 1984; Zakay & Block, 1997). The accumulation process could require attention, and transfer of this information from the accumulator to STM would require STM. A problem with this issue is that attention and STM are often closely related in executing a task, so that it may be difficult to obtain independent estimates of their contribution to time estimation. Another problem is the variety of mental phenomena with which attentional control may be concerned, which led some researchers to suggest that attention should be used not as defining a unitary concept, but as a complex field of study, where specific paradigms tap functionally different systems (see Neumann & Sanders, 1996). Thus, even if temporal production was insensitive to manipulations of complexity in visual attention tasks, this may not be the case with all forms of attentional control. Combinations of specific paradigms with time estimation in concurrent processing conditions that minimize interference from peripheral factors, as in the experiments summarized here, should be useful to examine further the role of cognitive factors in time estimation.

REFERENCES

Block, R.A. (1992). Prospective and retrospective duration judgment: The role of information processing and memory. In F. Macar, V. Pouthas, & W.J. Friedman (Eds.), *Time, action and cognition: Towards bridging the gap* (pp. 141–152). Dordrecht, The Netherlands: Kluwer.

Brown, S.W. (1997). Attentional resources in timing: Interference effects in concurrent temporal and nontemporal working memory tasks. *Perception and Psychophysics, 59,* 1118–1140.

Fortin, C., & Breton, R. (1995). Temporal interval production and processing in working memory. *Perception and Psychophysics, 57,* 203–215.

Fortin, C., & Champagne, J. (1998). *Order information in short-term memory and time interval production.* Quebec '98 conference on STM, Québec, June 1998.

Fortin, C., & Couture, E. (1997). *Interference between short-term memory processing and temporal reproduction.* 38th Meeting of The Psychonomic Society, Philadelphia, 1997.

Fortin, C., Duchet, M.-L., & Rousseau, R. (1996). Tapping sensitivity to processing in short-term memory. *Canadian Journal of Experimental Psychology, 50,* 402–407.

Fortin, C., & Massé, N. (1999). Order information in short-term memory and time estimation. *Memory and Cognition, 27,* 54–62.

Fortin, C., & Massé, N. (1998). Interruptions in time estimation during a time interval production. In S. Grondin & Y. Lacouture (Eds.), *Fechner Day 98* (pp. 219–224). Québec: International Society for Psychophysics.

Fortin, C., & Rousseau, R. (1998). Interference from short-term memory processing on encoding and reproducing brief durations. *Psychological Research, 61,* 269–276.

Fortin, C., Rousseau, R., Bourque, P., & Kirouac, E. (1993). Time estimation and concurrent nontemporal processing: Specific interference from short-term memory demands. *Perception and Psychophysics, 53,* 536–548.

Gibbon, J., Church, R.M., & Meck, W.H. (1984). Scalar timing in memory. In J. Gibbon & L. Allan (Eds.), *Timing and time perception* (Annals of the New York Academy of Sciences, Vol. 423, pp. 52–77). New York: New York Academy of Sciences.

Hicks, R.E., Miller, G.W., & Kinsbourne, M. (1976). Prospective and retrospective judgements of time as a function of amount of information processed. *American Journal of Psychology, 89,* 719–730.

Horowitz, T.S., & Wolfe, J.M. (1998). Visual search has no memory. *Nature, 394,* 575–577.

Kantowitz, B.H. (1985). Channels and stages in human information processing: A limited analysis of theory and methodology. *Journal of Mathematical Psychology, 29,* 135–174.

Logan, G.D. (1979). On the use of a concurrent memory load to measure attention and automaticity. *Journal of Experimental Psychology: Human Perception and Performance, 5,* 189–207.

Macar, F., Grondin, S., & Casini, L. (1994). Controlled attention sharing influences time estimation. *Memory and Cognition, 22,* 673–686.

Meck, W.H. (1984). Attentional bias between modalities: Effect on the internal clock, memory, and decision stages used in animal time discrimination. In J. Gibbon & L. Allan (Eds.), *Timing and time perception* (pp. 528–541). New York: New York Academy of Sciences.

Neumann, O., & Sanders, A.F. (1996). *Handbook of perception and action: Vol. 3. Attention.* London: Academic Press.

Predebon, J. (1996). The effects of active and passive processing of interval events on prospective and retrospective time estimates. *Acta Psychologica, 94,* 41–58.

Rousseau, R., Picard, D., & Pitre, E. (1984). An adaptive counter model for time estimation. In J. Gibbon & L. Allan (Eds.), *Timing and time perception* (pp. 639–642). New York: New York Academy of Sciences.

Schweickert, R., & Boggs, G.J. (1984). Models of central capacity and concurrency. *Journal of Mathematical Psychology, 28,* 223–281.

Sheppard, S., & Metzler, D. (1988). Mental rotation: Effects of dimensionality of objects and type of task. *Journal of Experimental Psychology: Human Perception and Performance, 14,* 3–11.

Thomas, E.A.C., & Weaver, W.B. (1975). Cognitive processing and time perception. *Perception and Psychophysics, 17,* 363–367.

Treisman, A., & Gelade, G. (1980). A feature integration theory of attention. *Cognitive Psychology, 12,* 97–136.

Zakay, D. (1998). Attention allocation policy influcences prospective timing. *Psychonomic Bulletin and Review, 5,* 114–118.

Zakay, D., & Block, R.A. (1997). The role of attention in time estimation processes. In M.A. Pastor & J. Artieda (Eds.), *Time, internal clocks and movement* (pp. 143–164).

Localizing Localization:
The Role of Working Memory in Auditory Localization

Natasha Merat
University of Leeds, UK

John A. Groeger
University of Surrey, Guildford, UK

Deborah J. Withington
University of Leeds, UK

It is unclear from current accounts of working memory which, if any, of its components might be involved in our ability to specify the location of a sound source. A series of studies were performed to assess the degree of interference in localization of broadband noise, by a concurrent articulatory suppression (articulatory loop—Experiment 1), serial recall (phonological store and articulatory loop—Experiment 2), and Paced Visual Serial Addition Test (central executive—Experiment 3). No significant disruption of auditory localization was revealed by the first two experiments, ruling out a role for the phonological loop in auditory localization. In Experiment 3, a large degree of error was exhibited in localization, when performed concurrently with the addition task, indicating a requirement for central resources. This suggestion is confirmed by comparison of localization performance across all three studies, which demonstrates a clear deterioration in performance as the demand of concurrent tasks on central resources increases. Finally, concurrent localization was shown to disrupt the primacy portion of the serial position curve, as well as performance on the Paced Visual Serial Addition Test.

Il est difficile de déterminer, sur la base du modèle de mémoire de travail, laquelle de ses composantes pourrait être impliquée dans notre capacité à localiser la provenance d'un son. Une série d'études évaluent le degré d'interférence dans la localisation d'un bruit, lors d'une suppression articulatoire simultanée (boucle articulatoire—Expérience 1), d'un rappel sériel (registre phonologique et boucle articulatoire—Expérience 2) et d'une tâche d'addition (unité de gestion central—Expérience 3). Aucune perturbation de la localisation auditive n'a été révélée dans les deux premières expériences, éliminant le rôle de la boucle phonologique dans la localisation auditive. Dans l'expérience 3, un grand nombre d'erreurs de localisation a été observé lorsque cette tâche était effectuée en même temps qu'une tâche d'addition, indiquant l'utilisation de ressources centrales. Ceci est confirmée lorsque la performance de localisation aux trois expériences est comparée. Cette comparaison montre une détérioration de la performance qui est fonction des ressources sollicitées par la tâche concurrente. Finalement, le fait d'effectuer la localisation simultanément avec une autre tâche nuit au rappel des premiers items ainsi qu'à la performance au test d'addition.

From a physiological perspective, auditory localization is assisted by the creation of a map of auditory space in the human midbrain. The formation of this map is brought about by differences in the *intensity* and *time of arrival* of sound to each ear (e.g. Middlebrooks & Green, 1991; Wightman & Kistler, 1993). Auditory localization is therefore a process that involves identifying the *spatial* location of a *sound* source.

Baddeley and Hitch's (1974) conceptualisation of working memory is a multi-component short-term memory system, consisting of a central executive, which controls information flow, and two subsidiary systems that deal with auditory (i.e. phonological loop), visual, and spatial information (i.e. visuospatial sketch pad, see Baddeley, 1998, for recent overview). Therefore, from a theoretical perspective, there is reason to expect that both spatially based, and sound-based subsidiary systems of the working memory model are required in auditory localization, and where this task increases in difficulty (e.g. when two sound sources are close in proximity), there may also be a requirement for executive processes. Indeed, there is some suggestion in the literature that localization is either a spatial task (e.g. Smyth, Pearson, & Pendleton, 1988), or one that is demanding of central resources (Klauer & Stegmaier, 1997), although these are not placed within the working memory framework.

Requests for reprints should be addressed to Natasha Merat, School of Psychology, University of Leeds, Leeds, LS2 9JT, UK.
This work was supported by a studentship award from the Economic and Social Research Council, and additional support from Sound Alert Ltd. We would like to thank John Varley and David Horton for their technical support.

© 1999 International Union of Psychological Science

This paper reports a series of studies that attempt to ascertain what role working memory might play in auditory localization. Specifically, three dual-task studies were conducted, each combining a sound localization task with an articulatory suppression, serial recall, or serial addition task. Our assumption was that an impairment in performance of the sound localization and/or the working memory task, during dual-task conditions, would indicate that auditory localization relied upon the phonological loop or central executive components of working memory.

METHOD

Participants

Twenty-four participants were recruited for each study, with an equal number of males and females in each group (mean age: 24.91 ± 0.54). Participants were undergraduate and postgraduate students, recruited at Leeds University, and were provided with a cash incentive after completion of the study.

Design and Procedure

Sound Localization. A burst of broadband noise (74 dB SPL), was delivered from one of five speakers, placed on a horizontal bar at 0° (directly ahead, at ear level), 15°, 30°, 330°, and 345° azimuth. Participants were seated in front of the speaker array, which was concealed by acoustically transparent material, and were required to aim a purpose-built pointer towards the perceived sound source position.

Working Memory. For all three experiments a digit was presented in the centre of a computer screen, which was placed between the participant and the speaker array. Although participant response was always verbal, the *type* of response changed in each experiment. In Experiment 1, participants simply articulated the digits as they appeared on the screen (articulatory suppression—AS). For Experiment 2, we asked participants to read out the name of the digit as it was delivered, and they were then required to recall digits after a string of seven had been presented (serial recall—SR). For the last experiment, participants were asked to add each digit to the one immediately preceding it, and utter the sum out loud (Paced Visual Serial Addition Test—PVSAT). This task is thought to rely on central resources, due to its attentional and information processing aspects (Channon, Baker, & Robertson, 1993).

Sound localization and each of the working memory tasks outlined previously were performed alone (once a second, or once every 2sec: L1 and M1 or L2 and M2) and then concurrently (see Fig. 1). The dual-task session was constructed by combining the four single-task sessions. Therefore, sound and digits were either presented together (L1M1 and L2M2), or sound localization was required every second while digits were displayed every 2sec (L1M2), and vice versa (L2M1). In each experiment, rate and order of stimulus presentation was counterbalanced across participants.

Results

Mean angular error of localization for all conditions (computed as the absolute difference between perceived and actual speaker position) is reported in Table 1.

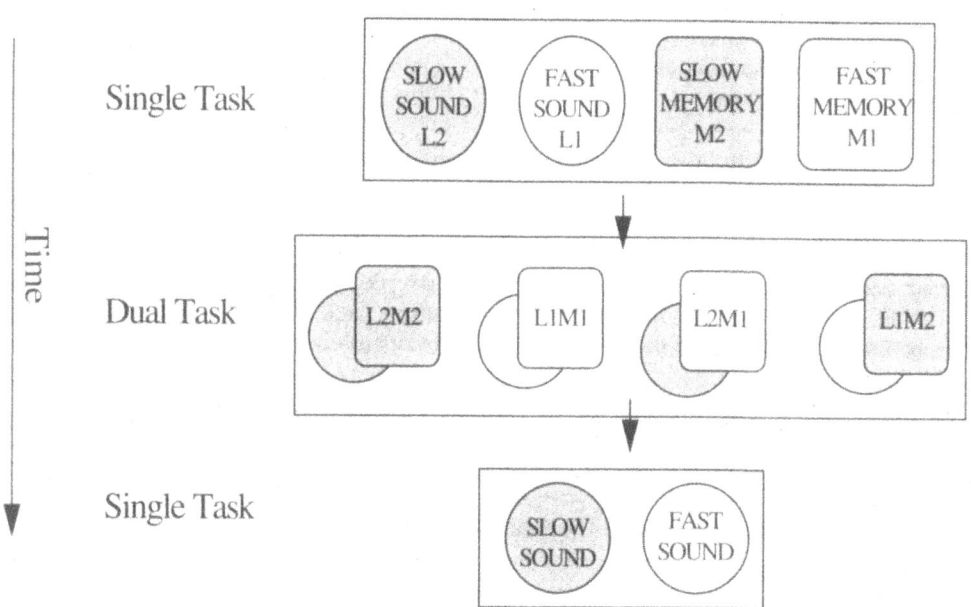

FIG. 1. A schematic of the design. Number of stimuli presented for each single- and dual-task trial: L1/L2: 25 bursts of noise (a 10sec gap introduced after every 5 bursts); M1/M2: 35 digits (a 10sec gap introduced after every 7 digits); L1M1/L2M2: 35 digits, 35 bursts of noise; L1M2: 35 digits, 70 bursts of noise (in each case, a 10sec gap was introduced after every 7 digits); L2M1: 70 digits, 35 bursts of noise (10sec gap introduced after every 14 digits). Each of these conditions was presented twice.

TABLE 1
Mean Angular Error of Localization for All Three Studies

	Localization[b]	Working Memory Condition[a]		
		M0	M1	M2
AS	L1	8.56 ± 2.48	8.02 ± 2.15	9.87 ± 3.07[c]
	L2	7.72 ± 2.18	7.42 ± 1.62	7.10 ± 1.45
SR	L1	10.24 ± 5.05	10.60 ± 2.97	13.70 ± 4.27[c]
	L2	7.89 ± 2.43	8.26 ± 2.71	8.72 ± 2.50
PVSAT	L1	9.28 ± 3.50	13.09 ± 4.58[c]	14.39 ± 4.08[c]
	L2	7.70 ± 2.16	10.25 ± 4.68[c]	9.00 ± 3.46[c]

[a] Working memory task: absent—M0; present every second—M1; present every 2 seconds—M2.
[b] Rate of sound localization: every second—L1; every 2 seconds—L2.
[c] Dual task is significantly impaired compared to equivalent single task ($P < .05$).

Impairment in localization was assessed by comparing the degree of error in the dual-task condition, with that of the second single-task session. Results were analyzed by means of a 2 (speed of localization) × 3 (working memory task: none, present every second, present every 2sec) repeated measures ANOVA.

Articulatory Suppression (AS). The main effect of speed of localization [$F(1,23) = 38.63$, $P < .001$] was statistically significant, with localization at a fast rate associated with more error than slow localization. The interaction between speed of localization and rate of suppression was also reliable [$F(2,46) = 8.74$, $P < .001$]. Post hoc Newman-Keuls' analyses revealed that the effect of suppression on localization was confined to when localization was fast and suppression was at a slow rate (L1M2 condition).

Serial Recall (SR). The main effect of speed of localization continued to be reliable [$F(1,23) = 40.00$, $P < .001$]. Results also revealed a reliable effect of serial recall [$F(2,46) = 11.79$, $P < .001$] and an interaction between speed of localization and requirement for serial recall [$F(2,46) = 5.38$, $P < .05$]. However, post hoc analyses showed that the only significant error in localization was once again confined to where participants were required to localize every second, but the digits for serial recall were delivered every 2sec.

Paced Visual Serial Addition Task (PVSAT). Speed of localization continued to show a reliable effect [$F(1,23) = 54.53$, $P < .001$]. Results also showed a reliable effect of serial addition on localization [$F(2,46) = 20.06$, $P < .001$], as well as a significant interaction between speed of localization and serial addition [$F(2,46) = 12.67$, $P < .001$]. Post hoc analyses revealed a significant impairment in localization during *all* dual tasks, when compared to single tasks.

Secondary Task Performance

AS. Localization was not found to interfere with articulatory suppression, and participants uttered the digits as many times as they were cued.

SR. A 2 (rate of digit presentation) × 3 (concurrent localization: none, present every second, present every 2sec) repeated measures ANOVA showed that participants remembered more digits in their correct serial positions in the absence of localization (mean = 65.09% ± 23.93), than with localization at a fast (mean = 49.17% ± 21.96) or slower rate [mean = 53.87% ± 22.06; $F(2,42) = 18.10$; $P < .001$]. However, overall, the speed at which digits were presented made little difference [$F(1,21) = 0.10$, $P > .05$]. Accuracy varied considerably across serial position [$F(6,126) = 22.75$; $P < .001$], but this depended on whether, and at what speed, localization was required, as well as the speed at which digits were presented [$F(12,252) = 4.16$; $P < .001$; Fig. 2]. Post hoc analyses of this interaction revealed that the recency effect was affected much less by concurrent localization than was the primacy effect. Memory for initial portions of the list was dramatically lower when localization was required at a fast rate, and also when to-be-remembered digits presented at a fast rate were coupled with localization at a slow rate. Where digit and sound bursts were presented simultaneously, performance was worse in every position when compared to single-task serial recall, but the overall shape of the serial position curve was maintained.

PVSAT. Performance was assessed by calculating the percentage of correct responses in both single- and dual-task conditions. A 2 (rate of digit presentation) × 3 (concurrent localization: none, present every second, present every 2sec) repeated measures ANOVA showed a main effect of rate of digit presentation [$F(1, 23) = 135.03$, $P < .001$] with better performance when digits

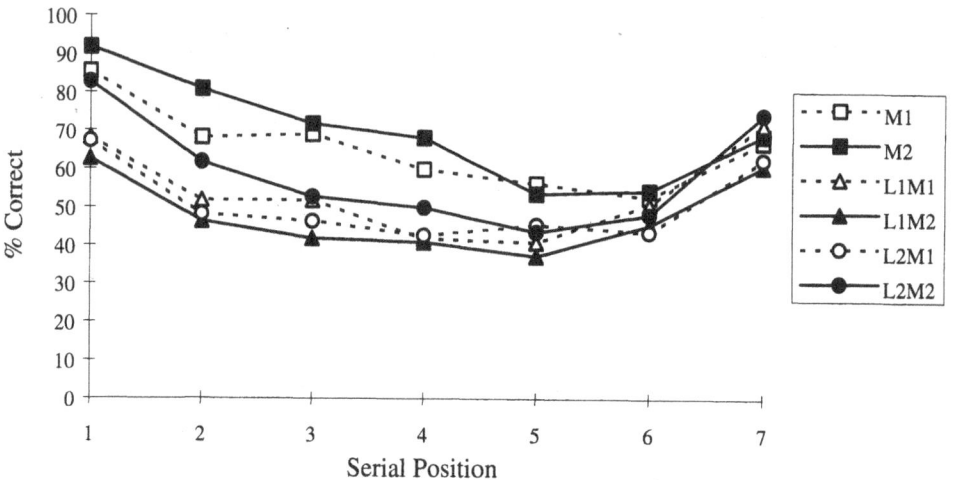

FIG. 2. Serial recall as a function of position, rate of digit presentation, and concurrent localization.

were presented at a slow rate [mean = 82.55% ± 11.59, vs. 65.00% ± 12.04). The effect of localization on PVSAT was found to be statistically reliable [$F(2,46)$ = 75.69, $P < .001$], and results also showed a reliable interaction between speed of localization and rate of digit presentation [$F(2,46)$ = 28.87, $P < .001$] (Table 2). The source of this interaction lay in the fact that whereas without concurrent localization, adding digits presented at one per second was worse than at the two per second rate, when localization was required at the faster rate, PVSAT deteriorated significantly at both speeds, while with slower localization, a deterioration in PVSAT was only observed when digits were delivered at a fast rate.

Comparison of Localization across Studies

An "index of decrement" in localization was achieved for each dual-task condition, by calculating the ratio between dual-task localization, and its comparable single task. A three-way analysis of variance (between-participant: factor of study; within-factors: rate of localization and digit presentation) revealed main effects of study [$F(2,69)$ = 6.78, $P < .05$], speed of localization [$F(1,69)$ = 12.64, $P < .05$] and rate of digit presentation [$F(1,69)$ = 14.71, $P < .001$]. Results also revealed an interaction between speed of localization and rate of digit presentation across the three studies [$F(1,69)$ = 33.68, $P < .001$]. In each case, when *fast* localization was required, the decrement in performance was significantly greater with SR and PVSAT, than with AS, with differences between the first of these two conditions also being statistically reliable. By contrast, reliable differences with *slow* localization only occurred when the working memory task had to be performed at the faster rate, and then only between suppression and PVSAT (Fig. 3).

TABLE 2
The Effect of Localization on Performance in PVSAT (% Correct)

Localization	Working Memory Condition	
	M1	M2
L0	77.92 ± 13.77	90.35 ± 12.81
L1	63.53 ± 14.37[a]	72.50 ± 15.41[a]
L2	53.56 ± 12.27[a]	84.79 ± 11.30

[a] Dual task is significantly impaired compared to equivalent single task ($P < .01$).
See Table 1 for abbreviations.

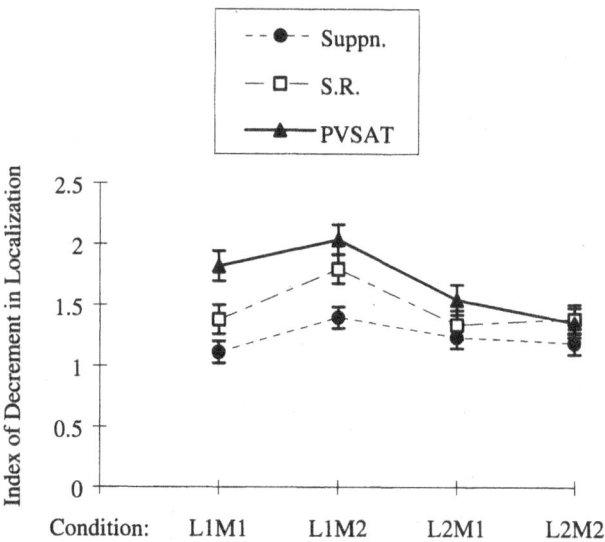

FIG. 3. A comparison of localization error across the three experiments.

DISCUSSION

In each of the experiments, greater error was observed when localization every second, rather than every 2 seconds, was required. We consider that this decrement in speeded localization reflects an increase in task difficulty, perhaps in part because of the difficulty in discriminating between a new stimulus from the fast-fading echoic image of a previous trial (e.g. Darwin, Turvey, & Crowder, 1972; Howell & Darwin, 1977). Since, in general, auditory localization was not impaired by concurrent suppression or serial recall, we conclude that neither the phonological loop, nor its individual components, play a role in the localization of sound. The effects of slow AS and SR on fast localization are more consistent with the suggestion that localization depends on central resources, and the incompatible rate at which the two tasks must be performed increases that demand still further. This suggestion implies that error in this condition would rise systematically, with increases in cognitive load imposed by the working memory task.

In Experiment 3, finding greater impairment of localization by a serial addition test, believed to engage central resources (Channon et al., 1993), provides further support for our contention that the central executive plays a role in auditory localization, as implied by results previously reported by Klauer and Stegmaier (1997). This is also evident from a contrast across the three studies, which demonstrates that imposing additional requirements on central resources leads to a clear (further) decrement in localization performance.

Analysis of secondary task performance also supported the conclusion that localization is centrally demanding. Close inspection of the serial position curve data demonstrates that simultaneous presentation of digits and broadband noise reduced performance across all positions, as would be expected on the basis of other studies showing effects of noise on serial recall (e.g. Surprenant, this issue). However, increasing demand on central resources, by increasing the rate at which localization is required, and especially pairing fast localization with slow digit presentation, appears to selectively impair the primacy effect. This also suggests that successful memory for earlier portions of a list itself depends on executive processes, probably at encoding, since retrieval was never accompanied by localization. Future studies will explore this effect further, as well as examining the extent to which auditory localization depends on visuospatial aspects of working memory.

REFERENCES

Baddeley, A.D. (1998). Recent developments in working memory. *Current Opinion in Neurobiology*, 8(2), 234–238.

Baddeley, A.D., & Hitch, G.J. (1974). Working memory. In G. Bower (Ed.), *The psychology of learning and motivation* (pp. 47–90.). New York: Academic Press.

Channon, S., Baker, J.E., & Robertson, M.M. (1993). Working memory in clinical depression: An experimental study. *Psychological Medicine*, 23, 87–91.

Darwin, C.J., Turvey, M.T., & Crowder, R.G. (1972). An auditory analogue of the Sperling partial report procedure: Evidence for brief auditory storage. *Cognitive Psychology*, 55, 104–126.

Howell, P., & Darwin, C.J. (1977). Some properties of auditory memory for rapid format transitions. *Memory and Cognition*, 5, 700–708.

Klauer, K.C., & Stegmaier, R. (1997). Interference in immediate spatial memory: Shifts of spatial attention or central-executive involvement. *Quarterly Journal of Experimental Psychology*, 50A(1), 79–99.

Middlebrooks, J.C., & Green, D.M. (1991). Sound localization by human listeners. *Annual Reviews in Psychology*, 42, 135–159.

Smyth, M.M., Pearson, N.A., & Pendleton, L.R. (1988). Movement and working memory: Patterns and positions in space. *Quarterly Journal of Experimental Psychology*, 40A(1), 497–514.

Surprenant, A.M. (this issue). The effect of noise on simulated hearing loss on memory for spoken syllables, *International Journal of Psychology*, 34, 329–334.

Wightman, F.L., & Kistler, D.J. (1993). Sound localization. In Y.A. Yost, A.N. Popper, & R.R. Fay (Eds.), *Human psychophysics* (pp. 155–192). London: Springer-Verlag.

Attentional Selectivity in Short-term Memory: Similarity of Process, Not Similarity of Content, Determines Disruption

William Macken, Sébastien Tremblay, David Alford, and Dylan Jones
Cardiff University, UK

Background sound substantially disrupts serial recall, even under conditions where participants are explicitly told to ignore it. Study of such a phenomenon may serve to illuminate the manner in which information from various sources interacts in memory, as well as the extent to which unattended information is processed. A review of the literature is presented that points to a number of conclusions. First, that interference occurs in memory, not on the basis of similarity of content between relevant and irrelevant material, but rather on the basis of similarity of process. Specifically, in a serial recall task, the key memory process is that of order retention, and therefore, order information in the sequence of auditory events interferes with the process of ordering within the rehearsal set. Second, that organisation and interference within memory are intimately connected with perceptual processes.

Un bruit de fond nuit au rappel sériel, même lorsque les participants ont pour instruction explicite de l'ignorer. L'étude d'un tel phénomène met en lumière la façon dont l'information provenant de plusieurs sources interagit en mémoire, ainsi que le degré de traitement de l'information ignoré. Une recension de la littérature est présentée ainsi que les conclusions qui en découlent. Premièrement, l'interférence en mémoire se produit sur la base de la similarité du traitement, plutôt que sur la base de la similarité du matériel pertinent et non pertinent. Par exemple, dans une tâche de rappel sériel, le processus mnémonique clé est la rétention de l'ordre. C'est donc l'information reliée à l'ordre d'une séquence d'éléments auditifs qui interfère avec le processus relié à l'ordre à l'intérieur de l'ensemble à retenir. Deuxièmement, l'organisation et l'interférence en mémoire sont intimement liées aux processus perceptifs.

BACKGROUND: THE IRRELEVANT SOUND EFFECT

The disruption of memory performance by task-irrelevant background sound, even when subjects are instructed to ignore that sound, is a well-established phenomenon in cognitive psychology (e.g. Colle, 1980; Colle & Welsh, 1976; Jones & Macken, 1993; Salamé & Baddeley, 1982). The typical experimental paradigm involves serial visual presentation of items such as letters or digits, which the subject is required to recall in serial order. Subjects are exposed to sound which they are assured is irrelevant to the task, and despite the attempt to ignore it, such sound produces substantial disruption of recall relative to performance in quiet control conditions. This phenomenon is of interest as it may illuminate the way in which unattended information is processed and the manner in which information from the eye and the ear converge in memory.

Early research focused on the disruptive effect of background speech on serial recall, and established that the level of disruption was independent of factors such as the intensity, meaning, and location of the sound (Colle, 1980; Colle & Welsh, 1976). Based on the finding that continuous broadband noise produced little or no disruption of recall, Salamé and Baddeley (1982, 1989) suggested that interference was occurring in a speech-specific phonological store to which the irrelevant speech gained automatic access through a selective filter. Since the verbal memory items are also represented in this phonological store, they are corrupted by the presence of the irrelevant speech to the degree that the content of the irrelevant material is phonologically similar to the memory items. More recent findings have shown this account to be unsatisfactory. First, the presence of speech is not a sufficient condition for the disruption to occur. Jones, Madden, and Miles (1992) found that a single repeated utterance, or a single sustained utterance

---

Requests for reprints should be addressed to Bill Macken, School of Psychology, Cardiff University, PO Box 901, Cardiff CF1 3YG, UK (E-mail: macken@cardiff.ac.uk).

Preparation of this paper was supported by funding from the Economic and Social Research Council of the UK and the Defence Evaluation & Research Agency. Dylan Jones is a Visiting Research Fellow at the Centre for Human Sciences, Defence Evaluation & Research Agency, Farnborough, UK.

© 1999 International Union of Psychological Science

(such as a vowel sound) produced little or no disruption of recall. Substantial disruption only occurred if the irrelevant speech comprised a sequence of different utterances. Further, speech is not a necessary condition for disruption to occur, as a sequence of tones changing in frequency also interfered with serial recall performance, but here again, a single repeated tone produced no disruption (Jones & Macken, 1993).

THE CHANGING-STATE HYPOTHESIS

Based on this finding, that a sequence of different sounds (speech or nonspeech) produces substantial disruption but a single repeated item produces little or none, we proposed an alternative account of the phenomenon that we refer to as the changing-state hypothesis (Jones & Macken, 1993; Jones et al., 1992). According to this view, the disruption of recall occurs, not as a result of interference between irrelevant and memory *items*, but rather as a result of two concurrent processes of seriation: one inherent in the temporal ordering of the sequence of different sounds in the irrelevant material, and one that arises from rehearsal within the memory set. One implication of this hypothesis is that short-term memory tasks that do not require the retention of serial order should not be subject to this changing-state effect. Jones and Macken (1993) showed that a missing item task, within which subjects were presented serially with all but one of the items of an overlearned set (e.g. days of the week, the digits 1 to 9) and required merely to report the missing one, was not disrupted by changing-state sequences of tones, but if the subject was required to recall the same items in serial order, then the normal pattern of disruption (i.e. the changing-state effect) was observed. Despite the fact that subjects would have to remember all the items in order to perform both tasks, they do not need to rehearse the order of items for the missing item task. Beaman and Jones (1997, 1998) have extended this finding and have shown that changing-state irrelevant sound interferes with order information in memory, rather than with memory for the items themselves (but see also LeCompte, 1994).

In this respect, the changing-state hypothesis represents a different kind of account of interference to those that see interference as being related to similarity of *content* between the primary and interfering material, such accounts often embodying the notion of modular processing of different types of stimuli (e.g. Deutsch, 1970; Salamé & Baddeley, 1982). Rather, the changing-state hypothesis emphasises the role of similarity of *process* within a nonmodular processing system (see also Crowder, 1993, for a similar argument). Specifically, since in the typical serial recall paradigm, the same memory items are presented on each trial, the key information that the participant has to retain is the order of those items. Thus the key determinant of disruption will be that the irrelevant material also involves the processing of order. More generally, where a memory task involves, for example, the processing of semantic information, then the semantic properties of interfering material will be important (see, e.g., Martin, Wogalter, & Forlano, 1988).

THE OBJECT-ORIENTED EPISODIC RECORD (O-OER) MODEL OF SHORT-TERM MEMORY

The changing-state effect provides the initial basis for a general model of short-term memory: the Object-oriented Episodic Record (O-OER) model (Jones, 1993; Jones, Beaman, & Macken, 1996). There are two basic components to this model. First, *objects*, which are assumed to be abstract representations of events in the world. These representations are object-oriented in that they are not modality specific, but rather they code all aspects of an event (its auditory characteristics, visual characteristics, etc.). Further, objects from all sources and modalities are represented in a functionally equivalent fashion in a single memory system. In this way, the O-OER model deviates from many models of short-term memory that posit separate processing systems for, for example, auditory and visual information (e.g. Baddeley, 1986, 1990). Second, the temporal ordering of objects is encoded in *episodic pointers* that point from object to object in a probabilistic manner. Within the irrelevant sound paradigm, such pointers are assumed to be established preattentively for the auditory material, and are established and maintained by a rehearsal process for the memory items. Serial recall involves navigating through the representational space from object to object using these pointers. The task of navigation is impeded by the presence in memory of other sequential pointers associated with other sets of objects. Whereas a sequence of changing auditory items will give rise to separate objects for each item and a chain of pointers linking successive objects, a single repeated item will give rise to only one object with a single self-referential pointer. Thus, the task of navigating through the target sequence is more likely to be affected by the presence of changing-state than steady-state (a single repeated item) auditory material.

It is important to reiterate here that this conception does not see disruption of recall as being due to interference between memory and irrelevant objects, but rather as being due to interference between the episodic pointers in the irrelevant sequence and those in the target sequence. One prediction that follows from this view is that the identity of the irrelevant objects, and their relationship to the target objects, does not influence the degree of disruption produced by the irrelevant sound. That this may be the case is already suggested by the fact that nonspeech, as well as speech, produces disruption of serial recall of verbal items (Jones & Macken, 1993). To test this proposition further, Jones and Macken (1995a) compared the disruptive effects of sounds that were either phonologically similar or dissimilar to the memory items. Subjects were presented visually with lists composed of random orderings of the letters F, K, L, M, Q, R, and Y, while being exposed to irrelevant sound composed of the spoken words *deaf, pay, bell, hem, shoe, car,* and *high* (phonologically similar) or *hat, cow, pin, nest, pier, boat,* and *top* (phonologically dissimilar). These two types of irrelevant sound sequence produced equivalent degrees of disruption of recall, strongly suggesting that the disruptive effect does not occur as a result of the relationship between irrelevant and memory items (see also LeCompte & Shaibe, 1997; Martin-Loeches, Schweinberger, & Sommer, 1997).

Taking this argument a step further, a changing-state effect should occur regardless of the origin of the irrelevant objects. For example, internally generated verbal events should show the same functional pattern of interference with recall as externally presented ones. A series of studies examining the effect of concurrent articulation on visual-verbal recall showed this to be the case (Macken & Jones, 1995), with both vocalised and silently mouthed changing-state articulatory activity (repeating the letters A through G) producing more disruption of recall than steady-state articulation (repeating the letter A). Further, this changing-state articulation effect was only found for tasks that required serial recall. Interference with visuospatial short-term memory by changing-state irrelevant sound and concurrent articulation also occurs (Jones, Farrand, Stuart, & Morris, 1995) as long as the visuospatial task requires the retention of order information. Thus it appears that the interaction of information in memory is not determined by modality or content, but rather by process. Further, an irrelevant sound effect has also been demonstrated when the memory items are presented auditorily, rather than visually (Hanley & Broadbent, 1987; LeCompte, 1996). Again, from the point of view of the O-OER model, this finding highlights the point that the relationship between the source of the irrelevant material and that of the memory material is not an important determinant of disruption of memory.

CHANGING-STATE: THE ROLE OF SEGMENTATION

Thus far, the evidence suggests that tasks that are susceptible to disruption are those that require retention of order information, and sounds that disrupt are those that contain changing-state information. It appears that changing state is registered when there is some degree of mismatch between separate items in a sequence of sound and that it is the mismatch between immediately successive items that is critical for disruption to occur (Tremblay & Jones, 1998). Therefore, in order for changing state to be registered some process of segmentation is required, since the critical change is that which occurs between two separate entities. For example, a continuous, randomly varying pitch glide produces no disruption of serial recall, but if the same pitch glide is regularly interrupted by short periods of silence, the usual disruption occurs (Jones, Macken, & Murray, 1993). Obviously, silent interruptions would not be the only means by which a sound could be segmented, since acoustically continuous signals, such as most narrative speech, nonetheless give rise to the perception of discrete units (e.g. syllables or phonemes). Abrupt changes in pitch and/or amplitude, which occur naturally within speech sounds, would seem likely candidates for the segmentation of both speech and nonspeech sounds (see Walsh & Diehl, 1991). Indeed, Jones et al. (1993) showed that a continuous sequence of synthesised vowel sounds was as disruptive as one in which formant transitions were removed to give an interrupted sequence. With these continuous speech stimuli, however, although acoustically continuous, marked changes in the pitch and amplitude characteristics of the signal occur at the boundaries between vowels, which may provide cues to segmentation. More recent research lends weight to this interpretation, as comodulating amplitude and frequency at critical rates within a nonspeech, continuous pitch glide also restores the disruptive effect of such stimuli (Alford, 1998).

This segmentation process is actually a necessary component of changing state, since the critical change in this respect is that between successive units in a sound sequence. This elaborated notion of changing state—that a sound will be disruptive if it is segmentable into discrete units, and each unit is different from the one preceding it—suggests that those passages of instrumental music will be most disruptive which lend themselves to easy segmentation. It also explains why humming a tune produces less disruption than either singing or speaking the words, since the continuously voiced humming will contain fewer abrupt transitions than speech or singing (Morris, Jones, & Quayle, 1989). Also, the finding that continuous broadband noise does not disrupt serial recall, a finding that contributed to Salamé and Baddeley's (1989) argument that speech has special status in memory, may be explained since such a signal will not contain cues to segmentation.

The important role of segmentation is also pointed to by experiments using "babble" speech (Jones & Macken, 1995b; Kilcher & Hellbrück, 1993; Klatte & Hellbrück, 1993). For example, the signal produced by recording 100 people speaking at once (babble) produces significant disruption relative to quiet, but produces significantly less disruption than a single voice. The reduced disruption found with babble speech can be produced with as few as eight voices (Kilcher & Hellbrück, 1993) and six voices (Jones & Macken, 1995b). In terms of the acoustic signal, a single voice will contain peaks and troughs of signal strength that may act as the basis for segmentation, but as further voices are added, these changes in the signal become less marked, until the signal appears to be of a constant amplitude. More specifically, as more voices are added, steady-state portions of each voice will mask the abrupt pitch/amplitude changes in other voices. The resulting compound signal contains fewer cues to segmentation than a single voice, thereby undermining this necessary precondition for changing state, and thereby leading to an attenuation in the disruptive capacity of the sound.

CHANGING-STATE: THE ROLE OF STREAMING

If the six voices which go to make up the babble are assigned to different locations by transmitting them through separate loudspeakers arranged around the subject's head, then the usual disruptiveness is re-established (Jones & Macken, 1995b, Expt. 3). The processes of auditory perception are such that the particular acoustic signal arriving at the ear is decomposed according to the various sources of the components of that signal in the environment. This process is referred to as auditory scene analysis, or streaming (see, e.g., Bregman, 1990; Handel, 1989). Signals are parsed according to environmental source on the basis of such aspects as spatial location, proximity, and continuity in the frequency domain, temporal characteristics, and so on. With regard to the results of Jones and Macken, the different spatial locations of the six voices allows the auditory system to deal with each one as if it was unaccompanied, and therefore the normal segmentation processes can take place, thus re-establishing the disruptiveness of the sound.

The role of streaming in the irrelevant speech effect has been examined in more detail by Jones and Macken (1995c). One of the critical comparisons was between two ways of presenting the same sequence of three syllables. In one case the three syllables were presented monophonically through headphones in a repeated loop. Thus, this condition involves presentation of a single changing-state stream. The second condition involved stereophonic presentation of the same three syllables such that one was presented to one ear, a second to the other ear, and a third to both ears at once. Thus on the basis of auditory streaming, this condition gives rise to the perception of three steady-state streams. Jones and Macken showed that this condition produced less disruption of serial recall than the condition comprising a single changing-state stream. Thus the changing-state concept must be elaborated further to include the importance of auditory streaming. Essentially, what this means is that changing state must occur within a stream in order to produce disruption of serial recall.

This leads to an important feature of the relationship between the degree of change within the auditory stream and its disruptive capacity. Certain levels of change within the auditory stream will give rise to segmentation and the registering of changing state, which provide the basis for the encoding of order information within the stream. However, above certain levels, mismatch serves to subsume another process, namely, that of stream segregation: If two temporally successive entities are sufficiently different from each other, then the auditory system will treat them as having arisen from different environmental sources. For example, participants are very poor at identifying the order of a rapidly repeated sequence of unrelated sounds, such as a buzz, a hiss, a tone, and a click (Warren, Obusek, & Farmer, 1969). Bregman and Campbell (1971) argued that this was because each of the sounds was allocated to a separate stream, and showed that although perception of order was good for items within a stream, subjects were unable to judge the relative ordering of items belonging to different streams (see also McNally & Handel, 1977). If the disruptive potency of sound is due to a clash between the order information within that sound and the order information that the participant is trying to retain within the memory set, then sound sequences within which order information is not encoded (even though those sequences contain distinct elements) should produce little or no disruption. This means that the relationship between mismatch and disruption should be nonmonotonic: Moderate degrees of mismatch lead to the encoding of order information and concomitant disruption of recall, but large degrees of mismatch will lead to each item being assigned to a separate stream, thus losing information about the order between them, and so disruption should diminish. For example, a sequence of tones alternating in frequency gives rise to substantial disruption of recall. However, when the difference in frequency between the two tones reaches the level at which they are now assigned to different perceptual streams, each one containing a repeated tone (see Van Noorden, 1975), the degree of disruption is attenuated (Jones, Alford, Bridges, Tremblay, & Macken, in press).

The relationship discussed between mismatch, streaming, and the encoding of order information provides us with a means of specifying in advance which sequences of sounds will or will not produce disruption of recall. If, for example, participants are unable to report the order in which events within a sequence occurred (such as happens with the stimuli examined by Warren et al., 1969, as mentioned earlier), then the changing-state hypothesis predicts that such sequences will lead to little or no disruption of recall. This is because if order information is poorly encoded in the auditory sequence, then there is no order information associated with the irrelevant sound to interfere with that in the memory set. Similarly, sequences of alternating sounds that, when in the focus of attention, perceptually split into separate, steady-state streams, will also be minimally disruptive of serial recall. Thus, by testing the perceptual properties of sequences of sounds, it should be possible to predict how disruptive they will be of recall when they are unattended.

CONCLUSIONS

Many theories in cognitive psychology posit a modular processing structure within which information interacts on the basis of similarity of content. Much of the literature on short-term memory is no exception to this trend. However, research on the irrelevant sound effect has cast doubts on such modularity assumptions, in showing that sound disrupts recall not on the basis of similarity of content between what is heard and what is being remembered, but rather because two concurrent processes of seriation are taking place: That involving the preattentive organisation of sounds in the irrelevant stream, and that involving the ordering of items within the memory set. This holds whether the sounds are similar or dissimilar to the to-be-remembered items, whether the irrelevant material is heard or internally generated, and even whether the to-be-remembered material is verbal or visuospatial in nature. Further, the organisation of information in memory is intimately related to the processes of perceptual organisation, such that the effects of irrelevant sound on memory are modulated by the processes of auditory stream formation. Taken together, these findings point to a nonmodular processing system that is object based; those objects, and the way in which they interact with each other, being the product of perceptual processes.

REFERENCES

Alford, D. (1998). *Pitch glides and the irrelevant sound effect: On the synergy of acoustic attributes*. Poster presented at Quebec '98 Conference on Short-term Memory, Quebec, June.

Baddeley, A.D. (1986). *Working memory*. Oxford: Clarendon Press.

Baddeley, A.D. (1990). *Human memory: Theory and practice*. Hove, UK: Lawrence Erlbaum Associates Ltd.

Beaman, C.P., & Jones, D.M. (1997). The role of serial order in the irrelevant speech effect: Tests of the changing state hypothesis. *Journal of Experimental Psychology: Learning, Memory and Cognition, 23*, 459–471.

Beaman, C.P., & Jones, D.M. (1998). Irrelevant sound disrupts order information in free as in serial recall. *Quarterly Journal of Experimental Psychology: Human Experimental Psychology, 51A*, 615–636.

Bregman, A.S. (1990). *Auditory scene analysis: The perceptual organisation of sound*. Cambridge, MA: MIT Press.

Bregman, A.S., & Campbell, J. (1971). Primary auditory stream segregation and perception of order in rapid sequences of tones. *Journal of Experimental Psychology, 89*, 244–249.

Colle, H.A. (1980). Auditory encoding in visual short-term recall: Effects of noise intensity and spatial location. *Journal of Verbal Learning and Verbal Behavior, 19*, 722–735.

Colle, H.A., & Welsh, A. (1976). Acoustic masking in primary memory. *Journal of Verbal Learning and Verbal Behavior, 15*, 17–31.

Crowder, R.G. (1993). Short-term memory: Where do we stand? *Memory and Cognition, 21*, 142–145.

Deutsch, D. (1970). Tones and numbers: Specificity of interference in short term memory. *Science, 168*, 1604–1605.

Handel, S. (1989). *Listening: An introduction to the perception of auditory events* (1st ed.). Cambridge, MA: MIT Press.

Hanley, J.R., & Broadbent, C. (1987). The effect of unattended speech on serial recall following auditory presentation. *British Journal of Psychology, 78*, 287–297.

Jones, D.M. (1993). Objects, streams and threads of auditory attention. In A. Baddeley & L. Weiskrantz (Eds.), *Attention: Selection, awareness and control* (pp. 87–103). Oxford: Clarendon Press.

Jones, D.M., Alford, D., Bridges, A., Tremblay, S., & Macken, W.J. (in press). Organisational factors in selective attention: The interplay of acoustic distinctiveness and auditory streaming in the irrelevant sound effect. *Journal of Experimental Psychology: Learning, Memory and Cognition*.

Jones, D.M., Beaman, C.P., & Macken, W.J. (1996). The object-oriented episodic record model. In S. Gathercole (Ed.), *Models of short-term memory* (pp. 209–238). Hove, UK: Lawrence Erlbaum Associates Ltd.

Jones, D.M., Farrand, P., Stuart, G., & Morris, N. (1995). Functional equivalence of verbal and spatial information in serial short-term memory. *Journal of Experimental Psychology: Learning, Memory and Cognition, 21*, 1008–1018.

Jones, D.M., & Macken, W.J. (1993). Irrelevant tones produce an irrelevant speech effect: Implications for phonological coding in working memory. *Journal of Experimental Psychology: Learning, Memory and Cognition, 19*, 369–381.

Jones, D.M., & Macken, W.J. (1995a). Phonological similarity in the irrelevant speech effect: Within- or between-stream similarity? *Journal of Experimental Psychology: Learning, Memory and Cognition, 21*, 103–115.

Jones, D. M., & Macken, W.J. (1995b). Auditory babble and cognitive efficiency: Role of number of voices and their location. *Journal of Experimental Psychology: Applied, 1*, 216–226.

Jones, D.M., & Macken, W.J. (1995c). Organisational factors in the effect of irrelevant speech: The role of spatial location and timing. *Memory and Cognition, 23*, 192–200.

Jones, D.M., Macken, W.J., & Murray, A.C. (1993). Disruption of visual short-term memory by changing-state auditory stimuli: The role of segmentation. *Memory & Cognition, 21*, 318–328.

Jones, D.M., Madden, C., & Miles, C. (1992). Privileged access by irrelevant speech to short-term memory: The role of changing state. *The Quarterly Journal of Experimental Psychology, 44A*, 645–669.

Kilcher, H., & Hellbrück, J. (1993). The irrelevant speech effect: Is binaural processing relevant or irrelevant? In A. Schick (Ed.), *Contributions to psychological acoustics. Results of the sixth Oldenburg Symposium on Psychological Acoustics* (pp. 605–613). Oldenburg, Germany: BIS.

Klatte, M., & Hellbrück, J. (1993). Der "irrelevant speech effekt": Wirkungen von Hintergrundschall auf das Arbeitsgedachtnis [The "irrelevant speech effect": Effects of background noise on working memory]. *Zeitschrift fur Larmbekampfung, 40*, 91–98.

LeCompte, D.C. (1994). Extending the irrelevant speech effect beyond serial recall. *Journal of Experimental Psychology: Learning, Memory and Cognition, 20*, 1396–1408.

LeCompte, D.C. (1996). Irrelevant speech, serial rehearsal, and temporal distinctiveness: A new approach to the irrelevant speech effect. *Journal of Experimental Psychology: Learning, Memory and Cognition, 22*, 1154–1165.

LeCompte, D.C., & Shaibe, D.M. (1997). On the irrelevance of phonological similarity to the irrelevant speech effect. *Quarterly Journal of Experimental Psychology: Human Experimental Psychology, 50A*, 100–118.

Macken, W.J., & Jones, D.M. (1995). Functional characteristics of the inner voice and the inner ear: Single or double agency? *Journal of Experimental Psychology: Learning, Memory and Cognition, 21*, 436–448.

Martin, R.C., Wogalter, M.S., & Forlano, J.G. (1988). Reading comprehension in the presence of unattended speech and music. *Journal of Memory and Language, 27*, 382–398.

Martin-Loeches, M., Schweinberger, S.R., & Sommer, W. (1997). The phonological loop model of working memory: An ERP study of irrelevant speech and phonological similarity effects. *Memory and Cognition, 25*, 471–485.

McNally, K.A., & Handel, S. (1977). Effect of element composition on streaming and the ordering of repeating sequences. *Journal of Experimental Psychology: Human Perception and Performance, 3*, 451–460.

Morris, N., Jones, D.M., & Quayle, A. (1989). Memory disruption by background speech and singing. In E. Megaw (Ed.), *Contemporary Ergonomics 1989*. London: Taylor & Francis.

Salamé, P., & Baddeley, A. (1982). Disruption of short-term memory by unattended speech: Implications for the structure of working memory. *Journal of Verbal Learning and Verbal Behavior, 21*, 150–164.

Salamé, P., & Baddeley, A.D. (1989). Effects of background music on phonological short-term memory. *Quarterly Journal of Experimental Psychology, 41A*, 107–122.

Tremblay, S., & Jones, D.M. (1998). Role of habituation in the irrelevant sound effect: Evidence from the effects of token set size and rate of transition. *Journal of Experimental Psychology: Learning, Memory and Cognition, 24*, 659–671.

Van Noorden, L.P. (1975). *Temporal coherence in the perception of tone sequences*. Unpublished doctoral dissertation, Eindhoven University of Technology.

Walsh, M.A., & Diehl, R.L. (1991). Formant transition duration and amplitude rise time as cues to the stop/glide distinction. *Quarterly Journal of Experimental Psychology: Human Experimental Psychology, 43A*, 603–620.

Warren, R.M., Obusek, C.J., & Farmer, R.M. (1969). Auditory sequence: Confusion of patterns other than speech or music. *Science, 164*, 586–587.

The Effect of Noise on Memory for Spoken Syllables

Aimée M. Surprenant
Purdue University, West Lafayette, USA

Two experiments explore the effects of noise on memory for spoken syllables. Participants identified and then recalled nonsense syllables under different levels of noise. There were significant decrements in memory, even in conditions where there was no effect of the noise on identification of the syllable. The experiments showed effects over all list positions as well as decreases in the final, or recency, portion of the curve. Results suggest that both capacity and dual-coding play a role in immediate memory.

Deux expériences explorent les effets du bruit sur la mémoire de syllabes présentées de façon auditive. Les participants devaient identifier, puis rappeler, des syllabes sans signification en présence de différents niveaux de bruit. Une diminution significative du rappel de syllabes a été observée, même pour les syllabes correctement identifiées en présence de bruit. Les résultats montrent des effets à toutes les positions serielles ainsi qu'une diminution de l'effet de récence. Ces résultats suggèrent que la capacité ainsi que le double encodage jouent un rôle en mémoire immédiate.

Some sort of noise is constantly present in today's society. The hum of machines, the noise of traffic, radios, TVs, etc., are all a constant accompaniment to our everyday tasks. Studies of the effects of low-level noise on memory for speech sounds have been few and far between, perhaps because of the impression that the speech signal is very robust and is intelligible despite a great deal of distortion (Hirsh, Reynolds, & Joseph, 1954). One common assumption is that if a speech sound is identified correctly, there is no effect of the noise. The experiments reported here are designed to question that assumption by providing evidence that background noise which is not severe enough to cause failures of identification does, in fact, affect memory performance. In addition, serial position functions will be reported that show differential effects of noise across list positions.

A number of studies have shown reduced memory performance when the stimuli are distorted in some way. For example, Luce, Feustel, and Pisoni (1983) demonstrated that memory for word sequences was substantially poorer for synthetic speech than for natural speech. However, this result is difficult to interpret because identification performance was very different for the two types of speech sounds (see also Humes, Nelson, Pisoni, & Lively, 1993).

More convincing evidence demonstrating that noise or distortion has a direct effect on memory, given correct identification, was reported by Rabbitt (1968, 1991) and Pichora-Fuller, Schneider, and Daneman (1995). Rabbitt (1968) showed overall decrements in memory for words that were presented to young normal-hearing listeners in white or broad-band noise. This overall decrement occurred even though the listeners were able to identify the stimuli perfectly. Rabbitt (1991) showed that even mild peripheral sensory hearing loss could result in a substantial reduction in the number of words recalled, compared to an age-matched control group with no hearing loss, even though identification performance (measured by shadowing the presented stimuli out loud) was essentially perfect for both groups. Similarly, Pichora-Fuller et al. (1995), using a variant of the speech-perception-in-noise test (Bilger, Nuetzel, Rabinowitz, & Rzeczkowski, 1984), showed that mildly impaired older participants recalled fewer items than young participants even when levels of identification were equated. Both Pichora-Fuller et al. (1995) and Rabbitt (1991) suggested that the added difficulty in interpreting the words for the listeners with distorted signals (i.e. white noise or mild hearing loss) took away from resources that might otherwise be used to elaboratively encode and rehearse the materials. Thus, even though the noise or distortion of the signal had no overt effect on identification (Rabbitt, 1968, 1991), and identification performance was equated (Pichora-Fuller et al., 1995), there were still effects of hearing loss and ageing on memory and comprehension (see also Rabbitt, 1990). Neither Rabbitt nor Pichora-Fuller et al. reported errors by serial position.

What happens when a person can identify a stimulus perfectly but there is some sort of distortion of the signal

---

Requests for reprints should be addressed to Aimée M. Surprenant, 1364 Psychological Sciences Bldg., Purdue University, West Lafayette, IN 47907–1364, USA (E-mail: aimee@psych.purdue.edu).

This research was supported, in part, by a Summer Faculty Grant from the Purdue Research Foundation. The author wishes to thank Dr. Ian Neath, Marie Poirier, and John Groeger for comments on the manuscript.

or some background noise? There are at least two possible ways that this could affect memory. When masking or distortion is not sufficient to produce errors of identification, a listener may nevertheless have to make more *effort* to distinguish what is said. This may reduce the resources available for more elaborative encoding and rehearsal of the stimulus. Alternatively, any *physical trace* that is used to help identify words can be less useful at discriminating the to-be-remembered item from the set of possibilities. These two factors are likely to result in different patterns of performance that would not be seen when the only reported measure is overall level of recall. The two types of explanations make different predictions as to how the noise will affect performance across serial positions.

When people are asked to recall a sequence of words in order and auditory—or vocalized—presentation is used, they generally recall the first few items well (the primacy effect) and the last few items well (the recency effect) relative to middle-list items (Crowder, 1976). When visual presentation is used, there is no recency effect (LeCompte, 1992), and this difference between auditory and visual presentation is known as the modality effect (see Penney, 1989, for a review). Although at the moment there is no single well-accepted explanation of the serial position curve and the modality effect, most theories of the recency and modality effect rely on some sort of dual-coding scheme: Items at the end of the list are remembered quite well because there is some extra advantage that auditory items have over visual items. This advantage is due to either lack of overwriting by successive items (e.g. Crowder, 1973; Nairne, 1990) or lack of decay of the final item(s) (Cowan, 1992), which linger in a sensory-based or phonological form.

Dual-coding theories (e.g. Crowder, 1973; Fujisaki & Kawashima, 1970; Nairne, 1990; Pisoni, 1973) suggest that each item results in more than one code, one that is somewhat abstract (i.e. the name of the word) and another that preserves more of the physical characteristics of the stimulus (i.e. a physical trace). As each new stimulus occurs, the physical trace may be overwritten if it is similar to the subsequent stimulus. The final item has an advantage because there is no subsequent stimulus and the physical trace is not subject to overwriting. Any sound appended to the end of the list, given that it is similar enough to overwrite the physical trace of the final item, will act as a suffix and reduce recall of that item (Crowder, 1973).

Surprenant and Neath (1996) argued that the addition of noise to the signal results in an impoverished or degraded sensory or physical trace. This reduces recall because that information is critical for recoding the perceptual representation into a more durable verbal code. Surprenant and Neath argue that recall is determined by the relative discriminability of the memory representation rather than by the relative discriminability of the actual physical stimulus. If the physical representation of the stimulus is degraded, such as when it is presented in noise, successful recall will depend almost exclusively on the abstract features of the stimulus. A simple dual-code theory would predict that noise would primarily affect the end of the list that relies more heavily on physical traces.

A capacity explanation such as those suggested by Rabbitt (1991) and Pichora-Fuller et al. (1995) could explain the effect of noise or distortion on memory by suggesting that the effect of the noise is to cause difficulty in encoding the stimulus and thus use up more of a limited pool of resources just to understand each word. Rabbitt (1968) suggested that when a person is listening to speech in noise they are essentially performing in a dual-task situation. Because the processing of the stimulus in noise is no longer automatic, some resources are being allocated to understand the stimulus and those resources cannot therefore be used in higher-level cognitive processing. What effect this decrease in resources might have on the recall of items by serial position is not explicitly stated and there have not been a great many studies of the effect of a secondary task on serial positions.

However, Baddeley, Scott, Drynan, and Smith (1969) showed that with auditory presentation, the addition of a secondary task affects recall of all the items with the exception of the recency item or items. Surprenant, LeCompte, and Neath (in press) showed that articulatory suppression, which might be considered to be a secondary task, decreased performance across serial positions but had no effect on recency. Thus a theory appealing to a capacity construct might predict that the effect of noise should be restricted to the beginning of the list and should not affect the recency portions of the curve.

The key difference between a capacity model and a dual-trace model lies in the cause of the deficit. According to a dual-code model, the primary determinant of recall is the discriminability of each of the codes in memory. Adding noise does not require more resources; rather, it degrades the physical traces, making them less useful at recall. The subject must then rely almost exclusively on the abstract features of the word in order to discriminate it from others in the search set. According to Nairne's (1990) feature model, for example, recall would be based mainly on modality-independent features and thus an auditory list would behave in the same way as a visual list (i.e. no recency). Within this view, any manipulation that degrades the auditory representation of a word will affect recall, whether it is noise, low-pass filtering, or irrelevant background speech (Neath, Surprenant, & LeCompte, 1998). A resource allocation or capacity view, on the other hand, emphasizes the amount of attention required to process and rehearse the sound. According to this view, adding noise should increase the resources required, and should impair memory performance.

EXPERIMENT 1

Rabbitt (1968) showed that recall of words in white or broad-band noise was substantially worse than that recall in the quiet, even though participants could identify the words perfectly. However, he reported only overall performance and did not show how the noise affected each serial position. In addition, Rabbitt used only one level of noise. The present experiment had three purposes: (1) to replicate and extend Rabbitt's (1968) study by demonstrating an effect of noise on memory in the absence of an effect on identification; (2) to determine whether noise has differential effects on recall across serial positions; and (3) to explore the effects of increasing the level of the noise on memory.

One of the questions posed in these studies is whether difficulty hearing a stimulus, at a fairly low level, can cause what look to be deficits in memory. They are meant to demonstrate that small difficulties in understanding sounds show their effect at more central cognitive processes. Thus, in the following experiments white, or broad-band, noise is used so that the majority of the effects are due to physical masking of the stimuli at a peripheral level. Broad-band noise is unlikely to affect trace formation or to interfere with a phonological or verbal trace in memory.

Method

Participants. Thirty Purdue University undergraduates volunteered to participate in exchange for credit in introductory psychology courses and were arbitrarily assigned to one of six counterbalancing orders.

Stimuli and Design. The stimuli were six consonant-vowel syllables (/ba/, /bæ/, /bi/, /bI/, /bo/, /bU/) digitized at 44 kHz and low-pass filtered at 10 kHz. The syllables were presented at 65 dB SPL in the quiet condition and were mixed with white or broad-band noise in two conditions that resulted in +10 and +5 dB speech-to-noise ratios[1]. The noise conditions were mixed together and presented randomly—participants were unable to predict the next condition.

Procedure. Participants were first allowed to listen to each stimulus twice. The name of the syllable was displayed on the computer screen while the stimulus was played. They were then given 30 identification trials. A syllable was presented and participants were asked to identify it by pressing one of six keys on the computer keyboard overlaid with the names of the syllables. Feedback was given. After the identification trials they were given 25 recall trials where each list consisted of a random permutation of all 6 syllables. Participants were instructed to respond in strict serial order. Again all responses were collected on the keyboard and participants were not allowed to go back and change any response. No feedback was given in the recall trials.

Results and Discussion

The left column of Table 1 shows the identification data for Experiment 1. There was a reliable difference in correct identification in this experiment [$F(2,58) = 3.93$, $MSe = 0.003$, $P < .05$]. Post hoc (LSD, $\alpha < .05$) tests show a reliable difference between only the quiet and the +5 S/N condition. As would be expected, the errors were not evenly distributed across the stimuli. The highest percentage of errors occurred with /bæ/ being misrecognized 25% of the time followed by /ba/ at 16% with /bI/, /bo/, and /bU/ all with about 12% errors and the fewest errors was /bi/, with 7%. This is essentially the order of confusions found by Peterson and Barney (1952) in their seminal work on vowel categorization. Even though the errors were not evenly spread among the syllables, any effect of this should be spread evenly across serial positions.

Figure 1 shows the serial position by noise interaction. There is an effect of noise that seems different for the overall list and the final recency item. Analysis of variance indicates a reliable main effect of noise [$F(2,58) = 18.14$, $MSe = 0.02$, $P < .01$], a main effect of serial position [$F(5,145) = 51.12$, $MSe = 0.01$, $P < .01$], and a small but still reliable interaction of noise and serial position [$F(10,290) = 1.88$, $MSe = 0.00$, $P = .05$]. Planned comparisons on the final positions of each condition show that the quiet and +10 S/N conditions are both different from the +5 S/N condition [$F(1,29) = 14.65$, $MSe = 0.01$, $P < .01$; $F(1,29) = 14.75$, $MSe = 0.01$, $P < .01$], respectively, but were not different from each other ($F < 1$).

The curves for the quiet and the +10 S/N ratio conditions are just what would be predicted by a theory which suggests that the noise is adding a secondary task: All serial positions with the exception of the final one are decreased. However, when more noise is added, as in the +5 S/N ratio condition, overall performance

---

[1] Note that speech- or signal-to-noise ratios, S/N, by convention, are calculated by subtracting the level of the noise from the level of the speech. Thus a S/N ratio of +10 means that the speech is 10 dB more intense than the noise. Because in this experiment the level of the speech signal is held constant, in the +5 condition the noise is 5 dB louder than in the +10 condition.

TABLE 1
Proportion Correct Identification of Nonsense Syllables (and Standard Errors of the Mean) for Different Levels of Noise

Noise Level	Experiment 1	Experiment 2
Quiet	.88	.94
MSe	.03	.01
+10 S/N	.86	.95
MSe	.04	.01
+5 S/N	.84	.93
MSe	.04	.01

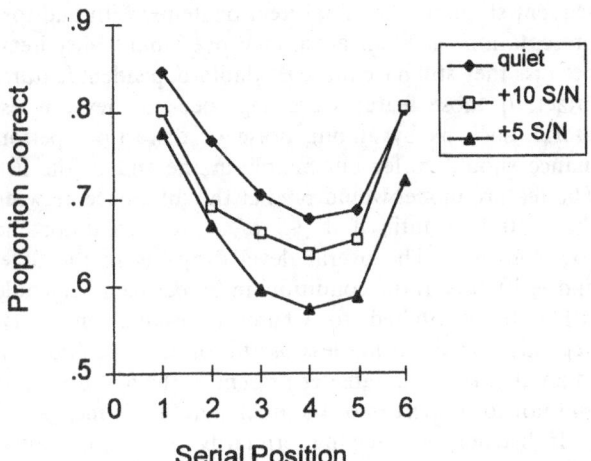

FIG. 1. Proportion correct recall as a function of serial position and speech-to-noise level for Experiment 1.

decreases even more and the final item is also affected, although there is still a substantial recency effect. This condition is a bit difficult to interpret given that the identification scores were significantly lower than those of the quiet condition.

EXPERIMENT 2

Experiment 1 showed that there were substantial effects of noise that occurred especially at the beginning of the serial position curve. However, the difference in identification level for the +5 S/N level condition is troubling. Given that the participants were less accurate in identifying the stimuli in that condition, it is difficult to interpret the memory functions resulting from them. The conditions in Experiment 1 were varied randomly and participants were not able to predict which noise condition would come next. This might have made both the identification and the recall trials more difficult. Trial-to-trial variability often results in much lower levels of performance than if the conditions are blocked (Watson, Kelly, & Wroton, 1976). Thus, Experiment 2 was a replication of Experiment 1 with the exception that the noise trials were blocked instead of randomly intermixed in order to reduce the trial-to-trial uncertainty and to equate the identification performance across the different noise conditions.

Method

Participants. Thirty different Purdue University undergraduates participated in this experiment in exchange for course credit.

Stimuli and Design. The stimuli were exactly the same as in Experiment 1. The design was also the same with the exception that noise level was blocked and blocks were counterbalanced across participants in a completely balanced Latin-square design such that each condition followed and preceded every combination of the other conditions.

Procedure. The procedure was the same as in Experiment 1 with the exception that participants were told that the noise would be the same within a condition.

Results and Discussion

Table 1 shows mean identification and standard error of the mean as a function of noise level for both experiments. The data from Experiment 2 are in the right column. As is evident from the table, identification was well above 90% correct in all conditions and there were no differences among the conditions. A one-way analysis of variance (ANOVA) confirms this observation [$F(2,58) < 1$]. Although there were very few errors in this experiment, the pattern of errors by syllable followed that of Experiment 1 exactly. The highest percentage of errors occurred with /bæ/ being misrecognized 10% of the time followed by /ba/, /bI/, /bo/, and /bU/, all with about 8% errors, and the fewest errors was /bi/, with 2%.

Although identification of the syllables was at the same level for all noise conditions, there were substantial effects of noise on recall (see Fig. 2). In particular, adding some noise (+10 S/N ratio) reduced performance at every single serial position. The addition of slightly more noise (+5 dB S/N ratio) further reduced performance but only at the final two positions. This latter decrement is rather reminiscent of the suffix effect.

All of these observations were supported by the statistical analysis: there was a main effect of noise [$F(2,58) = 3.17$, $MSe = 0.09$, $P < .05$], a main effect of serial position [$F(5,145) = 56.38$, $MSe = 0.01$, $P < .01$], and an interaction of the two [$F(10,290) = 3.11$, $MSe = 0.01$, $P < .01$]. Planned comparisons show that the final position for the quiet condition was marginally greater than the +10 S/N condition [$F(1,29) = 3.65$, $MSe = 0.01$, $P = .07$] and was significantly better than the +5 S/N condition

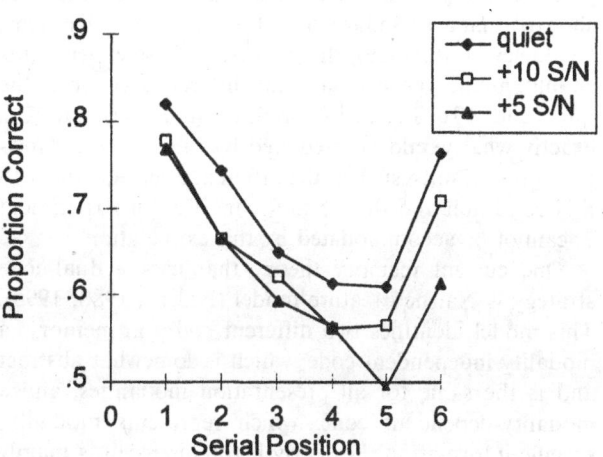

FIG. 2. Proportion correct recall as a function of serial position and speech-to-noise level for Experiment 2.

$[F(1,29) = 28.39, MSe = 0.05, P < .01]$. The final position was also different in the two noise conditions $[F(1,29) = 4.37, MSe = 0.03, P < .05]$, with performance on the final position in the +10 S/N condition being greater than the same position in the +5 S/N condition.

This experiment replicates Rabbitt (1968) but adds additional information on the effects of different levels of noise on specific portions of the serial position curve. Examining serial positions instead of just overall recall gives a more fine-grained analysis of what is occurring with the addition of noise. Looking at the serial position curves presented earlier, it seems that two processes are occurring—one that reduces overall recall when the stimuli are made a little more difficult to comprehend and one that reduces recall of the final items with further degradation. This is consistent with the hypothesis that both a reduction in attention or resources and a reduction in the usefulness of the physical trace play a role in reduced memory performance in noise.

GENERAL DISCUSSION

Experiments 1 and 2 demonstrated somewhat independent decrements in overall recall and recency for speech stimuli presented in noise, even when overall level of identification was (mostly) equated. Both experiments implicate a two-process account of memory: One which operates over the early list positions and another which operates at the final or recency portion of the curve. Neither a simple capacity nor a simple dual-code model can easily accommodate all aspects of these data.

The most influential current model that uses a capacity construct is Working Memory (Baddeley, 1986, 1992). The original Working Memory theory does not address serial position effects. However, researchers like Rabbitt (1991) and Pichora-Fuller et al. (1995) have suggested that working memory can account for these sorts of data by assuming that the addition of noise or distortion causes difficulty in encoding the stimulus words and thus adds a second task for the subject to perform along with the memory task. Given the data showing that a secondary task affects only early list items (Baddeley et al., 1969), the data from these experiments should mimic those data. The difference between the quiet and +10 S/N ratio condition in Experiment 1 is exactly what would be predicted by this analysis. However, other results, such as the difference between the +10 S/N condition and the +5 S/N condition in Experiment 2, cannot be accommodated by this explanation.

One current memory theory that uses a dual-code strategy is Nairne's feature model (Nairne, 1988, 1990). This model identifies two different codes in memory: a modality-independent code, which is somewhat abstract and is the same for all presentation modalities, and a modality-dependent code, which represents modality-specific information. For early list items recall is mainly dependent on modality-independent codes because the modality-dependent codes are overwritten by each subsequent stimulus. The final item or items, with auditory presentation, have an advantage over middle-list items because they still have those modality-dependent features intact. If those features are degraded so they are less useful, such as by adding noise or distortion, performance should suffer but mainly at the end of the list. The feature model would predict the difference between the +10 S/N ratio and +5 S/N ratio conditions in Experiment 2. The overall level drop, as in the quiet and +10 S/N ratio condition in Experiment 2, could either be attributed to whatever residual modality-dependent traces being less useful for early positions or to an attentional parameter present in the feature model and not to properties of the dual-coding scheme.

If listeners are relying primarily on the modality-independent features of the list items for most of the list items, then it follows that if the identity of the stimulus is known there should be no effect of noise at the beginning positions—the noise should affect only the recency portion of the curve. This is exactly the pattern of data reported by Frankish (1996). Frankish presented listeners with nine-item lists of digits in noise accompanied by a visual display of the numeral. The result of degrading the digits was seen only on the final few positions. Frankish suggested that this implied a memory representation including perceptual features found in the acoustic signal.

Regardless of the final theoretical interpretation, these data show that intelligibility tests provide a crude and sometimes inaccurate index of the extent to which noise may limit the efficiency of the encoding of information. The effect of noise cannot be disregarded until a point is reached at which recognition errors occur. Even levels of noise that do not have measurable effects on intelligibility may cause measurable decrements in the ability of listeners to remember spoken discourse. Noise may, in effect, impose an additional, "secondary task" that must be carried out whenever speech has to be understood.

REFERENCES

Baddeley, A.D. (1986). *Working memory.* Oxford: Oxford University Press.

Baddeley, A.D. (1992). Is working memory working? The fifteenth Bartlett Lecture. *Quarterly Journal of Experimental Psychology, 44,* 1–31.

Baddeley, A.D., & Hitch, G. (1974). Working memory. In G.H. Bower (Ed.), *The psychology of learning and motivation: Advances in research and theory, Vol. 8* (pp. 47–89). New York: Academic Press.

Baddeley, A.D., Scott, D., Drynan, R., & Smith, J.C. (1969). Short-term memory and the limited capacity hypothesis. *British Journal of Psychology, 60,* 51–55.

Bilger, R.C., Nuetzel, J.M., Rabinowitz, W.M., & Rzeczkowski, C. (1984). Standardization of a test of speech perception in noise. *Journal of Speech and Hearing Research, 27,* 32–48.

Cowan, N. (1992). Verbal memory span and the timing of spoken recall. *Journal of Memory and Language, 31,* 668–684.

Crowder, R.G. (1973). The representation of speech sounds in Precategorical Acoustic Storage. *Journal of Experimental Psychology, 98,* 14–24.

Frankish, C. (1996). Auditory short-term memory and the perception of speech. In S. Gathercole (Ed.), *Models of short-term memory* (pp. 179–207). Hove, UK: Psychology Press.

Fujisaki, H., & Kawashima, T. (1970). Some experiments on speech perception and a model for the perceptual mechanism. *Annual Report of the Engineering Research Institute, Faculty of Engineering, University of Tokyo, 29,* 207–214.

Hirsh, I.J., Reynolds, E.G., & Joseph, M. (1954). Intelligibility of different speech materials. *Journal of the Acoustical Society of America, 26,* 530–538.

Humes, L.E., Nelson, K.J., Pisoni, D.B., & Lively, S.E. (1993). Effects of age on serial recall of natural and synthetic speech. *Journal of Speech and Hearing Research, 36,* 634–639.

LeCompte, D.C. (1992). In search of a strong visual recency effect. *Memory and Cognition, 20,* 563-572.

Luce, P.A., Feustel, T.C., & Pisoni, D.B. (1983). Capacity demands in short-term memory for synthetic and natural speech. *Human Factors, 25,* 17–32.

Nairne, J.S. (1988). A framework for interpreting recency effects in immediate serial recall. *Memory and Cognition, 16,* 343–352.

Nairne, J.S. (1990). A feature model of immediate memory. *Memory & Cognition, 18,* 251–269.

Neath, I., Surprenant, A.M., & LeCompte, D.C. (1998). Irrelevant speech eliminates the word length effect. *Memory and Cognition, 26,* 343–354.

Penney, C.G. (1989). Modality effects and the structure of short-term verbal memory. *Memory and Cognition, 17,* 398–422.

Peterson, G.E., & Barney, H.L. (1952). Control methods used in a study of the vowels. *Journal of the Acoustical Society of America, 32,* 693–703.

Pichora-Fuller, M.K., Schneider, B.A., & Daneman, M. (1995). How young and old adults listen to and remember speech in noise. *Journal of the Acoustical Society of America, 97,* 593–608.

Pisoni, D.B. (1973). Auditory and phonetic memory codes in the discrimination of consonants and vowels. *Perception and Psychophysics, 21,* 253–260.

Rabbitt, P.M.A. (1966). Recognition: Memory for words correctly heard in noise. *Psychonomic Science, 6,* 383–384.

Rabbitt, P.M.A. (1968). Channel capacity, intelligibility and immediate memory. *Quarterly Journal of Experimental Psychology, 20,* 241–248.

Rabbitt, P.M.A. (1990). Applied cognitive gerontology: Some problems, methodologies and data. *Applied Cognitive Psychology, 4,* 225–246.

Rabbitt, P.M.A. (1991). Mild hearing loss can cause apparent memory failures which increase with age and reduce with IQ. *Acta Otolaryngology Supplement, 476,* 167–176.

Surprenant, A.M., LeCompte, D.C., & Neath, I. (in press). Manipulations of irrelevant information: Suffix effects with articulatory suppression and irrelevant speech. *Quarterly Journal of Experimental Psychology.*

Surprenant, A.M. & Neath, I. (1996). The relation between discriminability and memory for vowels, consonants, and silent-center vowels. *Memory and Cognition, 24,* 356–366.

Watson, C.S., Kelly, W.J., & Wroton, H.W. (1976). Factors in the discrimination of tonal patterns. II. Selective attention and learning under various levels of stimulus uncertainty. *Journal of the Acoustical Society of America, 61,* 1176–1186.

Semantic Contribution to Immediate Serial Recall Using an Unlimited Set of Items: Evidence for a Multi-level Capacity View of Short-term Memory

Nicole Caza and Sylvie Belleville
Université de Montréal, Canada

The purpose of this study was to assess the respective roles of lexical and semantic levels of representations in immediate serial recall, by testing participants with items that varied on both these dimensions. Contrary to most studies where a small fixed set of words are repeated over trials, the current items were tested once by sampling them from an unlimited set of items without replacement. Participants recalled three classes of words under articulatory suppression: nonwords, function words, and content words. Results indicated an advantage for function words over nonwords, confirming a specifically lexical contribution to immediate serial recall. Additionally, content words were more frequently recalled than function words, confirming a semantic contribution. These results imply that non-phonological factors influence immediate serial recall and are consistent with a multi-level capacity view of short-term memory.

Cette étude a pour but d'évaluer les contributions respectives des représentations lexicales et sémantiques lors du rappel sériel immédiat. Trois catégories de mots ont été utilisées: des mots abstraits (ayant des représentations lexicales et sémantiques), des mots grammaticaux (possédant des représentations lexicales mais peu de représentations sémantiques) et des non-mots (sans représentation lexico-sémantique). Contrairement à la plupart des études qui utilisent un petit groupe d'items, les listes de mots ont été créées à partir d'un grand ensemble d'items de sorte qu'ils n'étaient pas répétés d'un essai à l'autre. Les sujets devaient rappeler les mots en condition de suppression articulatoire. Les résultats montrent que les mots grammaticaux sont mieux rappelés que les non-mots ce qui indique une contribution spécifiquement lexicale lors du rappel sériel immédiat. De plus, un avantage est observé pour les mots abstraits comparativement aux mots grammaticaux ce qui confirme une contribution des représentations sémantiques. Ces résultats démontrent que des facteurs non-phonologiques influencent le rappel sériel immédiat et sont compatibles avec une approche voulant que la capacité de mémoire à court terme soit déterminée par plusieurs niveaux de représentations.

Performance in immediate serial recall of short verbal sequences has traditionally been recognized as a measure of verbal short-term memory (STM) capacity. Though it is widely used, researchers still do not fully understand the underlying mechanisms involved in this task. Two important theoretical conceptions have guided a large number of studies concerned with this issue. One very influential proposal is Baddeley's (1986; Baddeley & Hitch, 1974) phonological loop model. According to this view, verbal STM is essentially determined by a phonological store and a rehearsal process, thus by phonological factors. Central to this model is the assumption that verbal STM is a distinct and independent cognitive subsystem. An alternative view assumes that the processing of any type of information involves different but interactive domain-specific subsystems, each having a temporary storage capacity (Craik & Lockhart, 1972; Crowder, 1989; N. Martin & Saffran, 1997; R.C. Martin, Shelton, & Yaffee, 1994; Monsell, 1984). Accordingly, verbal STM is seen as having common underlying mechanisms with language processing rather than construed as an isolated memory system. Since most theories of language assume the existence of different representational levels, such representations are further assumed to be reflected in the immediate serial recall performance of verbal information.

The debate between these two theoretical conceptions has currently been revived by recent research showing that immediate serial recall performance is influenced by long-term memory (LTM) information. Indeed, several researchers have reported lexical effects on immediate serial recall tasks (Besner & Davelaar, 1982; Gregg, Freedman, & Smith, 1989; Hulme, Maughan, & Brown, 1991; Hulme, Roodenrys, Brown, & Mercer,

---

Requests for reprints should be addressed to Nicole Caza or Sylvie Belleville, Centre de recherche, Institut Universitaire de Gériatrie de Montréal, 4565 Queen Mary, Montréal, Québec, Canada, H3W 1W5 (E-mail: cazan@magellan.umontreal.ca).

The stimuli used in this study are available from NC. This work was supported by an NSERC grant and a FRSQ Chercheur-boursier fellowship (obtained by SB), and by NSERC and FRSQ scholarships (obtained by NC). We would like to thank Len Caza and Daniel Saumier for help in editing the paper.

© 1999 International Union of Psychological Science

1995; Roodenrys, Hulme, Alban, Ellis, & Brown, 1994; Tehan & Humphreys, 1988). Within the context of Baddeley's theory, a LTM influence must be independent of the phonological loop. These lexical effects have been obtained under articulatory suppression or found not to be mediated by differences in speech rate. These LTM effects are attributed to the knowledge participants have of the phonological form of the words stored in LTM, thus to the lexical level (word level) of representations.

The observation of a LTM contribution to immediate serial recall tasks has different implications for these two theoretical proposals. In the case of Baddeley's framework, a lexical effect from stored phonological forms of words cannot be accounted for without modifying his current model. In a recent paper, Baddeley, Gathercole, and Papagno (1998) proposed a new version of the phonological loop model in order to accommodate the growing evidence of a LTM contribution. The authors suggested that the phonological store interacts with the phonological form of words stored in LTM. This new version can thus account for lexical (or LTM phonological form) effects that indicate LTM contributions of a phonological nature.

Contrary to the original phonological loop proposal, evidence for a LTM contribution to immediate serial recall is quite compatible with the multi-level capacity approach. As mentioned before, this proposal assumes that different levels of representations will be reflected in recall performance. According to most theories of language, linguistic comprehension and production require the processing of phonological, lexical, syntactic, and semantic representations. However, since participants performing an immediate serial recall task must produce a list of discrete words, and not complete sentences, it is assumed that the levels of representations implicated exclude syntactic knowledge. Hence, a multi-level capacity approach to immediate serial recall would predict not only a phonological effect on immediate recall, but also lexical and semantic contributions.

In the studies mentioned earlier, the LTM contribution has been attributed to lexical representations. However, in two of these studies (Besner & Davelaar, 1982; Hulme et al., 1991), a LTM contribution was inferred from a difference in performance found between words and nonwords. Since words usually convey meaning, they possess semantic representations in addition to lexical representations. Therefore, one cannot be sure that the effects found were solely mediated by lexical knowledge: The semantic representations might also have contributed to producing the effect.

The issue of whether the LTM contribution is arising from lexical or semantic levels of representations is not trivial. Implications stemming from the two theoretical conceptions are quite different. In the latest version of the phonological loop model (Baddeley et al., 1998), only a lexical contribution could be accounted for. Unless some modifications are made, evidence for a semantic contribution to immediate serial recall cannot be explained by this new version of the phonological loop model. On the other hand, the multi-level capacity view specifically predicts that semantic representations are used in immediate serial recall. However, convincing evidence for such a contribution is required in order to support this view. Because these two models make distinct predictions regarding the role of semantic representations in immediate serial recall, we believe that this issue is of important theoretical relevance.

A review of the literature suggests that few attempts have been made to set apart the semantic and lexical effects on immediate serial recall. Tehan and Humphreys (1988) indirectly provided a first demonstration when they compared recall performance across three classes of words; nouns, adjectives, and function words (e.g. articles, prepositions, conjunctions). It is assumed that since the meanings of function words are better established within the context of a sentence, they have less semantic content than nouns and adjectives when presented in isolation. Tehan and Humphreys showed that nouns and adjectives were better recalled than function words and interpreted this as suggesting a semantic contribution to immediate serial recall. However, this word-class effect was later challenged by Bourassa and Besner (1994), who controlled for the imageability value of the test items. In this later study, no advantage was found for content over function words.

Unfortunately, some methodological problems were noted in both these studies. First, neither experiment used lists of nonwords. When compared with nonwords, function words can reflect the specific contribution of lexical representations, independently of semantic knowledge. Additionally, there is a methodological issue related to the size of the pool of items used. Given that all but one of the studies mentioned previously were based on the use of small fixed sets of items, it is possible that participants learned certain fixed sets of items more rapidly. For instance, the repetition of small sets of items may result in facilitating the recall of words over nonwords, thus contributing to the exaggeration of a lexical effect. Indirect evidence for this was obtained in a study by Lapointe and Engle (1990), who found differences in word-length effects in span tasks when comparing small fixed pools of repeated words with large unlimited sets of items sampled without replacement.

The experiment reported here was designed to explore the respective involvement of semantic and lexical levels of representations in immediate serial recall, as expected by the interactive multi-level capacity approach. For this purpose, items that differ according to their LTM representations were compared. Abstract content words were used to counter a possible imageability effect. Words were chosen without replacement from an unlimited set so that no item was presented more than once. If immediate serial recall is mediated by the different subsystems involved in processing verbal information, performance should be better when items possess both lexical and semantic representations than when they possess only lexical representations, and these latter items should be better recalled than those lacking lexical (and semantic) representations. Participants were evaluated under articulatory suppression so that any effect found could not be attributed to the phonological loop.

METHOD

Participants

Twenty-one French-speaking students participated voluntarily in this experiment. Participants (12 women) had an average age of 21.67 years ($SD = 3.01$; range = 18–28) with an average level of education of 14.29 years ($SD = 2.08$). Their mean score on a French version of the Mill Hill Vocabulary Test (Gérard, 1983) was 24.43/34 ($SD = 3.91$), which is within normal range. Their average word span was 4.81 ($SD = 0.75$; range = 4–6), which indicates normal verbal STM capacity.

Material

All stimuli were presented visually on a Macintosh computer screen. Each word was presented at the centre of the screen in lower-case letters using a Times 36 font. Three sets of 40 items were constructed such that each set contained content words, function words, and nonwords. Eight lists of five items were created by drawing items randomly without replacement from each word-class set. Some lists were modified to control for semantic and phonological similarity. It should be noted that, unlike English function words (e.g. then, that, thus), French function words are not phonologically similar. All 24 lists were matched according to number of syllables, phonemes, letters, and bigram frequency. For content and function words, lists were also matched for word frequency (Baudot, 1992). The content words were abstract. Since there was no imagery and concreteness values available for these French content words, we used English indices when available (Friendly, Franklin, Hoffman, & Rubin, 1982; Paivio, Yuille, & Madigan, 1968).

Procedure

The experiment was conducted during a single session. Each trial began with the presentation of a visual cue (three stars) in the centre of the screen, followed by the five-item sequence. The items were presented individually at a rate of one every 1500msec, each item remaining on screen for 1250msec. At the end of the sequence, when a question mark appeared, the participant attempted to recall the words. Recalled items were written on a response sheet containing five lines placed one under the other. Participants were asked to write down the entire item to be remembered (not only the first letters), from top to bottom, on the line that corresponded to the serial order of the item in the sequence. Participants crossed out a line when they could not remember an item. Articulatory suppression was performed during both presentation and recall of the items. Articulatory suppression involved having participants count repeatedly from one to eight when the cue appeared, and continue counting until the last item was recalled. The order of presentation of the different word-classes was counterbalanced across participants according to a Latin Square design. Prior to the memory task, participants received a practice trial.

RESULTS

An analysis of variance was performed on the proportion of items correctly recalled. Responses were scored according to a strict serial recall criterion. Preliminary analyses were first performed to assess the effect of position in the Latin Square design and of fatigue or practice within a given word-class. No such effects were found.

Table 1 shows the mean proportions of words recalled in the correct serial position for each word-class. Both content and function words yielded better recall than nonwords. Furthermore, content words were better recalled than function words, although this advantage is of smaller magnitude than the one between function words and nonwords. A repeated-measures ANOVA including the word-class factor confirmed that the main effect was reliable, $F(2, 40) = 131.696$, $P < .0001$, $MSe = 0.00255$. A Newman-Keuls analysis ($P < .05$) indicated that recall of the nonwords was reliably lower than the recall of function words, and that these later items were less well recalled than content words.

DISCUSSION

The recall advantage of function words over nonwords is interpreted as a lexical effect given the lexical difference between these two word-classes. Considering the semantic difference between content and function words, the recall advantage of content words over function words is interpreted as a semantic effect. Since these effects were obtained under articulatory suppression, they are also interpreted as being independent of the phonological loop. Furthermore, since items were not repeated, the results may not be attributed to a learning effect.

The observation of a lexical and/or semantic contribution to immediate serial recall that is not mediated by the phonological loop has previously been demonstrated in several studies involving normal participants (Gregg et al., 1989; Hulme et al., 1997; Roodenrys et al., 1994; Tehan & Humphreys, 1988). Although the present results

TABLE 1
Mean Proportions of Words Recalled in the Correct Serial Position

Word-class	Mean	SD
Content word	.405	.089
Function word	.367	.065
Nonword	.169	.061

are consistent with these studies, our study establishes the independence of the lexical contribution from semantic representations by using items that are devoid of semantic properties (function words).

Our results also show a semantic effect on immediate serial recall. This is consistent with a recent study by Poirier and Saint-Aubin (1995), which demonstrates an advantage for homogenous semantic category word-lists over heterogeneous category word-lists, thus providing indirect evidence for the involvement of semantic representations in immediate serial recall. Neuropsychological studies also provide some converging evidence as to the existence of a semantic influence on immediate serial recall in brain-damaged patients unable to use phonological codes (Belleville, Peretz, Fontaine, & Caza, 1997; N. Martin & Saffran, 1997; R.C. Martin et al., 1994).

The latest version of the phonological loop (Baddeley et al., 1998) can now account for lexical contributions to immediate serial recall by postulating that the phonological store interacts with a phonological long-term system. However, this proposal has two important inconsistencies with our findings. The first problem concerns how a lexical or LTM phonological contribution obtained under suppression in the visual modality could be accounted for by the phonological loop model. According to this model, when items are presented visually, articulatory suppression blocks access to the loop. LTM effects could not be mediated via this system. However, an alternative account provided by Baddeley (1996) postulates that the central executive is involved in holding and manipulating verbal information from long-term memory. Unfortunately, it is unclear how this relates to immediate serial recall. A second inconsistency stems from the fact that the phonological loop model makes no prediction concerning the contribution of semantic representations to immediate serial recall.

On the other hand, the demonstration of lexical and semantic effects on immediate serial recall is consistent with the multi-level capacity view. This proposal assumes that the different subsystems responsible for processing these representations also have storage capacities and are thus contributing to their recall. The finding of a lexico-semantic contribution to immediate serial recall in brain-damaged patients has led N. Martin and Saffran (1997) to propose a theoretical framework based on a model of language production (Dell & O'Seaghdha, 1992; N. Martin, Dell, Saffran, & Schwartz, 1994). Dell and O'Seaghdha's model is particularly relevant because it assumes that word processing is temporally graded, where processing output needs to be stored until it is complete. However, Dell and O'Seaghdha's model is limited to single word repetition tasks. N. Martin and Saffran (1997) further developed this model to provide an account for multi-word utterances.

The present study leaves some issues unresolved. The method of articulatory suppression was used in order to gather evidence for a LTM contribution that was independent of the phonological loop. However, it would be interesting to assess the effect of the different word-classes without suppression, when participants have complete access to the phonological level of representations, in order to evaluate the two models described earlier. Although an unlimited set of words was used to demonstrate LTM contributions, it would be of interest to show if the same effects would be found with smaller word-pools or if our semantic effect depended on using the current paradigm. Indeed, since smaller word sets require repeated presentations, participants can focus more on the position of the items and less on their identity (i.e. meanings). Additionally, one should address the issue of why the semantic effect is smaller than the lexical effect. One possibility is that activation is faster for lexical than for semantic representations, which would favour lexical effects on immediate serial recall (in spite of the fact that an unlimited set of words was used). Obviously, the details needed to account for the complex processing of word sequences have not yet been fully worked through. Thus, further research concerning these issues is needed.

In conclusion, the stance taken here is that performance in immediate serial recall tasks at span or near span of verbal information may be seen as deriving from distinct representational levels involved in language processing. New evidence from normal participants has been provided to include semantic representations and also to establish the specific contribution of lexical knowledge.

REFERENCES

Baddeley, A.D. (1986). *Working memory.* Oxford: Oxford University Press.

Baddeley, A. (1996). Exploring the central executive. *Quaterly Journal of Experimental Psychology, 49A,* 5–28.

Baddeley, A., Gathercole, S., & Papagno, C. (1998). The phonological loop as a language learning device. *Psychological Review, 105,* 158–173.

Baddeley, A.D., & Hitch, G.J. (1974). Working memory. In G.H. Bower (Ed.), *The psychology of learning and motivation, Vol. 8* (pp. 47–90). New York: Academic Press.

Baudot, J. (1992). *Fréquence d'utilisation des mots en français écrit contemporain* [Frequency of usage for words in contemporary written French]. Montréal: Presses de l'Université de Montréal.

Belleville, S., Peretz, I., Fontaine, F., & Caza, N. (1997). Neuropsychological argument for the activation approach to memory: A case of phonological memory deficit. *Brain and Cognition, 35,* 382–385.

Besner, D., & Davelaar, E. (1982). Basic processes in reading: Two phonological codes. *Canadian Journal of Psychology, 36,* 701–711.

Bourassa, D., & Besner, D. (1994). Beyond the articulatory loop: A semantic contribution to serial order recall of subspan lists. *Psychonomic Bulletin and Review, 1,* 122–125.

Craik, F.I.M., & Lockhart, R.S. (1972). Levels of processing: A framework for memory research. *Journal of Verbal Learning and Verbal Behavior, 11,* 671–684.

Crowder, R.G. (1989). Modularity and dissociations in memory systems. In H.L. Roediger III & F.I.M. Craik (Eds.), *Varieties of memory and consciousness: Essays in*

Dell, G.S., & O'Seaghdha, P.G. (1992). Stages of lexical access in language production. *Cognition, 42,* 287-314.

Friendly, M., Franklin, P.E., Hoffman, D., & Rubin, D.C. (1982). The Toronto word pool: Norms for imagery, concreteness, orthographic variables, and grammatical usage for 1080 words. *Behavior Research Methods & Instrumentation, 14,* 375-399.

Gérard, M. (1983). *Contribution à l'évaluation de la détérioration mentale chez l'adulte à l'aide du test de vocabulaire Mill Hill* [Contribution of the assessment of mental deterioration in the adult with the Mill Hill vocabulary test]. Unpublished master's thesis, University of Liège.

Gregg, V.H., Freedman, C.M., & Smith, D.K. (1989). Word frequency, articulatory suppression and memory span. *British Journal of Psychology, 80,* 363-374.

Hulme, C., Maughan, S., & Brown, G.D. (1991). Memory for familiar and unfamiliar words: Evidence for a long-term memory contribution to short-term memory span. *Language, 30,* 685-701.

Hulme, C., Roodenrys, S., Brown, G., & Mercer, R. (1995). The role of long-term memory mechanisms in memory span. *British Journal of Psychology, 86,* 527-536.

Hulme, C., Roodenrys, S., Schweickert, R., Brown, G.D.A., Martin, S., & Stuart, G. (1997). Word-frequency effects on short-term memory tasks: Evidence for a redintegration process in immediate serial recall. *Journal of Experimental Psychology: Learning, Memory, and Cognition, 23,* 1217-1232.

Lapointe, L.B., & Engle, R.W. (1990). Simple and complex word spans as measures of working memory capacity. *Journal of Experimental Psychology: Learning, Memory, and Cognition, 16,* 1118-1133.

Martin, N., Dell, G.S., Saffran, E.M., & Schwartz, M.F. (1994). Origins of paraphasias in deep dysphasia. Testing the consequences of decay impairment to an interactive spreading activation model of lexical retrieval. *Brain and Language, 47,* 609-660.

Martin, N., & Saffran, E.M. (1997). Language and auditory-verbal short-term memory impairments: Evidence for common underlying processes. *Cognitive Neuropsychology, 14,* 641-682.

Martin, R.C., Shelton, J.R., & Yaffee, L.S. (1994). Language processing and working memory: Neuropsychological evidence for separate phonological and semantic capacities. *Journal of Memory and Language, 33,* 83-111.

Monsell, S. (1984). Components of working memory underlying verbal skills: A distributed capacities view. In H. Bouma & D.G. Bouwhuis (Eds.), *Attention and performance X: Control of language processes.* Hove, UK: Lawrence Erlbaum Associates Ltd.

Paivio, A., Yuille, J.C., & Madigan, S.A. (1968). Concreteness, imagery, and meaningfulness values for 925 nouns. *Journal of Experimental Psychology Monograph Supplement, 76,* 1-25.

Poirier, M., & Saint-Aubin, J. (1995). Memory for related and unrelated words: Further evidence on the influence of semantic factors in immediate serial recall. *The Quaterly Journal of Experimental Psychology, 48A,* 384-404.

Roodenrys, S., Hulme, C., Alban, J., Ellis, A.W., & Brown, G.D. (1994). Effects of word frequency and age of acquisition on short-term memory span. *Memory and Cognition, 22,* 695-701.

Tehan, G., & Humphreys, M.S. (1988). Articulatory loop explanations of memory span and pronunciation rate correspondences: A cautionary note. *Bulletin of the Psychonomic Society, 26,* 293-296.

Effects of Word Processing and Short-term Memory Deficits on Verbal Learning: Evidence from Aphasia

Nadine Martin and Eleanor M. Saffran

Temple University and Moss Rehabilitation Research Institute, Philadelphia, USA

We report two experiments that investigate the abilities of aphasic subjects with lexical and short-term memory impairments to learn supraspan lists of 10 words. We examined effects of stimulus factors (characteristics of words and lists to be learned) and subject factors (verbal and nonverbal STM span, nature of language impairment). Learning ability was influenced by the imageability and frequency of the words to be learned (Experiment 1) and by the linguistic relationship among words in a list (Experiment 2). Additionally, learning ability was affected by the nature of a subject's word processing deficit (whether it involved semantic and/or phonological processes). Phonological ability was positively associated with learning in both experiments, and semantic ability was associated with learning when words in a list were high in both frequency and imageability (Experiment 1) or were contextually related to one another (Experiment 2). Finally, verbal STM span was positively related to learning performance, but the effect was more pronounced for word span than digit span. These relationships among word processing ability, verbal STM span, and learning ability are discussed with reference to learning in aphasia and to models of learning more generally.

Nous présentons deux expériences où des sujets aphasiques, présentant des déficits lexicaux et de mémoire à court terme, tentent apprendre des listes de dix mots. L'effet de facteurs reliés aux stimuli (caractéristiques des mots et des listes à apprendre) ainsi que de facteurs reliés aux sujets (empan à court terme verbal et non verbal, nature des déficits de langage) sont examinés. La capacité d'apprentissage est influencée par l'imagerie et la fréquence des mots à apprendre, par la relation linguistique entre les mots d'une liste ainsi que par la nature des déficits des sujets (si ceux-ci impliquent un processus sémantique ou phonologique). L'habileté phonologique et l'habileté sémantique sont associées positivement avec l'apprentissage dans les deux expériences. Finalement, l'empan verbal en mémoire à court terme est relié à l'apprentissage mais cet effet est plus prononcé pour l'empan de mots que pour l'empan de chiffres. Ces relations entre la capacité à traiter les mots, l'empan verbal en mémoire à court terme et la capacité d'apprentissage sont discutées en faisant référence à l'apprentissage chez les aphasiques ainsi que selon les modèles d'apprentissage plus généraux.

The capacity to learn verbal information depends on the integrity of word processing and verbal short-term memory (STM) abilities. In the present study, we examine the relationships of these abilities to learning in aphasic individuals with both word-processing and verbal STM deficits. Evaluation of the learning abilities in this population is important for two reasons. First, aphasic individuals with word-processing deficits invariably exhibit reduced verbal STM capacities. Thus, their performance on learning tasks could potentially reveal interrelated effects of STM and lexical processes that would inform models of verbal learning. Second, remediation of language disorders would benefit from an understanding of factors that influence learning in this population.

Verbal STM ability has been linked to verbal learning in normal adults (Papagno, Valentine, & Baddeley, 1991) and to the development of vocabulary in children (e.g. Gathercole & Baddeley, 1989; Service, 1992). Learning in standard long-term memory tasks is also influenced by the integrity of language processing, but this relationship is less well understood. To date, many studies of learning involve populations without language impairment (normal adults and children). Moreover, those studies that include language-impaired subjects (acquired or developmental) have focused predominantly on the relationship between learning and the verbal STM impairments that accompany the language delay or deficit (e.g. Gathercole & Baddeley, 1989; Warrington & Shallice, 1969).

Investigations of verbal learning abilities of aphasic individuals began in earnest in the late 1960s. Early studies focused on the relationship between verbal learning and the phonological STM impairment that accompanied their language deficit (e.g. KF: Warrington & Shallice, 1969) and often involved subjects with minimal

---

Requests for reprints should be addressed to Nadine Martin, PhD, Department of Neurology, Center for Cognitive Neuroscience, Temple University School of Medicine, 3401 N. Broad St, Philadelphia, PA 19140, USA (E-mail: nmartin@astro.ocis.temple.edu).

This study was supported by grants from the National Institutes of Health, DC 01924–05 (N. Martin) and DC 00191–17 (E. Saffran). Many thanks go to Jennifer Lowery, Kim Feldman, Karin Altshuler, Lani Habibullah, and Jason Smith for their assistance in completing this project.

© 1999 International Union of Psychological Science

language impairment (e.g. JB: Warrington, Logue, & Pratt, 1971; PV: Basso, Spinnler, Vallar, & Zanobio, 1982). An important finding of these studies was that subjects demonstrated long-term learning despite restrictions in phonological STM.

Trojano, Stanzione, and Grossi (1992) investigated another aspect of learning in a patient (SC) with phonological processing and short-term memory impairments. They examined effects of phonological (word length) and lexical-semantic (concreteness, word category) variables on learning supraspan word lists and found that their subject's performance was most affected by word category. This suggested a role of lexical-semantic coding in verbal learning.

The primary impairment of the subjects just described was a reduced phonological STM capacity. The selection of such patients for the study of verbal STM reflected the predominant viewpoint in the 1970s and 1980s that representations in verbal STM were purely phonological (e.g. Baddeley, 1986) and that lexical-semantic influences on STM capacity reflected input from long-term memory. The performances of PV and SC on learning tasks indicate that some learning is possible even when phonological STM is impaired. Trojano et al.'s (1992) study of SC suggests further that relatively intact lexical-semantic processes might play a role in that learning. These and other studies of STM and learning in patients with acquired brain damage (N. Martin & Saffran, 1997; R.C. Martin, Shelton, & Yaffee, 1994; Saffran & Martin, 1990) indicated that studies of this population could potentially provide insight into the relationship between language processing, verbal STM, and verbal learning (Saffran, 1990).

In the present study, we examine the role of lexical and verbal STM processes in verbal learning by examining learning abilities of individuals with acquired aphasia who demonstrate impairments of both word processing and verbal STM. Lexical impairments can result from a breakdown of semantic or phonological processing of words or some combination of these abilities (e.g. Ellis, 1985). Additionally, there is mounting evidence that verbal STM is influenced by both lexical-semantic and phonological factors in normal (Walker & Hulme, 1999) and language-impaired individuals (e.g. R.C. Martin et al., 1994), and that these factors differentially affect characteristics of verbal STM performance (e.g. serial position effects) in aphasia (N. Martin & Saffran, 1997).

Our subjects all have acquired deficits of word processing (semantically and/or phonologically based) and verbal STM (mild to severe). To examine learning in this population, we employed a standard word list learning paradigm used in several studies of verbal learning in neurologically impaired subjects (Trojano et al., 1992). This task assesses the ability to learn associations among familiar words rather than the ability to learn new vocabulary and can be used to study effects of stimulus factors (word, list characteristics) and subject factors (kind and severity of language impairment) on learning.

EXPERIMENTAL INVESTIGATION

In two experiments we investigate four factors that potentially influence verbal learning in individuals with acquired impairments of word processing and verbal STM.
1. Stimulus factors:
   a. Experiment 1: Characteristics of the words to be learned (imageability and frequency).
   b. Experiment 2: Characteristics of the lists to be learned (relationships among words in the list—semantic, phonological, no relationship).
2. Subject factors (Experiments 1 and 2):
   c. Primary source of word processing impairment (semantic or phonological).
   d. Verbal STM span.

Subjects

Eighteen aphasic subjects participated in one or both of the experiments. All subjects had left-hemisphere lesions resulting from a CVA or, in one case, a gunshot wound and exhibited word retrieval difficulties and a verbal STM deficit. All subjects were at least 1 year post onset and ranged in age from 26 to 77. The sample included a variety of aphasia types and a wide range of severity (very mild to severe). With one exception, DB, all of the patients would be classified as fluent. We excluded subjects with nonfluent aphasia only if they exhibited articulatory disturbances (apraxia, dysarthria) that might mask evidence of learning. Background data on all aphasic subjects are shown in Table 1.

Both experiments were administered to normal subjects (12 in Experiment 1 and 11 in Experiment 2), ranging in age from 18–63 years, who were recruited from Temple University (employees and students) and paid $7.50 per session for their participation.

Procedure

Evaluation of Short-term Memory and Lexical Processing

Each subject's word-processing and verbal STM abilities were examined with standardized and laboratory-developed tests. From these tests, a profile of each subject's semantic and phonological abilities and verbal STM capacities was assembled. These measures were correlated with performance on the learning tasks. The background examination is described next.

Short-term Memory

1. *Digit and word span.* Auditory span for digits (from 1–9) and for words (drawn from a set of nine high-frequency concrete words) was assessed using a pointing response and, in a second condition, using a repetition response. Spans tested ranged from one to five items. Twenty strings of each length were presented. Digit and word stimuli were audiotaped and presented free-field. Subjects were instructed to recall the items in serial order.

TABLE 1
Subject Background Information

Subject	Age at Testing	Aetiology	Language Profile
GL	47	Left thalamic haemorrhage s/p section meningioma	Wernicke resolved to conduction
RWB	60	Left temporo-parietal haemorrhage	Wernicke resolved to conduction
VP	63	LCVA-inferior frontal, pre-central gyrus and anterior superior temporal gyrus	Anomic
DB	45	LCVA secondary to cerebral aneurysm; extensive frontal and parietal involvement	Nonfluent, anomic
WR	61	LCVA-left middle cerebral artery	Anomic
NC	30	LCVA secondary to cerebral aneurysm; mid to posterior superior temporal gyrus	Conduction
RD	75	LMCA infarct; temporal-parietal regions	Conduction
JW	26	Gunshot wound—left temporo-parietal cranial defect; fragments in L occipital lobe	Anomic
RR	56	LMCA infarcts in occipital, parietal, and frontal lobes	Transcortical sensory
EG	61	L frontal, bilateral lacunar infarct, R watershed	Anomic
IG	74	L posterior parietal infarct	Anomic
GN	52	L middle cerebral artery infarction	Conduction
AK	75	L lacunar infarct	Anomic
ED	74	Small infarct near L sylvian fissure	Conduction
MB	74	L CVA, atrophy	Transcortical sensory
AH	62	L middle cerebral artery infarct	Wernicke
DK	34	LCVA following cardiac arrest	Conduction
FK	68	Left occipital, left precentral, and right parietal infarcts	Anomic

2. *Spatial span.* (Corsi Block Span Task; De Renzi & Nichelli, 1975). In this task, the examiner points to a series of blocks among nine arrayed randomly on a board, and the subject points to the same blocks in serial order. Block sequences range from one to nine, with five sequences tested at each length. The test proceeds through successively longer sequences until the subject makes errors on two items of a particular sequence length. Normal span performance on this task is 5.92.

3. *Scoring.* Spans for each modality and response condition were estimated using a metric devised by Shelton, Martin, and Yaffee (1992). The span estimates are shown in Table 2.

TABLE 2
Estimates of Verbal and Nonverbal Short-term Memory Span

	Span Task and Response Condition				
	Digit Span		Word Span		Corsi Block Span Task
Subject	Pointing	Repetition	Pointing	Repetition	Pointing
GL	1.9	2.0	1.8	1.6	3.8
RWB	4.0	–	2.5	–	–
VP	1.6	2.5	1.6	2.0	–
DB	1.5	1.8	2.0	1.3	3.8
WR	1.2	–	1.2	–	–
NC	3.1	3.8	2.4	2.6	6.8
RD	3.0	3.0	2.3	2.3	5.4
JW	–	2.2	2.0	2.0	4.8
RR	–	3.0	–	–	4.0
EG	5.0	4.4	2.9	2.3	4.8
IG	5.0	5.0	2.9	2.8	4.0
GN	3.0	2.8	3.6	1.8	3.4
AK	5.0	3.7	5.0	3.8	5.0
ED	3.3	3.5	3.9	4.0	4.0
AH	1.7	0.0	2.2	1.9	5.4
MB	4.0	1.7	5.0	3.7	4.8
DK	2.3	2.5	2.3	2.1	4.0
FK	5.0	3.8	5.0	3.8	5.0

Span measure from Shelton et al. (1992): Span = list length at which at least 50% of the lists are recalled correctly + (proportion of lists recalled when length is one item greater) / (.50).

4. *Assessment of lexical-semantic and phonological abilities.* We used three measures to evaluate the lexical-semantic abilities and three to assess phonological abilities. These measures, discussed in detail elsewhere (N. Martin & Saffran, 1992, 1997) are described briefly below. Performance by normal subjects on the laboratory-developed tests is noted in the task descriptions below.

Lexical-semantic Measures

1. *Peabody Picture Vocabulary Test* (Form L; Dunn & Dunn, 1981). This is a standardized measure of word comprehension abilities using a spoken word-to-picture matching format.

2. *Lexical comprehension* (from the Philadelphia Comprehension Battery. Saffran, Schwartz, Linebarger, Martin, & Bochetto, 1988). This test also uses a spoken word-to-picture matching format. Of the four choices, three are semantically related distractors ($N = 16$). Normal subjects ($N = 5$) averaged .9918 correct ($SD = .0211$).

3. *Synonymy judgements.* The task is to decide which two of three written (and spoken) words are most similar in meaning ($N = 78$). Two tests were administered contrasting knowledge of noun and verb meanings ($N = 30$) in one and concrete and abstract words in the other ($N = 48$). Normal subjects ($N = 5$) averaged .9686 correct ($SD = .0415$) on the noun/verb synonymy and .9507 correct ($SD = .0521$) on the concrete/abstract synonymy test.

Phonological Measures

4. *Phoneme discrimination.* Subjects must decide whether two spoken words or nonwords that differ by one or two phonemes are the same or different ($N = 160$ per condition). There are two conditions:

a. No delay—items in a pair are presented one immediately following the other. Normal subjects ($N = 5$) averaged .9920 correct ($SD = .0084$).

b. Filled delay—5-second filled interval (examiner and subject counting to five) between presentations of each item in the pair. Normal subjects ($N = 5$) averaged .9880 correct ($SD = .0084$).

5. *Auditory rhyme judgments* ($N = 64$). The task is to listen to two spoken words and decide whether they rhyme or not. Normal subjects ($N = 5$) averaged .9790 correct ($SD = .0202$) on the rhyming pairs and .9880 correct ($SD = .0200$) on the nonrhyming pairs.

In order to establish an estimate of each subject's semantic and phonological abilities, we first converted raw scores on each of the background tests to rating scores between 1 and 4 using a method described in N.

TABLE 3
Composite Semantic and Phonological Ratings of Each Subject

Subject	Composite Phonological Rating	Composite Semantic Rating
GL	0.84	3.53
RWB	2.94	3.18
VP	1.96	2.45
DB	2.37	2.11
WR	2.06	1.40
NC	1.69	2.58
RD	1.08	3.08
JW	1.73	2.28
RR	1.99	0.16
EG	1.97	2.42
IG	2.89	3.58
GN	0.68	3.34
AK	3.62	3.02
ED	1.71	3.11
AH	0.85	1.73
MB	2.38	1.04
DK	2.17	3.31
FK	3.54	3.37

Martin and Saffran (1997). We then computed a composite semantic (S) and a composite phonological (P) score by averaging the ratings on individual lexical-semantic and phonological measures (Table 3)[1]. The composite S and P scores did not correlate with each other ($r = -.03$), indicating that the two measure different abilities. To evaluate the influences of semantic and phonological abilities on learning, we correlated the composite scores with performance on the verbal learning measures. As Table 3 indicates, all subjects demonstrated some difficulty in processing single words, but their impairments vary in severity and in the pattern of underlying semantic and phonological deficits. For some individuals semantic or phonological impairment is relatively exclusive, while for others, semantic and phonological deficits are both present.

Experimental Task: Learning Lists of 10 Words

The stimulus materials, procedures, and scoring for each experiment are described below.

Stimulus materials

Experiment 1: Effects of Frequency and Imageability. Four lists of 10 words varied for frequency and imageability were created: high frequency-high imageability (HF-HI), low frequency-high imageability (LF-HI), high frequency-low imageability (HF-LI), and low frequency-low imageability (LF-LI). Words occurring more often than 40 times per million (Kuçera &

---

[1] The composite rating scores reported for some subjects in this study differ slightly from those reported in N. Martin and Saffran (1997). This is because the composite ratings are based on the range of scores of only and all subjects within a study. The present experiments include additional subjects, not reported in N. Martin and Saffran (1997), whose scores expanded the range of scores for some of the tests used to calculate the composite ratings.

Francis, 1982) were classified as high frequency, and those occurring less often than 25 times per million as low frequency. Using Paivio, Yuille, and Madigan (1968) imageability ratings, a word rated higher than 4.97 (on a scale of 1–7) was labelled high imageability and less than 4.97 low imageability.

Experiment 2: Effects of Inter-item Relationships on Learning. Stimulus lists consisted of 10 concrete words related to each other semantically, phonologically, or not at all. Semantic relatedness was defined as membership in a semantic category (e.g. body parts) and phonological relatedness as a common initial phoneme. Six lists of words were created, two in each condition (one with high- and one with low-frequency words). Learning performance did not differ as a function of frequency, thus learning performance was averaged across the high- and low-frequency lists within a condition.

Testing Procedure (Experiments 1 and 2)

The procedure for each experiment was the same. The examiner read the list of words to the subject with the instructions to repeat as many words as he or she could recall in any order. This procedure was repeated a maximum of 10 times. If the subject produced all 10 items on 2 consecutive trials before the 10th trial, the experiment was terminated.

Scoring and Data Analysis (Experiments 1 and 2)

For all subjects, the number correct per trial was recorded.

Aphasic Subjects. The dependent measure was the greatest number of items recalled on any one trial within a condition. If a response deviated from the target word by one or two phonemes, and the target word was recognizable, it was considered an accurate response. The effects of imageability, frequency, and interrelations among words in a list were examined using one factor, repeated measures ANOVAs and Tukey HSD post hoc comparisons (for both aphasic and normal subjects). The relationships between measures of learning and estimates of semantic and phonological abilities and span were examined using Pearson's correlations (for aphasic subjects only).[2]

Normal subjects. The normal subjects invariably learned all 10 words in a list and often did this in less than 10 trials. Therefore we evaluated their performance using the number of trials needed to learn a list as the dependent measure. Although this precludes a direct comparison of normal and aphasic performance, we can observe any similarities in the patterns of stimulus effects in the two groups.

Results

Experiment 1. Learning Lists of Words Varied for Their Frequency and Imageability

Effects of Frequency and Imageability. Sixteen aphasic subjects participated in this experiment (all those in Table 1 except RR and GN). The average number of words learned under each list condition was as follows: HF-HI 6.9, LF-HI 5.9, HF-LI 4.8, LF-LI 4.3. A one-factor, repeated measures ANOVA indicated that overall performance on these four conditions differed $[F(3,15) = 15.021, P < .0001]$. Post hoc comparisons revealed a significant effect of imageability on learning both high-frequency (HF-HI vs. HF-LI) and low-frequency (LF-HI vs. LF-LI) words $(P < .01)$. There were no differences between those list conditions that contrasted frequency categories (HF-HH vs. LF-HH and HF-LI vs. LF-LI).

The normal subjects showed a somewhat similar pattern of results. The average number of trials that it took them to learn a list on each condition was as follows: HF-HI 4.9, LF-HI 6.3, HF-LI 7.2, LF-LI 7.8. A one-factor, repeated measures ANOVA indicated that performance on the four list conditions was significantly different $[F(3,15) = 5.595, P < .0032]$. Post hoc comparisons indicated that imageability influenced performance on lists of high-frequency words $(P < .05)$ but not low-frequency words. As in the case of the aphasic subjects, frequency did not affect normal performance.

Relationship between Semantic and Phonological Abilities and List-learning. Table 4 shows the correlations between Composite S and P scores and performance on each condition of the experiment. Phonological abilities are associated with learning when the words in the list are low in imageability or frequency. In contrast, the ability to learn lists of frequent and highly imageable words is positively associated with semantic abilities.

TABLE 4
Correlations between Composite Language Measures and Number of Words Learned (Experiment 1)

Composite Measure	List Type			
	HF-HI	LF-HI	HF-LI	LF-LI
Composite P	.46	.61*	.86*	.91*
Composite S	.50*	.25	.19	.27

$N = 16$, $df = 14$.
*$P < .05$; = .497 (two-tailed).

---

[2] Raw data from the verbal learning experiments are available from the authors. Also, we correlated verbal learning performance with the individual semantic and phonological tests that comprised the composite scores. These data are also available form the authors.

TABLE 5
Correlations between Auditory Span Estimates and Number of Words Learned (Experiment 1)

Span Measure	List Type			
	HF-HI	LF-HI	HF-LI	LF-LI
Pointing (df = 14)				
Digit	.23	.32	.48	.61*
Word	.64*	.53*	.50*	.66*
Repetition (df = 11)				
Digit	.20	.36	.56*	.60*
Word	.35	.52	.61*	.60*
Corsi Block Spatial Span *(df = 11)*	.06	.04	−.01	.20

* $df = 14$, $P < .05$; = .497 (two-tailed). $df = 11$, $P < .05$; = .553 (two-tailed).

Relationship between Span Performance and List Learning. Table 5 shows the correlations between five measures of span and list learning. Digit span is associated with learning performance only when words are of low imageability. Word span is consistently associated with list learning when measured with a pointing response. When it is measured using a repetition format, it is more strongly associated with performance on lists of words low in frequency and imageability. Finally, the measure of nonverbal span did not correlate with any of the list-learning conditions. Thus, performance on these tasks is not related to the subjects' nonverbal STM abilities.

Experiment 2. Learning Lists of Words that are Semantically or Phonologically Related or Unrelated

Effects of Linguistic Relationship among Words to Be Learned on List Learning. Eighteen subjects participated in Experiment 2 (all subjects listed in Table 1). A one-factor, repeated measures ANOVA indicated that the average number of words learned under each list-relatedness condition differed [means: Semantic 7, Phonological 5.5, Unrelated 6.4; $F(2,17) = 8.962$, $P < .0007$]. Although more words were learned on semantically related lists than unrelated word lists, post hoc comparisons indicated that this difference was not significant ($P < .10$). Phonological similarity among words in the list had a detrimental effect on learning relative to the unrelated lists ($P < .05$).

Normal performance on this task parallelled that of the aphasic subjects in that phonologically related lists were more difficult to learn. The average number of trials needed to learn each condition was as follows: Semantic 3.6, Phonological 7.0, Unrelated 4.2. These means were significantly different [$F(2,10) = 22.962$, $P < .00001$]. Post hoc comparisons indicated that lists that were phonologically similar required more trials to learn than unrelated lists or semantically related lists ($P < .01$). Performance on semantically related and unrelated lists did not differ.

Relationship between Semantic and Phonological Abilities and List Learning. Table 6 shows the correlations between composite S and P scores and performance on semantically and phonologically related and unrelated word lists. Semantic abilities are strongly associated with learning lists of related and unrelated words. Phonological abilities correlate with this task when the words to be learned are phonologically related or unrelated.

Although phonological abilities show a trend of association with list learning, the measures most strongly associated with performance on this task are tests of lexical and semantic ability. The linguistic relationships among words in the list may promote the use of lexical-semantic coding to facilitate recall. Although the effect was present in the unrelated condition, the context of the experiment (learning related and unrelated lists) may have encouraged such a strategy. Additionally (or alternatively), the link between semantic abilities and learning may be related to the imageability of words used in this experiment. In Experiment 1, semantic abilities were associated with better learning of high-frequency, imageable words. Although both high- and low-frequency words were used in Experiment 2, their high imageability may have been a contributing factor to the overall association with semantic abilities.

Relationship between Span Performance and List Learning. Table 7 shows the correlations between five measures of span and list learning as a function of relationship among words in the list. Word span, whether assessed with a pointing response or repetition response,

TABLE 6
Correlations between Composite Language Measures and Number of Words Learned (Experiment 2)

Composite Measure	List Relationship		
	Semantic	Phonological	Unrelated
Composite P	.44	.60*	.49*
Composite S	.52*	.70*	.68*

* $df = 16$, $P < .05$; = .468 (two-tailed).

TABLE 7
Correlations between Auditory Span Estimates and Number of Words Learned (Experiment 2)

Span Measure	List Relationship		
	Semantic	Phonological	Unrelated
Pointing (df = 16)			
Digit	.41	.45	.44
Word	.53*	.66*	.64*
Repetition (df = 13)			
Digit	.20	.39	.29
Word	.55*	.66*	.61*
Corsi Block Spatial Span *(df = 13)*	−.16	.01	.02

* $df = 16$, $P < .05$; = .468 (two-tailed).
  $df = 13$, $P < .05$; = .514 (two-tailed).

is strongly associated with performance on the list-learning task. In contrast, digit span is not associated with learning ability regardless of the task used to assess span, although there is a trend when digit span is measured with a pointing response. As in Experiment 1, the measure of nonverbal span shows no relationship with performance on list-learning tasks.

GENERAL DISCUSSION

We have investigated effects of four factors on learning abilities in aphasia: characteristics of words to be learned, linguistic relationship among words-to-be learned, kind of lexical impairment (semantic or phonological), and verbal STM impairment. All of these factors play some part in the effective completion of a verbal learning task, and there appears to be some interaction among these variables.

The characteristics of words to be learned influence the ease with which a supraspan list of words can be learned. Words of high imageability and high frequency are easiest to learn while lists of low frequency and low imageability are more difficult to learn. This finding was true for normal and aphasic subjects.

The linguistic relationship among words in a list also affects learning. For both normal and aphasic subjects, learning was adversely affected when words in the list were related phonologically. In this experiment, we defined phonological similarity as sharing an initial phoneme. Prior research indicates that a rhyming relationship among words facilitates recall (Conrad, 1964). Fallon and Groves (1998) recently demonstrated that when words to be recalled are phonologically similar, but nonrhyming, item recall is worse than conditions in which words rhyme or are phonologically dissimilar. The data from this study are consistent with this finding.

The aphasic subjects in this study were similar in that they all had word processing deficits and verbal STM impairments. They were heterogeneous with respect to the origin of the lexical processing impairment (semantic and/or phonological deficit). These experiments reveal some interesting patterns of association between learning and the semantic and phonological abilities underlying word processing. Phonological abilities were strongly related to learning performance when words in a list were unrelated (Experiment 1), regardless of the frequency or imageability of the words. Semantic abilities were related to learning performance only when the words to be learned were high in both frequency and imageability. In Experiment 2, we found a slightly different pattern. Here, the subject was presented with a random grouping of high-imageability words that either have a context (they share meaning or form) or they do not (they are unrelated). Correlations of semantic abilities with performance on this task were all positive and significant. A possible interpretation of this finding is that semantic processes are deployed in list-learning tasks when the words bear a contextual relationship, even if the context is not semantic in nature (as in the phonologically related condition). It is also possible that the high imageability of the words in this experiment contributed to the association with semantic abilities. These relationships between learning and semantic abilities require further investigation.

Relationships between STM Span and Learning Ability

We also found some associations between span performance and learning that could have implications for how we measure these abilities in aphasia. In both normal and aphasic populations, auditory-verbal span is measured with different kinds of stimuli (e.g. digits, letters, words, nonwords) and often varies depending on the items to be recalled. What stimuli are most closely associated with learning performance? A second factor to consider in the aphasic population is the response format used to assess auditory-verbal span. Two common formats are repetition and pointing to items in a visual display. Probe recall and recognition recall are also used. Whereas the repetition task engages both input and output word processing, the others involve primarily input processing of words. Performance on these various measures of span is not necessarily uniform within a subject, suggesting that measurement of span in this population is confounded with modality-related word processing effects. What format of span measurement is most closely associated with learning? Some aspects of the data from the present experiment are informative. We found in Experiment 1, for example, that digit span did not correlate with list learning ability unless the words were low in imageability. In Experiment 2, there was no relation between list learning and digit span, although correlations are in the predicted direction and, when measured with a pointing response, nearly significant. Word span measures show a more consistent relationship with learning ability, especially when measured with a pointing response. Two tentative predictions can be drawn from these data: (1) Word span is more closely linked with learning ability than digit span and (2) span, as measured with auditory input and pointing response, is a better predictor of learning ability than span measured in a repetition paradigm.

These predictions are theoretically motivated as well. First, it is likely that word span tasks engage lexical and semantic processes more than digit span tasks do, perhaps because digits are overlearned or because words have more complex lexical-semantic representations. Second, repetition span tasks (digit or word) are less likely to engage lexical-semantic processes than are span tasks that use an auditory stimulus and pointing response format, because the latter task requires mapping of the auditory input on to some lexical-semantic representation. We know from several aphasic syndromes that repetition of a sequence neither precludes nor requires lexical-semantic processing and that underlying representations that support repetition vary across aphasic syndromes (N. Martin & Saffran, 1997). Transcortical sensory aphasia, a syndrome in which failure on simple auditory word comprehension tests does not preclude repetition of a near normal span of digits, indicates that repetition can proceed almost entirely on the basis of activated phonological (and, perhaps, lexical) representations. In contrast, deep dysphasia, a syndrome in which semantic substitutions are produced in repetition of a single word, indicates that semantic information can be accessed in a repetition task. The data from this study suggest that repetition span is not the most reliable indicator of span capacity in aphasia. Moreover, they are consistent with the idea that span capacity is not fixed but varies depending on the task, the items in the sequence, and the available linguistic processes to support storage and retrieval of the input sequence.

CONCLUSIONS

The aphasic population offers a potential source of insight into the relationships between word processing, verbal STM, and verbal learning. Our understanding of these relationships has both clinical and theoretical implications. We used a supraspan list-learning task to explore influences of lexical processing ability and verbal STM on learning. This task requires the subject to recall known words and presumably encourages the use of a context-formation strategy. The context could be simply that these words are heard together or it could draw on relationships among the words in the list. Our data suggest that phonological abilities support learning and that, under certain circumstances, semantic processes also play a role. Further exploration of these and other factors that might affect learning is needed, particularly in the context of other learning paradigms that examine the ability to learn new words (e.g. paired associate tasks).

REFERENCES

Baddeley, A.D. (1986). *Working memory*. Oxford: Clarendon Press.

Basso, A., Spinnler, H., Vallar, G., & Zanobio, M.E. (1982). Left hemisphere damage and selective impairment of auditory-verbal short-term memory. A case study. *Neuropsychologia, 20*, 263–274.

Conrad, R. (1964). Acoustic confusion in immediate memory. *British Journal of Psychology, 55*, 75–84.

De Renzi, E., & Nichelli, P. (1975). Verbal and nonverbal short-term memory impairment following hemispheric damage. *Cortex, 11*, 341–354.

Dunn, L., & Dunn, L. (1981). *Peabody Picture Vocabulary Test-Revised*. Circle Pines, MN: American Guidance Service.

Ellis, A.W. (1985). The production of words: A cognitive neuropsychological perspective. In A.W. Ellis (Ed.), *Progress in the psychology of language*, Vol. 2 (pp. 107–145). London: Lawrence Erlbaum Associates Ltd.

Fallon, A.B., & Groves, K. (1998). *Phonemic similarity and immediate serial recall: Different materials produce different effects*. Paper presented at Quebec STM Conference, Quebec, June.

Gathercole, S., & Baddeley, A.D. (1989). Evaluation of the role of phonological STM in the development of vocabulary in children: A longitudinal study. *Journal of Memory and Language, 28*, 200–213.

Kuçera, H., & Francis, W.N. (1982). *Computational analysis of present-day American English*. Boston, MA: Houghton Mifflin.

Martin, N., & Saffran, E.M. (1992). A connectionist account of deep dysphasia: Evidence from a case study. *Brain and Language, 43*, 240–274.

Martin, N. & Saffran, E.M. (1997) Language and auditory-verbal short-term memory impairments: Evidence for common underlying processes. *Cognitive Neuropsychology, 14* (5), 641–682.

Martin, N., Saffran, E.M., & Dell, G.S. (1996). Recovery in deep dysphasia: Evidence for a relationship between auditory-verbal STM capacity and lexical errors in repetition. *Brain and Language, 52*, 83–113.

Martin, R.C., Shelton, J., & Yaffee, L. (1994). Language processing and working memory: Neuropsychological evidence for separate phonological and semantic capacities, *Journal of Memory and Language, 33*, 83–111.

Paivio, A., Yuille, J., & Madigan, S. (1968). Concreteness, imagery and meaningfulness values for 925 nouns. *Journal of Experimental Psychology Monograph, 76*, 1 (Pt. 2).

Papagno, C., Valentine, T., & Baddeley, A.D. (1991). Phonological short-term memory and foreign language learning. *Journal of Memory and Language, 30*, 331–347.

Saffran, E.M. (1990). Short-term memory impairment and language processing. In A. Caramazza (Ed.), *Advances in cognitive neuropsychology and neurolinguistics*. Hillsdale, NJ: Lawrence Erlbaum Associates Inc.

Saffran, E.M., & Martin, N. (1990). Neuropsychological evidence for lexical involvement in short-term memory. In G. Vallar & T. Shallice (Eds.), *Neuropsychological impairments of short-term memory*. Cambridge: Cambridge University Press.

Saffran, E.M., Schwartz, M.F., Linebarger, M., Martin, N., & Bochetto, P. (1998). *The Philadelphia Comprehension Battery*. Unpublished test.

Service, L. (1992). Phonology, working memory, and foreign-language learning. *Quarterly Journal of Experimental Psychology, 45A*, 21–50.

Shelton, J., Martin, R.C., & Yaffee, L. (1992). Investigating a verbal short-term memory deficit and its consequences for language processing. In D. Margolin (Ed.), *Cognitive neuropsychology in clinical practice*. New York: Cambridge University Press.

Trojano, L., Stanzione, M., & Grossi, D. (1992). Short-term memory and verbal learning with auditory phonological coding defect: A neuropsychological case study. *Brain and Cognition, 18*, 12–33.

Vallar, G., & Baddeley, A.D. (1984). Fractionation of working memory: Neuropsychological evidence for a phonological short-term store. *Journal of Verbal Learning and Verbal Behavior, 23*, 151–161.

Walker, I., & Hulme, C. (1999). *Concrete words are easier to recall than abstract: Evidence for a semantic contribution to short-term serial recall*. Manuscript submitted for publication.

Warrington, E.K., Logue, V., & Pratt, R.T.C. (1971). The anatomical localisation of selective impairment of short-term memory. *Neuropsychologia, 9*, 377–387.

Warrington, E.K., & Shallice, T. (1969). The selective impairment of auditory verbal short-term memory. *Brain, 92*, 885–896.

The Influence of Long-term Memory Factors on Immediate Serial Recall: An Item and Order Analysis

Jean Saint-Aubin
Université de Moncton, Nouveau-Brunswick, Canada

Marie Poirier
Université Laval, Sainte-Foy, Québec, Canada

In immediate serial recall, an error can occur because the presented item is not recalled (item error) or because it is recalled at the wrong serial position (order error). Even if these two types of information can be selectively influenced, in most current studies, a global performance measure confounding item and order information is used. Here, the issues associated with the measure of memory for item and order information are discussed. First, it is argued that in some circumstances it is very important that item information be controlled for when measuring order retention, by for example, conditionalizing order memory on memory for item information. Second, using such measures, it is shown that long-term memory factors recently investigated in immediate serial recall produce a different pattern of results than what is predicted by most current models: Semantic similarity, word frequency, and lexicality all influence item recall, but only lexicality affects order information. These findings are discussed in the light of a retrieval-based account suggesting that degraded phonological traces must undergo a reconstruction process calling upon long-term knowledge of the to-be-remembered items.

En rappel sériel immédiat, une erreur survient si l'item présenté n'est pas rappelé (erreur d'item) ou s'il est rappelé à la mauvaise position (erreur d'ordre). Même si des effets différents sont parfois observés pour ces deux types d'information, la plupart des études contemporaines utilisent une mesure globale qui ne permet pas de les distinguer. L'examen des facteurs associés à l'évaluation du rappel des items et de leur ordre est effectué. Il est d'abord établi qu'il est important d'utiliser des mesures du rappel de l'ordre exemptes de l'influence du rappel des items, comme par exemple les probabilités conditionnelles d'erreurs d'ordre. Deuxièmement, l'utilisation de mesures adéquates révèle que l'influence des facteurs de mémoire à long terme, récemment étudiés en rappel sériel immédiat, diffère de celle prédite par la plupart des modèles contemporains. Ainsi, la similarité sémantique, la fréquence et la lexicalité influencent toutes le rappel des items, mais seule la lexicalité affecte le rappel de l'ordre. Les résultats sont interprétés à la lumière d'une hypothèse de récupération selon laquelle les connaissances à long terme des items à rappeler supporteraient l'interprétation des représentations phonologiques dégradées.

When a list of items must be recalled immediately after its presentation, it is well known that different kinds of errors can occur. For example, a presented item may not be recalled or it may be recalled in the wrong position. The aim of the present paper is to reaffirm that considering item and order information recall separately has many advantages at the empirical and theoretical levels. This strategy would benefit most if not all situations involving ordered recall tasks. Here, its benefits will be examined in recent work on the influence of long-term memory factors on immediate serial recall (ISR) performance.

We first discuss some methodological issues involved in this more detailed analysis of performance in ordered recall tasks. The effects of semantic similarity, word frequency, and lexicality on item and order information in ISR are then examined. Some of the implications for theoretical accounts in the field are then briefly discussed, and a retrieval-based hypothesis accounting for all these results is presented.

DISSOCIATING EFFECTS ON ITEM AND ORDER INFORMATION

In ISR, the analysis of item information recall is best attempted through the use of an open word pool. This implies that different items are presented on every trial. Performance is then scored by computing the number of presented items recalled regardless of the accuracy of their order. This measure is often referred to as a free recall score. Another popular measure is to compute the number of item errors: omissions or reported items that have not been presented on that trial. When recall is restricted to the size of the list, both measures produce identical results.

The analysis of order information is more complex. When subjects are performing an ISR task with an open word pool, order information is usually measured by computing the number of items reported at the wrong serial position (the absolute number of order errors). However, it can be argued that the absolute number of order errors is an appropriate measure only when the level of item recall is similar in all conditions. When item recall levels vary across conditions, the absolute number of order errors can be a misleading score, because of the influence of the overall level of item recall. Simply put, one can only be sure that an order error was made for reported items that were part of the presented list. If more items are recalled in one condition, then strictly speaking, a greater number of order errors are possible. For example, if no item is recalled, order errors are not a possibility. If two items are recalled, the number of possible order errors is less than if four items are recalled. Consequently, if item recall accuracy varies across conditions, an appropriate measure of order errors should control for item recall (Murdock, 1976; Poirier & Saint-Aubin, 1996).

The theoretical processes hypothesized to be responsible for the maintenance of item and order information might in some cases predict a specific dependency between item and order errors and influence the way an error is scored. When such a theoretical framework is under investigation, the measure of order retention must not necessarily control for item recall, since the main objective is to test the predicted dependency. However, in many cases, the issue of the most appropriate means of measuring order recall without the confounded influence of item recall must be addressed.

To eliminate the item recall confounding, the conditional probability of order errors per item recalled is perhaps the most straightforward solution (Murdock, 1976; Poirier & Saint-Aubin, 1996; Saint-Aubin & Poirier, in press 1999). These conditional probabilities are simply derived by dividing the total number of order errors in a list by the total number of items recalled for that list, regardless of their order. However, it can be argued that a linear transformation of this kind is not the most appropriate correction. For instance, as the number of reported items increases, the number of mathematically possible transpositions—reporting two items at each other position—increases nonlinearly. The number of ways of reporting two items at each other position, given n items are reported (regardless of their order), is equal to $[n! \div 2((n-2)!)]$. Thus, it might seem wiser to divide the absolute number of order errors by the number of possible transpositions given the number of items recalled. However, in our view, this solution is not the best one because order errors are of many kinds. They include: (1) transpositions (123456 given as 1*32*456), (2) displacement where a group of items are reported at the wrong positions, but their inter-item order was preserved (123456 given as 1*34562* or 1*62345*), and (3) simple order errors where, due to the presence of omissions (a blank was left in the reported list), an item is reported at the wrong serial position without disturbing the order of the remaining items (123456 given as 1_ 3*4*26 or 1 _ *2* _ _ 6). Consequently, to develop a finer-grained measure of order information recall uncontaminated by item information, a different correction must be applied to each kind of order error. This is necessary because the number of opportunities to make each kind of error does not increase at the same rate as the number of reported items. It appears more parsimonious and straightforward to use a conditional probability like the one suggested above unless a given hypothesis, prediction, or theoretical view calls for a finer-grained analysis.

In the work carried out in our laboratory, we have relied on simple conditional probabilities. Although this solution is perhaps not perfect, it has proven helpful in accounting for inconsistent effects in the literature, and it has produced the same pattern of results as obtained with tasks that are thought to rely more heavily on memory for order. Such tasks include serial reconstruction of order and ISR with the same words presented in a different order on every trial (Saint-Aubin & Poirier, 1999). Because, at recall, the presented words are made available to the participants (in a new random order), or because the same items are presented on every trial, it is typically assumed that performance on these tasks mainly reflects order retention (Whiteman, Nairne, & Serra, 1994). However, it should be noted that Neath (1997) has recently shown that the serial reconstruction of order task does not provide a functionally pure measure of order memory.

THE EFFECT OF SEMANTIC SIMILARITY ON ORDER RECALL REVISITED

Recently, many studies have investigated the influence on ISR of factors traditionally associated with long-term memory. Usually, performance is assessed with a strict serial recall criterion: An item must be recalled in its exact serial position to be considered correct, and item and order information are not differentiated. Better ISR performance has been found whenever the to-be-remembered items are associated to better, richer, or more easily accessed long-term memory representations. For example, ISR performance is better for words than for nonwords (Hulme, Maughan, & Brown, 1991) and for high- than for low-frequency words (Hulme et al., 1997).

However, one long-term memory factor has produced inconsistent results. Semantic similarity—where all items of a to-be-remembered list are taken from the same semantic category—has been found to increase, decrease, or to have no effect on ISR performance (Crowder, 1979;

Murdock, 1976). In order to account for these inconsistent effects, it has been argued that semantic similarity produces opposite effects on item and order information.

The beneficial effect of semantic similarity on item recall is both reliable and sizable (Crowder, 1979; Poirier & Saint-Aubin, 1995; Saint-Aubin & Poirier, 1999). On the other hand, although it is often taken for granted, the detrimental effect of semantic similarity on order recall is not consistently found (see, e.g., Crowder, 1979; Murdock, 1976). Here it is argued that the order retention measures used could well account for the inconsistencies in previous studies.

A study by Murdock and vom Saal (1967), using a Brown-Peterson task, is perhaps the most frequently cited concerning the detrimental effect of semantic similarity on order information recall. In effect, Murdock and vom Saal examined order errors while attempting to control for item information. This was done by comparing order recall for the subset of lists where all items had been reported. Based on these trials, they found a higher conditional probability of order errors for semantically similar trigrams. However, in a replication of this experiment, Murdock (1976) examined conditional probabilities for all trials and found that semantic similarity had no effect on order recall.

STUDIES USING ISR AND AN OPEN WORD POOL

Using an ISR task with different words presented on every trial, Crowder (1979) reported a similarity advantage when a free recall score was applied—where only item recall is considered—that was not present with a strict scoring criterion factoring in order information. He argued that this implied a semantic similarity disadvantage for order information, a disadvantage that overshadowed the advantage found for item information. This conclusion must be considered with caution, because it is based on indirect evidence.

More recently, Poirier and Saint-Aubin (1995) used an ISR task with an open word pool and reported a semantic similarity disadvantage only under articulatory suppression. However, they did not control for item recall level; they used the absolute number of order errors instead of conditional probabilities. Based on their raw data, we computed conditional probabilities of order errors, presented in Table 1. None of the experiments showed a semantic similarity effect or the previously reported interaction with articulatory suppression. The only result that was close to significance was the *smaller* conditional probability of order errors for semantically similar lists in the third experiment. In two further ISR experiments, using conditional probabilities, Saint-Aubin and Poirier (1999) also failed to find a detrimental effect of semantic similarity on order information recall.

Hence, when conditional probabilities are used for all trials and conditions, no semantic similarity disadvantage is found for order information recall. As we will see

TABLE 1
Conditional Probability of Order Errors Based on Poirier and Saint-Aubin's (1995) Data

Viewing Conditions	List Type	
	Similar	Dissimilar
Experiment 1 (N=24)		
Quiet	.143	.164
Experiment 2 (N=16)		
Quiet	.107	.145
Suppression	.261	.253
Experiment 3 (N=16)		
Quiet	.087	.102
Suppression	.199	.298

There was no suppression requirement in Experiment 1; suppression was performed during presentation in Experiment 2, and during presentation and recall in Experiment 3.

below, this finding is echoed in the results reported with tasks thought to rely more heavily on order information recall.

SERIAL ORDER RECONSTRUCTION

In two distinct experiments, Crowder (1979) used a serial order reconstruction task to investigate the effect of semantic similarity. He reported a slight significant disadvantage in one of them. Nairne and Neumann (1993), as well as Saint-Aubin and Poirier (1999), also used a serial order reconstruction task and failed to observe an effect of semantic similarity—there was even a slight nonsignificant advantage for similar lists in the latter study. Finally, Murdock (1976) also failed to find an effect of semantic similarity on order information recall with a recognition of order task that can be considered to involve similar processes as order reconstruction tasks (Neath, 1997).

STUDIES USING ISR AND A LIMITED WORD POOL

Baddeley (1966a) used an ISR task where, on each trial, a list of five words drawn from the same pool of eight was presented. He observed a slight disadvantage for similar lists. However, he used a general performance measure factoring in item and order information. Moreover, there is the possibility of a ceiling effect, given that 90% of the dissimilar lists were perfectly recalled. Baddeley (1966b) closely replicated this design in another study (Experiment 1, first trial), and failed to observe a semantic similarity disadvantage for order information. Using a procedure very close to the one of Baddeley (1966a), but with additional methodological controls and a separate examination of item and order recall, Saint-Aubin and Poirier (1999) also found no detrimental effect of semantic similarity on order information recall.

In sum, the case of semantic similarity illustrates well the usefulness of separately measuring memory for item and order information and the importance of using a proper measure of order information, that is to say, a measure uncontaminated by item information recall: Contrary to the frequently accepted view, the evidence indicating that semantic similarity hinders order information recall is very weak at best. In fact, the bulk of the evidence indicates no such effect. In every instance where item recall is controlled for systematically, no effect of semantic similarity is found.

BEYOND SEMANTIC SIMILARITY: OTHER FACTORS, OTHER EFFECTS

In ISR, word frequency is one of the most extensively studied long-term memory factor (see, e.g., Hulme et al., 1997). The frequency effect is characterized by the better recall of high- than low-frequency words. However, to the best of our knowledge, only one study has examined its influence on item and order recall. Poirier and Saint-Aubin (1996) contrasted performance with high-, medium-, and low-frequency words. Better item recall was found for high-frequency words than for the medium-frequency words, which in turn were better recalled than the low-frequency words. However, conditional probabilities of order errors did not vary as a function of frequency (see Whiteman et al., 1994, for related results).

In the light of the results with semantic similarity and word frequency, it is tempting to hypothesize that the effects of long-term memory factors are restricted to item recall. However, the effect of lexicality must also be considered. This effect is considered by most theoretical proposals accounting for the influence of long-term memory factors. Also, as will be discussed shortly, according to some of these proposals, lexicality should affect order recall.

Saint-Aubin and Poirier (in press) compared ISR for words and nonwords (CVC) equated for pronunciation duration. As in previous studies, overall, with a strict serial recall criterion that factors in item and order information, words were better recalled than nonwords (Hulme et al., 1991). However, a detailed analysis revealed that words were associated with better item recall, but with poorer order recall as measured by conditional probabilities of order errors.

All long-term memory factors investigated as of yet produce differential effects on item and order information recall, and the pattern of item and order errors varies across factors. This cannot be captured by a global performance measure like the strict serial recall criterion where all long-term memory factors produce the same results. The more detailed pattern of results provided by the separate measure of memory for item and order information may allow a more stringent test of the theoretical proposals accounting for the influence of long-term memory factors in ISR, a topic to which we now turn.

THEORETICAL ACCOUNTS

A number of theoretical proposals can account for the influence of one or more long-term memory factors on ISR, as measured with a global score factoring in item and order information (see, e.g., Burgess & Hitch, 1996; Hulme et al., 1991; Lewandowsky & Murdock, 1989; Nairne, 1990; Saint-Aubin & Poirier, 1999; Schweickert, 1993). However, the influence of long-term memory factors is implemented quite differently by each proposal as well as the maintenance of item and order information. These differences translate into diverging predictions with regards to the impact of long-term memory factors on item and order information. Space precludes a detailed presentation of all major proposals accounting for the influence of long-term memory factors on ISR. Here, the implications of some to the findings reviewed earlier for a few models will be presented. Finally, a tentative framework will be presented that accounts for the effects of all long-term memory factors reviewed here, as well as other classical effects in ISR.

The Feature Model

Recently, Nairne (1990; Neath & Nairne, 1995) proposed a feature model of immediate memory that can account for the effects of a wide range of factors. In this model, list items are represented in both primary and secondary memory as a series of features that can be of different types, such as phonological and semantic. Degradation occurs only in primary memory, and recall is achieved by sampling an intact item in secondary memory with a degraded trace from primary memory. This model could account for lexicality and word frequency by assuming more complex features for words than for nonwords and for high- than for low-frequency words, resulting in better overall recall. Semantic similarity could be modelled by assuming that it restricts the secondary memory search set to the presented items on that trial, resulting in better recall.

It is difficult to evaluate how the feature model could account for the influence of long-term memory factors on item and order information because it has just been recently extend to make distinct predictions about order information (Neath, this issue). However, predictions can be derived for semantic similarity. Because the model uses a similarity-based interference rule, and because recall likelihood is based on a ratio of similarities, the ensuing prediction is that, just as with phonological similarity, semantic similarity will be detrimental to order information recall. Because, as shown earlier, semantic similarity does not hinder order information recall when it is properly measured, it must be assumed that there are very few semantic features or that they are not subject to similarity-based interference. In any case, the simplifying assumption that similarity per se, be it phonological or semantic, is detrimental to order recall must be qualified.

TODAM

When performance in ISR is measured with a global score, Murdock's Theory Of Distributed Associative Memory (TODAM) can account for the effects of all long-term memory factors reviewed here (Lewandowsky & Murdock, 1989). However, the effects of word frequency and semantic similarity on order information recall are more problematic. For instance, word frequency has been modelled by increasing the value of the associative information for high-frequency words, resulting in better recall for high-frequency items. This way of implementing the effect of frequency is appealing, because it generates the appropriate pattern for modelling recognition memory data, where low-frequency words are usually better recognized than high-frequency words. This occurs because in TODAM item and associative information are the complement of each other, and recognition is attributed to item information: Low-frequency items have higher values on item information because of order information on which they have lower values than high-frequency items. However, the effects of frequency in ISR must be modelled differently to produce the appropriate pattern of results on item and order information. The results reviewed earlier show a null effect on order information, and better item recall for high-frequency words. One possibility, as suggested by Lewandowsky and Murdock, would be to change the number of features in the memory vector as a function of the item frequency or to introduce another parameter. Another possibility calls upon the deblurring mechanism of TODAM, where more frequent items would benefit from a more efficient deblurring mechanism (see Saint-Aubin & Poirier, 1999).

The Reconstruction and Retrieval-based Hypotheses

To account for the effects of long-term memory factors on ISR, the most frequently called-upon mechanism is some form of reconstruction process. This reconstruction hypothesis is applied to the effects appearing with a global score factoring in item and order information (Hulme et al., 1991; Poirier & Saint-Aubin, 1995; Schweickert, 1993). This framework has been formalized by Schweickert and has also been implemented in the formal model of Brown and Hulme (1995). According to this proposal, the presentation of a list sets up phonological representations of the to-be-remembered items. At recall, these representations are likely to be degraded because of either decay or interference. The degraded phonological representations must undergo a reconstruction process before being output as a response. The reconstruction process would be based on the long-term phonological knowledge of the to-be-recalled items. This process would be less efficient for nonwords and for low-frequency and semantically dissimilar words, because the long-term memory representations of the to-be-recalled items are more difficult to access, which in turn will decrease the probability of a successful reconstruction, and consequently of a correct response.

Poirier and Saint-Aubin (1996; Saint-Aubin & Poirier, in press, 1999) have recently proposed a version of this general proposal that takes item and order information into account independently. According to this hypothesis, at recall, degraded phonological traces are output in their presentation order. Order errors are attributed to trace interpretation problems during the recall process, as is often suggested (see, e.g., Lewandowsky & Murdock, 1989; Nairne, 1990). For instance, if the degraded trace of a list item contains mainly features shared with other list items, then the probability would be high that another item within the list would be erroneously recalled. Consequently, the probability of order errors would be higher when list items share more phonological features or when the phonological trace has lost many unique features due to degradation. On the other hand, the probability of an item error would be higher when the long-term representation of the to-be-remembered item is harder to access or when the phonological trace has lost many features—as might be produced by articulatory suppression—thus becoming an inefficient retrieval cue.

Although not on the same level of theorizing as previous models, the framework described here can successfully account for the effects of semantic similarity, word frequency, and lexicality on item and order information recall. Better item recall is observed for semantically similar items because the semantic category shared by the to-be-remembered items would enhance the probability of accessing the relevant long-term memory representation, perhaps by reducing the pool of recall candidates (see Crowder, 1979, for a related idea). On the other hand, semantic similarity would not influence order retention, because it affects neither the nature nor the degradation of phonological features. The same logic can be applied to word frequency effects. The long-term representations of high-frequency items would be easier to access, thus entailing better item recall (Hulme et al., 1997; Poirier & Saint-Aubin, 1996). Because word frequency does not affect phonological features, order retention would be unaffected. Finally, lexicality is expected to influence both item and order information recall. More words should be recalled than nonwords because the former, but not the latter, would benefit from adequate long-term memory representations. With respect to order errors, because they are attributed to the reconstruction process, and because this process cannot operate, for all practical purposes, in the case of unfamiliar nonwords, then a strict interpretation of the framework presented here predicts that order errors will be extremely infrequent for nonwords. Consequently, as observed by Saint-Aubin and Poirier (in press), a higher proportion of order errors is anticipated for words than for nonwords.

CONCLUSION

In sum, this brief review of the influence of long-term memory factors on ISR illustrates the importance of measuring item and order information recall separately. This provides a more accurate picture that cannot be anticipated on the sole basis of a global performance measure factoring in item and order information. For instance, from the results of previous empirical studies where lexicality was manipulated, it was impossible to anticipate the better order recall of nonwords. In addition, results with semantic similarity and word frequency illustrate the need to use an adequate measure of order retention, that is to say, a measure uncontaminated by item recall information. Finally, the measure of memory for item and order information allows more stringent tests of theoretical proposals than the usual global score.

REFERENCES

Baddeley, A.D. (1966a). Short-term memory for word sequences as a function of acoustic, semantic, and formal similarity. *Quarterly Journal of Experimental Psychology, 18A*, 362–365.

Baddeley, A.D. (1966b). The influence of acoustic and semantic similarity on long-term memory for word sequences. *Quarterly Journal of Experimental Psychology, 18A*, 302–309.

Brown, G.D.A., & Hulme, C. (1995). Modeling item length effects in memory span: No rehearsal needed? *Journal of Memory and Language, 34*, 594–621.

Burgess, N., & Hitch, G.J. (1996). A connectionist model of STM for serial order. In S.E. Gathercole (Ed.), *Models of short-term memory* (pp. 51–72). Hove, UK: Psychology Press.

Crowder, R.G. (1979). Similarity and order in memory. In G.H. Bower (Ed.), *The psychology of learning and motivation: Advances in research and theory: Vol. 13* (pp. 319–353). New York: Academic Press.

Hulme, C., Maughan, S., & Brown, G.D.A. (1991). Memory for familiar and unfamiliar words: Evidence for a long-term memory contribution to short-term memory span. *Journal of Memory and Language, 30*, 685–701.

Hulme, C., Roodenrys, S., Schweickert, R., Brown, G.D., Martin, A., & Stuart, G. (1997). Word-frequency effects on short-term memory tasks: Evidence for a redintegration process in immediate serial recall. *Journal of Experimental Psychology: Learning, Memory, and Cognition, 23*, 1217–1232.

Lewandowsky, S., & Murdock, B.B. (1989). Memory for serial order. *Psychological Review, 96*, 25–57.

Murdock, B.B. Jr. (1976). Item and order information in short-term serial memory. *Journal of Experimental Psychology: General, 105*, 191–216.

Murdock, B.B. Jr., & vom Saal, W. (1967). Transpositions in short-term memory. *Journal of Experimental Psychology, 74*, 137–143.

Nairne, J.S. (1990). A feature model of immediate memory. *Memory and Cognition, 18*, 251–269.

Nairne, J.S., & Neumann, C. (1993). Enhancing effects of similarity on long-term memory for order. *Journal of Experimental Psychology: Learning, Memory, and Cognition, 19*, 329–337.

Neath, I. (1997). Modality, concreteness, and set-size effects in a free reconstruction of order task. *Memory and Cognition, 25*, 256–263.

Neath, I. (1999). Modelling the disruptive effects of irrelevant speech on order information. *International Journal of Psychology, 34*, 416–424.

Neath, I., & Nairne, J.S. (1995). Word-length effects in immediate memory: Overwriting trace decay theory. *Psychonomic Bulletin and Review, 2*, 429–441.

Poirier, M., & Saint-Aubin, J. (1995). Memory for related and unrelated words: Further evidence on the influence of semantic factors in immediate serial recall. *Quarterly Journal of Experimental Psychology, 48A*, 384–404.

Poirier, M., & Saint-Aubin, J. (1996). Immediate serial recall, word frequency, item identity and item position. *Canadian Journal of Experimental Psychology, 50*, 408–412.

Saint-Aubin, J., & Poirier, M. (in press). Immediate serial recall of words and nonwords: Tests of the retrieval based hypothesis. *Psychonomic Bulletin and Review*.

Saint-Aubin, J., & Poirier, M. (1999). Semantic similarity and immediate serial recall: Is there a detrimental effect on order information? *Quarterly Journal of Experimental Psychology, 52A*, 367–394.

Schweickert, R. (1993). A multinominal processing tree model for degradation and redintegration in immediate recall. *Memory and Cognition, 21*, 168–175.

Whiteman, H.L., Nairne, J.S., & Serra, M. (1994). Recognition and recall-like processes in the long-term reconstruction of order. *Memory, 2*, 275–294.

The Microanalysis of Memory Span and Its Development in Childhood

Nelson Cowan, J. Scott Saults, Lara D. Nugent, and Emily M. Elliott

University of Missouri, Columbia, USA

It is not clear from the literature why, as children develop, there are important increases in memory span, the number of just-presented items that the participant can repeat in the correct serial order. To understand this, some recent results on capacity limits and processing rates were re-analyzed. We first describe results using a conventional measure of performance in immediate memory tasks that is affected by the list length (proportion correct). Next we describe results using a less conventional measure (number correct) that is unaffected by list length under circumstances in which attention to the list during its presentation is curtailed. This measure can estimate an individual's limited-capacity storage ability. Last, we examine measures of spoken response timing that do and do not change with list length. We show that unconventional measures that do not change with list length, but do change with development, are especially useful in assessing basic changes in information processing parameters, including increases in memory capacity and processing speed.

Il existe une augmentation importante de l'empan au cours du développement de l'enfant, mais les raisons de cet accroissement demeurent incertaines. Afin de comprendre les causes de ce phénomène, de nouvelles analyses ont été effectuées sur des résultats récents concernant les limites de capacité et la vitesse de traitement. Nous décrivons tout d'abord les résultats en utilisant une mesure conventionnelle de la performance qui est affectée par la longueur de la liste (proportion correcte) dans des tâches de mémoire immédiate. Nous décrivons ensuite ces mêmes résultats en utilisant une mesure moins conventionnelle (nombre correct) qui n'est pas affectée par la longueur de la liste dans des conditions où l'attention est réduite. Finalement, nous examinons les mesures d'organisation temporelle des réponses orales qui changent ou non avec la longueur de la liste. Nous montrons que des mesures non conventionnelles qui ne changent pas avec la longueur de la liste, mais qui changent avec le développement, sont particulièrement utiles afin d'évaluer les changements se produisant au niveau du traitement de l'information.

In memory span tasks, lists of words or digits are presented with a serial recall period immediately following each list, and what is measured is how long the list can be before the participant makes errors in recalling the list. Performance on memory span tasks increases markedly with development in childhood, is related to performance on a number of more complex comprehension and problem-solving tasks (Dempster, 1985), and is even included in tests of intelligence. This makes sense because comprehension and problem solving require that propositions or premises be kept in the mind until additional information is presented and all of the information can be processed together. Memory span tasks provide one index of the ability to hold multiple items in the mind at one time (another practical example being addends within a math problem).

Although memory span tasks are procedurally simple, it is far from clear what mental processes contribute to performance on these tasks and how they operate together. To answer that question, what would appear to be needed is a detailed analysis or "microanalysis" of performance on memory span tasks. Siegler and Crowley (1991) proposed a microgenetic analysis of the time course of developmental growth in cognitive tasks, and what we are proposing is, in a complementary fashion, a microanalysis of the *processes* involved in span and its development. Baddeley, Thomson, and Buchanan (1975) initiated one such approach by determining that people could recall about as many items as they could pronounce in about 2sec, and by suggesting a phonological loop process consisting of a fading, 2-sec passive phonological store along with an active rehearsal process that is used in an attempt to refresh information in the store before it fades away. Hulme, Maughan, and Brown (1991) demonstrated that there is an additional, independent role of lexical knowledge, with words being recalled better than nonwords that could be spoken just as quickly as the words. We fully acknowledge such factors but have found that there are still other factors that appear important and yet have been studied far less often with reference to memory span. We have studied (1) the role of attention in an immediate, serial verbal recall task

---

Requests for reprints should be addressed to Nelson Cowan, Department of Psychology, University of Missouri, 210 McAlester Hall, Columbia, MO 65211, USA (Tel: 573-882-4232; Fax: 573-882-7710; E-mail: CowanN@missouri.edu).

This research was supported by NIH Grant HD-21338. We thank Nathaniel Fristoe and an anonymous reviewer for comments.

© 1999 International Union of Psychological Science

(Cowan, Nugent, Elliott, Ponomarev, & Saults, in press), and (2) the speed of spoken recall in a memory span task (Cowan et al., 1998), and it is these experimental situations that we will re-examine here.

The main thesis of this article is that one can identify two different types of measures of immediate memory that change with development: those that are affected by list length and those that are unaffected by list length. The list length manipulation is a well-known way to influence the difficulty of a memory test, both in adult research (e.g. Raaijmakers & Shiffrin, 1981) and developmentally (e.g. Engle & Marshall, 1983). Moreover, for measures affected by list length, one can individually adjust the list lengths so as to equate the task difficulty level and reduce or eliminate age differences in performance. However, there are other, less conventional memory measures that are unaffected by list length and do not tap difficulty level per se, yet still reveal age differences. We show that such measures can index basic aspects of the processing capacities of individuals that are independent of the specific task parameters. One such aspect is the immediate memory storage capacity, which will be explored with respect to the memory for unattended speech procedure of Cowan et al. (in press). Another such aspect is processing speed, which will be examined with the spoken recall timing procedure of Cowan et al. (1998).

MEMORY FOR ATTENDED AND UNATTENDED DIGIT LISTS

The experiment by Cowan et al. (in press) showed that proportion correct and number correct measures yield different types of information about recall. First, let us describe the rationale and results of the experiment. Cowan et al. highlighted two components of memory span. One component is a capacity to hold in mind a certain number of unrelated items (e.g. three or four random digits). Another component is the use of attention to engage in mnemonic strategies (e.g. grouping and semantic elaboration) that enable the participant to chunk or link items together so that they are no longer unrelated (see Miller, 1956). Cowan et al. set out to separate these components in a participant sample including first-graders, fourth-graders, and adults ($N = 24$ per age group). In one part of the experiment, lists of spoken digits were attended, as in an ordinary span task. In another part of the experiment, lists of spoken digits were ignored as the participant carried out a silent video game in which a central picture on each trial was to be matched to one of four surrounding pictures on the basis of a rhyme between their names. Although there were no responses to most of the spoken lists, occasionally the video game was replaced on the computer screen with a series of empty boxes, one box per item in the most recent list, and the participant was to use the keypad to recall the digits from this most recent list in the presented serial order. The cue to recall came only 2sec after the most recent list. The lengths of the lists within the attended-speech and ignored-speech sessions varied and were adjusted to equal the maximal number of items that the child could repeat (termed Span Length), or one, two, or three items less (Lengths Span-1, Span-2, and Span-3).

It was expected that the response to unattended lists followed by a recall cue would have to be based on a vivid sensory memory of the list, as in the previous studies using visual spatial arrays (Sperling, 1960) and auditory spatiotemporal arrays (Darwin, Turvey, & Crowder, 1972). From these studies it can be assumed that the amount of information in auditory sensory memory is very large and extends backward several seconds in time. Therefore, memory for unattended speech should be limited not by this store, but by how much information could be transferred to a more categorical, limited-capacity store (e.g. the focus of attention; see Cowan, 1988) without exceeding its capacity. The results suggested that this analysis is appropriate. Sperling (1960) found that people could recall about 4 items in his "whole report" condition regardless of the array size and, similarly, Cowan et al. (in press) found that adults could recall about 3.5 items in the unattended speech condition no matter whether the list length was equal to Span, Span-1, Span-2, or Span-3. Children also displayed a constant memory for unattended speech across list lengths, but the limit was significantly smaller (with first-graders recalling only about 2.5 items and fourth-graders recalling about 3.0 items).

It is important to consider why it is impossible for participants to increase the number correct through mnemonic strategies such as covert verbal rehearsal or memorization as the display size increases. In Sperling's (1960) study, the whole report limit could not benefit from these strategies because the array sizes were too large, and the arrays presented too briefly, for participants to get a chance to use strategies. In our study the items were presented one at a time but, in the unattended speech condition, the absence of attention severely limited the use of strategies.

In contrast to unattended speech, the number correct for attended speech increased steadily as a function of list length. However, the age differences were about the same size as in the unattended speech condition, showing that age differences in recall have little to do with the use of attention-demanding mnemonic strategies during the presentation of the list. This finding is in contrast to the classic emphasis on the importance of rehearsal during reception of the list in short-term memory tasks (Flavell, Beach, & Chinsky, 1966; Ornstein & Naus, 1978), though it does agree with several other previous analyses of memory span that questioned the central importance of rehearsal in span tasks (Dempster, 1981; Huttenlocher & Burke, 1976).

We now consider what proportion correct and number correct scores tell us about the processes involved in our task. Figure 1 plots the results for the attended- and unattended-speech conditions in terms of the proportion correct. (An item was counted correct only if it was

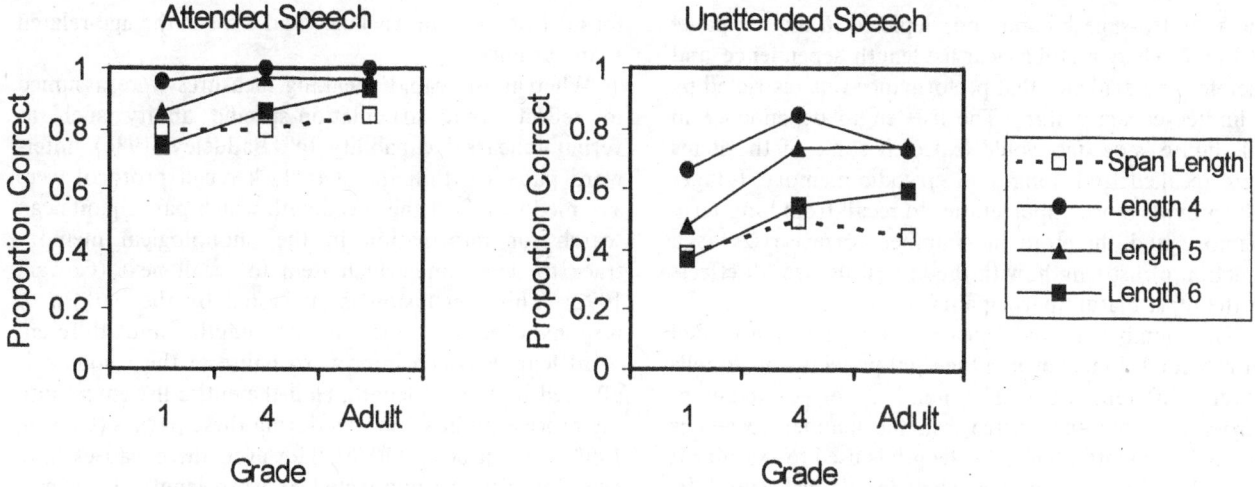

FIG. 1. For participants of three ages, proportion correct in two immediate memory tasks for three list lengths (solid lines) and for lists with a length equal to the maximum that the participant recalled correctly (dashed lines). *Left panel*: attended-speech task. [In that task, standard errors in the three age groups (youngest to oldest) were: for List Length 4, .01, .00, & .00; for List Length 5, .03, .01, & .01; for List Length 6, .03, .02, & .02; and for span-length lists, .03, .04, & .02.] *Right panel*: unattended-speech task, in which lists were unattended during their presentation and recalled only occasionally, if a post-list visual cue was presented. [In that task, standard errors in the three age geoups were: for List Length 4, .05, .04, & .04; for List Length 5, .05, .04, & .04; for List Length 6, .04, .04, & .04; and for span-length lists, .04, .05, & .03.] Data from Cowan et al. (in press).

recalled in the correct serial position.) The left panel shows the attended condition. Although performance levels are high, they strongly conform to the list length dependent pattern. The solid lines show performance for List Lengths 4, 5, and 6, the only list lengths available for a large enough number of participants in each age group. Performance levels are higher for the shorter list lengths, performance increases as a function of age, and the age effect is largest for the longest list length. Most importantly, as shown by the dashed lines, the increase in proportion correct across ages is basically eliminated when each participant is examined with lists of his or her own span length. The right panel of Fig. 1 shows much the same thing for the unattended speech condition, at a lower level of performance. Thus, the proportion correct measure is nicely sensitive to the list length in relation to the participant's span.

From the proportion correct scores, one could be led to suppose that the processes taking place in the attended- and unattended-speech conditions are fundamentally the same, with just an overall impairment in the unattended-speech condition. Evidence against this belief, in the form of number correct scores based on the same data as the proportion correct, appears in Fig. 2. If the recalled items have to be drawn from sensory memory into a capacity-limited store, with little chance of rehearsal or memorization during the presentation of the list, then the number reported should not exceed the capacity of the store no matter how many items are in the list. This is not the pattern shown for

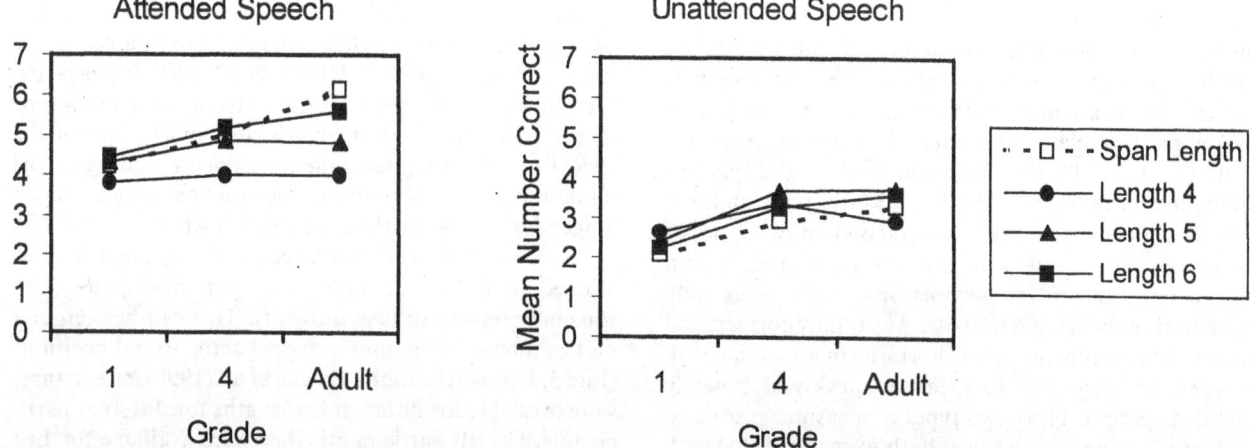

FIG. 2. For participants of three ages, number correct in two immediate memory tasks for three list lengths (solid lines) and for lists with a length equal to the maximum that the participant recalled correctly (dashed lines). *Left panel*: attended-speech task. [In that task, standard errors in the three age groups (youngest to oldest) were: for List Length 4, 0.05, 0.00, & 0.01; for List Length 5, 0.14, 0.05, & 0.06; for List Length 6, 0.30, 0.17, & 0.11; and for span-length lists, 0.17, 0.19 & 0.22.] *Right panel*: unattended-speech task. [In that task, standard errors in the three age groups were: for List Length 4, 0.19, 0.18, & 0.19; for List Length 5, 0.24, 0.23, & 0.23; for List Length 6, 0.42, 0.29, & 0.24; and for span-length lists, 0.19, 0.25, & 0.23.] Data from Cowan et al. (in press).

the attended-speech condition, depicted in the left panel of Fig. 2. There is still a clear list length dependence, and therefore no evidence that performance was restricted by a limited-capacity store. The list length dependence in this figure is as one would expect if some of the items were recalled from long-term episodic memory. Longer lists provide more opportunities to recall from long-term memory and therefore the number correct rises as a function of list length, with the largest list length effects in the most mature participants.

The number correct measure for the unattended speech condition, shown in the right panel of Fig. 2, tells a very different story. The number correct increases across ages, but that increase in the number correct is the same no matter which list length is used to examine it and, therefore, no matter whether the list length is adjusted to match the participant's span or not. We can think of the basic memory capacity that shows up in this condition as an age-dependent capacity that is rather distinct from what is observed in an ordinary span task. (The correlation between the pretested span and the mean number correct for unattended speech was $r = .52$, but the correlation between the pretested span and the number correct for attended speech was much larger at $r = .94$.) As noted, the number correct measure for unattended speech may reflect a limit to how many items can be drawn from sensory memory into the focus of attention at the same time. Assuming that far more than that number of items are available within an unanalyzed sensory memory, the limit in capacity of the focus of attention can be observed in the same way for all lists that contain at least as many items as the participant's capacity limit.

SILENT PERIODS WITHIN SPOKEN RESPONSES IN A DIGIT SPAN TASK

We now turn to a second area that can benefit from an empirical analysis similar to the one described earlier, in which a measure that is not affected by list length is derived. In an attempt to determine how the timing of spoken recall is related to recall itself in a digit span task, Cowan et al. (1998, Exp. 1) investigated several types of timing measures in first-, third-, and fifth-grade children ($N = 24$ per age). The article was focused on two types of measures: the duration of inter-word pauses within spoken responses in the memory span task, using only those trials in which the response was totally correct; and the duration of repetitions of short lists in a separate task in which the child was to speak as quickly as possible (speeded speech). These two types of measures proved to be very revealing because they both were correlated with memory span (at moderate levels of about .4), whereas they were not correlated with each other at all. Together, in a structural equation model including multiple measures of the two types of processing duration contributing to two separate latent variables, they accounted for 60% of the span variance and 87% of the age-related span variance.

Whereas the rapid speaking measures were assumed to reflect some articulation-specific ability such as verbal rehearsal capability (cf. Baddeley, 1986), inter-word pauses within the span task recall protocol were assumed to reflect the speed with which participants can search for information in the phonological memory trace to determine which item to recall next (Cowan, 1992). This conclusion is suggested by the pattern of responses across different list lengths and different word lengths. Each inter-word pause in the response is affected by the list length, as if the entire list enters into the processing in some way during these pauses (Cowan, 1992; Cowan et al., 1998). However, these pauses have been found to be unaffected by word length (Cowan et al., 1994; Hulme, Newton, Cowan, Stuart, & Brown, in press). The process accounting for our inter-word pauses thus did not appear to be rehearsal, which occurs at a slower rate for sets of words that take longer to pronounce (Baddeley et al., 1975; Baddeley, 1986; Landauer, 1962) and presumably would have produced a word length effect on pauses.

Other evidence strengthens the analogy between the processes taking place during inter-word pauses and during memory search tasks. Adults' rapid pronunciations of subspan lists (Sternberg, Monsell, Knoll, & Wright, 1978; Sternberg, Wright, Knoll, & Monsell, 1980) similarly have been explained according to a memory search process. An analogy with memory search is further strengthened in that, similar to the pauses in serial recall (but unlike serial recall performance levels), word length has no effect in standard memory search procedures in which a list is followed by a probe item (Chase, 1977; Clifton & Tash, 1973).

The work of Hulme et al. (in press), which used adult participants, further strengthens the hypothesis that inter-word pauses are times when some kind of memory search process takes place, in that memory search times (using a procedure in which a list was followed by a probe) were found to be correlated with inter-word pauses in the span task recall period. Hulme et al. further suggested that during the pauses, in addition to carrying out a type of memory search, participants also must identify the lexical node in long-term memory corresponding to the phonological representation, given that pauses were much longer for nonwords than for English words.

The list length dependence of inter-word pauses alluded to here is an indication that these pauses are somehow related to task difficulty. This can be seen in a plot of inter-word pauses averaged across serial positions (Fig. 3, left panel). In the Cowan et al. (1998) data, pauses were available for different list lengths for different participants. For all participants, they were available for List Lengths 2, 3, and 4 (solid lines); and for all but one participant (who had a maximal span of 8 items), they were available for a relative list length of Span-2 (dashed line), which equalled a List Length of 2 (for Span = 4), 3 (for Span = 5), 4 (for Span = 6), or 5 (for Span = 7).

Longer list lengths were recorded but the meticulous timing analyses were not carried out on them. The results depicted in the left panel of Fig. 3 show the typical list length dependent pattern in which performance was better (i.e. in this case, contained shorter pauses) for shorter lists and in which the age effect was diminished by examining each participant on a list length linked to his or her own memory span (in this case, Span-2).

An important issue related to inter-word pauses and other measures of processing speed is that it is often unclear whether speed is the cause of capacity differences, whether it is the result of these differences, or whether both are affected by a third factor. Exquisite fits between speeds and span, with other variables controlled, have tended to lead to the suggestion that processing speed limits cause capacity limits (e.g. see Fry & Hale, 1996; Kail & Park, 1994; Salthouse, 1996). However, given the multiplicity of processing speeds, as demonstrated for example by Cowan et al. (1998), it is possible that some processing speed limits have a different causal path than others. We will use a new measure to gain insight into the nature of the inter-word pause measure.

Assume for the time being that participants must in some sense process the entire list in a search process taking place during each inter-word pause in the recall period (cf. Cowan, 1992; Hulme et al., in press). Further assume that the processing time for each item does not depend on the difficulty of the task, but depends only on the participant's intrinsic speed of processing that is not influenced by task load. If these assumptions are met, then the processing speed *per item* should not vary with list length, whereas it should vary among individuals.

This proposition is examined in the right panel of Fig. 3. This panel shows each mean pause time (averaged across serial positions) divided by the list length, providing an estimate of the mean pause time on a per-list-item basis. As the figure shows, this type of metric eliminates list length effects. This suggests the plausibility of the notion that an individual has a certain per-list-item pause time that stays the same no matter how many items are in the list.

CONCLUSION

It can be argued that measures of immediate memory that produce a list length effect are potentially ambiguous in developmental studies. They display age effects that differ depending on what list length is examined. Therefore, it is not clear how to map the complex age effects that are found onto underlying theoretical variables. In the present study, we have illustrated the use of measures that are derived in such a way that they are not influenced by list length, but nevertheless are influenced by age. We are hopeful these measures might be useful in identifying basic processes underlying immediate memory performance. A measure of the number correct based on data from Cowan et al. (in press) showed a complex pattern for attended lists, but an exquisitely simple pattern for unattended lists (Fig. 2, right). In that pattern, the number correct was the same regardless of the list length and was taken to indicate a developmental growth in the capacity limit of the store to which sensory memory of items from ignored lists must be transferred to allow recall. A newly derived speech recall timing measure, of the pause duration per item in the list, showed a pause-per-list-item time that was fixed across list lengths but sped up with development (Fig. 3, right). This measure was taken as a possible indication of developmental growth in an underlying speed of processing. Although this conclusion requires the acceptance of

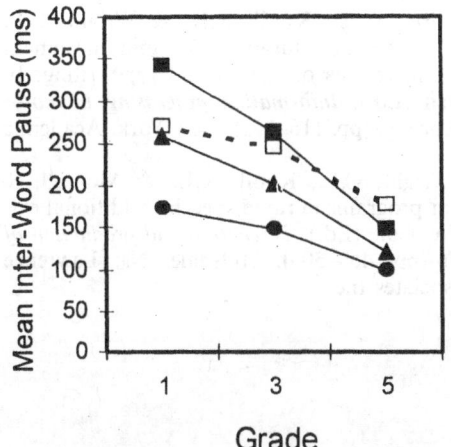
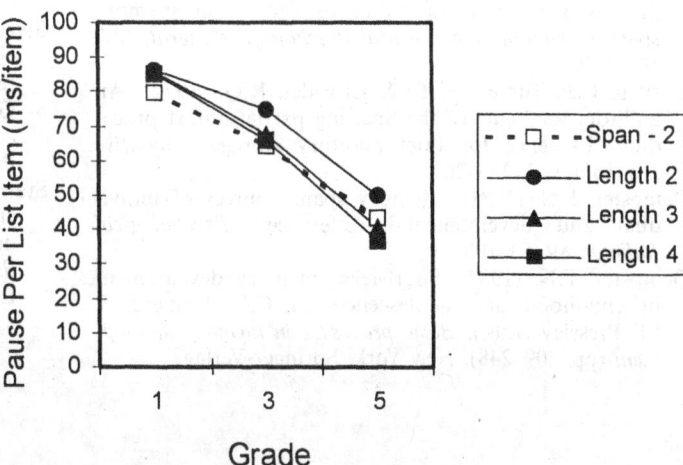

FIG. 3. For children of three ages, timing measurements within correctly repeated lists of three different fixed lengths (solid lines) and lists of a length two below the maximum that the participant recalled correctly (dashed lines). *Left panel*: inter-word pause times averaged across serial positions. [For this measure, standard errors in the three age groups (youngest to oldest) were: for List Length 2, 18.85, 23.98, & 20.95; for List Length 3, 26.93, 27.49, & 30.16; for List Length 4, 35.11, 28.77 & 32.75; and for List Length (Span-2), 27.11, 29.52, & 33.74.] *Right panel*: Pause per list item, calculated as the mean inter-word pause time (averaged across serial positions) divided by the list length. [For this measure, standard errors in the three age groups were: for List Length 2, 9.43, 11.99, & 10.48; for List Length 3, 8.98, 9.16, & 10.05; for List Length 4, 8.78, 7.19, & 8.19; and for List Length (Span-2), 8.09, 8.15, & 9.15.] Means calculated from the data set used by Cowan et al. (1998).

some uncertain assumptions about information processing that were described earlier, we feel that the present data and new measures warrant further investigation in the near future.

REFERENCES

Baddeley, A.D. (1986). *Working Memory.* Oxford: Clarendon Press.

Baddeley, A.D., Thomson, N., & Buchanan, M. (1975). Word length and the structure of short-term memory. *Journal of Verbal Learning and Verbal Behavior, 14,* 575–589.

Chase, W.G. (1977). Does memory scanning involve implicit speech? In S. Dornic (Ed.), *Attention and performance VI* (pp. 607–628). Hillsdale, NJ: Lawrence Erlbaum Associates Inc.

Clifton, C., & Tash, J. (1973). Effect of syllabic word length on memory-search rate. *Journal of Experimental Psychology, 99,* 231–235.

Cowan, N. (1988). Evolving conceptions of memory storage, selective attention, and their mutual constraints within the human information processing system. *Psychological Bulletin, 104,* 163–191.

Cowan, N. (1992). Verbal memory span and the timing of spoken recall. *Journal of Memory and Language, 31,* 668–684.

Cowan, N. (1998). What is more explanatory, processing capacity or processing speed? [Commentary on target article by Graham Halford.] *Behavioral and Brain Sciences, 21,* 835–836.

Cowan, N., Keller, T., Hulme, C., Roodenrys, S., McDougall, S., & Rack, J. (1994). Verbal memory span in children: Speech timing clues to the mechanisms underlying age and word length effects. *Journal of Memory and Language, 33,* 234–250.

Cowan, N., Nugent, L.D., Elliott, E.M., Ponomarev, I., & Saults, J.S. (in press). The role of attention in the development of short-term memory: Age differences in the verbal span of apprehension. *Child Development.*

Cowan, N., Wood, N.L., Wood, P.K., Keller, T.A., Nugent, L.D., & Keller, C.V. (1998). Two separate verbal processing rates contributing to short-term memory span. *Journal of Experimental Psychology: General, 127,* 141–160.

Darwin, C.J., Turvey, M.T., & Crowder, R.G. (1972). An auditory analogue of the Sperling partial report procedure: Evidence for brief auditory storage. *Cognitive Psychology, 3,* 255–267.

Dempster, F.N. (1981). Memory span: Sources of individual and developmental differences. *Psychological Bulletin, 89,* 63–100.

Dempster, F.N. (1985). Short-term memory development in childhood and adolescence. In C.J. Brainerd & M. Pressley (Eds.), *Basic processes in memory development* (pp. 209–248). New York: Springer-Verlag.

Engle, R.W., & Marshall, K. (1983). Do developmental changes in digit span result from acquisition strategies? *Journal of Experimental Child Psychology, 36,* 429–436.

Flavell, J.H., Beach, D.H., & Chinsky, J.M. (1966). Spontaneous verbal rehearsal in a memory task as a function of age. *Child Development, 37,* 283–299.

Fry, A.F., & Hale, S. (1996). Processing speed, working memory, and fluid intelligence: Evidence for a developmental cascade. *Psychological Science, 7,* 237–241.

Hulme, C., Maughan, S., & Brown, G.D.A. (1991). Memory for familiar and unfamiliar words: Evidence for a long-term memory contribution to short-term memory span. *Journal of Memory and Language, 30,* 685–701.

Hulme, C., Newton, P., Cowan, N., Stuart, G., & Brown, G. (in press). Think before you speak: Pause, memory search and trace redintegration processes in verbal memory span. *Journal of Experimental Psychology: Learning, Memory, and Cognition.*

Huttenlocher, J., & Burke, D. (1976). Why does memory span increase with age? *Cognitive Psychology, 8,* 1–31.

Kail, R., & Park, Y.-S. (1994). Processing time, articulation time, and memory span. *Journal of Experimental Child Psychology, 57,* 281–291.

Landauer, T.K. (1962). Rate of implicit speech. *Perceptual and Motor Skills, 15,* 646.

Miller, G.A. (1956). The magical number seven, plus or minus two: Some limits on our capacity for processing information. *Psychological Review, 63,* 81–97.

Ornstein, P.A., & Naus, M.J. (1978). Rehearsal processes in children's memory. In P.A. Ornstein (Ed.), *Memory development in children* (pp. 69–99). Hillsdale, NJ: Lawrence Erlbaum Associates Inc.

Raaijmakers, J.G.W., & Shiffrin, R.M. (1981). Search of associative memory. *Psychological Review, 88,* 93–134.

Salthouse, T.A. (1996). The processing-speed theory of adult age differences in cognition. *Psychological Review, 103,* 403–428.

Siegler, R.S., & Crowley, K. (1991). The microgenetic method: A direct means for studying cognitive development. *American Psychologist, 46,* 606–620.

Sperling, G. (1960). The information available in brief visual presentations. *Psychological Monographs, 74* (Whole No. 498).

Sternberg, S., Monsell, S., Knoll, R.L., & Wright, C.E. (1978). The latency and duration of rapid movement sequences: Comparisons of speech and typewriting. In G.E. Stelmach (Ed.), *Information processing in motor control and learning* (pp. 116–152). New York: Academic Press.

Sternberg, S., Wright, C.E., Knoll, R.L., & Monsell, S. (1980). Motor programs in rapid speech: Additional evidence. In R.A. Cole (Ed.), *Perception and production of fluent speech* (pp. 469–505). Hillsdale, NJ: Lawrence Erlbaum Associates Inc.

Measuring Memory Span

John A. Groeger and David Field
University of Surrey, Guildford, UK

Sean M. Hammond
Clinical Decision Support Unit, Broadmoor Hospital, Crowthorne, UK

This study, conducted on a sample of 403 adult subjects, set out to explore the relationships between measures of digit span (forward and reversed), motor and spatial span, and their dependence on a broad range of measures of cognitive function. The results revealed that measures of digit span are closely related, as are measures of motor and spatial span, but these pairs of memory span measures are relatively independent of each other. Furthermore, reverse digit span, motor span, and spatial span appear to rely on what might be regarded as intellectual or executive cognitive functions. As such, the results provide little support for accounts of serial recall, which suggest that order and/or item information are more adequately modelled in a modality-independent form.

Cette étude explore les relations entre des mesures d'empan de chiffre (avant et inversé), d'empan moteur et spatial, et leur relation, avec un ensemble de mesures de fonctions cognitives. Les résultats révèlent que les mesures d'empan de chiffres sont fortement reliées entre elles, tout comme l'empan moteur et spatial, mais que ces deux paires de mesures d'empan mnésiques sont relativement indépendantes l'une de l'autre. De plus, l'empan de chiffre inversé, l'empan moteur et l'empan spatial semblent être basés sur des fonctions cognitives intellectuelles ou exécutives. Ces résultats ne soutiennent pas les hypothèses suggérant que l'information reliée à l'ordre ou aux items est modélisée de façon plus adéquate lorsque les modalités sont considérés indépendantes.

Measures of memory span are widely used as measures of specific memory functioning, and of more general cognitive functioning (e.g. Lezak, 1995; Wechsler, 1987). Typically the tasks used rely on the presentation of items, at a relatively rapid rate, with the requirement that these are to be reported immediately after all items have been presented, usually, but not always, in the same order as the original presentation. The requirement for maintaining serial order is the main focus of the present paper, since although maintenance or manipulation of serial order has been regarded as a "problem" for over 50 years (Lashley, 1951), the raft of papers within the past 2 or 3 years makes clear that it remains one that has not been solved. Recent interest in the issue has been reawakened by a number of empirical and theoretical developments (e.g. Burgess & Hitch, 1992, 1996; Henson, Norris, Page, & Baddeley, 1996; Houghton, Hartley, & Glasspool, 1996). These show convincingly, we believe, that traditional accounts of serial behaviour in terms of "chaining", are no longer sustainable. Here our interest lies in a different aspect of serial recall, that is, the extent to which it is similar across different modalities and directions of recall. Specifically, we explore the degree to which different measures of serial span predict each other, and are in turn predicted by the same, non-memory indices of cognitive performance—reasoning that if strong relationships of this sort exist they lend support to arguments which stress the modality-independent nature of serial recall.

Within the Working Memory tradition, digit span is assumed to depend principally on an aspect of Working Memory that is dedicated to the maintenance of phonological information (i.e. the phonological loop). It is also assumed that modality-free strategic control executive processes are required to maintain the operation of the phonological loop, especially when errors in serial recall begin to occur and need to be "repaired" if performance is not to disintegrate (Hitch & Baddeley, 1976). Hence (Baddeley, 1996, p. 11), "as the digit load increases, the demands made on the Central Executive will increase, resulting in a general impact of concurrent span on any task that demands working memory capacity" and "It seems likely that level of performance on a task such as digit span which involves relatively little complex processing will be determined by storage rather than executive limitations."

Precisely what is involved in the maintenance of serial order among visual or spatial stimuli is rather less clear. It has frequently been shown that maintenance of visual information and maintaining information about the order in which stimuli were presented are influenced by different variables. However, the purpose of this research has been to establish a difference between "visual" and "spatial" components of Working Memory (see Logie,

---

Requests for reprints should be addressed to J.A. Groeger, Department of Psychology, University of Surrey, Guildford, GU2 5JA, UK (E-mail: j.groeger@surrey.ac.uk).

© 1999 International Union of Psychological Science

1995, for extensive discussion), rather than to explore *how* the serial order of spatial materials is maintained. Despite this lacuna, it would be consistent with the Working Memory framework to assume that memory for serial spatial positions might reflect the operation of a similar, visuospatial, active rehearsal process, with the Central Executive helping out as the span increases. Given this assumption, one might expect differential involvement of the Central Executive in forward and reverse versions of the task. However, at least for children, Isaacs and Vargha-Khadem (1989) have shown that serial spatial performance for forward and reversed recall are similar. In support of this, Smyth and Scholey (1992) claim that spatial items are encoded merely in relation to the position of other items in the display, and that additional executive resources are not required to reverse the order of Corsi Blocks (see also Schofield & Ashman, 1986). It is worth noting in this respect that typically verbal forward and reversed report show differences across the whole adult age-range, whereas the direction of report differences with Corsi Blocks only emerge strongly among middle-aged and older subjects (see Wechsler, 1987, p. 52).

Further difficulties arise with the traditional account of memory span because of the findings reported recently by Farrand and Jones (1996). Here, by presenting items serially, and then sometimes re-presenting all list items simultaneously before recall, it was possible to contrast recall when only serial order, or serial order plus item information, was required. The results showed that there were no differences between forward and reversed recall of serial order, for lists of auditory-verbal, visual-verbal, and spatial stimuli, when only order information had to be recalled. When recall of both order and item information was required (i.e. simultaneous re-presentation did not occur before recall), "recall in the backward direction of report was significantly worse than in the forward direction of report, both in spatial and verbal tasks" (Farrand & Jones, 1996, p. 140).

This study is important in a number of respects. First, it confirms differences between forward and reversed report requirements in spatial tasks, attributing the Isaacs and Vargha-Khadem findings to the requirement to retain both item and order information rather than to differences in the modality of the memory requirement. More crucially for the present study, Farrand and Jones emphasise the similarity of verbal and spatial serial recall.

This is a controversial claim, given the weight of evidence for the separation of verbal and spatial spans. For example, De Renzi and Nichelli (1975) have reported patients with very low verbal spans and normal spatial spans, and patients with very low spatial spans and normal verbal spans. Similarly, the patients described by Vallar and Baddeley (1984) and Hanley, Young, and Pearson (1991) reflect a similar double dissociation. The work of Smyth and colleagues (e.g. Smyth & Scholey, 1992; Smyth, Pearson, & Pendelton, 1988) appears to show convincingly that concurrent articulation during presentation of a list of spatial items to be recalled does not interfere with performance, that spatial interference tasks did not affect memory for verbal items unless the interference tasks involved verbal labels for the spatial stimuli, and that verbal interference tasks did not affect spatial memory unless the verbal tasks were dealing with spatial stimuli. Although we would not wish to go as far as Jones and colleagues elsewhere (e.g. Jones, 1993; Jones, Beaman, & Macken, 1996) and suggest that the fractionation of Working Memory advocated by many is unwarranted (because of the equivalence of spatial and verbal tasks and representations), it does behove us to make clear the differences between serial verbal and spatial tasks, as well as the representational systems used to perform them.

Here, we take a different approach in order to address the issues raised earlier, i.e. what the differences are between digit and spatial span, whether the requirement to maintain serial order is best conceptualised as a process distinct from these modality-dedicated stores and processes, and the role of the Central Executive in memory span tests. Specifically, we have measured the memory spans, using successively longer sequences until failure at longer sequences occurs, of a large group of adult volunteers, as part of a larger study of cognitive and affective correlates of driving behaviour. We then use a regression approach, attempting to predict each span measure from all other variables, including or excluding the remaining memory span measures as appropriate.

METHOD

Sample

Four hundred and three adult volunteers took part in three 1-hour sessions of testing, with all tests being completed on the same day. The 200 men taking part ranged in age from 17 to 74 years (average: 31.3), the 203 women who took part ranged from 17 to 77 years of age (average: 35.3).

Procedure

All adults took part in three sessions of approximately 1 hour of mainly computer-based tests of a range of cognitive functions, thought to relate to driving ability (see Groeger, Hammond, & Field, 1998). The data reported here relate to a subset of these tests.

Span Measures Employed. These were forward and reversed digit span, traditionally administered, with digits read to subjects at a rate of one per second; a computerised version of the forward Corsi Blocks task, in which one of a set of squares on a screen temporarily changes colour, and the subject's task is to tap these squares in the order in which they changed colour; and a computerised motor sequence task. This final task merits more detailed description. The subject sits in front of a steering wheel, on which are located two buttons, with his feet resting near foot pedals. A series of directional instructions (i.e. "right" or "left") accompanied by a motor instruction (such as "pedal", "steer" or "button") are presented on a computer screen in front of the subject. Ascending sequences of instructions are presented, after which the subject responds by performing the designated actions. Before the task is used to assess retention (where commands are issued successively but are no longer available before performance commences), in order to familiarise the subject with the apparatus, commands are issued and acted upon one at a time. Performance on the acquisition version of the task is the time taken to reproduce a sequence of 30 actions, while the retention version of the task records the largest number of correctly remembered and performed actions. All span measures reflected the maximum length at which two successes occurred, and were derived by presenting two successive strings at each level until two failures at a particular level occurred.

Reaction Time Measures. These included: simple alerted finger and foot reaction time, separating initiation and movement time components, surprise foot reaction time (i.e. single trial reaction time measured in response to a randomly occurring signal before or after other tasks began or were completed); two- and three-alternative choice reaction time. Motor performance measures included: ability to respond to random sequence of 30 motor commands, performed twice (actions as for motor span but with instruction always available); and ability to track an on-screen object, using steering wheel (horizontal) or foot pedals (vertical), performed separately and combined. Visual trajectory and time of collision estimation was also assessed.

Measures of Intellectual Functioning. These included: a visual version of Baddeley's (1968) verbal reasoning task; inspection time tasks (minimum exposure time required to determine which of three rapidly presented and masked lines was the longest); symbol-digit conversion (after digit-symbol task in Wechsler, 1987); and a standard Stroop task. Further details of these and other measures taken in the study as a whole are available from the first author.

RESULTS AND DISCUSSION

Table 1 presents the average performance on the four serial recall tasks. Further analyses involved separate regression analyses, carried out in an attempt to identify the best predictors of each of the four memory span measures. For each span measure, we attempt to predict it from all other span measures simultaneously entered, in order to assess the unique contribution to span performance of each, with all other measures being entered subsequently. An alternate version of this analysis in which non-memory measures are entered simultaneously, with the other span measures being entered subsequently,

TABLE 1
Memory Span Performance

	Mean	SD	Min	Max	N
Digits (forward)	6.96	1.27	4.00	9.00	403
Digits (reversed)	5.30	1.35	2.00	8.00	403
Motor (forward)	5.04	1.03	2.00	6.00	324
Corsi (forward)	6.63	1.24	2.00	9.00	381

was also carried out in each case. For all analyses, variables with missing values were deleted in a listwise fashion.

Forward Digit Span

The first analyses deal with forward digit span. Reversed digit span, spatial span, and motor span together account for 31% of the variance in forward digit span [adjusted R-square: 0.301; $F(3,259) = 38.551$; $P < .001$]. The unique contributions of the three span measures are 26%, 0.5%, and 0.1% respectively. Adding all the other indices of cognitive performance increases R-squared to 0.367 [adjusted R-square: 0.294; $F(27,235) = 5.041$; $P < .001$], but the incremental F ratio [$F(24,235) = 0.966$], is not statistically reliable. If, instead, non-memory indices are all included simultaneously first, the R-square value 0.128 [adjusted R-square: 0.040; $F(24,238) = 1.451$; $P > .08$] is not statistically reliable. Subsequently adding the memory span measures increases explanatory power [R-square = 0.367; adjusted R-square = 0.294; $F(27,235) = 5.041$; $P < .001$]. This increase in variance accounted for is statistically reliable [incremental $F(3,238) = 29.942$; $P < .001$], with reverse digit span (21%), but neither spatial (0.01%) nor motor (0.03%) span adding reliably to the unique variance accounted for.

Thus, forward and reverse digit span are highly related, but forward span is virtually unrelated to forward spatial or motor span performance. Although the multiple regression is not statistically reliable, approximately 13% of variance in forward span is accounted for by non-memory-based indices of cognitive function.

Reverse Digit Span

Reverse digit span was considered next. Forward digit span, spatial span, and motor span together account for 31% of the variance in reverse digit span [adjusted R-square: 0.306; $F(3,259) = 39.544$; $P < .001$]. The unique contributions of the three span measures are 26%, 0.6%, and 0.3% respectively. Adding all the other indices of cognitive performance increases R-squared to 0.399 [adjusted R-square: 0.330; $F(27,235) = 5.782$; $P < .001$], but the incremental F ratio [$F(24,235) = 1.385$] narrowly failed to reach statistical reliability ($P < .09$). In contrast to what occurs with forward digit span, when non-memory indices are all included simultaneously first, the R-square value 0.158 [adjusted R-square: 0.073; $F(24,238) = 1.854$; $P < .01$) is statistically reliable. Those indices of cognitive performance that contribute reliably to the regression equation are time taken to perform motor sequences (1.8% of unique variance), symbol-digit recoding (1.2%), verbal reasoning (3.7%), and age (1.9%).

Two aspects of this are worthy of comment. First, measures of intelligence are the most important of the non-memory measures of cognitive function that relate to reverse digit span, and second, a substantial amount of variance in reverse digit span performance is accounted for by the combination of all the measures taken. Subsequently adding the memory span measures increases explanatory power [R-square = 0.399; adjusted R-square = 0.330; $F(27,235) = 5.782$; $P < .001$]. This increase in variance accounted for is statistically reliable [incremental $F(3,235) = 30.199$; $P < .001$], with forward digit span (20%), but neither spatial (0.04%) nor motor (0.08%) span adding reliably to the unique variance accounted for. In short, reverse digit span is most closely related to other measures of memory span, but is also independently related to indices that measure intellectual or executive function.

Spatial Span

Turning to performance on the computerized version of the Corsi Blocks task (forward), we find that although measures of memory span again reliably predict (spatial) span [R-square: 0.151, adjusted R-square: 0.141; $F(3,259) = 15.296$; $P < .001$], only motor span (10%; $t = 5.484$; $P < .001$), but not forward digit (0.6%) or reverse-digit span (0.7%) contribute reliably to the variance accounted for. Subsequently adding all other measures of cognitive function increases R-square [0.336; $F(27,235) = 4.407$; $P < .001$], the additional variance explained being statistically reliable [incremental $F(27,235) = 2.738$; $P < .001$].

When the regression analysis is repeated, but this time non-memory measures are added first, the R-square [0.301; adjusted R-square: 0.230; $F(24,238) = 4.264$; $P < .001$] is again statistically reliable. Several variables, finger-based reaction time (1.1%; $t = 1.898$; $P < .05$), foot initiation time (1.2%; $t = 2.053$; $P < .05$), symbol-digit conversion (1.1%; $t = 1.882$; $P < .05$), verbal reasoning (1.9%; $t = 2.557$; $P < .01$), and ability to control vertical tracking (4.2%; $t = 3.249$; $P < .001$), all contribute uniquely to explaining variance in spatial span, but obviously a large amount of the remaining variance explained by non-memory span measures is accounted for jointly by the other indices of cognitive function. Allowing the other memory span measures to enter subsequently increases the R-square value [R-square: 0.336; adjusted R-square: 0.260; $F(27,235) = 4.217$; $P < .001$], the increase in incremental $F [F(3,235) = 4.179; P < .001]$ being statistically reliable, but almost entirely due to the additional unique variance accounted for by motor span (2%; $t = 2.637$; $P < .01$; reverse digit span: 0.4%; forward digit span: 0.1%). Thus, as these results indicate, spatial span, as measured by the Corsi Blocks task, relies on more general cognitive functioning, and only minimally on the memory systems that support performance in the digit span tasks.

Motor Span

Finally, performance on our motor span task was predicted by performance on the other memory span tasks [R-square: 0.132; adjusted R-square: 0.122; $F(3,259) = 13.168$; $P < .001$], but only spatial memory span (10.1%; $t = 5.484$; $P < .001$) accounts for any substantial amount of variance in motor span (forward digit span: 0.1%; reverse digit span: 0.4%). Adding the other measures of cognitive performance to the regression equation increases the variance in motor span accounted for [R-square: 0.338; adjusted R-square: 0.262; $F(27,235) = 4.445$; $P < .001$; incremental $F(24,235) = 3.047$; $P < .001$]. By entering the non-memory measures first, 29% of the variance in motor span performance is accounted for [R-square: 0.292; adjusted R-square: 0.220; $F(24,238) = 4.084$; $P < .001$]. Although some tests contribute reliably to the variance explained (Tracking, 1.4%, $t = 2.196$, $P < .05$; Choice reaction time, 1.1%, $t = 2.014$, $P < .05$; Verbal reasoning, 2.0%, $t = 2.651$, $P < .01$; Stroop interference, 1.3%, $t = 1.889$; $P < .05$], in excess of 20% of the variance in motor span performance is accounted for by the non-memory tests. Adding memory span measures increases the variance explained [incremental $F(3,235) = 5.443$; $P < .01$], with only spatial span (2.0%), contributing reliably to the additional variance explained (forward digit span, 0.2%; reverse digit span, 0.8%).

This particular pattern of relationships suggests that the motor span task introduced here is more or less independent of verbal memory, which in turn suggests that the task is carried out by performing sequences of learned motor responses, rather than by memorizing sequences of verbal instructions which are subsequently performed. It is also clear that the task depends on a broad range of cognitive function, not only motor control and intellectual function, but also attentional switching or interference.

CONCLUSION

We set out to address three issues, by attempting to assess the degree to which a range of variables predicted performance on four memory span tasks. The results presented here make clear that spatial span, as operationalized by the Corsi Blocks task, is more or less independent of digit span, whether the latter is measured in its forward or reversed form. Because maximum digit span was measured, at which item information for digits is more or less redundant, we do not believe that the differences between digit span and spatial and motor span arise because of their differential requirement to maintain item information. We consider that the results add further weight to counter-suggestions that emphasize the equivalence of visual and verbal span tasks (e.g. Farrand & Jones, 1996; Isaacs & Vargha-Khadem, 1989). Even though each of the memory span tasks studied requires recall in a serial fashion, the tasks appear to be strongly divided in terms of modality, and the pattern of results reported offer very little evidence for some modality-independent serial ordering mechanism. Because of this, we consider that at this stage it is more appropriate to model serial order as an integral aspect of memory performance within that modality, rather than as a separate process. The final issue addressed here was the extent to which memory span depends on what some conceptions of Working Memory would style as Central Executive processes. Although we have not measured Central Executive processing using dual-task methodology, it is striking that verbal reasoning, which is regarded as a task requiring considerable Central Executive involvement (see Baddeley, 1986; Hitch & Baddeley, 1976), predicts a significant and usually distinct portion of memory span performance, irrespective of the modality in which serial span is measured. Although these are not necessarily measures of Central Executive functioning, it should be noted that other measures of intellectual functioning (e.g. inspection time) do not show this pattern. It may thus be that the verbal reasoning test correlates with ability to maintain serial order, because it itself requires sensitivity to order, although only of two items. The importance of selective functions, as reflected in performance of the Stroop task, the pursuit tracking task, and the choice reaction task, is also made clear by the present results, but only for visuomotor memory span tasks.

REFERENCES

Baddeley, A.D. (1968). A 3 minute reasoning test based on grammatical transformation. *Psychonomic Science*, *10*, 341–342.

Baddeley, A.D. (1996). The concept of working memory. In S.E. Gathercole (Ed.), *Models of short-term memory*. Hove, UK: Psychology Press.

Bjork, E.L., & Healy, A.F. (1974). Short-term memory and item retention. *Journal of Verbal Learning and Verbal Behaviour*, *13*, 80–97.

Burgess, N., & Hitch, G.J. (1992). Toward a network model of the articulatory loop. *Journal of Memory and Language*, *31*, 429–460.

Burgess, N., & Hitch, G.J. (1996). A connectionist model of STM for serial order. In S.E. Gathercole (Ed.), *Models of short-term memory*. Hove, UK: Psychology Press.

De Renzi, E., & Nichelli, P. (1975). Verbal and nonverbal short-term memory impairment following hemispheric damage. *Cortex*, *11*, 341–354.

Ebbinghaus, H. (1885/1964). *Memory: A contribution to experimental psychology*. New York: Dover.

Farrand, P., & Jones, D. (1996). Direction of report in spatial and verbal serial short-term memory. *Quarterly Journal of Experimental Psychology*, *20*, 80–115.

Groeger, J.A., Hammond, S.E., & Field, D. (1998). *Processes involved in responding to risk. Vol 2: Computerised assessment of drivers' skills: relationships between measures*. Project report TT/124/98. Crowthorne, UK: Transport Research Laboratory.

Hanley, J.R., Young, A.W., & Pearson, N.A. (1991). Impairment of the visuo-spatial scratch pad. *Quarterly Journal of Experimental Psychology*, *43*, 101–125.

Healy, A.F. (1974). Separating item from order information in short term memory. *Journal of Verbal Learning and Verbal Behaviour*, *13*, 80–97.

Henson, R.N.A., Norris, D.G., Page, M.P.A., & Baddeley, A.D. (1996). Unchained memory: Error patterns rule out chaining models of immediate serial recall. *Quarterly Journal of Experimental Psychology*, *20*, 80–115.

Hitch, G.J., & Baddeley, A.D. (1976). Verbal reasoning and working memory. *Quarterly Journal of Experimental Psychology*, *28*, 603–621.

Houghton, G., Hartley, T., & Glasspool, D.W. (1996). The representation of words and non-words in short-term memory: Serial order and syllable structure. In S.E. Gathercole (Ed.), *Models of short-term memory*. Hove, UK: Psychology Press.

Isaacs, E.B., & Vargha-Khadem, F. (1989). Differential course of development of spatial and verbal memory span. *British Journal of Developmental Psychology*, *7*, 377–380.

Jones, D. (1993). Objects, streams and threads in auditory attention. In A.D. Baddeley & L. Weiskrantz (Eds.), *Attention: Awareness, selection and control (A tribute to Donald Broadbent)*. Oxford: Clarendon Press.

Jones, D., Beaman, C.P., & Macken, W.J. (1996). The object-oriented episodic record model. In S.E. Gathercole (Ed.), *Models of short-term memory*. Hove, UK: Psychology Press.

Lashley, K.S. (1951). The problem of serial order in behaviour. In L.A. Jeffress (Ed.), *Cerebral mechanisms in behaviour: The Hixon Symposium*. New York: Wiley.

Lezak, M.D. (1995). *Neuropsychological assessment*. New York: Oxford University Press.

Logie, R.H. (1995). *Visuo-spatial working memory*. Hove, UK: Lawrence Erlbaum Associates Ltd.

Schofield, N.J., & Ashman, A.F. (1986). The relationship between digit span and cognitive processing across ability groups. *Intelligence*, *10*, 59–73.

Shiffrin, R., & Cook, J. (1978). Short-term forgetting of item and order information. *Journal of Verbal Learning and Verbal Behaviour*, *17*, 189–218.

Smyth, M., & Scholey, K.A. (1992). Determining spatial memory span: The role of movement time and articulation rate. *Quarterly Journal of Experimental Psychology*, *45*, 479–501.

Smyth, M.M., Pearson, N.A., & Pendelton, L.R. (1988). Movement and working memory: Patterns and positions in space. *Quarterly Journal of Experimental Psychology*, *49*, 497–514.

Vallar, G., & Baddeley, A.D. (1984). Fractionation of working memory: Neuropsychological evidence for short-term store. *Journal of Verbal Learning and Verbal Behaviour*, *23*, 151–161.

Wechsler, D. (1987). *Wechsler Memory Scale—Revised: Manual*. San Antonio, TX: Harcourt Brace Jovanovich.

Working Memory and Spoken Language Comprehension in Young Children

Anne-Marie Adams and Lorna Bourke
University of Manchester, UK

Catherine Willis
Liverpool Hope University College, UK

This study has two theoretical dimensions: (a) to explore which components of Baddeley's (1986) working memory model are associated with children's spoken language comprehension, and (b) to compare the extent to which measures of the components of this fractionated model and an index of a unitary model (listening span) are able to predict individual differences in spoken language comprehension. Correlational analyses revealed that within a group of 66 4- and 5-year-old children both listening span and phonological memory, but not visuospatial memory, were associated with vocabulary knowledge and spoken language comprehension. However, of the proposed measures of central executive function—dual task coordination, sustained attention, verbal fluency—only the latter was related to children's ability to understand spoken language. Hierarchical regression analyses indicated that variance in vocabulary knowledge was best explained by phonological memory skills, whereas individual differences in spoken language comprehension exhibited unique and independent associations with verbal fluency.

Cette étude s'intéresse à deux aspects théoriques distincts: (a) vérifier quelles composantes du modèle de mémoire de travail de Baddeley (1986) sont associées à la compréhension du langage parlé chez les enfants et (b) comparer la valeur de prédiction, au niveau des différences individuelles dans la compréhension du langage, des différentes mesures des composantes du modèle de mémoire de travail et d'un indice de modèle unitaire (empan d'écoute). Des analyses corrélationnelles montrent que dans un groupe de soixante-six enfants de 4 et 5 ans, l'empan d'écoute et la mémoire phonologique sont associés à la connaissance du vocabulaire et à la compréhension du langage. Par contre, la mémoire visuo-spatiale n'est pas reliée à ces deux habiletés. Cependant, parmi les mesures de l'unité de gestion centrale proposées (coordination de double tâche, attention soutenue et fluidité verbale) seule la fluidité verbale est reliée à la capacité de compréhension de langage chez les enfants. Des analyses de régression hiérarchique indiquent que la variance dans la connaissance du vocabulaire est mieux expliquée par les habiletés de mémoire phonologique, alors que les différences individuelles dans la compréhension du langage montrent des associations spécifiques avec la fluidité verbale.

Children learn to talk and to understand language at widely different rates. However, despite a wealth of information about the cognitive processes in skilled language processing there has been comparatively little investigation of the cognitive processes implicated in the development of expressive and receptive language skills. The present study aimed to integrate research examining the relationship between children's phonological memory and their expressive language development, with research into individual differences in adult comprehension, proposed to reflect variation in working memory capacity. Since these various studies reflect two traditions within working memory research, the models of working memory that underlie them, and the assessment tasks derived from these, will be considered next.

Daneman and her colleagues proposed that individual differences in language comprehension reflect individual differences in working memory capacity (Daneman & Carpenter, 1980). Their preferred measure of working memory is the reading span, or complex span task. Various versions of this task exist; however, all share the basic premise that the subject is required to process a series of sentences, and then to recall their final words. This task was designed to directly model the postulated functions of working memory, the simultaneous processing and storage of information. Total memory capacity is not proposed to vary between individuals, with comprehension differences arising as a result of variation in the efficiency with which information can be processed (Daneman & Tardif, 1987). Inefficient processing is

---

Requests for reprints should be addressed to Anne-Marie Adams, Department of Applied Psychology, Liverpool John Moores University, Trueman Building, 15-21 Webster Street, Liverpool, L3 2ET, UK.

This research was supported by a research grant from the Economic and Social Research Council. The authors would like to thank the children and the teachers who gave so willingly and patiently of their time to assist in the study.

© 1999 International Union of Psychological Science

considered to demand more of the limited working memory resources that could otherwise be used for storage. Thus the association between reading span and comprehension is proposed to reflect language processing differences that lead to impaired short-term retention of the sentence-final words.

This interpretation of the task and its association with comprehension has not, however, been unanimously accepted (Engle, Cantor, & Carullo, 1992). One of the most serious criticisms of this view is that an association between reading span and comprehension is potentially theoretically vacuous, since essentially what has been demonstrated is the language comprehension element in both tasks. Further to this individual differences in verbal processing skills may not best characterise individual differences in working memory abilities. Comparable associations have been obtained between a complex span task that did not require language processing skills (arithmetic processing combined with word recall) and reading comprehension (Engle et al., 1992). The model of working memory developed to account for these and related findings differentiated long-term memory (the "permanent" knowledge store), working memory (the proportion of this that can be simultaneously activated through relatively automatic processes), and short-term memory (a subset of working memory that is the current focus of attention) (Conway & Engle, 1994). Individual differences in working memory capacity are proposed to reflect differences in general attentional resources that have implications for the efficiency of inhibition processes (Engle, 1996). These inhibition processes filter out activated but irrelevant long-term memory information that would otherwise congest the limited capacity working memory. The principal aim of the current study was not, however, to choose between these theories, but to compare such theories, (here termed "unitary" models of working memory) with an alternative view of working memory resources, Baddeley's (1986) "fractionated" model. The present study investigated whether the association between complex span and adult comprehension was also evident in young children, and whether such unitary models provide a more coherent account than a "fractionated" model.

Daneman and Blennerhasset (1984) tried to measure the listening span performance of young children and relate this to their listening comprehension skills. It proved impossible, however, to prevent the children from imitating the entire sentence rather than recalling only the sentence-final words. They therefore merely demonstrated that children's ability to repeat sentences was related to their ability to understand language. In an attempt to resolve such difficulties the present study employed a sentence completion task (Towse, Hitch, & Hutton, 1998), in which the processing component requires that the child supply the missing final word of a spoken sentence. Such self-generation may help children to identify and recall the sentence-final words.

The impetus for Daneman and Carpenter's adoption of the complex span task was the desire to develop a task that reflected both the storage and processing functions of working memory. However, other researchers incorporated the contrast between processing and storage into their models and explicitly employed these distinctions to derive more constrained models of working memory. One such model, here termed the "fractionated" model, is the working memory model of Baddeley (1986). Within this model storage capabilities are disseminated to the phonological loop and the visuospatial sketch pad, specifically designed to store phonological and visuospatial information respectively. The processing function of working memory is ascribed to a separate component termed the central executive, which provides the interface with information in long-term memory and also coordinates the distribution of the limited resources throughout the memory system. Although both classes of theories of working memory have specified its importance in higher-level cognitive functions, and have actively explored the relation between working memory and language, in contrast to the work outlined above, research within the latter tradition has focused on the relationship between language and the storage capabilities of the model, particularly phonological memory skills (see Baddeley, Gathercole, & Papagno, 1998, for a review).

Associations have been identified between children's phonological memory and their vocabulary knowledge (Gathercole, Willis, Emslie, & Baddeley, 1992), with better phonological memory being associated with better vocabulary knowledge. Links have also been demonstrated between children's phonological memory and their expressive language skills (Blake, Austin, Canon, Lisus, & Vaughan, 1994), and it has proved possible to differentiate the spoken language profiles of young children grouped in terms of their phonological memory skills (Adams & Gathercole, 1995). Although evidence of phonological memory involvement in adult comprehension is weak and it is generally accepted that understanding is predominantly achieved without the need for short-term phonological storage (Caplan & Waters, 1990), a different picture may be evident during the development of comprehension skills. Four-year-old children classified as having relatively poor phonological memory abilities exhibited impaired performance on a standardised task of spoken language comprehension (Willis, 1996).

The evidence from unitary models of working memory suggests that the working memory resources implicated in comprehension may extend beyond the phonological domain, however. Independent evidence also exists that children's spoken language development (Gerken, 1991), and performance (Caramata & Schwartz, 1985) may be constrained by across-domain processing limitations. The current study will therefore consider whether associations between working memory and receptive language skills are confined to the phonological component of Baddeley's model, or whether they are also found with visuospatial memory, and perhaps particularly with central executive functions.

One factor that is likely to have contributed to the distinct focus of previous investigations of the working memory/language relationship is the imprecise characterisation of the modality-free central executive. However, recent advances in ascribing specific functions to the central executive, and the development of appropriate assessment techniques (Baddeley, 1996) may afford the opportunity to examine whether individual differences in central executive function are also related to spoken language abilities. In the present study tests modified for use with children which reflect three postulated central executive functions were examined in order to determine whether associations exist between children's receptive language abilities and central executive skills.

The executive functions examined were the search and retrieval of information from long-term memory, dual-task coordination, and sustained attention. Verbal fluency was used to assess long-term memory search and retrieval processes. The dual-task paradigm of Baddeley, Della Sala, Gray, Papagno, and Spinnler (1997a), which compares the relative detriment in performance between levels achieved when conducting two tasks in isolation to levels achieved when they are conducted simultaneously, was taken as an index of the central executive function of coordinating the simultaneous execution of two tasks. The final executive function assessed was sustained attention to response task (SART) using the task designed by Robertson, Manly, Andrade, Baddeley, and Yiend (1997). This task, developed to identify adults with impaired frontal lobe function, requires the inhibition of a highly practised response to a relatively rare target. The hypothesis tested is that individual differences in such central executive functions are associated with individual differences in children's ability to understand spoken language.

The research questions addressed in the present study can therefore be summarised as follows. Are individual differences analyses able to confirm previous evidence from group studies of associations between spoken language comprehension skills and phonological memory abilities? Are these associations limited to the phonological component of working memory or are they also associated with visuospatial memory? Since the mechanisms postulated to form the basis of the association tend not to include a visuospatial component (Adams & Gathercole, 1995) this relationship was not expected to be significant. Further questions included whether, like adults, children's language comprehension skills are associated with complex span performance and whether these associations are stronger than those found with simple span performance? Finally, is the index of "unitary" working memory (complex span) a better predictor of individual differences in language skills than phonological memory or central executive functions?

METHOD

Phase One: Screening

Participants

Children, excluding any who were receiving speech therapy or who had a history of hearing problems, were recruited from schools in the North-West of England. Three hundred and ten children (147 male and 163 female), aged between 47 and 63 months (mean age 58.28 months), produced data for each measure in the initial phase of testing.

Materials and Procedure

Phonological Memory Tests

1. *Nonword repetition.* The Children's Test of Nonword Repetition (Gathercole & Baddeley, 1996), in which the child is encouraged to copy the "funny made-up words" that the experimenter has said, was presented to each child. The number of phonemically correct repetitions was recorded (maximum = 40). The mean score on this test was 29.19 ($SD = 6.14$) ranging from 11–40 items correct.

2. *Memory span for words and digits.* Stimuli for the word span task were 12 phonologically dissimilar, single-syllable words, appropriate for children of this age (*cake, pig, box, fork, bag, bed, sun, egg, mouse, coat, duck, dog*), and for the digit span task stimuli were the digits from 1–9 (excluding the bisyllabic digit 7). Presentation lists ranged in length from two to six items with three lists at each list length. Items were presented at the rate of one item per second. Correct repetition of two of the three lists at a given length resulted in the length of the next list being increased by one item. Testing ceased when the child failed two of the three lists at a given length. Memory span (for both words and digits) was scored as the maximum length at which the child was able to repeat two lists correctly. Mean memory span for words was 3.30 ($SD = 0.69$) and for digits was 3.78 ($SD = 0.80$).

3. *Composite phonological memory score.* All three measures of phonological memory were highly intercorrelated, significant at the level $P < .001$. Nonword repetition was correlated with both word span and digit span ($r = .478$, and $r = .444$ respectively), and both measures of span were also significantly correlated ($r = .536$). To produce a composite measure of phonological memory, the scores on each of the three phonological memory measures were converted to a z score, and the mean of these scores was calculated. This value is referred to as the phonological memory score.

Nonverbal Ability. Four subscales (*Object assembly, Block design, Mazes,* and *Animal pegs*) from the Wechsler Preschool and Primary Scale of Intelligence (Wechsler, 1990) provided a Performance IQ for each child. Mean

Performance IQ, subsequently referred to as the nonverbal ability score, was 105.92 ($SD = 15.19$) ranging from 69–143.

Phase Two: Assessment

Participants

Children were selected to take part in the second phase of the study on the basis of their nonverbal ability and their phonological memory skills. All 310 children were ranked according to their composite phonological memory score, and every third child in this ranking took part in Phase Two of the study. The data are reported from 66 of these children from whom complete data sets are currently available. The mean age of these children was 60.65 ($SD = 3.05$ months) ranging between 54–66 months. Due to the number of tests to be administered, Phase Two testing was conducted in two sessions between 4 to 8 weeks apart. In the first session visual short-term memory and language skills were assessed. In the second session the children were given a listening span task and three tasks to assess central executive functions. Within each session the order of presentation of the tests was counterbalanced across children.

Materials and Procedure

Visuo-spatial memory ability

1. *Corsi blocks.* Short-term memory for visuospatial information was assessed using Corsi blocks (Isaacs & Vargha-Khadem, 1989), in which the child must replicate a sequence tapped out on a subset of randomly spaced blocks. Five sequences at each length from an initial length of two blocks were constructed. Successful completion of three sequences presented at a given length resulted in the number of blocks in the next sequence being increased by one block. Testing stopped with failure on three sequences at a given length. Span was recorded as the maximum sequence length at which three sequences were correctly reproduced.

2. *Visual pattern span.* Short-term memory for visual patterns was assessed using a paper and pencil version of the task developed by Wilson, Scott, and Power (1987). This task consisted of a series of matrices in which half the cells were randomly filled. Complexity in the task was indexed as the number of filled boxes with the initial level of complexity being two filled boxes (a 2×2 matrix). Five matrices were available for presentation at each level of complexity. The children's task was to recall the position of the filled cells in the matrices, making their responses in a booklet of blank matrices corresponding in size to each of the target patterns to be recalled. Each child was given a set of practice trials (two attempts at 2×2 and two attempts at 2×3 matrices) following the same procedure as the experimental trials. Continuation and cessation criteria were the same as those adopted for Corsi blocks. Span was calculated as the number of filled cells at which three matrices were correctly recalled.

3. *Listening span.* In this task the experimenter read out a series of sentences selected from those in Towse et al. (1998) and the child was asked to supply the missing word. At the end of a set of sentences the children were asked to recall, in the correct serial order, the words that they had supplied to complete the sentences. Initial set size was two sentences (recall two final words) with three sets of sentences available at each span length. Testing procedure followed that adopted for the word/digit span tasks—if the child correctly repeated two of the three sets of sentences at a given length then the number of sentences in the next set increased by one. The children, however, still found this task difficult, with some repeating the entire sentence rather than just the final words. Such complete imitations were scored as an incorrect response. Assessing span as the number of sentences in which the child correctly recalled the final words in two sets of sentences produced a very limited range of scores (0–2). A further score was therefore computed as per the absolute span procedure of Engle, Carullo, and Collins (1991) in order to reflect the variation between children more accurately. Absolute span was calculated as the total number of words recalled in correct trials. Thus if a child recalled two of the three words at set size two and one at set size three their absolute span score would be 7 [$(2 \times 2) + (3 \times 1)$]. Credit was not given for correct words in partially correct trials. This absolute span score is reported in the following analyses.

Central Executive. The central executive functions measured in the present study were: search and retrieval from long-term memory; dual-task coordination; and sustained attention.

1. *Search and retrieval from long-term memory (verbal fluency).* The number of exemplars from the two categories of animals and food and drink that the child was able to produce within a 30-second time limit was recorded. A practice category, items of clothing, was first presented to all the children to confirm that they understood the task requirements. Performance on the two measures of verbal fluency was highly associated, $r = .429$, $P < .001$, and in the following analyses the mean of these two verbal fluency measures is reported.

2. *Dual-task coordination.* This task was based on the dual-task paradigm of Baddeley et al. (1997a), modified for use with children. The two tasks are a tracking task and memory span for digits. First a conservative measure of the children's digit span, the longest list length at which they were able to repeat three out of three lists correctly, was obtained. The children were subsequently required to recall lists of digits at this span length for a period of 30 seconds. Performance was measured as the percentage of correctly repeated sequences (span single). For the tracking task each child was presented with an A4-size sheet of paper on which were $80 \times 2cm^2$ boxes linked by a line to form a path. The children were asked

to start at the beginning and to follow the path along by putting a mark in each of the boxes. They were told that they should try and do this as quickly as possible whilst making sure that they didn't miss any of the boxes out. A shortened version of the task formed a practice trial. Performance was assessed as the number of boxes that had been marked within the time limit of 30sec (tracking single). The children were then required to conduct both tasks simultaneously (span dual and tracking dual). The relative detriment in performance over both tasks was calculated using the mu score outlined in Baddeley et al. (1997a). This measure provides a single measure of dual-task performance as a percentage of single-task performance—a low score represents a large decrement and a high score a small decrement in performance.

3. *Sustained attention to response task (SART).* In this child's version of the task, random sequences of animals, *dog, frog, duck,* and *tortoise,* were presented singly at various locations on a computer screen for 0.5sec each. The location of the animals and the delay between successive stimulus presentations in the sequence was randomised (ranging from 1 to 2sec). Children were asked to press a computer key as soon as they saw one of these animals appear. The target animal (a dinosaur) was included in the sequence in a pre-fixed quasirandom fashion. The children were instructed not to press the space bar when the dinosaur appeared on the screen. They were asked to be as quick as they could but to be careful that they didn't press when they shouldn't. There were 60 stimulus events, in which the dinosaur appeared 5 times. A short practice trial was presented until the child was able to press for the other animals but inhibit their response to the dinosaur. For each child, target accuracy was recorded as the number of times on which they successfully refrained from pressing the key when the dinosaur appeared (maximum = 5).

Language Assessment

1. *Vocabulary comprehension.* The British Picture Vocabulary Scale (Dunn, Dunn, Whetton, & Burley, 1997), in which the child must choose which of a set of pictures represents the word spoken by the experimenter, was given to each child. Raw scores are reported, which reflect both the level reached and the number of errors made.

2. *Language comprehension.* The comprehension scale of the Reynell Developmental Language Scales (Edwards et al., 1997), a standard test of language development, was used to assess the children's spoken language comprehension skills. Toys and a picture book are employed, with the child being asked to demonstrate understanding of what the experimenter said either by pointing to a picture or by demonstrating the actions with the toys. Understanding of a range of linguistic components and constructions is tested including: single words, agents and actions, subject-verb-object constructions, adjectives, locative relations, passives and post-modifying clauses. The final section of the test assessed the children's ability to draw inferences based on real world knowledge. All the items in the test were presented to each child, resulting in a maximum score of 62.

RESULTS

Descriptive Statistics

Descriptive statistics for each of the measures assessed in Phase Two are shown in Table 1. Levels of performance in memory are comparable to previous studies (Adams & Gathercole, in press; Siegel, 1994) and in line with standardized scores for language abilities. Although each of the central executive tasks seemed to be sensitive to individual differences amongst the children, the standard on two of the tasks merits some comment. The mean target accuracy in the SART task of 44% (2.2/5 correct) compares with 70% (17.4/25 correct) for frontal lobe patients and 84% (21/25 correct) for adult controls (Robertson et al., 1997). The children are therefore performing worse than patients with impaired executive function. Dual-task coordination performance also seemed to be poor, with performance decrements in both tasks under dual-task conditions. Mu scores ranged from 29–126%, comparable to the range reported by Baddeley et al. (1997a, 54–120%) for adult control participants. However, the children's mean mu score of 71% is below the mean of the young adult controls (92%) and

TABLE 1
Descriptive Statistics for Nonverbal Ability, Phonological and Visuospatial Memory Measures, Listening Span, Central Executive Skills, and Language Abilities ($N = 66$)

Test	Mean (SD)	Range
Nonverbal ability	107.01 (14.29)	73–134
Verbal memory		
Nonword repetition (max 40)	28.42 (6.68)	11–40
Word span	3.36 (0.74)	2–5
Digit span	3.74 (0.79)	2–6
Visuospatial memory		
Corsi blocks	3.06 (1.21)	0–5
Pattern span	2.30 (0.76)	0–3
Listening span task		
Listening span	0.30 (0.72)	0–2
Absolute span score	1.56 (1.85)	0–7
Central executive skills		
Verbal fluency		
Animals	5.73 (1.87)	2–11
Food and drink	5.57 (1.98)	1–11
Mean verbal fluency	5.65 (1.63)	2–10
Sustained attention		
Target acc. (max 5)	2.20 (1.25)	0–5
Dual-task coordination		
Span single (% accuracy)	79 (23.10)	0–100
Span dual (% accuracy)	62 (34.40)	0–100
Tracking single (max 80)	39 (8.46)	22–60
Tracking dual (max 80)	22 (8.15)	6–48
Mu score	71 (22.78)	29–126
Language comprehension skills		
Vocabulary comprehension	55.79 (10.55)	34–80
Language comprehension	53.32 (3.72)	45–60

furthermore similar to that produced by dysexecutive patients (77%, Baddeley, Della Sala, Gray, Papagno, & Spinnler, 1997b). Two possibilities may explain the children's poor performance on these tasks. Either these tasks are not valid measures of central executive function in children of this age or these functions are as yet not consistently available to these children. These issues are considered further in the discussion.

Correlational Analyses

Within-domain Correlations

Table 2 reports the correlations between the phonological, visuospatial, listening span, and central executive memory measures and vocabulary and language comprehension scores. There were significant intercorrelations amongst the three phonological memory measures, and the two visuospatial memory measures were also significantly correlated. There were, however, no significant associations between absolute span and central executive skills. Nonsignificant, indeed minimal, correlations were observed between the assessments of central executive functions themselves. The implications of the relative independence of the central executive measures will be considered further in the discussion. Vocabulary comprehension showed a highly significant association with language comprehension.

Across-domain Correlations

Considering the relationship between the measures of phonological memory and visuospatial memory, Corsi blocks bore no association with any phonological memory measure whereas visual pattern span was associated only with nonword repetition skills. Absolute span was related to nonword repetition and word span, but not digit span. Of the measures of central executive function, only verbal fluency was associated with any other memory measure, being related to word span.

Hierarchical Regressions

Hierarchical regression analyses were conducted to examine these associations in more detail, primarily to consider whether any of the memory measures bore a unique association with language skills. In this technique variables that are proposed to predict variance in a criterion variable are added to the model in a theoretically constrained order. At each stage in this process the amount of variance in the criterion variable that can be accounted for by variables not yet included in the equation, or conversely the significant additional variance that they are able to explain when added to the equation, can be ascertained. In this way, it is possible to identify variables that are able to make significant and independent contributions to variance in the criterion variable. In order to limit the number of variables in these analyses, wherever possible, composite measures of the memory constructs were employed. Thus in the same way that the composite measure of phonological memory was constructed, a composite measure of visuospatial memory was created comprising the mean of the z scores for Corsi blocks and visual pattern span. Since the measures of central executive functions were not related to each other, it was not considered viable to incorporate these scores into a composite measure and they were entered into the regression equations as separate variables.

In the following analyses age and nonverbal ability were entered first to establish the degree of association between language and memory that was independent of these factors. Components of the fractionated model were entered next, with visuospatial memory first, since accounts of the association between limited capacity resources and language development do not specify a visuospatial mechanism. Central executive measures were entered next, to allow the contribution of phonological memory previously shown to be associated with language skills to be evaluated independently of this component. Absolute span as the index of unitary working memory was entered as the final variable. Alternative

TABLE 2
Correlations between the Memory and Language Measures Assessed in Phase Two ($N = 66$)

Variables	1	2	3	4	5	6	7	8	9	10	11	12
1 Age	1											
2 Nonverbal ability	.02	1										
3 Nonword repetition	.10	.25*	1									
4 Word span	.04	.18	.55**	1								
5 Digit span	−.04	.16	.41**	.56**	1							
6 Corsi blocks	.26*	.24	.11	−.08	.07	1						
7 Visual pattern span	.20	.28*	.29*	.08	.08	.30*	1					
8 Verbal fluency mean	−.07	.28*	.14	.24*	.10	.04	−.06	1				
9 Sustained attention target acc.	.14	−.05	−.07	.01	−.06	.10	.00	−.02	1			
10 Dual task (mu)	.29*	.16	.09	.14	.12	−.04	.02	.02	−.11	1		
11 Absolute span	.15	.31*	.31*	.27*	.14	.15	.17	.15	−.09	.067	1	
12 Vocabulary comprehension	.26*	.42**	.46**	.30*	.27*	.27*	.19	.21	−.06	−.00	.39**	1
13 Language comprehension	.21	.45**	.29*	.30*	.27*	.24	.13	.45**	−.07	.11	.30*	.65**

* $P < .05$; ** $P < .01$.

orderings were adopted to establish the degree of shared variance between significant predictors.

Vocabulary Comprehension as the Criterion Variable

The first regression equation (top panel of Table 3) was conducted with vocabulary comprehension as the criterion variable. Both age and nonverbal ability made significant contributions to variance in vocabulary knowledge. Neither visuospatial memory entered at the next step, nor any of the measures of central executive functions entered after this were able to predict further variance in vocabulary knowledge. Phonological memory entered at step seven explained a significant additional 9.9% of variance, while absolute span entered at step eight failed to account for a further significant proportion of variance in vocabulary knowledge. Reversing the order of the final two steps in the regression equation (see bottom panel of Table 3), absolute span entered at step seven accounted for an additional 4% of variance although this just failed to reach significance ($P = .056$). In contrast, even when the effects of all the other variables had been controlled, phonological memory remained a significant predictor, accounting for a further 8% of the variance in vocabulary knowledge. This pattern suggests that the predictive power of absolute span may merely reflect elements that it has in common with phonological memory skills.

Language Comprehension as the Criterion Variable

The first regression equation (top panel of Table 4) entered the independent variables in the same order as in the first regression in Table 3; however, this time language comprehension was the criterion variable. Nonverbal ability, but not age, predicted a significant amount of variance in language comprehension skills. Again the composite measure of visuospatial memory was unable to predict significant further variance and the same was true of the central executive measures of dual-task coordination and target accuracy in the sustained attention task. However, the central executive task of verbal fluency predicted an additional 13% of the variance in language comprehension. Neither phonological memory or absolute span entered after this could explain significant proportions of variance. In order to establish the degree of independence of verbal fluency from phonological memory and absolute span, alternative orderings of these variable were considered.

TABLE 3
Hierarchical Regressions: Vocabulary Comprehension as the Criterion Variable

Step	Inclusion Order	Total % Var.	Add. % Var.	F Value	P Value
1	Age	7	7	4.75	< .05
2	Nonverbal ability	24	17	13.95	< .01
3	Visual memory	25	1	0.70	n.s.
4	Central executive: mu	26	1	1.45	n.s.
5	Central executive: target acc.	27	1	0.87	n.s.
6	Central executive: verbal fluency	29	2	1.20	n.s.
7	Phonological memory	39	10	9.43	< .01
8	Absolute span	41	2	1.94	n.s.
7	Absolute span	33	4	3.81	.056 (n.s.)
8	Phonological memory	41	8	7.30	< .01

TABLE 4
Hierarchical Regressions: Reynell Language Comprehension as the Criterion Variable

Step	Inclusion Order	Total % Var.	Add. % Var.	F Value	P Value
1	Age	5	5	3.06	n.s.
2	Nonverbal ability	25	20	16.66	< .01
3	Visual memory	25	0	0.08	n.s.
4	Central executive: mu	25	0	0.03	n.s.
5	Central executive: target acc.	25	0	0.49	n.s.
6	Central executive: verbal fluency	38	13	12.25	< .01
7	Phonological memory	42	4	3.61	n.s.
8	Absolute span	42	0	0.37	n.s.
6	Absolute span	27	2	1.41	n.s.
7	Phonological memory	32	5	4.02	< .05
8	Central executive: verbal fluency	42	10	10.21	< .01
6	Absolute span	27	2	1.41	n.s.
7	Central executive: verbal fluency	39	12	11.59	< .01
8	Phonological memory	42	3	2.91	n.s.

The middle panel of Table 4 shows that absolute span, even when entered at step six, predicted only 2% of variance in language comprehension, with both phonological working memory and verbal fluency explaining significant further proportions of variance (5% and 10% respectively). This finding that verbal fluency makes an independent contribution to individual variation in language comprehension is highlighted by the pattern of relationships found in the final regression equation (bottom panel of Table 4). Reversing the order of the final two stages in the previous equation it is evident that the predictive power of verbal fluency does not arise merely from shared variance with phonological memory, since including phonological memory in the final stage, it is unable to predict a significant amount of variance further to that contributed by verbal fluency skills.

DISCUSSION

Working Memory and Vocabulary Comprehension

Individual differences in vocabulary knowledge were related to children's working memory skills. This was evident both when assessed by listening span and phonological memory tasks, although not generally with tasks assessing central executive function, and only weakly and inconsistently with visuospatial memory. Hierarchical regression analyses revealed that the link between vocabulary comprehension and phonological memory was significant even when individual differences in age, nonverbal ability, visuospatial memory, central executive functions, and listening span had been controlled. Such a distinct relationship confirms previous evidence of substantial links between children's vocabulary development and their phonological memory skills (Gathercole et al., 1992). The causal nature of this relationship has been the subject of much debate and the correlational nature of the present study is not informative in this regard. However, the most likely account now seems to be that the relationship is interactive; not only do phonological memory skills influence long-term learning, but word knowledge affects phonological memory performance (Baddeley et al., 1998). The specificity of these associations to the phonological component of working memory have been confirmed by the evidence presented here.

Working Memory and Language Comprehension

A rather different picture emerged with language comprehension skills. Language comprehension was again associated with both listening span and phonological memory skills and not at all related to visuospatial memory. However, although both sustained attention and dual-task coordination continued to vary independently of language comprehension, verbal fluency bore a high degree of association with this skill. The prior demonstration of differences in the language comprehension abilities of children grouped in terms of their phonological memory skills (Willis, 1996) was therefore also evident in this study at the level of the individual child. More detailed exploration of this pattern of associations in hierarchical regressions revealed that although phonological memory shared a significant degree of variance with language comprehension, this was not independent of the variance attributable to differences in verbal fluency skills. Verbal fluency was able to predict a unique and significant proportion of the variance in language comprehension.

Previous evidence of the relative ability of complex span compared to simple span to predict adult differences in reading comprehension has been equivocal. Whereas some studies have found that complex but not simple span is associated with measures of reading comprehension (Daneman & Carpenter, 1980), others have shown that simple span is able to predict reading comprehension (Engle et al., 1991). It has been suggested that a simple span/comprehension association may depend on using a sufficiently large pool of stimuli. Although the present study used a pool of only 12 stimuli, since the children made restricted progress through the possible combinations of the stimuli, relatively little repetition of items occurred in the lists presented to the children. Thus the task may well have functioned for each child as though a larger pool was available.

Although the correlation between Corsi blocks and vocabulary comprehension was significant it did not predict a significant proportion of variance in the hierarchical regression analyses. Neither of the measures of visuospatial memory were significantly related to language comprehension skills. Previous studies also suggest that the relationship between visuospatial memory skills and language abilities may be unclear. Raine, Hulme, Chadderton, and Bailey (1991) found that compared to controls, children with developmental disorders of language showed impaired memory for sequences of pictured cards, whereas with probed recall, Kushnir and Blake (1996) found no such differences. Adams and Gathercole (in press) recently noted associations between children's expressive language skills and Corsi blocks but not visual pattern span. Kushnir and Blake (1996) proposed that the discrepancy between their findings and those of Raine et al. (1991) arose from the requirement in Raine et al.'s task, but not theirs, to maintain serial order information. This is an intuitive account of the relationship between Corsi blocks but not visual pattern span in this study, however, such an account would predict a significant relationship between Corsi blocks performance and verbal span, which also requires memory for serial order that was not evident in this study. The reason for the tendency for Corsi blocks to associate with some measures of language abilities remains uncertain.

The Validity of the Central Executive

One of the aims of the present study was to compare unitary and fractionated working memory models not only on the issues on which they most markedly diverge, the assertion of independent modality-specific storage mechanisms, but also in the area in which they are most likely to converge, processing resource limitations and operations ascribed to the central executive. A particular aim was to determine the extent to which these models made relative contributions to the higher-level cognitive function of language comprehension. Such proposed theoretical convergence of unitary models and central executive function was not supported by the current empirical evidence, either in terms of associations between central executive functions and complex span assessment, or of comparable links with language comprehension skills. Although contrary to the current data, Rosen and Engle (1994, cited in Engle, 1996) showed that verbal fluency was linked to performance in a complex span task.

Perhaps a more serious problem arises when considering the theoretical validity of the central executive construct itself. Although previous work has demonstrated some degree of association between the postulated measures of executive function adopted in the present study, i.e. between dual-task coordination and verbal fluency (Baddeley et al., 1997b), no significant inter-correlations were observed in the present data. The lack of significant inter-relations between executive, frontal, and working memory tasks has been noted previously (Lehto, 1996). Finding inconsistent associations between various simple and complex span measures and executive measures taken from neuropsychological research, Lehto concluded that the evidence supported not a single executive system, but one whose component functions could be differentiated. Discussing such evidence and the interface between his model and unitary models of working memory, Baddeley conceded that more evidence was needed to determine whether a single executive should be postulated, or whether various functions may diverge to reveal an executive committee (Baddeley, 1996). The present findings, extending previous within-individual inconsistencies between performance on alternative executive tasks from adults to children, thus aligns more closely with the proposal of a central executive committee, rather than a single executive director. It is of course also possible that these functions may be differentially implicated in various higher-level cognitive tasks. To extend the metaphor further, one of the committee member's primary responsibilities may be the selection and manipulation of information maintained in the long-term store of knowledge (cf. Rosen & Engle, 1994). The evidence presented here, although only correlational, is consistent with the proposal that this executive function may have particular implications for the comprehension of spoken language in young children.

Alternative interpretations of the differences within individuals across the various executive tasks do exist, however. Despite attempts to reduce the difficulty of the tasks, they may simply not be valid indices of children's central executive functions. Further work is needed to address this and refine executive tasks to render them applicable for use with children. The challenge of measuring the degree of association between executive skills and language processing in children may be further complicated by the contention that executive skills may not yet be fully developed in children of this age—an implication of the late development of the frontal cortex (Johnson, 1997). In line with this the children's pattern of performance, although reflecting quite large individual differences, did attribute to children on both SART and dual-task coordination, mean achievement levels that were comparable to patients with executive impairment.

Verbal Fluency as a Measure of Working Memory

The executive function revealed as the most likely candidate for the mechanism that might underlie the association between working memory and language comprehension was verbal fluency. However, the particular process that it reflects remains unclear. One intuitive proposal, that individual differences in vocabulary knowledge may explain performance on both tasks, can, however, be discredited by the present data. If this were so, one would expect the contribution of word knowledge to verbal fluency skills to be represented in a significant relationship between verbal fluency and vocabulary comprehension, a relationship that was not evident in this study.

It is necessary, therefore, to identify another aspect of verbal fluency that may underlie its association with language comprehension abilities. Research by Engle and his colleagues exploring the nature of the mechanisms underlying performance in complex span tasks may provide some insight into this issue. This work developed from his account of memory divided into long-term memory, working memory—the activated proportion of long-term memory—and short-term memory—the proportion of working memory that is under the current focus of attention (Conway & Engle, 1994). On the basis of a series of experiments manipulating the "fan size effect" they concluded that differences in working memory capacity reflected not differences in the time to make long-term memory active but the time to conduct controlled processes to search, retrieve, or to focus attention on particular aspects of long-term memory that were already active in working memory.

Engle's (1996) model of working memory, which he accepts bears some comparison with the central executive, maintains that individual differences in working memory are due to individual differences not in the amount of information in long-term memory that can be activated at any one time, but to individual differences in attentional resources, which are required to inhibit irrelevant information in working memory. A central element of this research was that verbal fluency is intimately related to complex span assessment at least partly because it reflects the availability of such controlled attentional resources. Although the current correlational data are insufficient to confirm any particular account of the association between working memory and language comprehension, they are nevertheless consistent with the proposal that verbal fluency may bear a particular association with children's language processing skills since it reflects their ability to conduct controlled and hence effortful processing of long-term information. Specific processes may include activating the semantic correlates of the phonological forms that they perceive, manipulating or attending to these when they are activated in working memory, or inhibiting information which, although activated, is irrelevant to the current comprehension task.

REFERENCES

Adams, A.-M., & Gathercole, S.E. (1995). Phonological working memory and speech production in pre-school children. *Journal of Speech and Hearing Research*, 38(2), 403–414.

Adams, A.-M. & Gathercole, S.E. (in press). Limitations in working memory: Implications for language development. *International Journal of Language and Communication Disorders*.

Baddeley, A.D. (1986). *Working memory*. Oxford: Oxford University Press.

Baddeley, A.D. (1996). Exploring the central executive. *The Quarterly Journal of Experimental Psychology*, 49A(1), 5–28.

Baddeley, A., Della Sala, S., Gray, C., Papagno, C., & Spinnler, H. (1997a). Testing central executive functioning with a pencil-and-paper test. In P. Rabbitt (Ed.), *Methodology of frontal and executive function*. Hove, UK: Psychology Press.

Baddeley, A., Della Sala, S., Gray, C., Papagno, C., & Spinnler, H. (1997b). Dual-task performance in dysexecutive and non-dysexecutive patients with a frontal lesion. *Neuropsychology*, 11(2), 187–194.

Baddeley, A.D. Gathercole, S.E., & Papagno, C. (1998). The phonological loop as a language learning device. *Psychological Review*, 105(1) 158–173.

Blake, J., Austin, W., Canon, M., Lisus, A., & Vaughan, A. (1994). The relationship between memory span and measures of imitative and spontaneous language complexity in preschool children. *International Journal of Behavioural Development*, 17(1), 91–107.

Caplan, D., & Waters, G.S. (1990). Short-term memory and language comprehension: A critical view of the psychological literature. In G. Vallar & T. Shallice (Eds.), *Neuropsychological impairments of short-term memory* (pp. 337–389). Cambridge: Cambridge University Press.

Caramata. S.M., & Schwartz, R.G. (1985). Production of object words and action words: Evidence for a relationship between phonology and semantics. *Journal of Speech and Hearing Research*, 28, 323–330.

Conway, A.R.A., & Engle, R.W. (1994). Working memory and retrieval: A resource-dependent inhibition model. *Journal of Experimental Psychology: General*, 123, 354–373.

Daneman, M., & Blennerhassett, A. (1984). How to assess the listening comprehension skills of prereaders. *Journal of Educational Psychology*, 76(6), 1372–1381.

Daneman, M., & Carpenter, P.A. (1980). Individual differences in working memory and reading. *Journal of Verbal Learning and Verbal Behavior*, 19, 450–466.

Daneman, M., & Tardif, T. (1987). Working memory and reading skill re-examined. In M. Coltheart (Ed.), *Attention and performance XII: The psychology of reading* (pp. 491–508). Hove, UK: Lawrence Erlbaum Associates Ltd.

Dunn, L., Dunn, L., Whetton, C., & Burley, A. (1997). *The British Picture Vocabulary Scale* (2nd ed). Windsor, UK: NFER-Nelson.

Edwards, M., Fletcher, P., Garman, D., Hughes, D., Letts, P., & Sinka, S. (1997). *Reynell Developmental Language Scales, (III): The University of Reading Edition*. Windsor, UK: NFER-Nelson.

Engle, R.W. (1996). Working memory and retrieval: An inhibition-resource approach. In J.T.E. Richardson (Ed.), *Working memory and human cognition* (pp. 89–119). New York: Oxford University Press.

Engle, R.W., Cantor, J., & Carullo, J.J. (1992). Individual differences in working memory for comprehension: A test of four hypotheses. *Journal of Experimental Psychology: Learning Memory and Cognition*, 18, 972–992.

Engle, R.W., Carullo, J.J., & Collins, K.W. (1991). Individual differences in working memory for comprehension and following directions. *Journal of Educational Research*, 84, 253–262.

Gathercole, S.E., & Baddeley, A.D. (1996). *The Children's Test of Nonword Repetition*. London: Psychological Corporation.

Gathercole, S.E., Willis, C., Emslie, H., & Baddeley, A.D. (1992). Phonological memory and vocabulary development during the early school years: A longitudinal study. *Developmental Psychology*, 28, 887–898.

Gerken, L. (1991). The metrical basis for children's subjectless sentences. *Journal of Memory and Language*, 30, 431–451.

Isaacs, E.B., & Vargha-Khadem, F. (1989). Differential course of development of spatial and verbal memory span: A normative study. *British Journal of Developmental Psychology*, 7, 377–380.

Johnson, M.H. (1997). *Developmental cognitive neuroscience*. Oxford: Blackwell Publishers.

Kushnir, C.C., & Blake, J. (1996). The nature of the cognitive deficit in specific language impairment. *First Language*, 16(1), 21–41.

Lehto, J. (1996). Are executive function tasks dependent on working memory capacity? *Quarterly Journal of Experimental Psychology*, 49A(1), 29–50.

Raine, A., Hulme, C., Chadderton, H., & Bailey, P. (1991). Verbal short-term memory span in speech-disordered children: implications for articulatory coding in short-term memory. *Child Development*, 62, 415–423.

Robertson, I.H., Manly, T., Andrade, J., Baddeley, B.T., & Yiend, J. (1997). "Ooops!": Performance correlates of everyday attentional failures in traumatic brain injured and normal subjects. *Neuropsychologia*, 35(6), 747–758.

Rosen, V., & Engle, R.W. (1994). Working memory capacity and retrieval from long-term memory. Unpublished manuscript.

Siegel, L.S. (1994). Working memory and reading: A life-span perspective. *International Journal of Behavioural Development*, 17 (1), 109–124.

Towse, J., Hitch, G.J., & Hutton, U. (1998). A re-evaluation of working memory capacity in children. *Journal of Memory and Language*, 39(2), 195–217.

Wechsler, D. (1990). *Wechsler Preschool and Primary Scale of Intelligence* (revised UK ed.). London: Psychological Corporation.

Willis, C.S. (1996). *Working memory and children's language processing*. Unpublished PhD thesis, Lancaster University.

Wilson, J.T.L., Scott, J.H., & Power, K.G. (1987). Developmental differences in the span of visual memory for pattern. *British Journal of Developmental Psychology*, 5, 249–255.

Verbal and Spatial Short-term Memory: Two Sources of Developmental Evidence Consistent with Common Underlying Processes

Y. M. Lisa Chuah and Murray T. Maybery
The University of Western Australia, Australia

Developments in serial short-term memory (STM) typically have been assessed using verbal items, and mechanisms of development unique to the verbal system have been postulated. Here we review two studies of the development of spatial STM. The first (Chuah & Maybery, 1999) showed that variance in spatial span was partitioned among a set of predictor variables in a configuration very similar to that found for verbal span. The second (Maybery & Chuah, 1999) examined the timing of recall for spatial sequences. Intervals between touches as children recalled spatial sequences showed comparable effects to those reported for the oral recall of verbal sequences. Discussion focuses on processes that could serve both verbal and spatial memory and mediate span development.

Le développement de la mémoire sérielle à court terme (MCT) a typiquement été évaluée utilisant des items verbaux. De plus, l'existence de mécanismes uniques au développement du système verbal a été postulée. Nous revoyons ici deux études du développement de la MCT spatiale. La première (Chuah & Maybery, 1999) montre qu'on peut rendre compte de la variance dans une tâche d'empan spatial à l'aide d'une configuration de variables très similaire à celle que l'on trouve pour l'empan verbal. La seconde étude (Maybery & Chuah, 1999) examine l'organisation temporelle du rappel de séquences spatiales. Les intervalles entre les réponses de pointage des enfants sont comparables à ce qui est rapporté pour le rappel oral de séquences verbales. Ces données sont discutées en abordant les processus qui pourraient être à la base du développement de l'empan en soutenant à la fois la mémoire verbale et spatiale.

The development across childhood in short-term memory (STM) for sequences of verbal items is well documented; however, there remains considerable debate as to its source (Chuah & Maybery, 1999). On the other hand, the development in STM for spatial sequences has only recently attracted attention, and there is little debate as to its source. Here we review two studies that report similarities in the development of verbal and spatial STM.

APPLICATION OF THE WORKING MEMORY MODEL TO DEVELOPMENT

According to the working memory model (Baddeley, 1986), different classes of information are handled by different systems. The phonological loop maintains verbal information using two mechanisms, a phonological store and a subvocal rehearsal process. The speech-like representations held in the store decay within approximately 2sec unless refreshed by the rehearsal mechanism. Therefore verbal memory span should be restricted to the number of items that can be rehearsed in about 2sec. In relation to development, it has been argued that increases in rehearsal rate with age result in larger verbal spans because more items can be refreshed before they decay. This proposition has been supported by findings of a linear relationship between articulation rate and verbal span using different age groups (Hitch & Halliday, 1983).

Researchers have also proposed storage and rehearsal mechanisms for the visuospatial sketchpad. However, the structure of the purported visuospatial rehearsal mechanism is uncertain. Smith and Jonides (1997) argued for a rehearsal process that involves shifting attention between representations of location. This proposal derives from their neuroimaging work, which showed that spatial STM tasks that required rehearsal and tasks that required shifts in visual attention activated similar right-hemisphere regions. However, there is little direct evidence for this mechanism, and any limitations of the sketchpad due to developmental differences have not been enunciated clearly. Nevertheless, the proposition of separate specialized systems carries the implication of independent sources of limitations in verbal and spatial span that may be reflected in different patterns of change with age.

Requests for reprints should be addressed to Lisa Chuah, Psychology Department, The University of Western Australia, Western Australia 6907, Australia (Tel: +618 9380 1420; Fax: +618 9380 1006; E-mail: lisa@psy.uwa.edu.au).

© 1999 International Union of Psychological Science

Accepting that changes in the efficiency of specialized mechanisms contribute uniquely to the development of verbal and spatial STM, it may nevertheless be possible that the two forms of memory develop in concert if the major contribution to development comes from broad changes in neural efficiency. In several recent studies, Kail has investigated the relative contributions of broad indices of processing efficiency versus indices focused on purported rehearsal mechanisms in accounting for developments in verbal and spatial STM.

First, Kail and Park (1994) used indices of articulation rate and general speed of processing in investigating the development of verbal span. Their path analysis appeared to support the working memory account of verbal-span development because the only contribution of speed of processing to span appeared to be through articulation rate. However, the contribution of speed was tested only after controlling for articulation rate *and age*. This test would therefore fail to identify any age-related contribution of speed that was independent of articulation rate. It is likely that most of the change in processing speed is linked to maturation, so controlling for age may mask a substantial contribution to verbal span from global changes in speed. Furthermore, the contribution of articulation rate found by Kail and Park was independent of age as well as processing speed, so it reflects a source of individual differences other than age. This analysis is therefore not ideal in isolating the factors contributing to span development. Kail (1997) used a similar analytic approach in studying spatial memory, where the conclusion was that the efficiency of a mechanism for regenerating visuospatial images plays a critical role in mediating the effects of age and processing speed on spatial span.

AGE-RELATED AND AGE-INDEPENDENT CONTRIBUTIONS TO VERBAL AND SPATIAL SPAN

The aims of the first study we precis (Chuah & Maybery, 1999) were to (1) adapt a methodology that would better identify age-related and age-independent contributions to span, and (2) compare verbal and spatial span in a single study, with particular reference to the factors contributing to their development.

To evaluate the factors influencing the development of span, the variance of interest must be the *age-related* variance in span. Figure 1 illustrates how variance in span accounted for by three predictor variables, age, processing efficiency, and articulation rate, can be split into seven components. Some components represent age-related variance in span, others represent variance accounted for by predictor variables excluding age. Kail's analyses centred on the components of variance unique to the predictor variables, such as area c, an age-independent contribution of articulation rate. To estimate all the contributions, we employed a regression-based variance-partitioning procedure described by Salthouse (1994). Salthouse also developed a *quasi-partial* correlation coefficient (r_{qp}) based on the proportion of *age-related* variance in a criterion variable that is systematically related to a predictor variable.

The children in the Chuah and Maybery (1999) study were administered verbal and spatial span tasks, articulation and tapping rate tasks, and verbal and spatial speed of search tasks. The verbal span task used auditorily presented letter sequences, and recall was oral. The spatial span task used sequences of illuminating squares on a computer screen, and recall was by touch. Articulation rate involved rapid repetition of letters, whereas tapping rate involved repetitive tapping of computer-screen locations. The two search tasks used either letters or spatial locations as stimuli.

Age, articulation rate, and speed of search were regressed onto verbal span for comparison to Kail and Park's (1994) results. The major contribution to predicting verbal span was the component common to age, speed of search, and articulation rate (r_{qp} = .90 for region g in Fig. 1). There was little evidence that changes in articulation rate, other than those that can be accounted for by general changes in speed, are involved in the development of verbal span. There was a contribution of articulation rate that was independent of age, but this did not appear to be due specifically to rehearsal of verbal items because the same contribution appeared when spatial span was the criterion variable. In fact, the corresponding analysis of spatial span yielded a remarkably similar pattern of results. The main contributor was again the component common to age, speed, and articulation rate (r_{qp} = .88). When articulation rate was replaced with tapping rate, the patterns of results for verbal and spatial span were again very similar. In each case, the major component of predicted variance in span

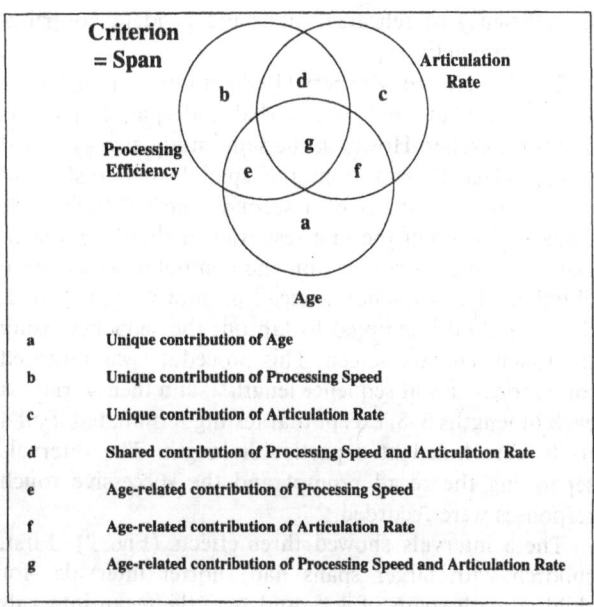

FIG. 1. Components of variance in span accounted for by age, processing efficiency, and articulation rate (from Chuah & Maybery, 1999).

was that common to age, speed, and tapping rate (r_{qp} = .89 for verbal span; r_{qp} = .91 for spatial span). Further analyses using predictors formed into verbal and spatial composites also generated very similar outcomes in predicting verbal and spatial span.

TIMING OF RECALL FROM SPATIAL STM

The preceding study showed that the same configuration of predictors accounted for variance in verbal and spatial span. This promotes the view that a common source of development underpins verbal and spatial STM, but does not compel the view that common *processes* subserve the two. It is plausible that independent modality-specific systems are subject to fundamental changes universal in scope, such as increases in neural efficiency (Case, 1985). The study reviewed next provides more direct evidence of processes common to verbal and spatial STM by showing that several timing-of-recall effects reported for verbal STM also exist for spatial STM.

Cowan et al. (1998) have argued that differences among individuals in verbal span are attributable to two independent sources, the efficiency of rehearsal and the efficiency of processes that operate when information is retrieved from memory. As a sequence of verbal items is reported orally, silent intervals occur between the production of neighbouring items. These intervals are assumed to reflect retrieval processes engaged in locating the next item to be reported. Individuals with larger spans show shorter silent intervals than do individuals with smaller spans. Also, the silent intervals are longer the larger the sequence to be reported (Cowan et al., 1994). In their most recent work, Cowan et al. (1998, Experiment 1) showed that the efficiency of retrieval and the efficiency of rehearsal made independent contributions to predicting span.

The Chuah and Maybery (1999) study was concerned principally with predicting verbal and spatial span, as described earlier. However, the same study also provided timing-of-recall data from the spatial span task, and these were the subject of a second report (Maybery & Chuah, 1999). On the first test trial of the spatial span task, 2 of the 19 squares on the computer screen were illuminated in sequence, a recall prompt was presented, then the child attempted to tap out the sequence using the touch-sensitive screen. This procedure was repeated for 3 more trials at sequence length 2, and then 4 trials at each of lengths 3–8, except that testing terminated if all 4 trials were failed at a particular length. The intervals separating the recall prompt and the successive touch responses were recorded.

These intervals showed three effects (Fig. 2). First, children with larger spans had shorter intervals—for children with spans of 4, 5, and ≥ 6, the mean intervals collapsed across sequence lengths 2–4 were 740msec, 714msec and 618msec, respectively. Second, the intervals increased with each increment in length of the sequence—for sequences of length 2–4, the mean intervals were 639msec, 700msec and 734msec, respectively. Furthermore, the increase in interval as a function of sequence length was smaller for children with larger spans (Fig. 2). These effects for spatial recall are consistent with Cowan's findings in the verbal domain, and therefore motivate a theoretical account that includes common processes subserving spatial and verbal STM.

THEORETICAL ACCOUNTS OF COMPARABLE DEVELOPMENTAL EFFECTS FOR VERBAL AND SPATIAL STM

In proposing that the silent intervals during recall are occupied by a memory-search process that locates the next item to be reported, Cowan et al. (1998) identified this search process with the (modality-independent) functioning of the central executive. This proposal is consistent with the evidence reviewed earlier that the timing-of-recall effects hold for spatial as well as verbal STM. It can also accommodate the regression analyses reported by Chuah and Maybery (1999) if it is assumed that the efficiency of the search process is critical to span, and that efficiency improves with age in concert with the efficiency of other processes.

Cowan et al. (1998) also suggested that this memory-search process is the same process that Sternberg (1966)

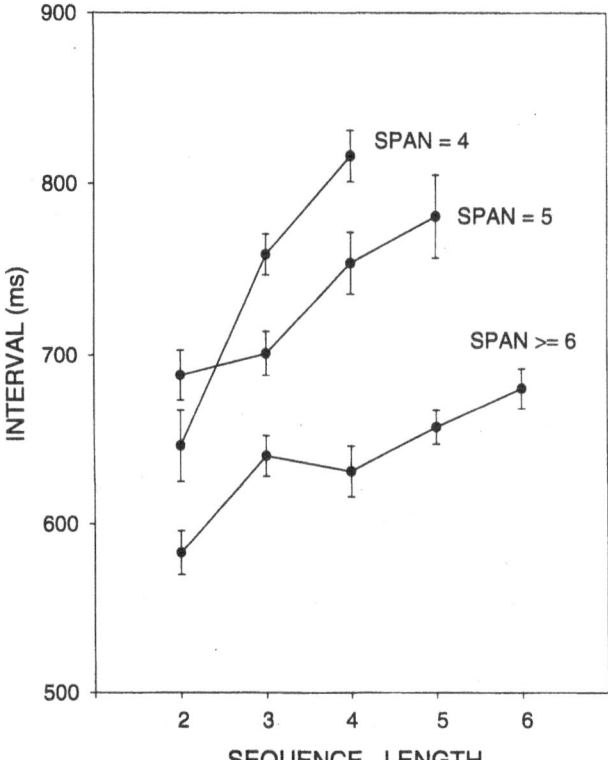

FIG. 2. Recall interval as a function of sequence length and span, where error bars index one standard error (from Maybery & Chuah, 1999).

isolated for a short-term recognition task. In a typical trial of the recognition task, a sequence of verbal items within the individual's span is studied and then a probe item, which may or may not be from the sequence, is presented. Sternberg reported that RT to the probe increased linearly as a function of sequence length. This effect is comparable in form to the effect of sequence length on the duration of the silent pauses when an entire sequence is recalled, as in span tasks. Sternberg argued that the increase in RT as a function of sequence length indexed the rate of the search process. However, Sternberg (1969) also established that the search process for his recognition task has different characteristics to that for a single-item recall task. In the latter task, the memory sequence is again followed by a probe item, but the probe is always contained in the sequence, and the participant reports the next item along in the sequence. This task provided a search rate substantially slower than the search rate for the recognition task. Also, for the single-item recall task, RTs increased the further along in the sequence the probe was positioned. No such serial position effect was found for the recognition task. Sternberg (1969) noted that the critical difference between the recognition and single-item recall tasks is that only the latter requires retention of the order of the sequence. Hence there appear to be two qualitatively different memory search processes—one operating when order information must be retained, the other when order information need not be retained.

In the tasks used by Cowan and ourselves in reporting the timing-of-recall effects, full and ordered recall of the memory sequences is required, so ordered search is presumed. Our tentative conclusion is therefore that an ordered search process common to verbal and spatial STM is likely to play a critical role in span development. Whether such a process is considered the province of the central executive in the tripartite working memory system (Baddeley, 1986) or part of a unitary memory system (Jones, Beaman, & Macken, 1996) is a moot point.

REFERENCES

Baddeley, A.D. (1986). *Working memory*. Oxford: Oxford University Press.

Case, R. (1985). *Intellectual development: Birth to adulthood*. Orlando, FL: Academic Press.

Chuah, Y.M.L., & Maybery, M.T. (1999). Verbal and spatial short-term memory: Common sources of developmental change? *Journal of Experimental Child Psychology, 73*, 7–44.

Cowan, N., Keller, T.A., Hulme, C., Roodenrys, S., McDougall, S., & Rack, J. (1994). Verbal memory span in children: Speech timing clues to the mechanisms underlying age and word length effects. *Journal of Memory and Language, 33*(2), 234–250.

Cowan, N., Wood, N.L., Wood, P.K., Keller, T.A., Nugent, L.D., & Keller, C.V. (1998). Two separate verbal processing speeds contributing to verbal short-term memory span. *Journal of Experimental Psychology: General, 127*(2), 141–160.

Hitch, G.J., & Halliday, M.S. (1983). Working memory in children. *Philosophical Transactions of the Royal Society (London), Series B, 302*, 325–340.

Jones, D.M., Beaman, P., & Macken, W.J. (1996). The object-oriented episodic record model. In S.E. Gathercole (Ed.), *Models of short-term memory*. Hove, UK: Psychology Press.

Kail, R. (1997). Processing time, imagery, and spatial memory. *Journal of Experimental Child Psychology, 64*, 67–78.

Kail, R., & Park, Y.-S. (1994). Processing time, articulation time, and memory span. *Journal of Experimental Child Psychology, 57*(2), 281–291.

Maybery, M.T., & Chuah, Y.M.L. (1999). *The timing of children's recall from spatial short-term memory*. Manuscript submitted for publication.

Salthouse, T.A. (1994). How many causes are there of aging-related decrements in cognitive functioning? *Developmental Review, 14*(4), 413–437.

Smith, E.E., & Jonides, J. (1997). Working memory: A view from neuroimaging. *Cognitive Psychology, 33*(1), 5–42.

Sternberg, S. (1966). High speed scanning in human memory. *Science, 153*, 652–654.

Sternberg, S. (1969). Memory-scanning: Mental processes revealed by reaction-time experiments. *American Scientist, 57*, 421–457.

Estimating the Capacity of Phonological Short-term Memory

Susan E. Gathercole and Susan J. Pickering
University of Bristol, UK

Two methods of assessing the capacity of phonological short-term memory that minimize support from long-term memory were compared in a sample of 7- and 8-year-old children. The children were tested on immediate serial recall of words and nonwords, and on the serial recognition of sequences composed of words and nonwords. Serial recognition scores were found to be highly related to children's accuracy of recall of nonwords composed of low-probability phonotactic combinations, but were independent of the long-term memory contributions to recall estimated in the serial recall experiment. Children with high vocabulary knowledge performed significantly better than low vocabulary children on both the recall and recognition measures. It is argued that the convergence of the two techniques lends substantial validity to their use as assessments of phonological storage capacity relatively free of long-term memory influence, and that the crucial difference between children varying in vocabulary knowledge lies in this storage capacity rather than the differential availability and use of long-term knowledge.

Deux méthodes permettant d'évaluer la capacité de la mémoire à court terme phonologique en minimisant la contribution de la mémoire à long terme (MLT) ont été comparées chez des enfants de 7 et 8 ans. Une tâche de rappel sériel ainsi qu'une tâche de reconnaissance sérielle de mots et de non-mots ont été utilisées. Les résultats montrent que les scores de reconnaissance sérielle sont fortement reliés à la capacité de rappeler des non-mots, mais qu'ils sont indépendants des contributions de la MLT. La performance des enfants ayant une bon vocabulaire était plus élevée aux mesures de rappel et de reconnaissance. Il est proposé que la convergence des deux techniques donne une validité substantielle à leur utilisation afin d'évaluer la capacité d'emmagasinage phonologique exempte des influences de la MLT. De plus, les résultats suggèrent que les différences observées dans la connaissance du vocabulaire chez les enfants résident dans la capacité d'emmagasinage plutôt que dans une différence au niveau de la disponibilité et de l'utilisation des connaissances en mémoire à long terme.

The extent to which permanent knowledge structures contribute to immediate verbal memory performance has been a topic of considerable interest in recent years. The memory mechanisms responsible for the temporary storage of verbal material are known to be highly sensitive to the physical properties of memory items such as articulatory duration and acoustic similarity (see Baddeley, 1997, for review). It has, however, become increasingly apparent that serial recall is also strongly influenced by properties of the to-be-remembered stimuli that are related to non-physical dimensions of memory stimuli: These dimensions include lexicality (Hulme, Maughan, & Brown, 1991), word frequency (Hulme et al., 1997), and imageability (Bourassa & Besner, 1994). Even memory for unfamiliar nonword stimuli is not free of potential long-term memory support: Recall of nonwords is affected by the phonotactic frequency of their phonological segments (Gathercole, Frankish, Pickering, & Peaker, 1999; Vitevitch, Luce, Charles-Luce, & Kemmerer, 1997). The impact of these variables on memory performance must necessarily arise from the contact made with stored knowledge about the memory items at some point between their presentation and their recall, as they are not signalled by the physical properties of the stimuli. The contribution of these sources of long-term knowledge to memory performance is substantial. Consider lexicality: It is not unusual to find that serial recall accuracy diminishes by more than 50% when the memory lists are composed of unfamiliar nonwords rather than familiar words (Gathercole, Pickering, Hall, & Peaker, 1998).

These findings of robust contributions of nonphysical dimensions of memory stimuli to immediate memory performance indicate the need for caution in interpreting poor scores on verbal short-term memory tests. Low scores may reflect either restricted storage capacity of the temporary memory mechanisms or weak support from long-term memory. The issue is an important one. Performance on tests of immediate verbal memory is known to relate closely to abilities to learn the phonological forms of language (see Baddeley, Gathercole, & Papagno, 1998, for review). There is now substantial evidence that individuals with reduced capacities for

---

Requests for reprints should be addressed to Susan E. Gathercole, Department of Experimental Psychology, University of Bristol, 8 Woodland Road, Bristol BS8 1TN, UK (Tel: +117 9288449; Fax: +117 9288588; E-mail: sue.gathercole@bristol.ac.uk).

This research was supported by a Medical Research Council programme grant G9423916 on "Working Memory and Learning Disability," awarded to Alan Baddeley and Susan Gathercole.

immediate recall, as a consequence of either developmental or acquired problems, encounter highly selective deficits in learning the sound patterns of new words (e.g. Baddeley, Papagno, & Vallar, 1988; Baddeley & Wilson, 1994; Gathercole & Baddeley, 1990). Before this natural relationship can adequately be explained, it is crucial that methods are developed that permit evaluation of whether the low scores obtained by such individuals on conventional tests of immediate memory such as word recall and digit span reflect diminished capacities in the phonological short-term memory system or reduced contribution of long-term knowledge to immediate memory.

The present study compared two methods of measuring immediate verbal memory, both of which were designed to minimize the contribution of long-term knowledge and hence to provide relatively pure assessments of the capacity of the temporary phonological memory system. The first method involved measuring serial recall for spoken lists composed of three types of one-syllable items: words, and nonwords composed of segments which were either low or high in phonotactic frequency. Testing 7- and 8-year-old children on these list types, Gathercole, Frankish et al. (1999) devised a method of obtaining separate estimates of the contributions made to recall of (1) the basic capacity of the phonological memory system to store verbal material, (2) the contribution of stored lexical knowledge, and (3) the contribution of knowledge concerning phonotactic probabilities of the language. Phonological storage capacity free of lexical support was indexed by the child's recall performance on lists containing low probability nonwords: It was reasoned that as these stimuli benefited from neither the possibility for lexical support or from favourable phonotactic frequencies, recall was mediated by the temporary phonological memory system. The contribution of phonotactic knowledge to recall was estimated by calculating the difference in recall scores for high- and low-probability nonwords, and lexical support was calculated in terms of the recall difference for lists composed of words and high-probability nonwords. Applying this subtractive technique to recall scores in the three list conditions, Gathercole, Frankish et al. (1999) estimated that approximately 50% of immediate recall of words in their experiments was supported by temporary phonological memory, 40% by lexical knowledge, and 10% by phonotactic knowledge.

The second method is serial recognition, a variant of a procedure also known as matching span. Like serial recall, serial recognition involves sequential presentation of to-be-remembered items. Following a brief interval after presentation of the list, the same set of items is re-presented either in the identical sequence to the first list, or with two of the adjacent items in the original sequence transposed. The participant's task is to judge whether the two sequences were the same or different. This paradigm has proved useful in the study of immediate memory capacities of individuals with language and speech-motor pathologies: Unlike serial recall, it places few demands on spoken output processes, and so provides an assessment of phonological storage capacity that is uncontaminated by compromised output abilities (e.g. Allport, 1984; Campbell & Butterworth, 1985; Martin & Breedin, 1992; Shallice & Warrington, 1977). Evidence that serial recognition is indeed a valid test of phonological short-term memory is provided by a recent report by Gathercole, Hitch, Service, Adams, and Martin (1999) that serial recognition scores correlate highly both with two recall-based measures of immediate memory (digit span and nonword repetition), and with measures of receptive vocabulary knowledge.

The serial recognition paradigm is not only appealing because of its lack of reliance on potentially artifactual speech output skills. It also appears that serial recognition performance is relatively impervious to lexicality, a variable which, as discussed earlier, has a substantial impact on recall accuracy. Gathercole, Pickering, Hall and Peaker (1999) found very little difference in the accuracy of serial recognition judgements for lists composed of either words or nonwords. These findings indicate that long-term knowledge may not be tapped in serial recognition as strongly as in serial recall, possibly because participants do not have to reconstruct the memory sequence for output in serial recognition. This reconstructive process has been suggested to be the source of the lexicality effect (Brown & Hulme, 1992; Hulme et al., 1991), so any procedure that diminishes reliance on this process may indeed be expected to show reduced sensitivity to the lexicality of the memory stimuli.

According to the theoretical analysis presented earlier, two techniques provide relatively pure estimates of the functional capacity of phonological short-term memory: serial recall of low-probability nonwords and serial recognition. If this is the case, the two measures should correlate highly with one another. Estimates of lexical and phonotactic contributions to recall, in contrast, should be independent of serial recognition ability. In this article, data are presented from a single sample of 7- and 8-year-old children whose phonological memory abilities were assessed using the two techniques: serial recall and serial recognition. The sample was composed of two groups of children, selected on the basis of having either relatively high or low vocabulary knowledge, although matched for general nonverbal intelligence. Detailed analyses of the results from the two experiments are reported by Gathercole, Frankish et al. (1999) and Gathercole, Pickering et al. (1999). In the present report, the main focus is on the interrelationships between the three parameter estimates obtained from the serial recall paradigm (phonological memory, lexical, and phonotactic) and scores on the serial recognition test.

METHOD

Participants

Twenty-nine children with a mean chronological age of 8 years 1 month (range 7 years 6 months to 8 years 6 months) participated in the two experiments.

The children were selected from a larger sample of 102 children attending a large state primary school in Bristol, England, who were given the British Picture Vocabulary Scale-Long Form (Dunn, Whetton, Dunn, & Pintilie, 1983) receptive vocabulary test. Fifteen children were selected on the basis of obtaining relatively low scores on the vocabulary test; this group had a mean standardized score of 96.7 ($SD = 7.0$). The remaining 14 children were high scorers on the vocabulary measure: This group had a mean standardized score of 121.4 ($SD = 6.8$). A further vocabulary test administered following group selection confirmed the reliability of membership of the two vocabulary groups. On the Expressive One-Word Picture Vocabulary Test (Gardner, 1990), mean standardized scores were 103.6 ($SD = 7.7$) for the low vocabulary children and 11.7 ($SD = 7.0$) for the high vocabulary group. The two groups were matched on a measure of nonverbal ability, Raven's Progressive Matrices (Raven, 1986). The mean raw score on this test was 27.3 ($SD = 3.0$) for the low vocabulary group, and 27.8 ($SD = 3.4$) for the high vocabulary children.

Each child was tested individually in a quiet area of the school. The two experiments were administered on separate days, separated in each case by an interval of less than 2 weeks.

Design and Procedure

Full details of the design and procedure for the serial recall experiment are provided by Gathercole, Frankish et al. (1999), and for the serial recognition experiment by Gathercole, Pickering et al. (1999). The basic structure of the two experiments is described next.

Serial Recall

Each child was tested on immediate serial recall of four kinds of lists, each containing monosyllable CVC items. The list types were words (e.g. *hip*, *van*), and three sets of nonwords: nonwords composed of high probability biphones (e.g *bip,*), nonwords composed of low-probability biphones (e.g. *keb*, *vook*), and nonwords with extremely low-probability final biphones (e.g. *bez*, *chorg*). The high- and low-probability nonwords were matched for initial consonants, vowels, and final consonants, and were distinguished only in the sequence of combination of the consonants and vowels. Seven lists were presented for each list type, sampling randomly and without replacement from each stimulus pool, and list type was blocked across successive trials. Order of testing list types was counterbalanced across participants. Presentation was auditory, at the rate of one every .75sec.

Following spoken presentation of each four-item list, the child was required to attempt immediate recall of the items in the same sequence as they were presented. The testing session was recorded onto an audiocassette, which was used as the basis for later scoring of the recall protocols on a phoneme-by-phoneme basis. For the present purposes, recall accuracy was scored at the item level: Each item was scored as correct if it was spoken accurately (i.e. all three phonemes correct in identity and sequence) and recalled in the correct position in the sequence. For each participant, the number of items correctly recalled was scored in each condition (maximum score = 28).

Serial Recognition

Each child received 30 lists of 1-syllable words and 30 lists of 1-syllable nonwords for serial recognition. Presentation was auditory, at the rate of one item every .75sec with a .75sec additional delay prior to the first item in the second sequence. Within each list type, there were six lists each containing two, three, four, five, and six items. At each length, half of the lists were the same (i.e. same words presented in same sequence on both occasions) and half of the lists were different (same items, order of one pair of adjacent items transposed on second presentation). List type (words and nonwords) was blocked and order of testing counterbalanced across participants. Length of list was also blocked, and increased successively by one item after each block of six trials. For each child, the number of lists correctly recognized as either same or different was scored. The maximum score was therefore 60.

RESULTS

Mean scores in the serial recall and serial recognition experiments as a function of vocabulary group are shown in Table 1. Serial recall data for the nonwords with very low-probability final biphones are not reported, as they were not used in the parameter estimation procedure. Recall accuracy was consistently higher for the children with high than low vocabulary. Data analysis reported by Gathercole, Frankish et al. (1999) established a main effect of vocabulary group on serial recall scores, with no interaction between group and list type. Recall was significantly greater for words than high-probability non-

TABLE 1
Summary of Scores on the Principal Measures for the Two Vocabulary Groups

| | Vocabulary Group | | | |
| | Low | | High | |
Measure	Mean	SD	Mean	SD
Chronological age (months)	96.0	4.1	98.1	2.5
Serial recall				
Words	17.5	5.3	24.0	4.8
High-probability nonwords	9.3	4.5	17.1	6.0
Low-probability nonwords	7.5	4.4	13.6	5.9
Serial recall parameter estimates				
I (intact)	7.5	4.4	13.5	5.9
L (lexical)	8.3	4.5	6.9	5.0
P (phonotactic)	1.8	3.6	3.6	3.6
Serial recognition				
Lists correct	48.6	5.6	54.6	4.2

words, and for nonwords containing high-probability rather than low-probability biphones.

The three parameters were estimated in the following method, for each participant. I (recall of intact memory trace) corresponded to recall score for the low-probability nonwords. P (phonotactic parameter) was the difference between recall scores for high- and low-probability nonwords. L (lexical parameter) was calculated as the high-probability nonword recall score subtracted from the word recall score. An analysis of covariance was performed on the I scores as a function of group, with age in months and nonverbal ability score (Raven) covaried. A highly significant effect of group was found [$F(1,25) = 7.96$, $MSe = 26.57$, $P < .01$]. Corresponding analyses of covariance established no such vocabulary group differences for either the L parameter [$F(1,25) = 1.43$, $MSe = 22.17$, $P > .05$] or the P parameter [$F(1,25) = 2.36$, $MSe = 13.4$, $P > .05$].

Analysis of covariance performed on the serial recognition scores as a function of group, with age and Raven score covaried, showed a significant effect of group [$F(1,25) = 7.16$, $MSe = 20.76$, $P < .05$]. This reflects the higher levels of recognition accuracy for the high than low vocabulary group.

Of primary interest are the interrelationships between the serial recall parameter estimates and the serial recognition scores. Table 2 shows the simple correlation coefficients and the partial correlation coefficients, with age and scores on the nonverbal ability test partialled out. A very clear pattern of associations and dissociations emerged, both for the simple and partial correlational analyses. The I serial recall parameter (the estimate of basis phonological storage capacity) correlated very highly with accuracy of serial recognition for both words and nonwords, with simple correlation coefficients of .50 and .66 ($df = 27$, $P < .001$), respectively. These relationships remained significant when differences attributable to age and nonverbal ability were partialled out. Significant although somewhat weaker negative correlations were found between the two serial recognition measures and the M (missing) parameter: for word recognition, $r(27) = -.37$, $P < .05$, and for nonword recognition, $r(25) = .59$, $P < .001$. The negative correlation coefficient between word recognition and the M parameter was reduced to a nonsignificant level when age and nonverbal ability were taken into account.

No significant associations were, however, found between the serial recognition measures and either the L (lexical) parameter or the P (phonotactic) parameter. The same pattern of a highly positive association of serial recognition scores with I but not L or P was found when differences attributable to age and nonverbal scores were partialled out.

The only other significant association was the strongly negative correlation coefficient between the L and P parameters, as noted by Gathercole, Service, Hitch, Adams, and Martin (1999). This feature of the serial recall results suggests that there may be a tradeoff between the use of lexical and phonotactic knowledge to support recall. It should, however, be noted that the L and P parameters are not statistically independent, as increases in performance on the highly wordlike nonword lists diminish the L parameter but increase the P parameter. Further independent assessment of the strength of the lexically and phonotactically mediated routes to recall are therefore required to explore this possible tradeoff between the two strategies further.

DISCUSSION

Children's scores on two tests of immediate verbal memory, recall of nonwords composed of low-probability phoneme combinations and the recognition of sequences of word and nonword stimuli, were highly correlated with one another: Individuals with high levels of accuracy in nonword recall also performed well at judging the order of sequences in the serial recognition task. Significant links were not, however, found between serial recognition performance and the extent to which the children used either lexical or phonotactic knowledge to support immediate serial recall. These findings lend substantial support to the validity of serial recall of low-probability nonwords and serial recognition of verbal sequences as methods of assessing the storage capacity of phonological short-term memory that effectively bypass the sometimes substantial contributions to immediate recall of long-term knowledge.

TABLE 2
Correlations between Parameter Estimates Derived from Serial Recall and Serial Recognition Measure

	1	2	3	4	5	6
1 I (intact)	—	-.30	-.12	-.72	*.41*	*.61*
2 L (lexical)	-.19	—	-.54	.09	-.06	-.24
3 P (phonotactic)	-.12	-.54	—	-.15	.21	.12
4 M (missing)	-.75	.01	-.12	—	-.28	-.54
5 Serial recognition—words	*.50*	.07	.16	-.37	—	*.65*
6 Serial recognition—nonwords	*.66*	-.07	.06	-.59	*.72*	—

Lower triangle shows zero-order correlation coefficients, $df = 27$.
Upper triangle shows partial correlation coefficients, with age and Raven scores partialled out, $df = 25$.
Coefficients printed in italic are significant at 5% level.

Importantly, the two assessment techniques provide convergent evidence that the close developmental associations between vocabulary knowledge and phonological memory skills that have been discovered in recent years reflect the common contribution of the temporary phonological memory system rather than long-term knowledge. In both experiments, children with superior vocabulary knowledge performed substantially better on the measures believed to provide the most sensitive indicators of storage capacity: recall of low-probability nonwords and serial recognition. In combination, these two techniques appear to provide a simple and reliable method of investigating the source of low performance on tests of phonological short-term memory that is appropriate for use with both developmental and adult participant populations.

REFERENCES

Allport, D.A. (1984). Auditory-verbal short-term memory and conduction aphasia. In H. Bouma and D.G. Bouwhuis (Eds.), *Attention and performance X: Control of language processes* (pp. 313–326). Hove, UK: Lawrence Erlbaum.

Baddeley, A.D. (1986). *Working memory*. Oxford: Oxford University Press.

Baddeley, A.D. (1997). *Human memory: Theory and practice* (2nd ed.). Hove, UK: Psychology Press.

Baddeley, A.D., Gathercole, S.E., & Papagno, C. (1998). The phonological loop as a language learning device. *Psychological Review, 105*, 158–173.

Baddeley, A.D., & Hitch, G. (1974). Working memory. In G.A. Bower (Ed.), *Recent advances in learning and motivation, Vol. 8*. New York: Academic Press.

Baddeley., A.D., Papagno, C., & Vallar, G. (1988). When long-term learning depends on short-term storage. *Journal of Memory and Language, 27*, 586–595.

Baddeley, A.D., & Wilson, B.A. (1993). A developmental deficit in short-term phonological memory: Implications for language and reading. *Memory, 1*, 65–78.

Bourassa, D.C., & Besner, D. (1994). Beyond the articulatory loop: A semantic contribution to serial order recall of subspan lists. *Psychonomic Bulletin and Review, 1*, 122–125.

Brown, G.D.A., & Hulme, C. (1992). Cognitive psychology and second language processing: The role of short-term memory. In R.J. Harris (Ed.), *Cognitive approaches to bilingualism* (pp. 105–122). Amsterdam: North Holland/Elsevier Science Publishers.

Campbell, R., & Butterworth, B. (1985). Phonological dyslexia and dysgraphia in highly literate subjects: A developmental case with associated deficits of phonemic processing and awareness. *Quarterly Journal of Experimental Psychology, 37A*, 435–476.

Dunn, L.M., Whetton, C., Dunn, L.M., & Pintilie, L. (1983). *The British Picture Vocabulary Scale*. Windsor, UK: NFER-Nelson.

Gardner, F.M. (1990). *The Expressive One-Word Picture Vocabulary Test (Revised)*. Novato, CA: Academic Therapy Publications.

Gathercole, S.E., & Baddeley, A.D. (1990). The role of phonological memory in vocabulary acquisition: A study of young children learning new names. *British Journal of Psychology, 81*, 439–454.

Gathercole, S.E., & Baddeley, A.D. (1993). *Working memory and language*. Hove, UK: Lawrence Erlbaum Associates Ltd.

Gathercole, S.E., Frankish, C.R., Pickering, S.J., & Peaker, S.H. (1999). Phonotactic influences on serial recall. *Journal of Experimental Psychology: Learning, Memory, and Cognition, 25*, 84–95.

Gathercole, S.E., Hitch, G.J., Service, E., & Martin, A.J. (1997). Phonological short-term memory and new word learning in children. *Developmental Psychology, 33*, 966–979.

Gathercole, S.E., Pickering, S.J., Hall, M., & Peaker, S.M. (1999). Lexical and phonological influences on serial recognition and serial recall. Manuscript undergoing revision.

Gathercole, S.E., Service, E., Hitch, G., Adams, A.M., & Martin, AJ. (1999). Phonological short-term memory and vocabulary development: Further evidence on the nature of the relationship. *Applied Cognitive Psychology, 13*, 65–77.

Hulme, C., Maughan, S., & Brown, G.D.A. (1991). Memory for familiar and unfamiliar words: Evidence for a longer term memory contribution to short-term memory span. *Journal of Memory and Language, 30*, 685–701.

Hulme, C., Roodenrys, S., Schweikert, R., Brown, G.D.A., Martin, S., & Stuart, G. (1997). Word-frequency effects on short-term memory tasks: Evidence for a redintegration process in immediate serial recall. *Journal of Experimental Psychology: Learning, Memory, and Cognition, 23*, 1217–1232.

Martin, R.C., & Breedin, S.D. (1992). Dissociations between speech perception and phonological short-term memory deficits. *Cognitive Neuropsychology, 9*, 509–534.

Raven, J.C. (1986). *Coloured Progressive Matrices*. London: H.K. Lewis.

Shallice, T., & Warrington, E.K. (1977). Auditory-verbal short-term memory impairment and conduction aphasia. *Brain and Language, 4*, 479–491.

Vitevitch, M.S., Luce, P.A., Charles-Luce, J., & Kemmerer, D. (1997). Phonotactics and syllable stress: Implications for the processing of spoken nonwords. *Language and Speech, 40*, 47–62.

Phonological Short-term Memory and Foreign Language Learning

Elvira V. Masoura and Susan E. Gathercole
University of Bristol, UK

This study investigated links between short-term memory skills and children's abilities to learn the vocabulary of a foreign language taught in school. Forty-five Greek children who were learning English as a foreign language were assessed on their short-term memory in both languages, and on their knowledge of both native and foreign vocabulary. Knowledge of native and foreign vocabulary shared highly significant associations with the phonological short-term memory measures. However, vocabulary scores in the two languages shared a close relationship that could not be explained exclusively in terms of phonological loop capacity. Implications of these findings for theoretical accounts of how words are learned in the native and foreign language are considered.

Cette étude explore les liens entre les habiletés de mémoire à court terme et la capacité des enfants à apprendre le vocabulaire d'une langue étrangère. Quarante-cinq enfants grecs ont été évalués au plan de leur mémoire à court terme et de leur connaissance du vocabulaire dans les deux langues (grec et anglais). La connaissance du vocabulaire dans les deux langues est fortement associée aux mesures de mémoire à court terme phonologique. Cependant, même si la relation entre les deux scores de connaissance du vocabulaire est très forte, celle-ci ne peut être expliquée exclusivement en terme de capacité de la boucle phonologique. La discussion porte sur les implications de ces résultats pour des hypothèses théoriques expliquant l'apprentissage des mots dans une langue maternelle et dans une langue étrangère.

Recent research has revealed a close link between language acquisition and the capacity of the verbal component of working memory, the phonological loop (see Baddeley, Gathercole, & Papagno, 1998, for review). There is evidence indicating that the phonological loop plays an important role in supporting the long-term learning of the phonological forms of previously unfamiliar words in the acquisition of vocabulary in foreign as in native languages. Service (1992) found that the single best predictor of success in learning English at school was the children's accuracy in repeating unfamiliar nonwords and established that nonword repetition was specifically associated with foreign language vocabulary acquisition rather than with other aspects of foreign language learning (Service & Kohonen, 1995). Learning of foreign words has found to be benefited by repetition at initial presentation in several studies (Ellis & Beaton, 1993a; Ellis & Sinclair, 1996).

Evidence that phonological short-term memory representations contribute significantly to native vocabulary learning is provided by both longitudinal and experimental studies with children. Gathercole and Baddeley (1989) reported that children's abilities to repeat unfamiliar nonwords at 4 years of age significantly predicts their vocabulary a year later, at age 5. In a further study, it was found that children with relatively good phonological short-term memory skills for their age were also better and faster at learning previously unfamiliar names of toy animals (Gathercole & Baddeley, 1990).

Recent investigations indicate that long-term knowledge of the structure of the language may also influence ease of learning new lexical material. The predictors of success in learning new foreign words in an experimental task were found to vary with the amount of vocabulary children had already acquired in that language (Cheung, 1996). However, new word learning ability in children with low vocabulary scores in their second language was best predicted by their phonological short-term memory skills. The same dependency upon short-term memory was not detected for children who had already acquired an extensive vocabulary in their foreign language (Chen & Leung, 1989). A decreasing reliance of vocabulary learning upon short-term memory, possibly due to a concomitant increase in support from the substantial base of existent word knowledge, has been found also in development of native vocabulary. Gathercole, Willis, Emslie, and Baddeley (1992) studied the native vocabulary acquisition of a cohort of children aged between 4 and 8 years of age, and found beyond 5 years of age clear evidence that existing vocabulary determines both phonological memory performance and further vocabulary development.

Requests for reprints should be addressed to Elvira V. Masoura, Department of Experimental Psychology, University of Bristol, Bristol BS8 1TN, UK (Tel: +1179288564; Fax: +1179288588; E-mail: E.Masoura@bristol.ac.uk).
The first author of this article is funded by the State Scholarship Foundation in Athens, Greece.

© 1999 International Union of Psychological Science

Another indication that long-term memory contributes to immediate memory is provided by the findings that memory span is greater for lists composed of native than foreign words (Hulme, Maughan, & Brown, 1991), a phenomenon that seems likely to reflect the lack of phonological lexical representations for unfamiliar words (Brown & Hulme, 1992). Long-term knowledge may also contribute to the recall of nonwords. Gathercole, Frankish, Pickering, and Peaker (1999) found that children recalled nonword sequences more accurately if the nonwords contain high than low-probability phonotactic segments, suggesting that knowledge of the probabilistic structure of the language may support memory performance (see also Gathercole, Willis, Emslie, & Baddeley, 1991; Vitevitch, Luce, Charles-Luce, & Kemmerer, 1997). Those findings suggest that the children's knowledge about rules and constraints of the phonological system of the native language can be used to enhance short-term memory performance.

The relationship between short-term memory and long-term knowledge therefore appears to be reciprocal: Phonological loop capacity promotes learning of phonological patterns of new words, and stored knowledge of the phonological structure of the language supplements the phonological loop. One implication of this analysis is that existing vocabulary knowledge will itself indirectly contribute to the learning of new vocabulary.

The possible trade-off between long-term vocabulary knowledge and phonological short-term memory is investigated in the present study of a group of Greek children learning English as a foreign language in school. The children were aged between 9 and 11 years, and had been studying English on a regular basis for 3 years on average. Previous investigations of the relationship between short-term memory and vocabulary acquisition have investigated either native vocabulary (e.g. Gathercole & Baddeley, 1989; Michas & Henry, 1994) or foreign vocabulary (e.g. Papagno, Valentine, & Baddeley, 1991; Papagno & Vallar, 1995; Service & Kohonen, 1995). A novel feature of the present study was that vocabulary knowledge of both languages was assessed, enabling us to make direct comparisons of the degree of dependency upon phonological short-term memory of native and foreign vocabulary acquisition.

Phonological short-term memory skills were also measured in both languages: The children were tested on their immediate repetition of both Greek (native) and English (foreign) nonwords. Three other factors that may contribute to ease of learning foreign vocabulary were also assessed: chronological age, nonverbal ability, and period of study of the foreign language.

In the present report, an additional focus concerned the association between knowledge of native and foreign vocabulary. We aimed to assess whether vocabulary knowledge was strongly related across the two languages and if so, whether this relationship could be accounted for simply in terms of the mediating influence of phonological short-term memory skills.

METHOD

Participants

Forty-five children attending a public primary school in Greece participated in this experiment. The mean age of the group was 10 years 3 months (range: 8 years 8 months to 11 years 8 months). All children were being taught English as a foreign language by the same teacher at their school. The mean period of study of English was 3 academic years (range from 1 to 5 years). The time children had spent learning English was estimated by a short interview with the parents, and confirmed by checking the school records. Every full academic year the child had been taught English was counted as 1 year of study, and children who had dropped the English classes for more than 5 months considered as having missed a year.

Design and Materials

Phonological Short-term Memory Measures

Repetition of English nonwords was assessed using the Children's Test of Nonword Repetition (CNRep; Gathercole & Baddeley, 1996). The test was administrated by a Greek native speaker experimenter. Each of the 40 nonwords was scored as either correct or incorrect, with no penalty for the characteristic prosody of a Greek accent provided that the phonemes were correct. The total number of correct repetition attempts (maximum = 40) was scored for each child. *Wordlikeness* measures were obtained for all test items by a small group of 20 Greek adults who were asked to rate each spoken nonword on a 5-point scale ranging from 1 (very likely to pass for a real word in Greek) to 5 (very unlikely to pass for a real word in Greek). The instructions emphasized that the rating should not be based on how similar the nonword is with a particular word, but on the extent to which its sound structure would pass for a real Greek word. The mean rating for each nonword was calculated; the mean value was 1.88 (*SD* 0.50).

In order to test the repetition of Greek nonwords, a Greek version of the CNRep was constructed. The test contained 50 nonwords, 10 each containing 2, 3, 4, 5, and 6 syllables. Examples of nonwords are *lalmae* and *vokrietan*. All the test items were also assessed for *wordlikeness* by Greek adults (mean value 2.78, *SD* 0.71). The stimuli of the test were phonotactically legal in Greek and followed the dominant stress patterns of the language. The Greek nonwords were presented to the children following the procedure developed for the CNRep (Gathercole & Baddeley, 1996).

Nonverbal Ability

The revised booklet edition of the Coloured Progressive Matrices (Raven, 1986) was administered to each child. The total number of items correct was scored for each child.

Native Vocabulary Measures

Native vocabulary knowledge was assessed using two measures, a receptive and a productive test. Receptive vocabulary knowledge was tested using a Greek translation of the short form of the British Picture Vocabulary Scale (Dunn, Dunn, Whetton, & Pintilie, 1982). On each trial of this test, the child is shown a page containing four line drawings. The test administrator speaks a single word to the child, whose task is to point to the drawing that corresponds to the spoken word. The test was translated into Greek by a native Greek speaker (EM). It was necessary to replace a small number of test stimuli that were judged likely to be unfamiliar to Greek children. For example, the word *socket* was replaced because the drawing does not correspond to the Greek electric sockets.

Productive vocabulary was assessed using the Word Definition subtest of the WISC III-UK (Wechsler, 1974). The test was translated into Greek. In this test, 30 words are presented for definition by the child. Two credits are given for every response that indicates good understanding of the word, one credit for every response that shows poverty of content, and zero for every incorrect definition of the word. The total sum of credits was scored for each child.

Foreign Vocabulary Measures

Two tests of the children's knowledge of English vocabulary were given, both involving translation between the spoken English and Greek forms of words. In the native-to-foreign translation test, the children were asked to provide the best English translation for 60 Greek words. In the foreign-to-native test, the children attempted to provide the best Greek equivalent to 60 different English words. The items were presented auditorily by a native Greek experimenter with good knowledge of English. The vocabulary items included in both tests were selected from the English textbooks used by the children in school (Triandafellou, 1996). The items were arranged in order of difficulty, with words that had been taught at the initial stages of learning appearing earlier in the tests than the words introduced later in tuition. Translation attempts were counted as correct only if both meaning and part of speech were accurately represented. That is, for the Greek word *ksafneka*, the English translation *suddenly* would count as correct, but not the English word *sudden*. One credit for every correct translation and zero for every incorrect translation of the word were given to each child. The total number of correct translation attempts of each child in each test was scored (maximum = 60).

Procedure

Children were tested individually in a single session lasting for about 1 hour. The order of the tests was held constant across all children. The order of administration of the tasks was as follows: nonverbal ability, Greek nonword repetition, English nonword repetition, translation foreign-to-native, translation native-to-foreign, native vocabulary receptive, native vocabulary productive.

RESULTS

Descriptive statistics for each measure are provided in Table 1. Repetition accuracy scores for the native and foreign nonwords were compared by calculating the number of correct responses on each test for the 40 items containing 2, 3, 4, and 5 syllables. A two-way analysis of variance with language and length as the within-subject variables established highly significant effects of both language $[F(1,45) = 86.6, P < .001]$ and length $[F(1,45) = 73.72, P < .001]$, replicating the frequent finding that phonological memory performance is better for familiar rather than unfamiliar lexical material. The children performed comparably on translating between Greek and English words regardless of the direction of the translation, with the two translation measures correlated highly with one another $[r(45) = .95, P < .001]$.

The lower triangle of Table 2 shows the correlation coefficients between all principal test scores. A Greek (native) vocabulary composite score was obtained by averaging the z-scores of the two vocabulary tests. The same procedure was followed to obtain a composite foreign vocabulary score from the two word translation tasks.

The English (foreign) vocabulary measure was significantly correlated with both foreign and native nonword repetition measures. Similarly, the composite Greek

TABLE 1
Means, Standard Deviations, and Ranges for all Measures

Measures	Mean	SD	Range
English nonword repetition			
2-syllable nonwords	5.58	1.63	2–9
3-syllable nonwords	5.73	1.48	2–8
4-syllable nonwords	3.89	2.07	0–10
5-syllable nonwords	3.36	1.81	0–7
Total	18.56	4.73	6–26
Greek nonword repetition			
2-syllable nonwords	7.22	1.62	3–10
3-syllable nonwords	7.92	1.51	3–10
4-syllable nonwords	5.27	1.47	2–8
5-syllable nonwords	5.38	1.67	1–8
6-syllable nonwords	3.29	1.38	0–6
Total	29.09	5.33	11–37
Native vocabulary measures			
Productive vocabulary	29.45	7.74	13–52
Receptive vocabulary	20.44	5.5	4–29
Foreign vocabulary measures			
Translation foreign-to-native	22.78	15.87	0–54
Translation native-to-foreign	21.09	11.90	0–48
Translation total	43.57	27.27	0–120
General measures			
Nonverbal ability	24.71	5.41	12–35
Length of study	3.30	2.19	1–5
Chronological age (months)	123.87	12.11	106–142

TABLE 2
Correlations between Principal Measures

Measures	1	2	3	4	5	6	7
1 Greek nonword repetition total		.47**	.43**	.44**			
2 English nonword repetition total	.48**		.31*	.43*			
3 Greek (native) vocabulary	.50**	.35*		.56**			
4 English (foreign) vocabulary	.36*	.39**	.66**				
5 Nonverbal ability	.24	.24	.40**	.34*			
6 Length of study	.04	.16	.03	.73**	.05		
7 Chronological age (months)	.03	.31*	.36*	.32*	.34*	.43**	

Lower triangle presents simple correlations coefficients, $df = 45$; upper triangle presents partial correlations after nonverbal ability, length of study and age partialled out, $df = 39$.
* $P < .05$; ** $P < .001$; all others nonsignificant.

(native) vocabulary score was significantly correlated with both native and foreign nonword repetition. Composite Greek and English vocabulary scores were strongly associated with one another.

In order to explore the specific relationship between nonword repetition and vocabulary in both languages, the potentially confounding influences of chronological age, nonverbal ability, and length of study were partialled out. The partial correlations are shown in the upper triangle of Table 2. Both native and foreign vocabulary scores remained significantly correlated with the nonword repetition measures after age, nonverbal ability and length of study had been partialled out. No significant differences were found between these correlation coefficients ($P > .05$, in all cases), indicating comparable associations between nonword repetition accuracy and both native and foreign vocabulary knowledge. The partial correlation between native and foreign vocabulary scores remained highly significant.

Finally, we wished to establish whether the close association between native and foreign vocabulary is mediated by the common link shared with performance on nonword repetition task. In order to test this possibility, a composite repetition score was computed for each child, based on the mean z-score for each of the Greek and English nonword repetition scores. Combining these measures in this way was judged to be appropriate, as both individual measures had been shown to share equivalent strengths of association with the two measures of vocabulary knowledge. The unique associations between each of the three composite scores (nonword repetition, native vocabulary, and foreign vocabulary) were then explored by partialling out the third variable in each case by controlling at the same time for chronological age, nonverbal ability, and length of English study. Foreign and native vocabulary scores remained highly associated with each other after repetition scores had been partialled out [$r(43) = .42$, $P < .05$]. Foreign vocabulary scores remained significantly associated with repetition scores after native vocabulary had been taken into account [$r(43) = .32$, $P < .05$]. However, when foreign vocabulary scores were partialled out, native vocabulary scores no longer maintained a significant link with nonword repetition [$r(43) = .30$, $P > .05$].

DISCUSSION

Highly significant links were found between children's phonological memory skills, as assessed by nonword repetition accuracy, and their knowledge of vocabulary in both native and foreign languages. These findings confirm and extend previous studies charting associations between short-term memory and vocabulary knowledge in both the native language (e.g. Gathercole & Baddeley, 1990; Michas & Henry, 1994) and in foreign languages (Cheung, 1996; Service, 1992; Service & Kohonen, 1995). The relationship between phonological short-term memory and foreign vocabulary was found to be independent of more general factors such as chronological age, nonverbal ability, and length of time spent studying the foreign language.

A unique feature of the present study was that both phonological memory skills and vocabulary knowledge were assessed in both languages, enabling us to make direct comparisons of the strengths of the associations across languages. Two features of the findings are notable. First, there was evidence for language specificity in the link between scores on the nonword repetition and vocabulary knowledge tests. Knowledge of foreign but not of native vocabulary was associated with nonword repetition independently both of general factors (age and nonverbal ability) and also of vocabulary competence in the native language. That children's learning of foreign vocabulary may be particularly highly dependent upon temporary phonological memory rather than native vocabulary acquisition may be due to the greater unfamiliarity of foreign words. There is more opportunity for support from lexical phonological knowledge in the learning of native words, and this may reduce the dependency on phonological short-term memory. On the basis of previous evidence that long-term knowledge of the structure of the language boosts immediate memory performance for nonwords (Gathercole et al., 1991; Gathercole et al., 1999; Vitevitch et al., 1997), this feature of the data is not surprising. It should be also noted that the superior levels of repetition accuracy in all syllable lengths for native than foreign nonwords does lend further weight to previous evidence of language specificity in memory for nonwords (Thorn & Gathercole, 1999).

Second, it was found that knowledge of native and foreign vocabulary shared extremely close links, which cannot be accounted for simply in terms of shared contributions of phonological short-term memory to long-term learning in the two cases. An implication of this finding is that an individual's capacity to learn the sound system of a language is strongly influenced by factors other then phonological short-term memory and any full account of vocabulary acquisition needs to identify what these factors may be. One possible explanation for the present finding is that the children participating in this study had learned many of the foreign words by direct association with the equivalent native words, in line with the dominant method of foreign language teaching employed in Greek schools. This account is certainly consistent with previous evidence that in the initial stages of foreign language acquisition, new words are learned via associations with native words (Chen & Leung, 1989; Kolers, 1966). In later stages, in contrast, children appear to be able to acquire foreign words directly, without associating them with the corresponding native words (Horst, Cobb, & Meara, 1998).

In summary, the present study both supplies further evidence of close associations between phonological memory and vocabulary knowledge in both native and foreign languages, and demonstrates that factors other than short-term memory place important constraints on an individual's capacity to learn new words. The findings suggest that in a second language, new vocabulary can be acquired by a process of bootstrapping onto the secure knowledge base already established for the native language and, as a consequence, the ease of learning new words in a foreign language is strongly influenced by the stability and extent of representations of native vocabulary. For individuals learning new languages in different contexts such as total immersion, however, this degree of dependency of foreign vocabulary acquisition on native language may be significantly diminished.

REFERENCES

Baddeley, A.D. (1986). *Working memory.* Oxford: Clarendon Press.

Baddeley, A.D., Gathercole, S.E., & Papagno, C. (1998). The phonological loop as a language learning device. *Psychological Review, 105*(1), 158–173.

Baddeley, A.D., & Hitch, G.J. (1974) Working memory. In G. Bower (Ed.), *The psychology of learning and motivation, Vol. 8* (pp. 47–90). New York: Academic Press.

Brown, G.D.A., & Hulme, C. (1992). Cognitive psychology and second language processing: The role of short-term memory. In R.J. Harris (Ed.), *Cognitive approaches to bilingualism* (pp. 105–121). Amsterdam: Elsevier Science Publishers.

Chen, H.-C., & Leung, Y.-S. (1989) Patterns of lexical processing in a non-native language. *Journal of Experimental Psychology: Learning, Memory and Cognition, 15*(2), 316–325.

Cheung, H. (1996). Nonword span as a unique predictor of second-language vocabulary learning. *Developmental Psychology, 32*(5), 867–873.

Crothers, E., & Suppes, P. (1967). *Experiments in second-language learning.* New York: Academic Press.

Dunn, L.M., Dunn, L.M., Whetton, C., & Pintilie, D. (1982). *British Picture Vocabulary Scale.* Windsor: NFER-Nelson.

Ellis, N.C., & Beaton, A. (1993a). Psycholinguistic determinants of foreign language vocabulary learning. *Language Learning, 43*, 559–617.

Ellis, N.C., & Beaton, A. (1993b). Factors affecting the learning of foreign language vocabulary: Imagery, keyword mediators and phonological short-term memory. *Quarterly Journal of Experimental Psychology, 46A*, 533–558.

Ellis, N.C., & Sinclair, S.G. (1996). Working memory in the acquisition of vocabulary and syntax: Putting language in good order. *Quarterly Journal of Experimental Psychology, 49A.* 234–250.

Gathercole, S.E., & Baddeley, A.D. (1989). Evaluation of the role of phonological STM in the development of vocabulary in children: a longitudinal study. *Journal of Memory and Language, 28*, 1–14.

Gathercole, S.E., & Baddeley, A.D. (1990). The role of phonological memory in vocabulary acquisition: A study of young children learning new names. *British Journal of Psychology, 81*, 439–454.

Gathercole, S.E., & Baddeley, A.D. (1996). *The Children's Test of Nonword Repetition.* London: The Psychological Corporation.

Gathercole, S.E., Frankish, C.R., & Peaker, S.H. (in press). *Probabilistic constraints on nonword repetition.* Manuscript submitted for publication.

Gathercole, S.E., Frankish, C.R., Pickering, S.J., & Peaker, S.H. (1999). Phonotactic influences on serial recall. *Journal of Experimental Psychology: Learning, Memory and Cognition, 25*, 84–95.

Gathercole, S.E., Willis, C.S., Emslie, H., & Baddeley, A.D. (1991). The influences of syllables and wordlikeness on children's repetition of nonwords. *Applied Psycholinguistics, 12*, 394–367.

Gathercole, S.E., Willis, C.S., Emslie, H., & Baddeley, A.D. (1992). Phonological memory and vocabulary development during the early school years: A longitudinal study. *Developmental Psychology, 28*, 887–898.

Horst, M., Cobb, T., & Meara, P. (1998). Beyond a clockwork orange: Acquiring second language vocabulary through reading. *Reading in a Foreign Language, 11*(2), 207–223.

Hulme, C., Maughan, S., & Brown, G.D.A. (1991). Memory for familiar and unfamiliar words: Long-term memory contribution to short-term memory span. *Journal of Memory and Language, 30*, 685–701.

Kolers, P.A. (1966). Interlingual facilitation of short-term memory. *Journal of Verbal Learning and Verbal Behaviour, 5*, 314–319.

Lenneberg, E.H. (1967). *Biological foundations of language.* New York: John Wiley & Sons.

Long, M.H. (1990). Maturational constraints on language development. *Studies in Second Language Acquisition, 12*, 251–285.

Michas, I.C., & Henry, L.A. (1994). The link between phonological memory and vocabulary acquisition. *British Journal of Developmental Psychology, 12*, 147–163.

Papagno, C., Valentine, T., & Baddeley, A. (1991). Phonological short-term memory and foreign-language vocabulary learning. *Journal of Memory and Language, 30*, 331–347.

Papagno, C., & Vallar, G. (1995). Verbal short-term memory and vocabulary learning in polyglots. *Quarterly Journal of Experimental Psychology, 48A*(1), 98–107.

Raven, J.C. (1986). *Raven's Progressive Coloured Matrices.* London: H.K. Lewis.

Service, E. (1992). Phonology, working memory and foreign-language learning. *Quarterly Journal of Experimental Psychology, 45A*, 21–50.

Service, E., & Craik, F. (1993). Differences between young and older adults in learning a foreign vocabulary. *Journal of Memory and Language, 32*, 608–623.

Service, E., & Kohonen, V. (1995). Is the relation between phonological memory and foreign language learning accounted for by vocabulary acquisition? *Applied Psycholinguistics, 16,* 155–172.

Thorn, A.S.C., & Gathercole, S.E. (1999). Language-specific knowledge and short-term memory in bilingual and non-bilingual children. *Quarterly Journal of Experimental Psychology, 52A,* 303–324.

Triandafellou, T. (1996). *Fun way, Students book 1-pilot text book.* Athens: Organisation for School-book Publications.

Vitevich, M.S., Luce, P.A., Charles-Luce, J., & Kemmerer, D. (1997). Phonotactics and syllable stress: Implications for the processing of spoken words. *Language and Speech, 40,* 47–62.

Wechsler, D. (1974). *Wechsler Intelligence Scale for Children-Revised.* New York: Psychological Corporation.

The Development of Memory for Serial Order: A Temporal-contextual Distinctiveness Model

Gordon D.A. Brown, Janet I. Vousden, and Teresa McCormack
University of Warwick, Coventry, UK

Charles Hulme
University of York, UK

A model of adult human memory, OSCAR, is applied to the development of memory for serial order. In the model, development of serial order memory is assumed to result from age-related changes in a dynamic learning-context signal that underpins memory for serial order. Developmental improvement in this dynamic learning-context signal leads to more temporally distinctive representations in memory, and this leads in turn to a reduction in order errors. It is shown that the model correctly predicts developmental changes in the movement error gradients in children's serially ordered recall, as well as developmental changes in the number of movement errors obtained. The model is also applied to repetition errors across development.

Un modèle de mémoire humaine adulte, OSCAR, est appliqué à l'étude du développement de la mémoire de l'ordre sériel. Dans ce modèle, le développement de la mémoire sérielle est le produit de changement liés à l'âge au niveau d'un contexte dynamique d'apprentissage qui soutient la mémoire sérielle. Des améliorations lors du développement, dans ce contexte dynamique d'apprentissage, mènent à des représentations en mémoire qui sont plus distinctes au plan temporel, entraînant un diminution des erreurs d'ordre. Lors d'un rappel sériel, le modèle prédit adéquatement les changements liés au développement dans les gradients d'erreurs ainsi que dans le nombre d'erreurs observé chez les enfants. Le modèle est aussi appliqué aux erreurs de répétition observées en fonction de l'âge.

The aim of this paper is to develop and test a computationally explicit account of the development of short-term memory for serial order, as no such account is available at present. According to the model, the development of serial order memory results in part from improvements in a dynamic internal learning-context signal that is involved in representing information about serial order. This implements the idea that the serial order of items can be represented in terms of their location along a temporal dimension, and that younger children have less temporally distinctive representations available to them.

Existing Models

Recent models of children's memory for serial order have largely been developed to account for data collected using specific experimental paradigms. Here we focus on data from the most widely used paradigm: serially ordered recall (SOR).

The concept of *subvocal rehearsal* has been accorded a central role in recent accounts of SOR development. Initial accounts emphasized the role of developmentally increasing use of subvocal rehearsal in maintaining information in short-term memory. Consistent with the importance of rehearsal in SOR development, memory span for verbal materials is linearly related to the rate at which the to-be-remembered items can be rehearsed (Baddeley, Thomson, & Buchanan, 1975), with developmental increases in articulation rate being closely and linearly related to parallel developmental increases in memory span (Hulme, Thomson, Muir, & Lawrence, 1984; Hulme & Tordoff, 1989; Nicolson, 1981). The presence of word length effects (assumed to reflect the use of rehearsal) in the different age groups suggested that children as young as 4 years of age rehearse when verbal stimuli are presented auditorily (Hulme et al., 1984). When nameable pictures are used, however, effects of picture-name length on recall are not observed until later in development, suggesting that SOR for pictorial stimuli does not involve spontaneous use of rehearsal strategies in younger children (Hitch & Halliday, 1983; although cf. Hulme, Silvester, Smith, & Muir, 1986). Consistent with this account, Halliday, Hitch, Lennon, and Pettipher

---

Requests for reprints should be addressed to Gordon D.A. Brown, Department of Psychology, University of Warwick, Coventry, CV4 7AL, UK (E-mail: G.D.A.Brown@warwick.ac.uk).

The work reported here has benefited from discussions with many individuals. In particular we thank Sharon Swain, Elizabeth Maylor, George Houghton, and Rik Henson. This work was supported by grant R00023 6216 from the Economic and Social Research Council of the UK, and grant G9608199 from the Medical Research Council of the UK.

© 1999 International Union of Psychological Science

(1990) found that articulatory suppression (to prevent rehearsal) disrupted SOR of pictures in older but not younger children. Furthermore, Johnston, Rugg, and Scott (1987) found that rehearsal training led to improved SOR for pictures in children as young as 5 years of age, consistent with the suggestion that high-level executive or strategic function may be important in determining whether a rehearsal strategy is used spontaneously by young children.

Despite the considerable support for rehearsal-based accounts of SOR development, several difficulties have recently emerged for any simple rehearsal-based model. First, the development of computational models of short-term SOR in adults has demonstrated that item length effects may be explained more parsimoniously without the assumption of subvocal rehearsal (Brown & Hulme, 1995; Neath & Nairne, 1995; see also Gathercole & Hitch, 1993), and these theoretical developments undermine the inference from word length effects to rehearsal strategies in children. Second, the rehearsal-preventing manipulation of articulatory suppression does not severely disrupt SOR for auditorily presented verbal material in young children even though children of the same age are sensitive to word length (Henry, 1991). Third, it is clear that short-term SOR is sensitive to variables other than the rate of articulation of the material to be remembered, such as word frequency and lexicality, both in adults (e.g. Brown & Hulme, 1992; Hulme, Maughan, & Brown, 1991) and children (Henry & Millar, 1991; Hitch, Halliday, & Littler, 1989, 1993; Roodenrys, Hulme, & Brown, 1993), and this has been taken as evidence that phonological representations in long-term memory are important in determining SOR performance (Brown & Hulme, 1992, 1995; Hulme et al., 1991; Hulme, Roodenrys, Brown, & Mercer, 1995; Hulme et al., 1997; Schweickert, 1993). Finally, no computationally explicit version of the rehearsal-development account of children's SOR has been forthcoming.

In summary, there are inadequacies with specific rehearsal-based models of the development of memory for serial order, although rehearsal rate does correlate with some unique variance in memory span (see, e.g., Cowan et al., 1998; Kail & Park, 1994). Other accounts of SOR development have focused on processes occurring during output (Cowan et al., 1992, 1994; Henry, 1991). Thus both individual differences in span within an age group, and differences across age groups, are correlated with the length of pauses between successive item recalls (Cowan et al., 1992, 1994, 1998), consistent with the idea that memory search for each successive item during serial recall is an important factor contributing to individual differences. However, there are as yet no computationally explicit models of SOR that have incorporated such results into a complete developmental account.

A final possibility is that developmental differences in inhibition may be related to memory development (e.g. Harnishfeger, 1995; McCormack, Brown, Vousden, & Henson, 1999). McCormack et al. examined the specific hypothesis that SOR development might be related to developmental changes in the process of *post-output response inhibition* that plays a major role in many recent models of adult SOR (Brown, Preece, & Hulme, in press; Hartley & Houghton, 1996; Henson, 1998a; Houghton, 1990; Lewandowsky, this issue; Vousden & Brown, 1998), but a detailed analysis of errors found evidence against the claim that this particular type of inhibition is important in SOR development.

In summary, there remains a lack of well-specified (e.g. implemented) models of rehearsal-based SOR. Implemented models of short-term serial recall that do exist focus almost exclusively on the performance of skilled adults (e.g. Brown et al., in press; Burgess & Hitch, 1992, 1996; Estes, 1972; Henson, 1998b; Houghton, 1990; Johnson, 1991; Lewandowsky & Murdock, 1989; Nairne, 1990; Page & Norris, 1998) and it is unclear that such models could easily be extended to account for developmental phenomena (see Brown, Hulme, & Dalloz, 1996; Brown, Preece, & Hulme, 1995). In short, we are aware of no computationally explicit account of the development of short-term memory for serial order. Therefore, we develop such an account in the present paper. The developmental model is an extension of a dynamic computational model that addresses adult data from both immediate serial recall and recency memory paradigms (Brown et al., in press). The model is called OSCAR (for OSCillator-based Associative Recall). The core assumption of OSCAR is that items in a list become associated to states of a time-varying learning-context signal, and that retrieved states of this learning-context signal are used as probes to recall successive list items. When applied to the development of serial recall, the central assumption is that less accurate (less temporally distinctive) retrieval cues are available to younger children. This leads to order errors, because less distinctive cues are available to distinguish between the temporal positions of adjacent list items, and can also lead to slower output (increased inter-item pauses) to the extent that retrieval is slower when less discriminative retrieval cues are available.

The OSCAR Model

The model is similar to several other recent accounts in which successive items in a sequence become associated to successive states of a time-varying control or learning-context signal (Brown et al., in press; Brown & Vousden, 1998; Burgess, 1995; Burgess & Hitch, 1992, 1996; Glasspool, 1995; Gupta, 1996; Hartley & Houghton, 1996; Henson, 1998b; Hitch, Burgess, Towse, & Culpin, 1996; Houghton, 1990, 1994). In other words, a series of item-to-context associations is learned. OSCAR uses an array of oscillators, of different frequencies, to provide the dynamic learning-context signal to which successive items in a sequence become associated. Retrieval of the sequence involves reinstatement of the dynamic learning-context, allowing the item-to-context associations to be probed one after the other. The full implementation is described in Brown et al. (in press); here we attempt to give an intuitive flavour of the general principles of operation of the model. A motivation for the general approach is given in Brown and Vousden (1998).

Successive states of the dynamic learning-context signal can be seen as analogous to successive states of a clock face. Each one of the rotating hands on the clock face (the hour hand, the minute hand, and the second hand) is analogous to one of the larger number of oscillators that combine to make up the learning context as a whole in the implemented model. The representation of a sequence is analogous to a set of associations between successively presented list items and successive states of the clock face. This process is illustrated in Fig. 1(a). Here, the state of a clock face at 2 o'clock represents the learning-context at the start of list learning. An association between the first list item and the state of the clock face at 2 o'clock is formed, creating the first item-to-context association. By the time the second list item is presented, the oscillators (the hands on the clock) will have moved on, to (say) 2.05. The second item-to-context association can then be formed, linking the second list item to the state of the clock face at 2.05. For a six-item list presented at a constant rate, further item-to-context associations will be formed between the representations of 2.10 and item 3; 2.15 and item 4; 2.20 and item 5; and 2.25 and item 6.

The set of learned item-to-context associations is the stored representation of the sequence, and if the dynamic learning-context can be reinstated then the item-to-context associations can be used to reconstruct the sequence. This is analogous to rewinding the clock to its state at the start of list learning. After this initial state (2.00) has been specified, successive states (2.05, 2.10, etc.) are obtained "for free" as the clock runs forward under its own intrinsic dynamics. Thus there is no need to maintain an explicit memory of the dynamic contexts associated with each list position. Each state of the learning-context signal can be used as a probe to recall each successive list item. This process is illustrated in Fig. 1(b). So, for example, the state of the clock face corresponding to 2.05 can be used as a probe to recall the second list item, and 2.10 for the third list item. Other list items will become activated to the extent that they were associated with clock face states similar to the one used as a recall cue.

The basic model architecture of the implemented OSCAR model (Brown et al., in press) is shown in Fig. 2. Items (e.g. words or letters in a list to be learned), and also states of the learning-context, are represented as vectors. As in the clock face analogy, individual items in an incoming sequence (such as words in a serial list) become associated with a dynamic representation of the internal cognitive context at the time of learning. In OSCAR, this dynamic representation is made up from the output of an array of sine-wave oscillators (illustrated at the bottom of the figure). Some of these oscillators are low in frequency (i.e. they change their output by only a small amount in each unit of time); others are higher in frequency. The outputs of these oscillators combine to make up the learning-context signal as illustrated in the figure. The state of this learning-context vector changes over time, as the output of the oscillators changes over time. Successive items in a to-be-learned sequence are associated (via simple Hebbian association) to successive states of this time-varying learning-context signal. Thus the resulting memory contains a set of item-to-context associations. Recall involves reinstatement of the dynamic context of learning—successive states of the time-varying learning-context signal are used as probes to the multiple item-to-context associations. The reconstructed states of the learning-context signal are subject to noise, and so may lead to the retrieval of an item that was originally associated to a cue similar to the original learning-context signal rather than to retrieval of the correct item. Because there are both slow and fast oscillators contributing to the dynamic learning-context vector, the vector has both slow-moving and fast-moving underlying components. This can be seen as an approximate instantiation of the clock face analogy.

Furthermore, as with the clock face example earlier, states of the signal that are near to each other in time are more similar than are states separated in time; and consequently states of the signal never repeat themselves over arbitrary time periods provided the lowest-frequency oscillator is sufficiently slow (analogous to including an arbitrarily slow hand on the clock face). This leads to a

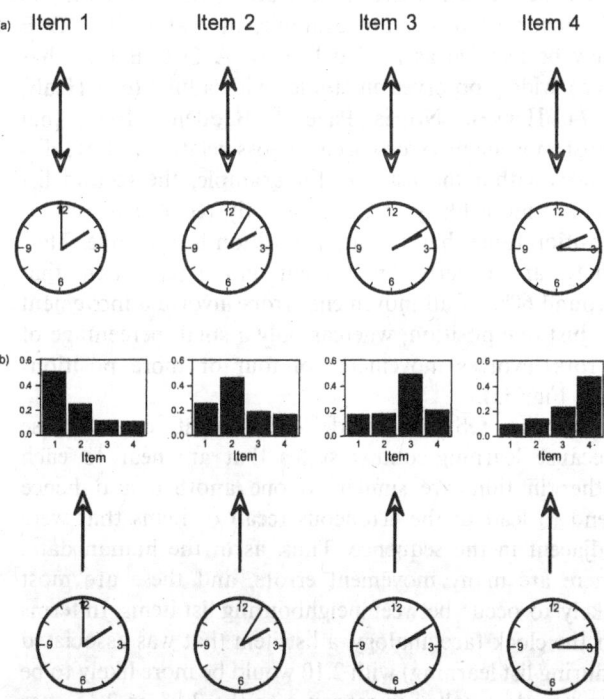

FIG. 1. (a) The association between four successive list items and four successive states of a learning-context signal, illustrated using the clock face analogy. (b) The retrieval of four successive list items from four successive states of a learning-context signal, illustrated using the clock face analogy.

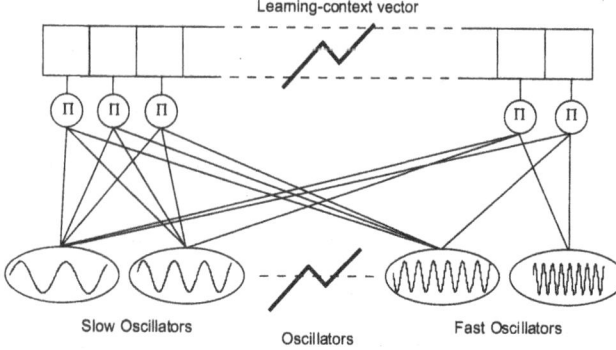

Fig. 2. The basic architecture of the OSCAR model, as described in the text.

The OSCAR Model, Temporal Distinctiveness, and Order Memory Development

Several models have suggested that items in memory are represented in terms of their absolute or relative temporal position within a list, such that the discriminability of items in memory will be determined by their proximity to other items and their temporal distance from the point of recall (see, e.g., Baddeley, 1976; Bjork & Whitten, 1974; Crowder, 1976; Crowder & Neath, 1991; Neath, 1993a, b; Neath & Crowder, 1990). The OSCAR model can be interpreted as a mechanism-level implementation of the same basic idea: In OSCAR the serial order of items in a list is represented in terms of the items' relative positions along a temporal dimen-

dynamic system with many of the necessary properties to account for serial list learning. Brown et al. (in press) apply the model to a range of serial order phenomena obtained from the study of adults; here we focus on the model's ability to account for *movement errors* in immediate serial recall, for these will underpin testing of the model as applied to the development of memory.

Movement Errors in the Model

In the immediate serial recall of short lists of items such as letters, many of the errors (often the majority) are order errors, where the correct items are recalled in the incorrect order. For example, the list A B C D E may be recalled as A C B D E or A D C B E. It has been widely observed in studies with adults (e.g. Healy, 1974; Henson, Norris, Page, & Baddeley, 1996) that most movement errors occur across relatively short distances within the list—so, for example, the second list item is more likely to be incorrectly recalled in output position three than in output position four or five. Thus there are orderly "movement gradients" such that around 60% of all movement errors involve a movement of just one position, whereas only a small percentage of errors involves movements of four or more positions (see Fig. 3a).

In the OSCAR model, movement errors arise because learning-context states that are near to each other in time are similar to one another, and hence tend to lead to the erroneous recall of items that were adjacent in the sequence. Thus, as in the human data, there are many movement errors, and these are most likely to occur between neighbouring list items. In terms of the clock face analogy, a list item that was associated (during list learning) with 2.10 would be more likely to be incorrectly recalled in response to the 2.05 or 2.15 cues than in response to the 2.00 or 2.20 cues. A typical movement gradient produced by the model in recalling six-item lists is shown in Fig. 3b, where it can be seen that a movement gradient similar to that observed in the empirical data is obtained.

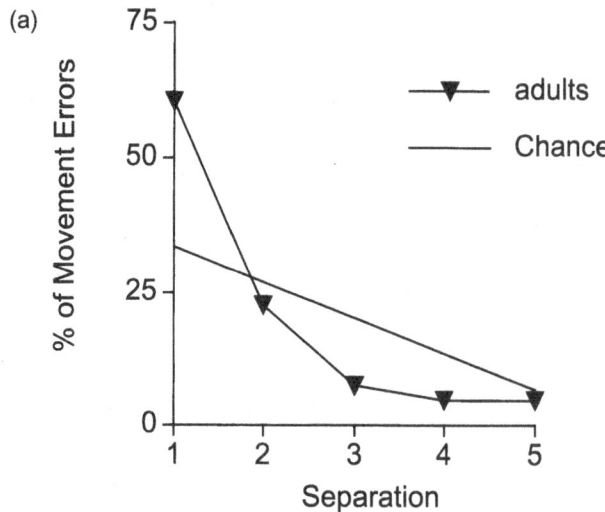

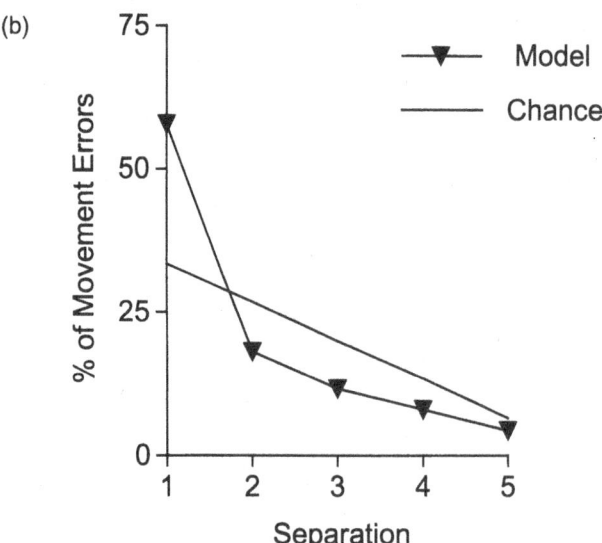

FIG. 3. The proportion of movement errors that occur over different distances in a short-term serial recall task. (a) Unpublished representative data from the authors' own laboratory. (b) Model. The error movement gradient that would be expected if errors were randomly distributed is also shown.

sion. Neighbouring items within a list will have memorial representations that are less temporally distinctive from one another, and therefore items close to one another in the list are more likely to be recalled in the wrong relative order, as illustrated by the error movement gradients described earlier. The examination of memory development within the OSCAR framework, as described later, can therefore alternatively be interpreted as an assessment of the idea that order memory develops as a result of the availability of memory representations of increasing temporal distinctiveness.

Sources of Possible Developmental Improvement in the OSCAR Model

Within the framework of the OSCAR model there are several possible sources of developmental improvement in the model (see Maylor, Vousden, & Brown, in press, for a discussion in relation to SOR in elderly adults). The availability of the implemented model allows us to examine the predictions of the model for developmental changes in overall performance and error movement gradients in terms of each hypothesized source of developmental improvement. Broadly speaking, sources of development in the model could be located within the learning-context signal (temporal distinctiveness of encoding); the accuracy of the reconstructed learning-context signal used as a retrieval cue (temporal distinctiveness of retrieval cue); the forgetting of the item-to-context associations, or the learning process itself (relative strength of initial encoding). We consider each source in turn in the model below.

EVALUATION OF THE MODEL

In order to evaluate these hypotheses, we applied the model to a subset of data from an experimental investigation of error movement gradients in the serial recall of six-item lists in three groups of children (of different ages) and adults (McCormack et al., 1999). Although some researchers have published detailed serial recall error data from children of different ages (e.g. Pickering, Gathercole, & Peaker, 1998; see also Healy, Cunningham, Gesi, Till, & Bourne, 1991), reports of error types and error movement gradients have not generally been reported in sufficient detail to be directly compared with the behaviour of the OSCAR model.

One of the experiments in the McCormack et al. (1999) study examined serial recall of six-item lists of confusable letters. (In order to compare error movement gradients across different age groups, it is necessary to use the same list length for all groups. This is because the movement gradient that would be expected by chance alone varies considerably with list length, and so it is difficult to compare movement gradients in a meaningful way across different list lengths. Fixing list lengths in this way has the consequence that overall levels of performance will not be equated in the different groups, but such performance level matching is in any case inappropriate in the present context as the developmental changes in overall performance form an important part of the data that the model seeks to explain.) The study, which employed visual presentation and written recall, examined error types and error movement gradients produced by adults and by three groups of children. The youngest group of children had verbal ages < 9 years; the middle group verbal ages between 9 and 11 years, and the oldest group > 11 years. The data of interest for present purposes involve error type proportions and movement error gradients, and we focus on these results while paying less attention to serial position effects. Comprehensive description and analyses of the data are reported by McCormack et al. (1999).

Errors were classified as follows. We illustrate with examples of recalls following a presented sequence of A B C D E F. *Omission errors* were recorded when a recall box was left blank (e.g. recall as A B – D E F involves one omission error). This therefore refers to the number of response boxes in which no item was recalled, rather than the number of presented list items that were not recalled (see McCormack et al., 1999, for separate examination of "input omissions" and "output omissions"). *Movement errors* were recorded when list items were recalled in incorrect positions, and the distance of the movement was also noted. For example, recall as A D C B E F involves two movement errors, each of distance 2. *Intrusion errors* were recorded whenever an extra-list item was recalled (e.g. recall as A B X D E F).

Repeat errors were also examined. The three error categories just given can be exhaustive and mutually exclusive, but it is also useful to examine separately errors where an item is erroneously recalled in two separate output positions (see Vousden & Brown, 1998, for detailed discussion of repeat errors in SOR and speech production). Recall as A C B C E F would qualify as a repeat error, as would recall as A B B D E F; this analysis took no account of whether or not one of the repeated items was recalled in the correct position. Repeat errors were not also classified as movement errors in the McCormack et al. (1999) study. We refer to these as repeat errors to distinguish them from "repetition errors"—failure to recall both occurrences of an item that occurred twice in the presented list (Henson, 1998a).

Figure 4 summarizes the error data from the McCormack et al. (1999) experiment. It is evident that percentage correct performance increases with age, that movement errors reduce very substantially with age, and that intrusion and omission errors also reduce with age although they are always at a much lower level than movement errors. Thus it is clear that a major part of the reduced performance of younger children in this serial order memory task is due to inability to remember the target items in the right order, in addition to inability to remember the items themselves. It is this deficit in order memory that the present model emphasizes.

Detailed information on movement errors is available from the McCormack et al. (1999) study, but some summary data are given here. Figure 5 shows the error

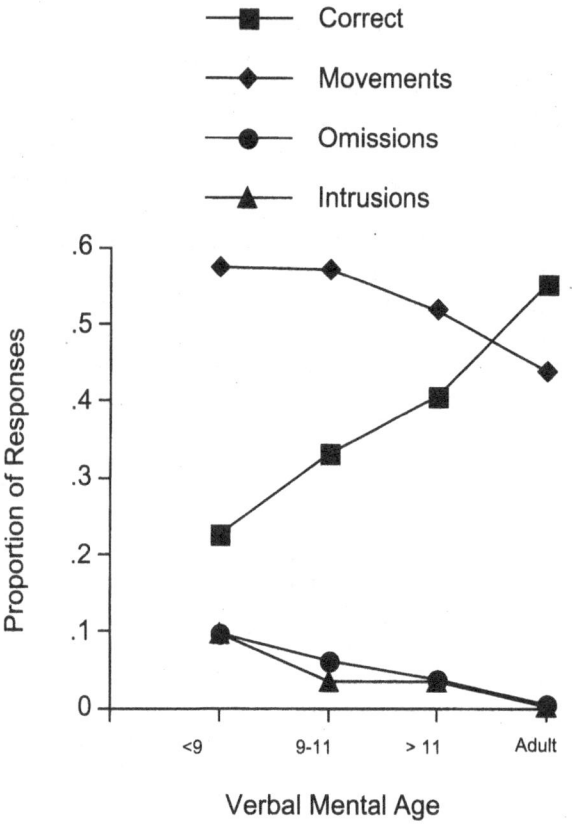

FIG. 4. Proportion of responses of different ages produced by different age groups (calculated from data reported by McCormack et al., 1999).

gradients for movement errors and repetition errors. The movement gradients express the proportion of all movement errors that occurred over each separation. Not only do older participants produce fewer movement errors overall (as indicated by Fig. 4); a much higher proportion of the movement errors that they do produce involve short movements (about 55% of the adults' movement errors involve a movement of just one position, compared with about 35% for the youngest children)[1].

The repetition error gradients show that most repetition errors occur over intermediate separations. This is assumed to be due to the time course of post-output response suppression (Houghton, 1994; McCormack et al., 1999; Vousden & Brown, 1998). If the representation of an item is suppressed or inhibited when that item has been output, as most current models of serial memory assume, then it is unlikely that an item will be recalled a second time very soon after it has been recalled once. The post-output response suppression must wear off over time, however, or it would not be possible ever to recall the same item twice. This would lead to an increasing proportion of repeat errors over larger separations. Offset against this, however, is the fact that long-distance repeat errors are unlikely for the same reason that long-distance movement errors are rare; i.e., there is little similarity between the contextual retrieval cues for temporally distal items. The combination of these two tendencies leads to the observed pattern, with relatively few repeat errors over either small or large within-list separations. McCormack et al. interpret these data as evidence that the time-course of inhibitory processes in serial recall is developmentally invariant.

In summary: McCormack et al. (1999) found a clear developmental increase in overall performance on the SOR task, with systematic developmental changes in the observed error movement gradients observed, while repeat errors occurred over intermediate separations for all age groups. In intuitive terms, the results seem likely to be consistent with a version of the OSCAR model in which developmental improvement is due to improvement in the quality of the oscillator-based dynamic learning-context signal used to underpin memory for serial order. If older children have available to them a better dynamic learning-context signal, they will be able to assign more temporally distinctive representations to each list item, and better order memory will result. We now examine the ability of the model to account for the detailed pattern of results obtained.

SIMULATION

In order to assess the predictions of the different possible developmental accounts within the OSCAR framework, we implemented a simple form of each hypothesis outlined earlier. In each case, we varied the relevant parameter (e.g. the parameter that determines context quality, or the parameter that determines relative encoding strength) over a range sufficient to cause overall level of performance (number of items recalled in their correct serial positions) to vary in accordance with that seen in the data. We then examined the error types and movement gradients produced by the model, with all other parameters being held constant.

The complete version of the OSCAR model (Brown et al., in press) has many parameters and is applied to a wide variety of different experimental paradigms, including studies of relative recency judgements, item and list grouping effects, list length effects, differential memory for item and order information, and probed serial recall. In the present extension of the model most of these parameters are absent or remained fixed in all simulations, as the demonstrations are concerned only with serial recall and we wished to use a simple version of the model. A full description of the operation and effects of all parameters is given in the Brown et al. paper; parameter values used in the present simulations are given in Table 1. One parameter of particular relevance to the present simulations, however, is the *output threshold,* which enables the possibility of omission errors. An omission error is recorded in the model whenever no potentially recallable vocabulary item exceeds the activation of its nearest competitor by more than a fixed amount; the output threshold parameter specifies this quantity. This parameter was held constant in all

---

[1] Although the steepness of movement error gradients will tend to correlate with overall level of performance, these can dissociate due to the possibility of other error types.

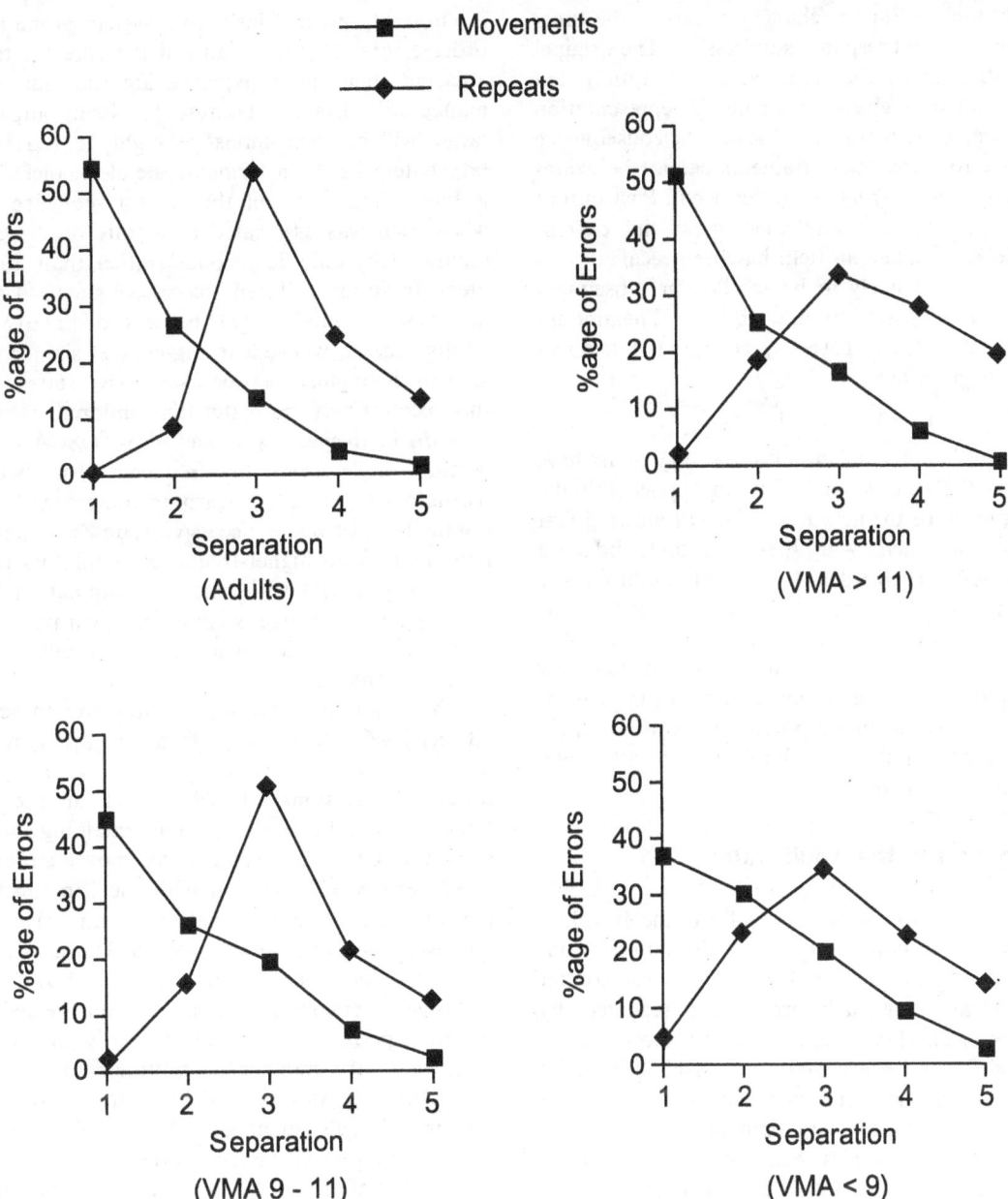

FIG. 5. Separation gradients for movement errors and repeat errors, for different age groups (calculated from data reported by McCormack et al., 1999).

TABLE 1
Values of Parameters Used in Demonstrations

Parameter	Value
D (distinctiveness of context)	Variable
	(4; 2; 1.2; 0.1)
Output threshold	.0007
Inhibition: I_0, d, I_b	−.8, .97, −.035
Retrieval cue noise parameter	Variable
	(0.65; 1.1; 1.5; 5.3)
Learning rate reduction	Variable
	(.8; .45; .25; .05)
No. of item vector elements similar	12
Weight Decay	Variable
	(.95; .6; .5; .3)

demonstrations here, as the aim was to gain a computational-level understanding of the effects of different manipulations, rather than the most impressive possible fit to the data by varying many parameters simultaneously. One change in the present version of the model, compared with the version reported in Brown et al. (in press), concerns the storage of associations. In the original OSCAR model, all item-to-context associations were stored in a single weight matrix. In the present version, each item-to-context association was stored separately, with the result that associations did not interfere with one another during encoding. This change makes no qualitative difference to the model's performance in most cases, including the serial ordered recall examined here, but enables the model to provide a better account of the recall of repeated items than did the original version[2]. A further change concerned the time-course of post-output response suppression. The original implementation made the simplifying assumption that during a recall of a given list an item's representation would be completely inhibited. This has the consequence that repeat error separation gradients cannot be examined, because repeat errors can never occur. Post-output response suppression is implemented in the current model as follows. When an item has been recalled, it is assumed to be less likely to be recalled in subsequent positions because its activation is inhibited. The amount of inhibition after s items have elapsed since the item was last output is given by:

$$I_s = I_0 * (1-d)^s + I_b$$

where I_s is the amount of inhibition after s items have passed, I_0 is the amount of inhibition applied initially (i.e. during recall of the item immediately following first recall of the item, when s = 0), I_b is a constant, and d is a decay rate parameter ($d \leq 1$). The amount of inhibition is simply subtracted from the level of activation that the previously output item would have had if no response suppression took place (see Vousden & Brown, 1998, for detailed exploration). In all other respects the implementation was identical to that reported in Brown et al. (in press); space does not permit duplication of all implementational details here.

Obtaining a Fit to the Adult Data

The first step was to choose a set of parameter values that would give a satisfactory fit to the adults' data. Figure 6a shows the serial position curves for correct performance and for each error type reported by McCormack et al. (1999), and Figure 6b shows the fit of the model. It can be seen that a reasonable fit to most aspects of the data was obtained, with an appropriate serial position curve and a predominance of movement errors at all serial positions. The next step was to take the parameter settings chosen to obtain the fit to the adult data, and vary one parameter at a time to examine the effects on error types and error separation gradients.

Temporal-contextual Distinctiveness

One possible source of developmental change located within the learning-context concerns the temporal distinctiveness of successive states of the signal. This distinctiveness is determined by the speed with which the learning-context vector evolves over time—the greater the rate of change, the less similar are states of the learning-context signal that become associated with successive items (assuming a constant rate of presentation). Use of a learning-context signal whose successive states are not very distinct leads to a system prone to making order errors. This is because if the cues for temporally adjacent items in a sequence are too similar, performance will decrease because list items adjacent to a target will be cued almost as highly at retrieval as the target item itself. In terms of the clock face analogy, it is like trying to recall the correct sequence of events when each was associated to a state of the clock face separated by only 30 seconds (rather than, say, 5 minutes). In young children, successive states of the learning-context signal might be less distinctive than in adults. Adults, whose learning-context signals are better able to distinguish between successive states, would on this account perform better than children. Variable context distinctiveness is modelled in OSCAR by using vectors made from low-frequency (slowly-changing) oscillators to provide a learning-context with poor discrimination between successive states, and context signals made from higher-frequency oscillators to provide a learning-context with better discrimination. Thus the developmental change is controlled by a parameter that determines the frequencies of the oscillators in the learning-context.

The results of varying this parameter to achieve the correct levels of overall performance are shown in column (a) of Fig. 7. The top panel shows the errors produced by versions of the model at the different "developmental stages," and the remaining three panels show the separation gradients for movement errors and repeat errors. Comparison with the experimental data (Figs. 4 and 5) reveals that the main features of the data were reproduced by the model. The error movement gradients became progressively shallower in the "younger" versions of the model, and the reduction in memory performance arose primarily due to a large increase in the number of movement errors. Furthermore, the separation gradients for the repeat errors remained largely unchanged. The main deviation from the data concerned the lack of developmental change in the number of omission and intrusion errors in the model as compared with the data. Although a better fit could easily be obtained by altering other parameters (e.g. by changing the output threshold parameter to produce more omissions), it was felt that introducing changes in several parameters simultaneously, although possibly plausible psychologically, would not add to the understanding of the model's behaviour.

Accuracy of Retrieval Cue

A second manipulation concerns the accuracy of the learning-context vector that is used as a retrieval cue for each item. The default assumption in the model is that retrieval cues are generated accurately, analogously to regenerating states of the clock face by allowing it to run forwards. However a parameter can be used to specify an amount of noise to be added to each element of each learning-context vector prior to its use as a retrieval cue; each learning-context vector element has added to it

---

[2] The original model, like several other similar models, sometimes has a tendency to recall repeated items too early due to the summation of associative strengths within a single weight matrix. This is obviated by the use of noninterfering associations.

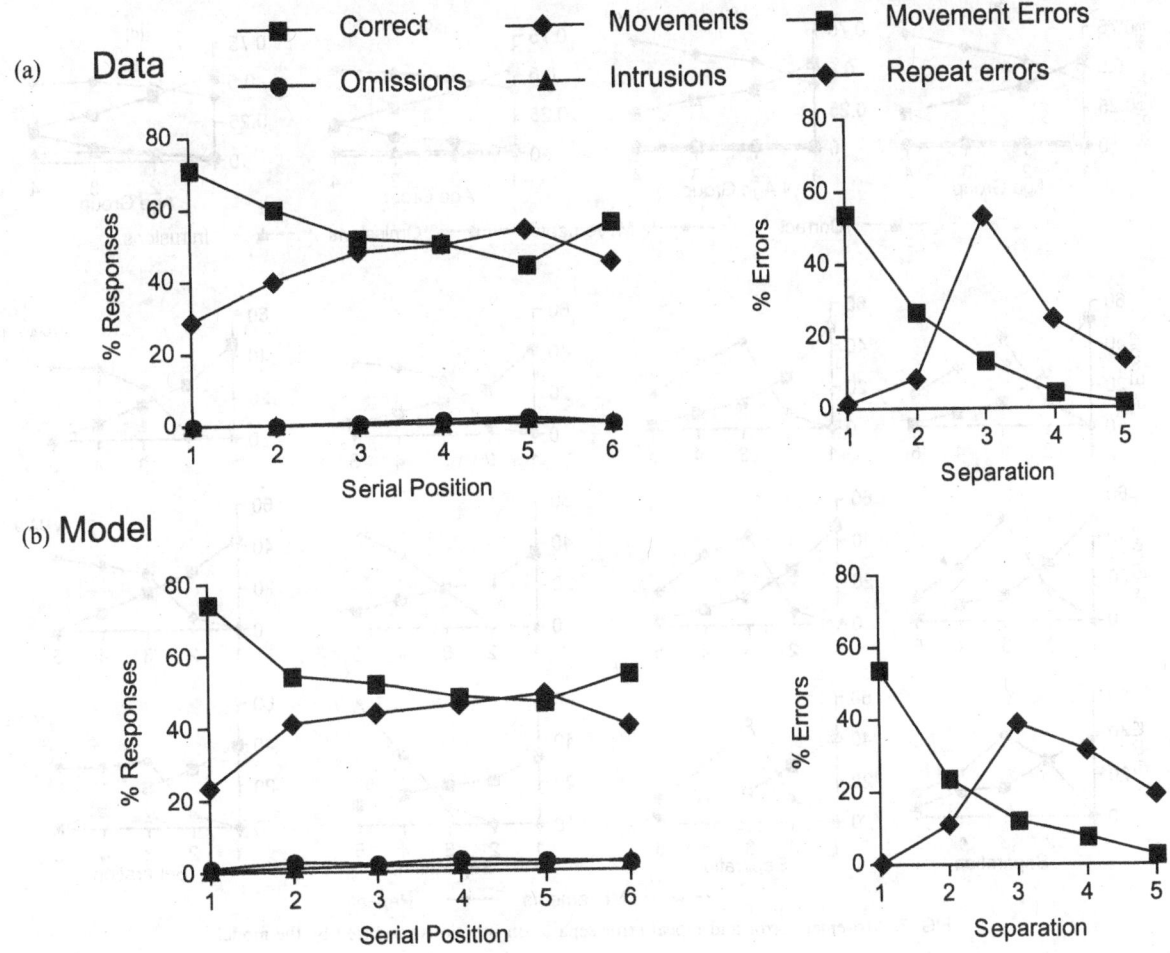

FIG. 6. (a) Serial position curves produced by adult participants in the McCormack et al. (1999) experiment. (b) Fit of the model.

a random number, drawn from a normal distribution with $SD = 1$ and $M = 0$, and multiplied by the parameter value. In psychological terms, this is equivalent to reducing the temporal-contextual specificity of the memory retrieval cues.

The results of this manipulation can be seen in the second column of Fig. 7, where it can be seen that the results are generally similar to those obtained in the previous demonstration. Detailed consideration is postponed to the General Discussion.

Forgetting Parameter

The standard version of the OSCAR model incorporates a weight decay parameter, which causes each item-to-context association to become weaker during encoding of each subsequent item-to-context association. Despite the name, this parameter could equally be thought of as representing the effects of interference; the result of its operation is that the learning of each new item reduces the quality of the representation of previously learned items. Each association is multiplied by a constant when each new association is learned, and the relevant parameter is simply the value of the constant.

The results of varying this parameter, such that greater trace degradation occurs in younger children, is shown in the third column of Fig. 7. This shows that variation in this parameter has effects that are rather different than those of the two context-distinctiveness manipulations described earlier. The error patterns are not too different from the data, with the main reduction in overall correct performance being due to increased movement errors and a rise in omissions (the latter of which could trivially be reduced by changing the output threshold parameter). However it is evident that the separation gradients for repeat errors are very different from those observed in the data; there are many more long-distance repeat errors in the model than in the data, especially at lower levels of performance. This is because the representations of early-presented items become so weak, compared with the representations of late-list items, that there are many anticipations of late-presented items into early recall positions, thus increasing the level of long-distance repeat errors to a level not seen in the data. It seems reasonable to conclude that any computational manipulation that has this effect on the errors can be ruled out as a plausible account of developmental change.

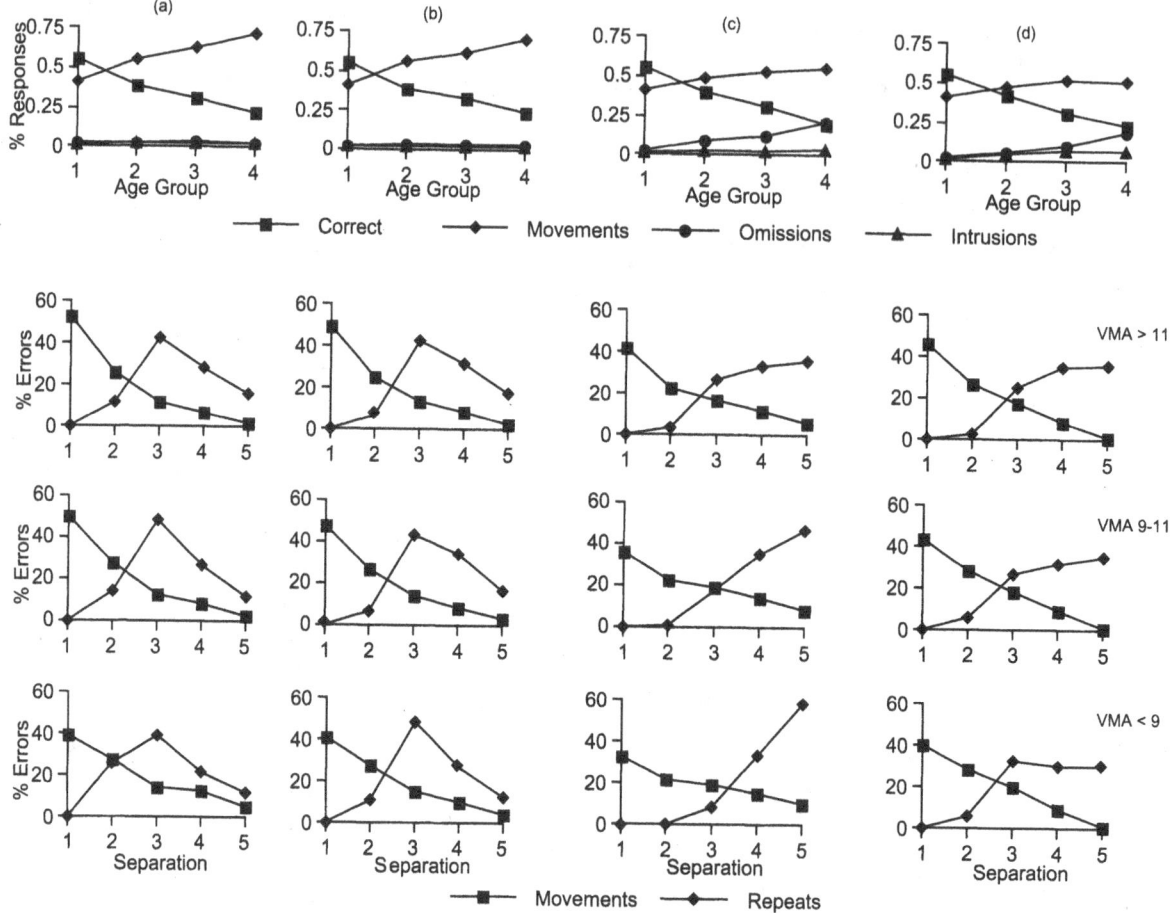

FIG. 7. Movement error and repeat error separation functions produced by the model.

Encoding Differences

Finally, we consider the process of encoding the item-to-context associations as a possible source of developmental improvement. In the OSCAR model, items in a serially ordered list are remembered by forming associations between the items and successive states of the learning-context. In common with other models (e.g. Lewandowsky & Murdock, 1989), OSCAR makes use of an attentional parameter that reduces the strength of encoding of item-to-context associations progressively through the list. If the value of this parameter is 0.9, for example, then the second item will be encoded with a strength of 0.9 times the strength of the first item; the third item with a strength of 0.9^2, and so on.

A reduction in this parameter to model development can be seen as an implementation of the idea that children pay less attention at encoding, particularly to items towards the end of the list. The results of this manipulation are shown in the rightmost column (d) of Fig. 7. Here it can be seen that a similar pattern was obtained to the one seen when the weight decay parameter was manipulated, with the separation gradients for repeat errors being very different from those seen in the data. However the reason is a different one: When attentional encoding reduces quickly throughout the list, as in the model of the youngest children's memory performance, the early-list items are very strongly encoded relative to the late-list items. This results in a relatively high number of long-distance perseverations compared to that seen in the data.

It seems, therefore, that manipulations that simulate reduced encoding of late-list items are unlikely to capture the relevant developmental data.

GENERAL DISCUSSION

In summary, the OSCAR model provides the best fit to developmental error patterns in serial recall tasks if it is assumed that developmental improvement is underpinned by changes in the effectiveness of a dynamic learning-context signal that is used to maintain information about serial order. Although changes in single parameters unsurprisingly failed to capture all aspects of the data, the only features of the data that were not duplicated by the two contextual distinctiveness manipulations (small developmental increases in the number of intrusions and omissions) seem less related than do movement and repeat errors to our central concern of the development of memory for serial order. It is in any case not difficult to capture these additional features of the data by incorporating additional parameter changes (e.g. increasing the similarity of item vector representations increases the number of intrusions; changing the output threshold increases the number of omission errors). We note that it is necessary to examine the developmental error data in considerable detail (e.g. the repeat error separation gradients) if models are to be constrained adequately.

The model can be seen as an implemented instantiation of the hypothesis that the development of memory for serial order is due to developmental increases in the temporal distinctiveness of items' representations in memory. However, further work will be needed to examine the relative merits of encoding-stage vs. retrieval-stage accounts; similar effects in the model were seen whether the temporal-contextual distinctiveness of cues was reduced at learning and retrieval, or just at retrieval.

Relationship to Other Accounts of the Development of Serial Memory

How does the OSCAR model of SOR development relate to the psychological accounts that we outlined in the introduction? The OSCAR model can be seen as a mechanism-level instantiation of a type of temporal distinctiveness model, for items that are assigned more temporally distinctive memorial representations will be more easily and accurately retrieved. Although a variety of temporal distinctiveness models have been applied to adult human memory (e.g. Crowder, 1976; Glenberg, 1987; Glenberg & Swanson, 1986; Neath, 1993a, b; Neath & Crowder, 1990, 1996), such models have not been used to account for the development of memory. Thus the claim embodied in the present developmental model, that the development of memory for serial order results at least in part from developmental increases in the temporal distinctiveness of retrieval cues, is a novel one. The OSCAR account of SOR development contrasts with rehearsal-based accounts, for no rehearsal process is included in the model. However we note the possibility that one function of rehearsal may be to increase the temporal distinctiveness of items' representations in memory. This is because recently encoded items will have more temporally distinctive representations (Crowder, 1976), and so the re-encoding of items enabled by rehearsal may serve to increase the temporal-contextual distinctiveness and diversity of the memory representations of rehearsed items. In the present paper we have focused on purely temporal distinctiveness, as this provides the main constraint on serial recall of unrelated items in the short term. However, contextual and other non-temporal cues also vary with the passage of time, and over longer time periods other aspects of temporal-contextual distinctiveness will assume greater importance in determining recall probability.

The OSCAR approach to SOR development can also be related to developmental accounts based on inter-item pauses (e.g. Cowan et al., 1992, 1998). Items with less distinctive cues will take longer to retrieve in any plausible associative-network memory system involving winner-take-all competition for response selection, and this is also true in the OSCAR model, although such simulations are not reported here. In terms of OSCAR, therefore, the longer inter-item pauses associated with reduced serial recall (Cowan et al., 1998) can be interpreted as the longer retrieval times for each item that will result when less temporally distinctive retrieval cues are available at recall. Our account therefore contrasts with that given by Cowan and his colleagues, for in a model such as OSCAR there is no separate "memory scanning" process occurring during the inter-item pauses other than the competitive winner-take-all process of selecting an item for output. This process will be faster (and hence the inter-item gaps will be shorter and span itself will be increased) just to the extent that the memory representation of the target item is distinctive. Thus there is no central executive involvement (Cowan et al., 1998) other than that involved in attention to the retrieval process itself; span and pause duration will both simply be affected directly by temporal-contextual distinctiveness.

The present version of OSCAR is limited in its ability to account for cross-list proactive interference effects, although later versions of the model accord a central role to such interference. Although proactive interference plays an important part in contributing to phenomena such as word length effects and phonemic similarity effects that are traditionally attributed to a short-term memory system (e.g. Nairne, Neath, & Serra, 1997), explanations of developmental increases in SOR have not generally focused on effects of proactive interference. In the context of a model such as OSCAR, however, proactive interference and temporal-contextual distinctiveness are closely related—proactive interference from temporally distal items in memory occurs just when insufficiently distinctive retrieval cues are available for target items. For example, proactive interference from items in previous lists will occur just to the extent that there is inadequate temporal-contextual distinctiveness at the level of lists.

How does the OSCAR account relate to that of other computational models of serial recall? Other models have not generally been applied to developmental data, although there is no reason in principle why they could not be extended to do so. Indeed, OSCAR is just one member of a family of recent computational models according to which the recall of items in correct serial position will be determined by the positional, temporal, or contextual distinctiveness of the item's representations in memory (e.g. Burgess & Hitch, 1992, 1996; Henson, 1998b; Houghton, 1990; Lewandowsky & Murdock, 1989; Neath, 1993a, b). Although these models differ from one another in a number of respects, in most cases the models could probably be modified to encompass a developmental distinctiveness account of some type.

Relation to Neurobiology

We have made no theoretical commitments regarding the neurobiological substrate of the developmental improvements in SOR. However, tentative relations between the development of frontal function and the availability of highly distinctive temporal-contextual memory representations can be outlined. Patients with frontal lobe lesions are known to have deficits in memory for serial order, at least as assessed by their ability to perform some temporal memory tasks (e.g. Milner, Corsi, & Leonard, 1991; Shimamura, Janowsky, & Squire, 1990; although cf. Hunkin & Parkin, 1993; Parkin, Leng, & Hunkin, 1990); imaging studies have related frontal activity to order memory (e.g. Cabeza et al., 1997), and frontal functioning generally is widely assumed to develop throughout childhood (e.g. Diamond, 1991). Furthermore, the context-providing role of the dynamic learning-context signal in OSCAR is highly similar to the role of maintaining representations of task-related contextual information assigned to pre-frontal cortex in several computational models of pre-frontal function (see, e.g., Cohen & Servan-Schreiber, 1992; Cooper & Shallice, 1997; Dehaene & Changeux, 1989; Levine & Prueitt, 1989). It is therefore possible that the developmental changes in OSCAR's learning-context signal assumed in the present account to underpin SOR development can be related to concomitant development in frontal lobe function. A similar interpretation of OSCAR has been given by Maylor et al. (in press) in applying the model to changes in memory for serial order in elderly adults. Such an account remains speculative at the present time, however.

Contrast with Connectionist Approaches to Cognitive Development

The mechanism that we have proposed contrasts strongly with the types of computational mechanisms that have been used to model developmental change within a more traditional connectionist framework. Although connectionist models have provided useful accounts of the development of low-level psychological processes such as verb-tense learning (Rumelhart & McClelland, 1986) or reading (Seidenberg & McClelland, 1989), the availability of gradient-descent learning algorithms has not led to adequate models of memory development. We have argued (e.g. Brown et al., 1996) that this is because of the types of learning algorithm that are available within connectionism. There are many extant associative mechanisms for forming associations within a single learning trial (e.g. standard Hebbian association) and also several variants of backpropagation and other gradient-descent learning procedures. But there has until recently been no exploration of how gradual development of the ability to perform one-shot learning could take place. OSCAR provides such an account, in terms of the development of the internal cognitive dynamics that can be used to represent structure in the world (Brown & Chater, 1999), rather than in terms of the increasing exposure to the learning task as is emphasized in many current connectionist accounts (e.g. Elman et al., 1996).

REFERENCES

Baddeley, A.D. (1976). *The psychology of memory.* New York: Basic Books.

Baddeley, A.D., Thomson, N., & Buchanan, M. (1975). Word length and the structure of short-term memory. *Journal of Verbal Learning and Verbal Behavior, 14,* 575–589.

Bjork, R.A., & Whitten, W.B. (1974). Recency-sensitive retrieval processes in long-term free recall. *Cognitive Psychology, 6,* 173–189.

Brown, G.D.A., & Chater, N. (1999). *Connectionist models of children's reading.* Manuscript submitted for publication.

Brown, G.D.A., & Hulme, C. (1992). Cognitive psychology and second language processing: The role of short-term memory. In R.J. Harris (Ed.), *Cognitive approaches to bilingualism* (pp. 105–122). Amsterdam: Elsevier, North Holland.

Brown, G.D.A., & Hulme, C. (1995). Modeling item length effects in memory span: No rehearsal needed? *Journal of Memory and Language, 34,* 594–621.

Brown, G.D.A., Hulme, C., & Dalloz, P. (1996). Modelling human memory: Connectionism and convolution. *British Journal of Mathematical and Statistical Psychology, 49,* 1–24.

Brown, G.D.A., Preece, T., & Hulme, C. (1995). Learning to learn in a connectionist network: The development of associative learning. In J.P. Levy, D. Bairaktaris, J.A. Bullinaria, & P. Cairns (Eds.), *Connectionist models of memory and language* (pp. 411–456). London: UCL Press.

Brown, G.D.A., Preece, T., & Hulme, C. (in press). Oscillator-based memory for serial order. *Psychological Review.*

Brown, G.D.A., & Vousden, J.I. (1998). Adaptive sequential behaviour: Oscillators as rational mechanisms. In M. Oaksford & N. Chater (Eds.), *Rational models of cognition* (pp. 165–193). Oxford: Oxford University Press.

Burgess, N. (1995). A solvable connectionist model of immediate serial recall of ordered lists. In G. Tesauro, D. Touretzky, & T.K. Leen (Eds.), *Neural information processing systems, 7.* Cambridge, MA: MIT Press.

Burgess, N., & Hitch, G.J. (1992). Towards a network model of the articulatory loop. *Journal of Memory and Language, 31,* 429–460.

Burgess, N., & Hitch, G.J. (1996). A connectionist model of STM for serial order. In S.E. Gathercole (Ed.), *Models of short-term memory* (pp. 51–72). Hove, UK: Psychology Press.

Cabeza, R., Mangels, J., Nyberg, L., Habib, R., Houle, S., McIntosh, A.R., & Tulving, E. (1997). Brain regions differentially involved in remembering what and when: A PET study. *Neuron, 19,* 863–870.

Cohen, J.D., & Servan-Schreiber, D. (1992). Context, cortex, and dopamine: A connectionist approach to behavior and biology in schizophrenia. *Psychological Review, 99,* 45–77.

Cooper, R., & Shallice, T. (1997). Modelling the selection of routine action: Exploring the criticality of parameter values. In M.G. Shafto & P. Langley (Eds.), *Proceedings of the 19th Annual Conference of the Cognitive Science Society* (pp. 131–136). Stanford, CA.

Cowan, N., Day, L., Saults, J.S., Keller, T.A., Johnson, T., & Flores, L. (1992). The role of verbal output time in the effects of word length on immediate memory. *Journal of Memory and Language, 31,* 1–17.

Cowan, N., Keller, T., Hulme, C., Roodenrys, S., McDougall, S., & Rack, J. (1994). Verbal memory span in children: Speech timing clues to the mechanisms underlying age and word length effects. *Journal of Memory and Language, 33*, 234–250.

Cowan, N., Wood, N.L., Wood, P.K., Keller, T.A., Nugent, L.D., & Keller, C.V. (1998). Two separate verbal processing rates contributing to short-term memory span. *Journal of Experimental Psychology: General, 127*, 141–160.

Crowder, R.G. (1976). *Principles of learning and memory.* Hillsdale, NJ: Lawrence Erlbaum Associates Inc.

Crowder, R.G., & Neath, I. (1991). The microscope metaphor in human memory. In W.E. Hockley & S. Lewandowsky (Eds.), *Relating theory and data: Essays on human memory in honor of Bennet B. Murdock* (pp. 111–125). Hillsdale, NJ: Lawrence Erlbaum Associates Inc.

Dehaene, S., & Changeux, J.-P. (1989). A simple model of prefrontal cortex function in delayed response tasks. *Journal of Cognitive Neuroscience, 1*, 244–261.

Diamond, A. (1991). Guidelines for the study of brain-behaviour relationships during development. In H.S. Levin, H.M. Eisenberg, & A.L. Benton (Eds.), *Frontal lobe function and dysfunction* (pp. 339–377). Oxford: Oxford University Press.

Elman, J.L., Bates, E.A., Johnson, M.H., Karmiloff-Smith, A., Parisi, D., & Plunkett, K. (1996). *Rethinking innateness: A connectionist perspective on development.* Cambridge, MA: MIT Press.

Estes, W.K. (1972). An associative basis for coding and organization in memory. In A.W. Melton & E. Martin (Eds.), *Coding processes in human memory* (pp. 161–190). Washington, DC: Winston.

Gathercole, S.E., & Hitch, G.J. (1993). Developmental changes in short-term memory: A revised working memory perspective. In A.F. Collins, S.E. Gathercole, M.A. Conway, & P.E. Morris (Eds.), *Theories of memory.* Hove, UK: Lawrence Erlbaum Associates Ltd.

Glasspool, D. (1995). Competitive queueing and the articulatory loop. In J.P. Levy, D. Bairaktaris, J.A. Bullinaria, & P. Cairns (Eds.), *Connectionist models of memory and language* (pp. 5–10). London: UCL Press.

Glenberg, A.M. (1987). Temporal context and recency. In D.S. Gorfein & R.R. Hoffman (Eds.), *Memory and learning: The Ebbinghaus Centennial Conference* (pp. 173–190). Hillsdale, NJ: Lawrence Erlbaum Associates Inc.

Glenberg, A.M., & Swanson, N.G. (1986). A temporal distinctiveness theory of recency and modality effects. *Journal of Experimental Psychology: Learning, Memory, and Cognition, 15*, 266–274.

Gupta, P. (1996). Verbal short-term memory and language processing—a computational model. *Brain and Language, 55*, 194–197.

Halliday, M.S., Hitch, G.J., Lennon, B., & Pettipher, C. (1990). Verbal short-term memory in children: The role of the articulatory loop. *European Journal of Cognitive Psychology, 2*, 23–38.

Harnishfeger, K.K. (1995). The development of cognitive inhibition: Theories, definitions and research evidence. In F.N. Dempster & C.J. Brainerd (Eds.), *Interference and inhibition in cognition* (pp. 176–204). San Diego, CA: Academic Press.

Hartley, T., & Houghton, G. (1996). A linguistically constrained model of short-term memory for nonwords. *Journal of Memory and Language, 35*, 1–31.

Healy, A.F. (1974). Separating item from order information in short-term memory. *Journal of Verbal Learning and Verbal Behavior, 13*, 644–655.

Healy, A.F., Cunningham, T.F., Gesi, A.T., Till, R.E., & Bourne, L.E. (1991). Comparing short-term recall of item, temporal, and spatial information in children and adults. In W.E. Hockley & S. Lewandowsky (Eds.), *Relating theory and data: Essays on human memory in honor of Bennet B. Murdock* (pp. 127–154). Hillsdale, NJ: Lawrence Erlbaum Associates Inc.

Henry, L.A. (1991). Development of auditory memory span: The role of rehearsal. *British Journal of Developmental Psychology, 9*, 493–511.

Henry, L.A., & Millar, S. (1991). Memory span increase with age: A test of two hypotheses. *Journal of Experimental Child Psychology, 51*, 459–484.

Henson, R.N.A. (1998a). Item repetition in short-term memory: Ranschburg repeated. *Journal of Experimental Psychology: Learning, Memory and Cognition, 24*, 1162–1181.

Henson, R.N.A. (1998b). Short-term memory for serial order: The start-end model. *Cognitive Psychology, 36*, 73–137.

Henson, R.N.A., Norris, D.G., Page, M.P.A., & Baddeley, A.D. (1996). Unchained memory: Error patterns rule out chaining models of immediate serial recall. *Quarterly Journal of Experimental Psychology, 49A*, 80–115.

Hitch, G.J., Burgess, N., Towse, J.N., & Culpin, V. (1996). Temporal grouping effects in immediate recall: A working memory analysis. *Quarterly Journal of Experimental Psychology, 49A*, 116–139.

Hitch, G.J., & Halliday, M.S. (1983). Working memory in children. *Philosophical Transactions of the Royal Society, London, B302*, 324–340.

Hitch, G.J., Halliday, M.S., & Littler, J.E. (1989). Item identification time and rehearsal rate as predictors of memory span in children. *Quarterly Journal of Experimental Psychology, 41A*, 321–338.

Hitch, G.J., Halliday, M.S., & Littler, J.E. (1993). Development of memory span for spoken words: The role of rehearsal and item identification processes. *British Journal of Developmental Psychology, 11*, 159–169.

Houghton, G. (1990). The problem of serial order: A neural network model of sequence learning and recall. In R. Dale, C. Mellish, & M. Zock (Eds.), *Current research in natural language generation* (pp. 287–319). London: Academic Press.

Houghton, G. (1994). Inhibitory control of neurodynamics: Opponent mechanisms in sequencing and selective attention. In M. Oaksford & G.D.A. Brown (Eds.), *Neurodynamics and psychology* (pp. 107–155). London: Academic Press.

Hulme, C., Maughan, S., & Brown, G.D.A. (1991). Memory for words and nonwords: Evidence for a long-term memory contribution to short-term memory tasks. *Journal of Memory and Language, 30*, 685–701.

Hulme, C., Roodenrys, S., Brown, G.D.A., & Mercer, R. (1995). The role of long-term memory mechanisms in memory span. *British Journal of Psychology, 86*, 527–536.

Hulme, C., Roodenrys, S., Schweickert, R., Brown, G.D.A., Martin, S., & Stuart, G. (1997). Word frequency effects on short-term memory tasks: Evidence for a multinomial processing tree model of immediate serial recall. *Journal of Experimental Psychology: Learning, Memory and Cognition, 23*, 1217–1232.

Hulme, C., Silvester, J., Smith, S., & Muir, C. (1986). The effects of word length on memory for pictures: Evidence for speech coding in young children. *Journal of Experimental Child Psychology, 41*, 61–75.

Hulme, C., Thomson, N., Muir, C., & Lawrence, A. (1984). Speech rate and the development of short-term memory span. *Journal of Experimental Child Psychology, 38*, 241–253.

Hulme, C., & Tordoff, V. (1989). Working memory development: The effects of speech rate, word length and acoustic similarity on serial recall. *Journal of Experimental Child Psychology, 48*, 1–19.

Hunkin, N.M., & Parkin, A.J. (1993). Recency judgements in Wernicke-Korsakoff and post-encephalitic amnesia: Influences of proactive interference and retention interval. *Cortex, 29*, 485–499.

Johnson, G.J. (1991). A distinctiveness model of serial learning. *Psychological Review, 98*, 204–217.

Johnston, R.S., Rugg, M.D., & Scott, T. (1987). Phonological similarity effects, memory span and developmental reading disorders: The nature of the relationship. *British Journal of Psychology, 78,* 205–211.

Kail, R., & Park, Y.S. (1994). Processing time, articulation time, and memory span. *Journal of Experimental Child Psychology, 57,* 281–291.

Levine, D.S., & Prueitt, P.S. (1989). Modeling some effects of frontal lobe damage: Novelty and perseveration. *Neural Networks, 2,* 103–116.

Lewandowsky, S. (this issue). Redintegration and response suppression in serial recall: A dynamic network model. *International Journal of Psychology, 34,* 435–447.

Lewandowsky, S., & Murdock, B.B. (1989). Memory for serial order. *Psychological Review, 96,* 25–57.

Maylor, E.A., Vousden, J.I., & Brown, G.D.A. (in press). Adult age differences in short-term memory for serial order: Data and a model. *Psychology and Aging.*

McClelland, J.L., McNaughton, B.L., & O'Reilly, R.C. (1994). Why there are complementary learning systems in the hippocampus and neocortex: Insights from the successes and failures of connectionist models of learning and memory. *Psychological Review, 102,* 419–457.

McCormack, T., Brown, G.D.A., Vousden, J., & Henson, R.N.A. (1999). *The development of serial recall: Implications for short-term memory development.* Manuscript submitted for publication.

Milner, B., Corsi, P., & Leonard, G. (1991). Frontal lobe contribution to recency judgements. *Neuropsychologia, 29,* 601–618.

Nairne, J.S. (1990). A feature model of immediate memory. *Memory and Cognition, 18,* 251–269.

Nairne, J.S., Neath, I., & Serra, M. (1997). Proactive interference plays a role in the word-length effect. *Psychonomic Bulletin and Review, 4,* 541–545.

Neath, I. (1993a). Contextual and distinctive processes and the serial position functions. *Journal of Memory and Language, 32,* 820–840.

Neath, I. (1993b). Distinctiveness and serial position effects in recognition. *Memory and Cognition, 21,* 689–658.

Neath, I., & Crowder, R.G. (1990). Schedules of presentation and temporal distinctiveness in human memory. *Journal of Experimental Psychology: Learning, Memory and Cognition, 16,* 316–327.

Neath, I., & Crowder, R.G. (1996). Distinctiveness and very short-term serial position effects. *Memory, 4,* 225–242.

Neath, I., & Nairne, J.S. (1995). Word-length effects in immediate memory: Overwriting trace-decay theory. *Psychonomic Bulletin and Review, 2,* 429–441.

Nicolson, R. (1981). The relationship between memory span and processing speed. In M. Friedman, J.P. Das, & N. O'Connor (Eds.), *Intelligence and learning.* New York: Plenum Press.

Page, M.P.A., & Norris, D. (1998). The primacy model: A new model of immediate serial recall. *Psychological Review, 105,* 761–781.

Parkin, A.J., Leng, N.R.C., & Hunkin, N. (1990). Differential sensitivity to contextual information in diencephalic and temporal lobe amnesia. *Cortex, 26,* 373–380.

Pickering, S.J., Gathercole, S.E., & Peaker, M. (1998). Verbal and visuo-spatial short-term memory in children: Evidence for common and distinct mechanisms. *Memory and Cognition, 26,* 1117–1130.

Roodenrys, S., Hulme, C., & Brown, G.D.A. (1993). The development of short-term memory span: Separable effects of speech rate and long-term memory. *Journal of Experimental Child Psychology, 56,* 431–442.

Rumelhart, D.E., & McClelland, J.L. (1986). On learning the past tenses of English verbs. In J.L. McClelland & D.E. Rumelhart (Eds.), *Parallel distributed processing: Explorations in the microstructure of cognition, Vol. 2* (pp. 216–271). Cambridge, MA: MIT Press.

Schweickert, R. (1993). A multinomial processing tree model for degradation and redintegration in immediate recall. *Memory and Cognition, 21,* 167–175.

Seidenberg, M.S., & McClelland, J.L. (1989). A distributed, developmental model of word recognition and naming. *Psychological Review, 96,* 523–568.

Shimamura, A.P., Janowsky, J.S., & Squire, L.R. (1990). Memory for the temporal order of events in patients with frontal lobe lesions and amnesic patients. *Neuropsychologia, 28,* 803–814.

Vousden, J., & Brown, G.D.A. (1998). To repeat or not to repeat: The time course of response suppression in sequential behaviour. In J.A. Bullinaria, D.W. Glasspool, & G. Houghton (Eds.), *Proceedings of the Fourth Neural Computation and Psychology Workshop: Connectionist representations* (pp. 301–315). London: Springer-Verlag.

Coding Position in Short-term Memory

Richard N.A. Henson
University College, London, UK

Many formal models of short-term memory have recently been proposed (e.g. Anderson & Matessa, 1997; Brown, Preece, & Hulme, in press; Burgess & Hitch, 1992; Henson, 1998; Lee & Estes, 1981; Lewandowsky & Murdock, 1989; Murdock, 1995; Nairne, Neath, Serra, & Byun, 1997; Neath, 1993; Page & Norris, 1998). An important issue addressed by these models is the problem of serial order: that is, how people store and retrieve a novel sequence of items in the appropriate order. A popular solution to this problem is to assume that each item is coded for its position within a sequence. The present article discusses three different means of coding position. It is argued that the pattern of errors people make when they misrecall a sequence supports the hypothesis that position is coded relative to the start and the end of a sequence. Other evidence, however, suggests that positional coding is also sensitive to temporal factors. A new model is described that reconciles these two strands of evidence.

Plusieurs modèles formels de mémoire à court terme ont été récemment proposés (Anderson & Matessa, 1997; Brown, Preece, & Hulme, sous presse; Burgess & Hitch, 1992; Henson, 1998; Lee & Estes, 1981; Lewandowsky & Murdock, 1989; Murdock, 1995; Nairne, Neath, Serra, & Byun, 1997; Neath, 1993; Page & Norris, 1998). Une question importante abordée par ces modèles est le problème de l'ordre sériel, c'est-à-dire comment les gens emmagasinent et récupèrent une nouvelle séquence d'items dans l'ordre approprié. Une solution populaire à ce problème est de supposer que chaque item est codé selon sa position dans une séquence. Cet article discute de trois façons différentes de coder la position. Il est proposé que le patron d'erreurs, lorsqu'une séquence n'est pas rappelée correctement, appuie l'hypothèse d'un codage de la position en rapport avec le début et la fin d'une séquence. D'autres données suggèrent que le codage de la position est aussi sensible à des facteurs temporels. Un nouveau modèle est décrit qui incorpore ces deux ensembles de résultats.

Models of serial order in short-term memory can be classified as *chaining*, *ordinal*, or *positional* models (Henson, 1998). Chaining models, such as TODAM (Lewandowsky & Murdock, 1989; Murdock, 1995), store order via associations between successive items. The order of items can be reconstructed by chaining along these associations, such that each item becomes the cue for retrieval of its successor. However, though a long-standing and recurring idea (e.g. Ebbinghaus, 1964; Jordan, 1986), there is in fact little evidence to support chaining models of short-term memory (Henson, 1996; Henson, Norris, Page, & Baddeley, 1996). Ordinal models, such as the Primacy Model (Page & Norris, in press) store order via the relative strengths of item representations in memory. These models escape many of the criticisms of chaining models. However, because order is stored relationally, ordinal models cannot account for positional errors in serial recall (see following). These errors demand some approximate coding of item positions in a sequence, as assumed in positional models, such as the List Memory Model (Anderson & Matessa, 1997), the Articulatory Loop Model (Burgess & Hitch, 1992, 1998), the OSCAR Model (Brown et al., in press), the Start-End Model (Henson, 1998), the Perturbation Model (Lee & Estes, 1981), and the Positional Distinctiveness Model (Nairne et al., 1997; Neath, 1993).

THREE CODINGS OF POSITION

The positions of items within a sequence can be defined in *temporal*, *absolute*, or *relative* terms. A coding of temporal position assumes that each item is associated with its time of occurrence (Yntema & Trask, 1963), perhaps relative to the start (Brown et al., in press) or end (Glenberg & Swanson, 1986; Neath, 1993) of a sequence. In the OSCAR model of Brown et al. (in press), for example, items are associated with the states of temporal oscillators of different frequencies (e.g. the hour and minute hands of a clock, Fig. 1a). By resetting the oscillators (rewinding the clock), the order of items can be recalled.

A coding of absolute position assumes that items are associated with their ordinal position (*first*, *second*, *third*, etc.), regardless of their time of occurrence (Anderson & Matessa, 1997; Burgess & Hitch, 1992). In the connectionist model of Burgess and Hitch, for example, items are associated with a context signal, implemented as a window of activity that moves across an array of nodes

---

Requests for reprints should be addressed to Dr R. Henson, Institute of Cognitive Neuroscience, University College London, 17 Queen Square, London WC1N 3AR, UK (Tel: +44 171 833 7483; E-mail: rhenson@fil.ion.ucl.ac.uk).

This work was supported by a BBSRC grant awarded to Neil Burgess and Graham Hitch.

from left to right (Fig. 1b). In one version of this model (Burgess & Hitch, 1992), the context signal is event-driven, in that the window only moves when a new item is presented, regardless of the delay between successive items. In other words, items are associated with their absolute position from the start of the list.

A coding of relative position assumes that items are coded with respect to both the start and the end of a sequence (Henson, in press; Houghton, 1990). The Start-End Model (SEM) of Henson (1998) for example, assumes a start marker, which is strongest at the start of a sequence and decreases in strength towards the end, and an end marker, which is weakest at the start of a sequence and increases in strength towards the end (Fig. 1c). The relative strengths of the start and end markers therefore provide an approximate two-dimensional code for each position within the sequence. Associating items with these marker strengths codes their position relative to the end as well as the start of a sequence.

A temporal coding of position is sensitive to presentation rate, such that items further apart in time are associated with more distinctive positional codes (cf. a line of telegraph poles receding into the distance, Neath & Crowder, 1990). An absolute coding of position, however, is insensitive to presentation rate, in that the code for the second item in a sequence presented rapidly is identical to the code for the second item in a sequence presented slowly. An absolute coding of position (relative to the start of a sequence) is also insensitive to the length of a sequence, in that the code for the third item in a sequence of three is identical to the code for the third item in a sequence of five. A relative coding of position, however, is sensitive to sequence length, in that the code for the third item in a sequence of three is different from the code for the third item in a sequence of five: The former item is coded at the end of the sequence, whereas the latter item is coded in the middle of the sequence.

EVIDENCE FROM ERROR PATTERNS IN SERIAL RECALL

Positional models of serial order derive support from two main types of error. The first occurs when a sequence is grouped into subsequences by, for example, inserting a pause every third item (e.g. Ryan 1969; Wickelgren, 1967). Though the total number of errors is reduced by grouping, one class of error actually increases (Lee & Estes, 1981; Nairne, 1991). These *interpositions* (Henson, 1996) are transpositions between groups that maintain their position within groups, such as the swapping of middle-group items illustrated in Fig. 2a. The relatively high incidence of isolated interpositions (Henson, 1996) indicates that items are somehow coded for their position within groups.

The second type of positional error occurs between recall of successive sequences. In a typical serial recall

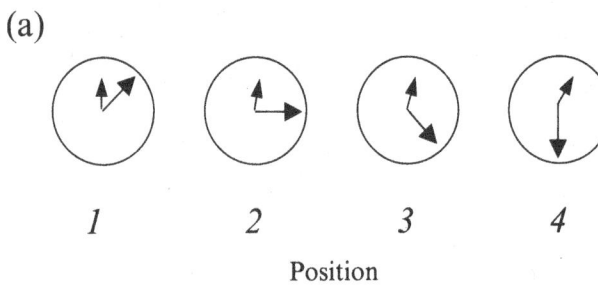
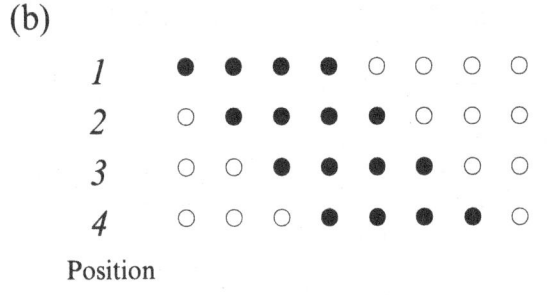
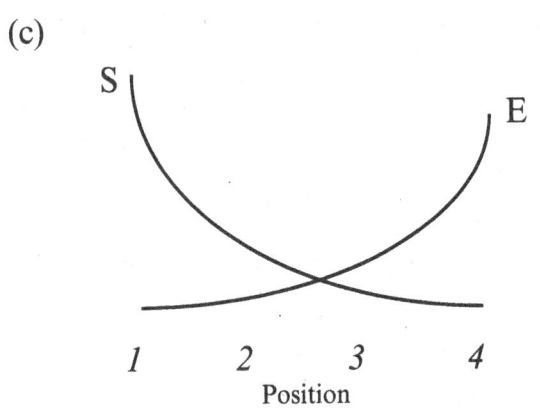

FIG. 1. Illustrations of positional coding in (a) the temporal terms of Brown et al. (in press), (b) the absolute terms of Burgess and Hitch (1992), and (c) the relative terms of Henson (1998).

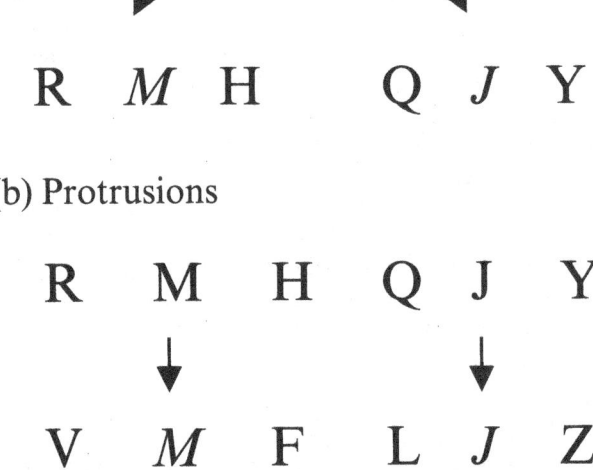

FIG. 2. Positional errors in serial recall: (a) interpositions between groups, and (b) protrusions between trials.

experiment, participants attempt multiple trials of presentation and recall. Detailed analyses of the errors in such experiments reveal that erroneous items are more likely than chance to occur at the same position in the previous trial (Conrad, 1960; Estes, 1991). Henson (1996) called such errors *protrusions* (Fig. 2b). Such proactive interference of positional information indicates that items are somehow coded for their position within trials.

Both interpositions and protrusions are examples of a general tendency for substitutions between sequences to maintain their position within a sequence. However, most previous demonstrations of such positional errors have used sequences of equal length presented at a constant rate, for which the definitions of temporal, absolute, and relative position are confounded. Only recently have these errors been used to investigate the nature of positional codes in short-term memory.

Temporal vs. Absolute Position

To test whether position within groups is coded in temporal or absolute terms, Ng (1996) examined the pattern of interpositions between groups presented at different rates. In one condition, the middle group in three groups of three items was presented twice as slowly as the first and last group. Considering only the first two groups for simplicity (Fig. 3a), the question was whether the third item in the first group was more likely to transpose with the third item of the second group (as predicted by an absolute coding of position from the start), or with the second item of the second group (as predicted by a temporal coding of position from the start, given that these items occurred at the same time relative to the start of a group). The former errors proved more common, favouring an absolute coding of position. This result held with both visual and auditory presentation of the stimuli (Ng & Maybery, 1999).

One problem with Ng's experiments is that participants may have rehearsed the items at rates that differed from the objective presentation rates. Indeed, it is possible that they rehearsed the groups at the same rate (e.g. their maximum rate of subvocal articulation), in which case the predictions of a temporal coding of position no longer differ from those of an absolute coding. One solution to this problem is to repeat the experiments with concurrent articulatory suppression, which should minimise any rehearsal (Baddeley, 1986). The results of such an experiment are currently being analysed (Ng & Maybery, 1999).

Absolute vs. Relative Position

Absolute and relative codings of position cannot be distinguished by Ng's experiments. To test whether position within groups is coded in absolute or relative terms, Henson (in press) examined the pattern of interpositions between groups of different sizes. In one condition

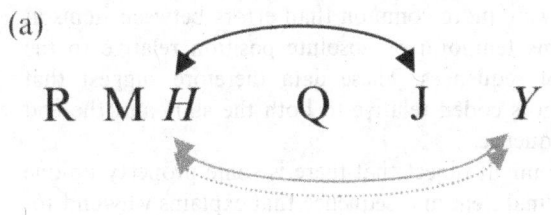

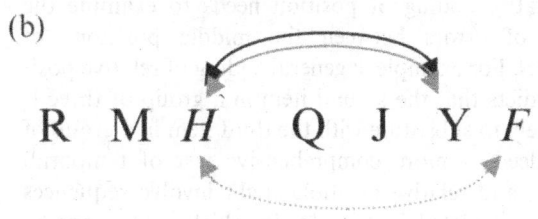

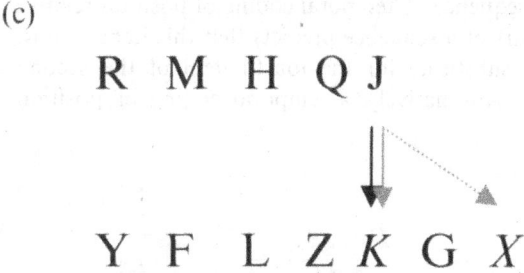

FIG. 3. Positional errors respecting temporal, absolute or relative position with (a) groups presented at different rates, (b) groups of different size, and (c) trials of different length. (Note: temporal and absolute position are defined relative to the start of a sequence in these examples.)

(Fig. 3b), a group of three items was followed by a group of four. The question was whether the third item in the first group was more likely to transpose with the third item of the second group (as predicted by an absolute coding of position from the start), or with the fourth item of the second group (as predicted by a relative coding of position, given that these items occurred at the end of a group). The latter errors proved more common, favouring a relative coding of position. In a second experiment, Henson examined the pattern of protrusions between trials of different length (Fig. 3c). A relative coding of position was again supported by the finding that items at the end of one report were more likely to have occurred at the end of the previous report than at the same absolute position in the previous report.

These results are difficult to explain in terms of different rehearsal rates, because there is no obvious reason for participants to rehearse longer sequences faster than shorter ones, such that the total rehearsal time for the different sequence lengths is equated. Furthermore, though the finding of end-to-end errors is not incompatible with a temporal or absolute coding of position defined relative to the end (rather than start) of a sequence, further analysis also revealed that start-to-start errors were more common than errors between items at the same temporal or absolute position relative to the ends of sequences. These data therefore suggest that position is coded relative to both the start and the end of a sequence.

One might object that there is some property unique to the final item in a sequence that explains why end-to-end substitutions were so common. A more general test of a relative coding of position needs to examine the pattern of errors between the middle positions of sequences. For example, a general coding of relative position predicts that the second item in a group of three is most likely to substitute with the third item in a group of five. Indeed, a more comprehensive test of temporal, absolute, and relative position might involve sequences like those depicted in Fig. 4a, in which a sequence of three items is followed by a sequence of five items presented three times as fast. Consider the second item in the first sequence: A temporal coding of position relative to the start of a sequence predicts that this item is most likely to substitute for the fourth item of the second sequence. Alternatively, a temporal coding of position relative to the end of a sequence predicts that this item is most likely to substitute for the second item of the second sequence. An absolute coding of position relative to the start of a sequence predicts that this item is most likely to substitute for the second item of the second sequence. Alternatively, an absolute coding of position relative to the end of a sequence predicts that this item is most likely to substitute for the fourth item of the second sequence. Only a relative coding of position predicts that the second item in the first sequence is most likely to substitute for the third item of the second sequence.

THE START-END MODEL

Of the three positional models outlined in Fig. 1, the results given favour the SEM (Henson, 1998). However, the data also raise questions regarding the nature of the end marker assumed by this model. First, there is the question of how the end marker grows in strength towards the end of a sequence, when that end has not yet occurred in time. One possibility is that the strength of the end marker corresponds to the degree of expectation for the end of the sequence (Henson, 1998). This is a plausible assumption when the sequence lengths are known in advance (such as the groups in Experiment 1 of Henson, in press). However, the length of the sequences used in Henson's Experiment 2 varied from trial to trial in an unpredictable manner. In other words, participants did not know the length of a sequence in advance, making an expectancy interpretation of the end marker strength less plausible. Another possible solution is described next.

OSCILLATOR-CODING OF RELATIVE POSITION

A model developed by Henson and Burgess (1997) demonstrates how a relative positional coding can be implemented with temporal oscillators. This model assumes that people possess a number of internal oscillators with a range of different frequencies. However, rather than combining the states of these oscillators to form a single timing signal, as in OSCAR (Brown et al., in press), Henson and Burgess assumed that each oscillator competes separately to best represent a sequence. The "best oscillators" are those with a half-period closest to the temporal duration of the sequence (see Fig. 5a). Thus sequences of different temporal durations are represented by different oscillators. Importantly, however, the positional codes associated with items are defined by the phase of the oscillators at the point in time when each item was presented. The use of phase information automatically defines position relative to both the start and the end of a sequence: The phase of an oscillator that is associated with an item at the end of a short sequence, for example, will be identical to the phase of a slower oscillator that is associated with an

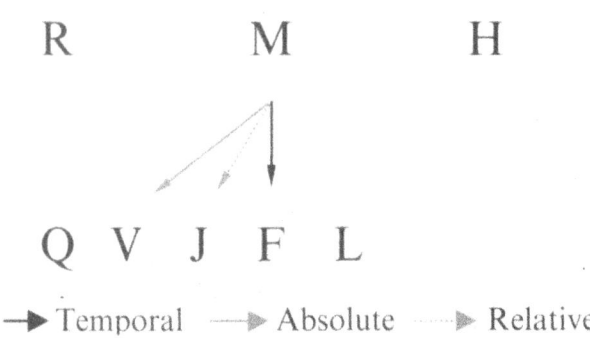

FIG. 4. Predictions for future experiments: (a) combined test of temporal, absolute and relative positional coding of nonterminal items (note: temporal and absolute position are defined relative to the start of a sequence in these examples), and (b) test for the effects of temporal spacing on serial recall performance.

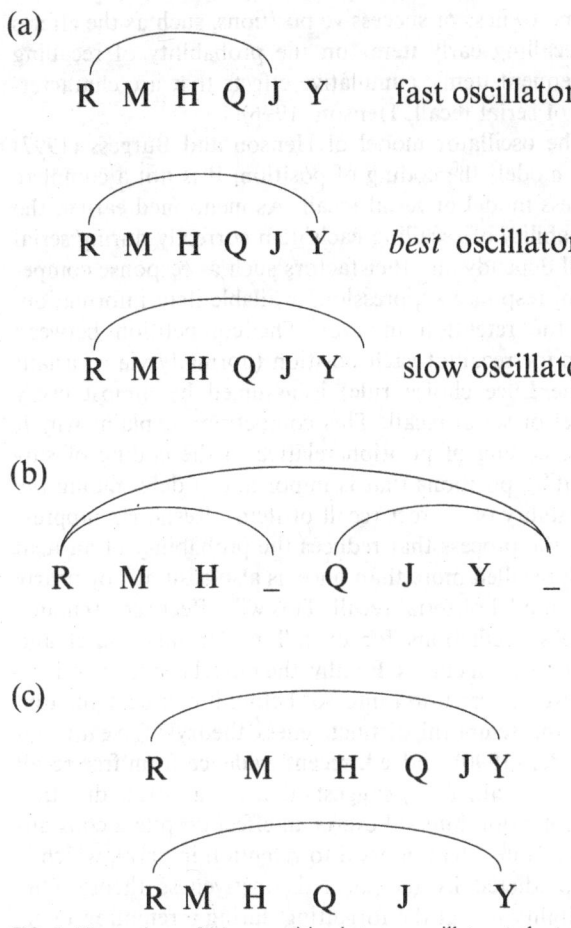

FIG. 5. Illustrations of (a) competition between oscillators to best represent a sequence (Henson & Burgess, 1997), (b) rhythmic parsing of grouped sequences, and (c) oscillator representations of increasing and decreasing schedules of Neath and Crowder (1996).

item at the end of a long sequence. Positional codes are therefore independent of both the number of items in a sequence and the rate of presentation of those items.

More precisely, the model assumes that items are associated with the phase of all oscillators as they are presented. When the sequence ends (as defined later), the oscillators with a frequency that means they are closest to completing a half-period (i.e. closest to their state at the start of the sequence) are selected to represent the sequence. An important advantage of this model over the SEM (Henson, 1998) therefore is that it does not need to know the length or duration of a sequence in advance. Because multiple oscillators compete during presentation, many possible "parsings" of a sequence are maintained in parallel, and only when a sequence ends is the correct "parsing" selected. At recall, oscillators of any frequency can be chosen in order to recall the items serially (depending on the desired speed of recall). The strength with which items are cued at each time point during recall is determined by the similarity in the phases of the recall oscillators and the oscillators that won the competition to represent the sequence. (For a more detailed mathematical formalization of this model, and demonstrations that it can reproduce appropriate similarity gradients, see Henson & Burgess, 1997.)

In order to detect the end of a sequence, Henson and Burgess assumed additional input from a rhythmic tracker. This tracker flags the end of a sequence whenever an item fails to occur in time with the beat defined by the previous items. Thus the pause after the third item in Fig. 5b will signal the end of the first group. (Surprisingly, the precise temporal characteristics that determine grouping in short-term memory do not appear to have been studied.) For such grouped sequences, oscillators compete to represent both the position of each item within a group, and the position of each group within the sequence. Structured sequences are therefore represented by oscillators of several different frequencies; fast ones coding item positions in groups, slower ones coding group positions in groups of groups, etc. In other words, the model is extendible to hierarchies of positional codes (Lee & Estes, 1981; though see Henson & Burgess, 1997, for the problems with synchronizing oscillators at each level of a hierarchy).

EVIDENCE FROM TEMPORAL PRESENTATION SCHEDULES

An alternative test of positional coding involves comparing serial recall performance as a function of different temporal presentation schedules. Several studies have shown that measures of the recency effect are sensitive to the ratio of inter-item interval to retention interval (e.g. Bjork & Whitten, 1974; Glenberg & Swanson, 1986; Neath & Crowder, 1990), consistent with the distinctiveness models of Neath (1993) and Nairne et al. (1997). However, these studies have used either free recall or recognition, for which the use of positional information is not strictly necessary. Moreover, the recency effect is not necessarily the best index of positional coding in short-term memory. The regression slope over the last few serial positions, for example, (Nairne et al., 1997) is likely to depend on several factors, including overall performance level. This is particularly relevant to serial recall, where other factors affecting recency include, for example, the suppression of previous responses (see Henson, 1998). These studies do not therefore provide direct evidence for temporal effects on positional coding in short-term memory for serial order.

One clear prediction of a temporal coding of position is that, all else being equal, items more widely separated in time will be coded more distinctively. This suggests that slower presentation rates should produce superior serial recall performance. However, one problem with this prediction is that rehearsal rates are again likely to differ from objective presentation rates. When rehearsal was prevented by articulatory suppression, Baddeley and Lewis (1984) found that serial recall was worse with slow presentation rates, contrary to what might be expected from a temporal coding of position. (Neath & Crowder, 1996, showed that slower presentation rates did aid performance when mean presentation rates were as fast as five items per second, but the danger with such rapid presentation rates is that they do not allow such effective encoding of items.)

A second problem with varying presentation rates is that other factors that affect serial recall may also be a function of time. For example, phonological information is often assumed to be rapidly forgotten from short-term memory (Tehan & Humphreys, 1995). The greater lag between presentation and recall of each item that is entailed by the slower presentation rates of Baddeley and Lewis (1984) might impair serial recall despite more distinctive positional codes. What is required is a comparison of serial recall performance when the temporal spacing between items is varied but the mean time between presentation and recall of items is kept constant. In Fig. 4b, for example, temporal distinctiveness theory predicts superior performance for the slower presentation rate. Assuming a linear relationship between lag and the recall probability of each item (and that rehearsal is prevented by articulatory suppression), the oscillator model of Henson and Burgess (1997), however, predicts no difference between the two presentation schedules, because the positional codes are equivalent in both cases.

A study by Neath and Crowder (1996) suggests that the timing of presentation can affect positional coding in other situations. They compared serial recall under two presentation schedules: an increasing schedule in which the interitem interval increased with serial position, and a decreasing schedule in which the interitem interval decreased with serial position (Fig. 5c). Performance with the increasing schedule was superior to that with the decreasing schedule. Because the total presentation time and mean lag between presentation and recall was equal in both schedules, this difference is difficult to attribute to encoding or rehearsal differences, or to decay of item information. The temporal distinctiveness explanation offered by Neath and Crowder was that participants adopted a forward perspective (from the start of the sequences), from which it is more beneficial for later items to be widely spaced in time than it is for early items (cf. the telegraph pole analogy).

This sensitivity to increasing and decreasing presentation schedules is not necessarily problematic for the oscillator model of Henson and Burgess (1997), however. Assuming that the rhythmic tracker does not identify any rhythm or grouping in either schedule, sequences will be coded by the same oscillators in both cases (Fig. 5c). Inter-item intervals that increase towards the end of a sequence will therefore be associated with increasing phase differences, whereas inter-item intervals that decrease towards the end of a sequence will be associated with decreasing phase differences. Larger phase differences between successive positions result in more distinctive coding of those positions, just as in temporal distinctiveness theory. Thus the model can appeal to the same explanation of a forward perspective that was proposed by Neath and Crowder (though one might also consider other consequences of changing the distinctiveness of successive positions, such as the effects of recalling early items on the probability of recalling subsequent items; cumulative effects that are characteristic of serial recall, Henson, 1996).

The oscillator model of Henson and Burgess (1997) only models the coding of position: It is not a complete process model of serial recall. As mentioned earlier, the probability of recalling each item correctly during serial recall depends on other factors such as response competition, response suppression, available item information, and the retention interval. The competition between items for recall at each position (normally via a variant of the Luce choice rule) is assumed by almost every model of serial recall. This competition explains why it is the coding of position relative to the coding of surrounding positions that is important in determining the probability of correct recall of items. Response suppression, the process that reduces the probability of an item being recalled more than once, is also assumed by nearly every model of serial recall. This will affect the oscillator model's predictions for overall performance level and serial position curves. Finally, the model needs to address the issue of retention interval before it can be compared with the temporal distinctiveness theory of Neath and Crowder (1990). Indeed, recent evidence from free recall (Nairne et al., 1997) suggests that the absolute duration of a retention interval exerts an effect despite a constant ratio of inter-item interval to retention interval, which is not predicted by temporal distinctiveness theory. One possibility is that the forgetting during a retention interval reflects the decay of the associations between items and the oscillators representing the sequence (cf. Burgess & Hitch, 1998). In this case, the effects of the retention interval are different from those of the inter-item interval: That is, there are effects of time on short-term memory for serial order that are distinct from its effects on positional coding.

CONCLUSION

A review of recent data suggests that models of short-term memory for serial order must include some form of positional information associated with the items in a sequence, and that this information should be defined relative to both the start and the end of that sequence. A new model was outlined that codes positions in such relative terms via the phases of oscillators. This model not only overcomes the problems associated with predicting the end of a sequence, but also allows some influence of temporal factors on positional coding, particularly when no rhythmic grouping is identified within a sequence. The challenge for future developments of this model is to specify more precisely how the timing of items effects their grouping and to address the issue of retention interval in order to compare the model to theories of temporal or positional distinctiveness.

REFERENCES

Anderson, J.R., & Matessa, M. (1997). A production system theory of serial memory. *Psychological Review, 104*, 728–748.

Baddeley, A.D. (1986). *Working memory*. Oxford: Clarendon Press.

Baddeley, A.D., & Lewis, V.J. (1984). When does rapid presentation enhance digit span? *Bulletin of the Psychonomic Society, 22*, 403–405.

Bjork, R., & Whitten, W.B. (1974). Recency-sensitive retrieval process in long-term free recall. *Cognitive Psychology, 6*, 173–189.

Brown, G.D.A., Preece, T., & Hulme, C. (in press). Oscillator-based memory for serial order. *Psychological Review.*

Burgess, N., & Hitch, G. (1992). Toward a network model of the articulatory loop. *Journal of Memory and Language, 31*, 429–460.

Burgess, N., & Hitch, G. (1998). *Memory for serial order: A network model of the phonological loop and its timing*. Manuscript submitted for publication.

Conrad, R. (1960). Serial order intrusions in immediate memory. *British Journal of Psychology, 51*, 45–48.

Ebbinghaus, H. (1964). *Memory: A contribution to experimental psychology*. New York: Dover.

Estes, W.K. (1991). On types of item coding and sources of recall in short-term memory. In W.E. Hockley & S. Lewandowsky (Eds.), *Relating theory and data: In honor of Bennet B. Murdock* (pp. 175–194). Hillsdale, NJ: Lawrence Erlbaum Associates Inc.

Glenberg, A.M., & Swanson, N.G. (1986). A temporal distinctiveness theory of recency and modality effects. *Journal of Experimental Psychology: Learning, Memory and Cognition, 12*, 3–15.

Henson, R.N.A. (1996). *Short-term memory for serial order*. Unpublished doctoral dissertation, University of Cambridge, UK.

Henson, R.N.A. (1998). Short-term memory for serial order: The Start-End Model of serial recall. *Cognitive Psychology, 36*, 73–137.

Henson, R.N.A. (in press). Positional information in short-term memory: Relative or absolute? *Memory and Cognition.*

Henson, R.N.A., & Burgess, N. (1997). Representations of serial order. In J.A. Bullinaria, D.W. Glasspool, & G. Houghton (Eds.), *4th Neural Computation and Psychology Workshop* (pp. 283–300). London: Springer.

Henson, R.N.A., Norris, D.G., Page, M.P.A., & Baddeley, A.D. (1996). Unchained memory: Error patterns rule out chaining models of immediate serial recall. *The Quarterly Journal of Experimental Psychology, 49A*, 80–115.

Houghton, G. (1990). The problem of serial order: A neural network model of sequence learning and recall. In R. Dale, C. Mellish, & M. Zock (Eds.), *Current research in natural language generation* (pp. 287–319). London: Academic Press.

Jordan, M.I. (1986). *Serial order: A parallel distributed approach* (ICS Report 8604). San Diego, CA: University of California, Institute for Cognitive Science.

Lee, C.L., & Estes, W.K. (1981). Item and order information in short-term memory: evidence for multilevel perturbation processes. *Journal of Experimental Psychology: Human Learning and Memory, 7*, 149–169.

Lewandowsky, S., & Murdock, B.B., Jr. (1989). Memory for serial order. *Psychological Review, 96*, 25–57.

Murdock, B.B., Jr. (1995). Developing TODAM: Three models for serial order information. *Memory and Cognition, 23*, 631–645.

Nairne, J.S. (1991). Positional uncertainty in long-term memory. *Memory and Cognition, 19*, 332–340.

Nairne, J.S., Neath, I., Serra, M., & Byun, E. (1997). Positional distinctiveness and the ratio rule in free recall. *Journal of Memory and Language, 37*, 155–166.

Neath, I. (1993). Distinctiveness and serial position effects in recognition. *Memory and Cognition, 21*, 689–698.

Neath, I., & Crowder, R.G. (1990). Schedules of presentation and temporal distinctiveness in human memory. *Journal of Experimental Psychology: Learning, Memory and Cognition, 16*, 316–327.

Neath, I., & Crowder, R.G. (1996). Distinctiveness and very short short-term serial position effects. *Memory, 4*, 225–242.

Ng, L.H.H. (1996). *Are time-dependent oscillators responsible for temporal grouping effects in short-term memory*. Unpublished Honors thesis, University of Western Australia.

Ng, L.H.H., & Maybery, M. (1999). *Temporal grouping effects in short-term memory: An evaluation of time-dependent models*. Manuscript submitted.

Page, M.P.A., & Norris, D.G. (1998). The primacy model: A new model of immediate serial recall. *Psychological Review, 105*, 761–781.

Ryan, J. (1969). Grouping and short-term memory: Different means and patterns of grouping. *The Quarterly Journal of Experimental Psychology, 21*, 137–147.

Tehan, G., & Humphreys, M.S. (1995). Transient phonemic codes and immunity to proactive interference. *Memory and Cognition, 23*, 181–191.

Wickelgren, W.A. (1967). Rehearsal grouping and hierarchical organization of serial position cues in short-term memory. *Quarterly Journal of Experimental Psychology, 19*, 97–102.

Yntema, D.B., & Trask, F.P. (1963). Recall as a search process. *Journal of Verbal Learning and Verbal Behavior, 2*, 65–74.

Modelling the Disruptive Effects of Irrelevant Speech on Order Information

Ian Neath
Purdue University, West Lafayette, USA

The feature model (Nairne, 1990) is extended to include order information by incorporating aspects of Estes' (1972, 1997) perturbation theory. Order information is encoded with other cues in primary memory and precision is gradually lost due to drift along the appropriate dimension. Recall begins with the cue whose positional uncertainty gradient indicates it was in the first position with the highest probability. Order errors occur primarily because cues can "perturb" to adjacent positions: Although the appropriate secondary memory target is sampled, it is sampled out of order. However, cues that have not perturbed can also sample an incorrect secondary memory item, which is then recalled out of order. Thus, both order errors and item errors can give rise to recalling an item from the list in an incorrect position. A simulation shows that with the addition of the perturbation mechanism, the feature model can produce the appropriate order error gradients for short and long words recalled in quiet, accompanied by irrelevant speech, or accompanied by articulatory suppression.

Certains aspects de la théorie de perturbation d'Estes (1972, 1997) ont été incorporés au modèle de caractéristiques (Nairne, 1990) afin d'inclure l'information reliée à l'ordre. L'information reliée à l'ordre est encodée avec d'autres indices en mémoire primaire et la précision est graduellement perdue en raison d'un déplacement le long de la dimension appropriée. Le rappel débute avec l'indice dont le gradient d'incertitude positionelle indique qu'il était à la première position avec la probabilité la plus élevée. Les erreurs d'ordre se produisent principalement parce que des perturbations amènent les indices à adopter des positions adjacentes: même si la cible appropriée est échantillonnée en mémoire secondaire, elle est échantillonnée dans le mauvais ordre. Par ailleurs, les indices n'ayant pas perturbé peuvent aussi échantillonner un item incorrect en mémoire secondaire, qui est alors rappelé dans le mauvais ordre. Donc, les erreurs d'ordre et les erreurs d'items peuvent produire le rappel d'un item à une position incorrecte. Une simulation montre qu'avec l'ajout du mécanisme de perturbation, le modèle de caractéristiques peut produire les gradients d'erreurs d'ordre appropriés pour des mots longs et courts rappelés en silence, accompagnés par des stimuli verbaux non pertinents ou accompagnés de suppression articulatoire.

Most tasks used to study immediate memory performance require the participant to recall the order in which the items were originally presented. Logically, two types of information contribute to accurate performance on this task, item information and order information. Although the feature model (Nairne, 1990) has been applied to many immediate memory phenomena, it lacks a satisfactory explanation of order information. In the current paper, I show that incorporating aspects of Estes' (1972, 1997) perturbation model within the feature model produces the appropriate error gradients observed in immediate memory tasks.

THE FEATURE MODEL

The feature model (Nairne, 1988, 1990) distinguishes between primary memory and secondary memory. Primary memory serves only as a place for maintaining and constructing cues; it has no capacity limits and does not involve the concept of decay. All information, regardless of the task, is recalled from secondary memory and all memory is cue driven. At test, each cue in primary memory is used to sample an item from secondary memory, with the best match for each cue being selected as the potential response. If a cue has some of its features interfered with, the probability of successful sampling is reduced. Matches are still possible, however, because the rule that determines the best match involves a variant of Luce's (1963) choice rule: The target that is selected is the best *relative* match. It is because of this property that the absolute number of features used in simulations is largely irrelevant (Neath, 1998, p. 97).

The feature model gets its name from the assumption that items in memory may be represented as vectors of features, a common assumption (Hintzman, 1991). An analogy is that each feature is like a pixel on a black-and-white television screen. If one were to begin in the upper left corner of the screen and transcribe +1 for a black pixel and −1 for a white pixel, one would end up with a vector of features that represent a particular item. By itself, a particular pixel (or feature) gives no information about the depicted item, but in conjunction with other pixels, the item is fully specified. Features typically take

---

Requests for reprints should be addressed to Ian Neath, 1364 Psychological Sciences Building, Purdue University, West Lafayette, IN 47907-1364, USA (Tel: 765 494 4607; Fax: 765 496 1264; E-mail: neath@pysch.purdue.edu).

the values of +1, −1, or 0, which can be thought of as corresponding to black, white, and broken pixels. A relatively large proportion of the pixels can be broken and the representation can still be identified correctly.

Two kinds of features are distinguished. Modality-independent features represent those aspects of a situation that remain the same regardless of presentation modality. Modality-dependent features represent those aspects of a situation that are determined by the modality of presentation. This follows a distinction, proposed by the broad class of dual-coding models, between an abstract form of representation and a form that more closely represents the physical characteristics (see Surprenant & Neath, 1996, for a brief review).

A fundamental assumption of the feature model is that different presentation modalities give rise to modality-dependent features that differ in terms of their discriminability. This assumption has been operationalized within the model by using more modality-dependent features for auditory items than for visual items. The important distinction is that auditory presentation gives rise to modality dependent features that are more useful in identifying the items that were presented than does visual presentation. Note that this idea could have been operationalized within the model using the exact same number of modality dependent features for both visual and auditory items but varying the discriminative information each provides. Both methods produce similar results. An extended discussion is provided by Nairne (1988) and Neath (in press).

Features are encoded in primary memory with a probability of L, which is usually set to 1.0. In primary memory, items become degraded due to retroactive interference: If feature x of item $n + 1$ is the same as feature x of item n, then feature x of item n is overwritten with a particular probability, F. There is no decay in the model and there is no formal limit on capacity.

The probability that a particular secondary memory trace, SM_j, will be sampled as a potential recall response for a particular primary memory trace, PM_i, is given by Equation (1), where w_{ij} and w_{ik} are possible response bias weights and n is typically the number of items presented on the current trial. The quantity $s(i,j)$ represents the computed similarity between primary memory trace PM_i and secondary memory trace SM_j, and is defined by Equation 2.

$$P_s(SM_j|PM_i) = \frac{w_{ij}s(i,j)}{\sum_{k=1}^{n} w_{ik}s(i,k)} \quad (1)$$

$$s(ij) = e^{-d_{ij}} \quad (2)$$

Distance, d, in Equation (2) is calculated by adding the number of mismatched features, M, and dividing by the number of compared features, N, as described in Equation (3). The value M_k is the number of times feature position x_{ik} does not equal feature position x_{jk}. The parameter a is a scaling parameter that can be mapped onto the overall level of attention, and b_k is used to weight particular comparisons if the task makes them more important than other comparisons.

$$d_{ij} = \frac{a \sum b_k M_k}{N} \quad (3)$$

$$P_r = e^{-cr} \quad (4)$$

Once an item has been sampled, it must also be recovered (see Raaijmakers & Shiffrin, 1981). The probability of recovery is related to the number of times the item has already been recalled, and is thus a form of output interference. Let P_r be the probability of recovering a sampled item, c be a scale constant, and r be the number of times a sampled item has already been recalled on the current trial. The probability of recovery is defined in Equation (4).

IMPLEMENTING ORDER INFORMATION

The sole difference between previous versions of the feature model and the one described here is that aspects of Estes' (1972, 1997) perturbation model have been incorporated. The idea is that the cues in primary memory contain information representing order information. One can think of position as being encoded as a point in multi-dimensional space. For each item, this point can drift (or perturb) along the relevant dimensions. For example, Nairne (1991) has shown data consistent with the idea that an encoded representation of an item can perturb from one position to the next within a list, and also from one list to another within an experiment.

During each particular interval, the probability that an item's encoded representation will drift (or perturb) along the position dimension is given by θ, which is typically set to .05 and is not considered a free parameter. It is assumed, for simplicity, that perturbations are equally likely in either direction. It is further assumed that an item cannot drift beyond the bounds imposed by the task; for example, an item cannot perturb to position 0 and cannot perturb beyond the last position. Formally, the probability that an item, I, will occupy a particular position, p, during the next time interval, $t+1$, is given by

$$I_{p,t+1} = (1 - \theta)I_{p,t} + \left(\frac{\theta}{2}\right)I_{p-1,t} + \left(\frac{\theta}{2}\right)I_{p+1,t} \quad (5)$$

For end items, slightly different equations are used to reflect the existence of boundaries. For position 1, Equation (6) is used whereas for the last position, n, Equation (7) is used.

$$I_{1,t+1} = \left(1 - \frac{\theta}{2}\right)I_{1,t} + \left(\frac{\theta}{2}\right)I_{2,t} \quad (6)$$

$$I_{n,t+1} = \left(1 - \frac{\theta}{2}\right)I_{n,t} + \left(\frac{\theta}{2}\right)I_{n-1,t} \quad (7)$$

Incorporating the perturbation process adds one free parameter to the feature model; this is π, the number of opportunities to perturb. For the simulations reported here, it was assumed for simplicity that each item had an equal number of opportunities to perturb. The rationale is that each item can begin perturbing during presentation and stops perturbing (or more accurately, perturbations stop having an effect) when it is recalled. The number of opportunities to perturb should be approximately equal if presentation time and recall time are similar. It turns out, however, that allowing different values of π for each list item did not substantially alter the basic qualitative predictions of the model.

The perturbation process produces a set of positional uncertainty distributions, a set of values that indicate the probability that a cue was initially encoded as representing each serial position. When recalling the order of a list of items, the cue that, according to its positional uncertainty distribution, has the largest probability of originally being in the first position will be used first. To recall the second item, the cue with the greatest probability of originally being in the second position will be used second. Because items can drift in either direction, most items will remain relatively close to the original position and few items will be in distant locations. This is the pattern of results typically observed (e.g. Nairne 1991).

The following is a description of the model as a typical visual trial proceeds. First, 20 modality-independent features and 2 modality-dependent features are randomly set to values of $+1$ or -1. Together, these 22 features represent the first item. (For an auditory list, 20 modality-dependent features would have been used.) The position of the item is encoded veridically (i.e. the position is 1), but opportunities for perturbation may begin. The same is done to generate the second item in the list, and its position is encoded as 2. At this point, overwriting of the first item occurs such that any feature in the first item that has the same value as the appropriate feature in the second item is set to 0 with a probability of F.

At the end of list presentation, primary memory contains a set of partially degraded cues and secondary memory contains undegraded representations. The modality-independent and modality-dependent features of all items except the final item will have undergone the process of overwriting. For the final item, internal rehearsal will overwrite some of the modality-independent features but the modality-dependent features will remain intact. The encoded position values will have had opportunities to perturb and for each item, a positional uncertainty distribution is calculated. This simply gives the probability that the encoded position value is equal to each of the available serial positions. Recall will begin by using the cue whose positional uncertainty gradient indicates it was originally in position 1 with the highest probability. This cue is then used to sample from secondary memory. In general, the item with the largest proportion of matching features in secondary memory will be sampled. The cue whose positional uncertainty gradient indicates it was originally in position 2 with the highest probability is used as the second cue, and secondary memory is again sampled. Order errors occur because of the perturbation process, in which a cue may be selected "out of order."

WORD LENGTH, ARTICULATORY SUPPRESSION, AND IRRELEVANT SPEECH

To demonstrate that the feature model produces appropriate error gradients, a set of simulations was run that examined the effect of articulatory suppression and irrelevant speech on recall of short and long words. The word length effect refers to the finding that performance on an immediate serial recall task is better when the words are short than when they are long (Baddeley, Thomson, & Buchanan, 1975). Articulatory suppression is a manipulation that requires the participant to say a word out loud repeatedly during list presentation (Murray, 1968). Articulatory suppression reduces the overall level of recall and also eliminates the word length effect (Baddeley, Lewis, & Vallar, 1984; Baddeley et al., 1975). The irrelevant speech effect refers to the finding that recall is impaired when presentation is accompanied by irrelevant background speech compared to a quiet control condition (Colle & Welsh, 1976). Just like articulatory suppression, irrelevant speech eliminates the word length effect (Neath, Surprenant, & LeCompte, 1998).

Neath and Nairne (1995) detailed how the feature model explains the word length effect, reporting several simulations. The feature model adapts an idea proposed by Melton (1963), that just as a list of words can be broken down into individual items, so too can an item be broken down into individual segments (see also Brown & Hulme, 1995). There are simply more opportunities to make an error recalling a word with more segments than a word with fewer segments. More generally, there will be more opportunities for errors for more complex items than for more simple items. Long words are usually more complex than short words: they have more syllables, more phonemes, or more "segments." Note that this need not always be the case: Caplan, Rochon, and Waters (1992) have shown that words that are complex from an articulation standpoint are not recalled as well as words that are more simple even though they are shorter temporally. If the probability of making an error during the output/response production stage of recall is the same for each segment, then there is a greater chance of an error for long than short words. It has been shown that this idea explains most of the basic word length effect findings in the literature, including the linear relationship between proportion recalled and pronunciation time, and the finding of a larger word length effect with visual presentation than auditory presentation (see Neath & Nairne, 1995).

Articulatory suppression is seen as adding noise to the modality-independent features, an idea also independently proposed by Murray, Rowan, and Smith (1988). When a participant repeatedly says a word out loud over and over, part of this information may be incorporated into the modality-independent features. This process is known as feature adoption. Feature adoption reduces the probability that a particular cue will sample the correct secondary memory item because some of the features of the cue no longer match the features of the target. The important consequence of articulatory suppression, then, is not that it affects rehearsal; rather, rehearsal, according to the feature model, is less important in determining the major effects of immediate memory than is usually thought. For example, Coltheart and Langdon (1998) demonstrated word length effects with presentation rates so fast they precluded rehearsal and Dosher and Ma (1998) have shown that output time is more predictive of recall levels than measures associated with rehearsal.

Irrelevant speech, according to the feature model, is very similar to articulatory suppression. When an irrelevant speech manipulation uses similar irrelevant items as an articulatory suppression manipulation, the only functional difference between the two is that more effort is required to produce irrelevant noises actively than merely to listen to them. The idea is that there is some component of articulatory suppression that serves as a general distractor over and above the deleterious mnemonic effects (see, for example, Parkin, 1993, p. 130). The difference in modelling the effects of articulatory suppression and irrelevant speech is that the parameter associated with overall attention or resource availability is less for the former than for the latter. The difference between levels of a for articulatory suppression and irrelevant speech is referred to as δ[1].

Evidence for similarities between articulatory suppression and irrelevant speech include their interactions with word length, phonological similarity, and presentation modality. Phonological similarity refers to the finding that lists of similar sounding items, such as the letters BCDGPTV, are harder to recall in order than lists composed of dissimilar sounding items, such as the letters FKLMQRY (Conrad, 1964). Both articulatory suppression and irrelevant speech eliminate the phonological similarity effect for visually presented items, but not for auditory items (Surprenant, Neath, & LeCompte, 1999). However, both articulatory suppression and irrelevant speech eliminate the word length effect for both visual and auditory items (Baddeley et al., 1984; Neath, et al., 1998)[2].

TABLE 1
Mean Proportion of Items Correctly Recalled as a Function of Word Length and Condition and Results from a Simulation

	Word Length	Condition		
		Quiet	Irrel. Speech	Artic. Supp.
Data	Short	.57	.46	.35
	Long	.48	.45	.34
Model	Short	.36	.28	.23
	Long	.29	.28	.23

Data from Experiment 1 of Neath et al. (1998).

SIMULATIONS

The data to be simulated were taken from Experiment 1 of Neath et al. (1998). They presented lists of eight short items and lists of eight long items followed by a serial reconstruction of order task. The words were drawn from a pool of 80 short and 80 long items (see LaPointe & Engle, 1990). The overall proportion of words correctly recalled in order is shown in Table 1 for each condition: In the quiet condition, the proportion of short words recalled was greater than the proportion of long words recalled, the standard word length effect. In both the irrelevant speech and articulatory suppression conditions, there was no difference in the proportion of short and long words recalled. Both articulatory suppression and irrelevant speech eliminated the word length effect.

For the current paper, the data from Experiment 1 of Neath et al. (1998) were re-scored and re-analyzed. The output order for each item was noted and position gradients were produced. These show the proportion of times that each item was recalled at each possible output serial position. The left column of Fig. 1 shows the gradients for short words and the right column shows the gradients for long words. The top row shows the gradients for the quiet condition, the middle row shows the gradients for the irrelevant speech condition, and the last row shows the gradients for the articulatory suppression condition. For example, the open diamond in the top left panel shows the proportion of times Item 1 was recalled in the first position, a correct response, and the proportion of times Item 1 was recalled in the second position, the third position, and so on, all incorrect responses.

There are five characteristics of the data to note. First, when an item is recalled in an incorrect position, it tends to be recalled most often in an adjacent position. Second, these error gradients are not symmetrical: The peaks decline through the list. Third, the gradients for the short words are steeper than those for the long words in the

---

[1] There are two equivalent ways of implementing the parameter δ. One is to use the original implementation of articulatory suppression but rename it as irrelevant speech, and then to decrement a by δ and call the result articulatory suppression. The problem with this method is that it would produce confusion when comparing simulations across papers (e.g. Nairne, 1990; Neath & Nairne, 1995). A second method, adopted by Neath (in press), keeps the implementation of articulatory suppression the same as in previous papers. To implement irrelevant speech, a is incremented by δ. This method captures the idea that the difference between articulatory suppression and irrelevant speech is that articulatory suppression entails more processing resources, but it keeps the newer simulations consistent with earlier simulations. Because the model is not used for quantitative fits, the choice of which method is used has no effect on the resulting simulations.

[2] Space limitations preclude a comparison between the feature model's account of the irrelevant speech effect with other accounts. The interested reader is referred to Neath (in press).

Data

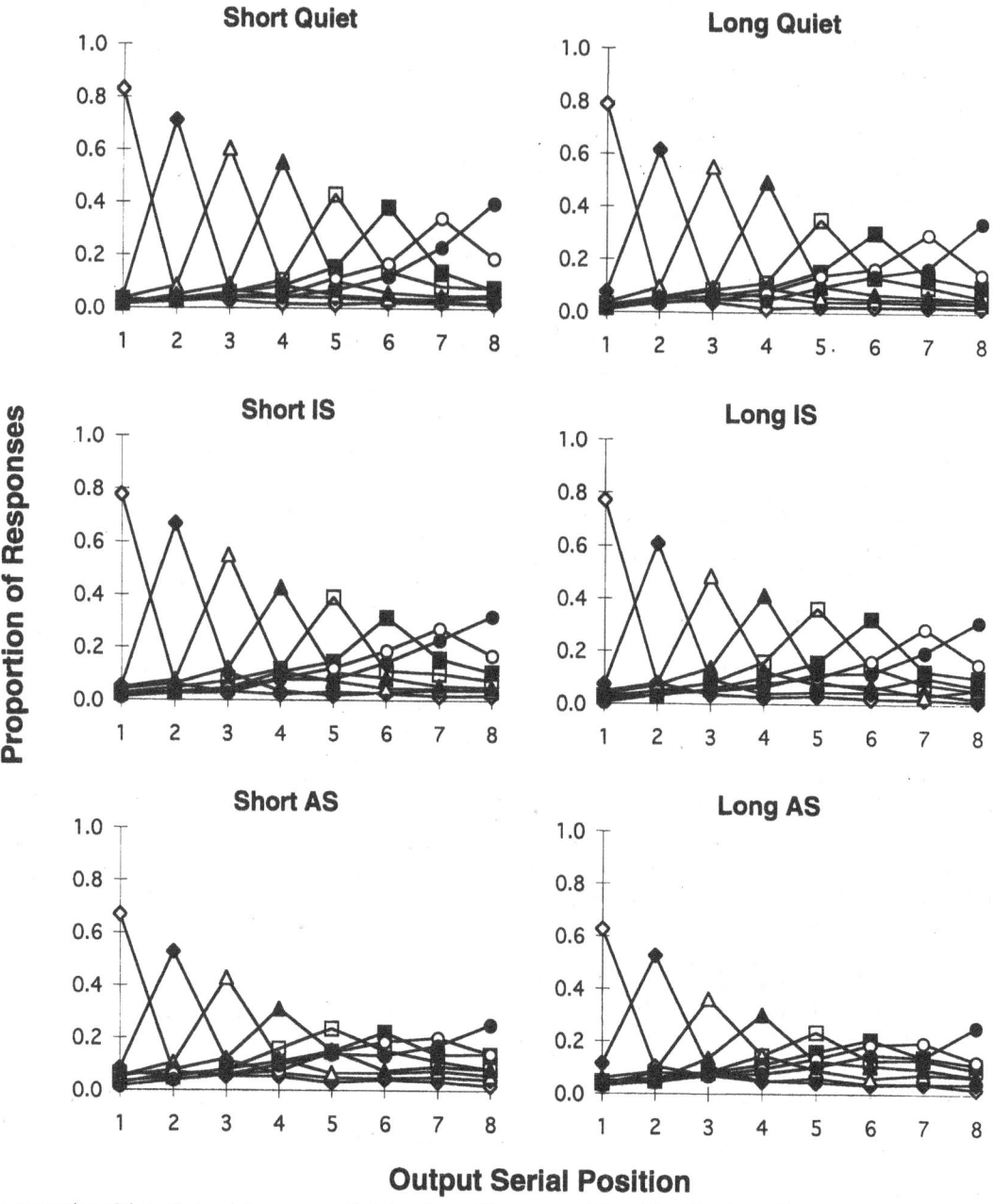

FIG. 1. The proportion of times that each item was recalled at each possible output serial position. The "peaks" are the correct responses; for example, the open diamond shows the proportion of times Item 1 was recalled in the first position (correct), the second position (incorrect), and so on. The left panel shows recall of short words, the right panel shows recall of long words. Note: IS = irrelevant speech; AS = articulatory suppression. Data from Experiment 1 of Neath et al. (1998).

quiet condition. This indicates more order errors occurred for long items than for short items[3]. Fourth, the gradients are flatter in the articulatory suppression condition than in the irrelevant speech condition. Fifth, the difference between short and long words disappears in both the irrelevant speech and articulatory suppression conditions. Not only is the proportion of total responses equivalent for short and long items for these two conditions, but also the proportion of correct (in position) responses is equivalent.

To simulate this experiment, the majority of the parameters (a full listing of parameter settings is shown in the appendix) were set to the same values as those used in the

---

[3] The proportion of total responses was equivalent in the short and long groups in each condition: .96 vs. .94 in the quiet condition, .95 vs. .94 in the irrelevant speech condition, and .94 vs. .93 in the articulatory suppression condition (all Fs < 1). However, the proportion of correct responses was lower for the long words than for the short words (see Neath et al., 1998, for the statistical analyses).

simulations reported by Neath and Nairne (1995) and Neath (in press), with the following exceptions. The parameters for list length (8) and modality (visual) were determined by the experiment. Theta, the probability of a perturbation, was set to .05; because this value is fixed, it is not considered a free parameter. The number of opportunities to perturb was set to 5 for each item in the list. This is a free parameter, and although it can be loosely mapped onto the time between the presentation and recall of an item, its value is somewhat arbitrary. This is not seen as a problem, however, because the model is now able to predict not only correct responses but also the full pattern of errors. Thus, for an 8-item list, the model is predicting 56 more data points at a cost of only 1 additional parameter. Finally, the probability of overwriting, F, was set to .5 rather than the usual 1.0 because of the addition of the perturbation process. Large values of F decrease overall performance and the perturbation process also decreases overall performance. If F had not been reduced, overall performance would have been too low to observe differences in the output error gradients. For the simulations reported here, the pattern of results is identical whether F is set to 1.0 or 0.0; only the absolute level varies.

As in previous work with the feature model, the goal is not to produce the best possible quantitative fit of the data by tweaking a large number of parameters. Rather, the approach is to demonstrate the appropriate pattern of results by changing only those parameters associated with the particular psychological processes implicated. Thus, although the overall level of performance differs between the data and the simulation, the pattern of results is correct. As can be seen in Table 1, the simulation produced the appropriate main effects and interactions at a global level: There is a word length effect in the quiet condition that is eliminated in both the irrelevant speech and articulatory suppression conditions. Furthermore, both irrelevant speech and articulatory suppression result in lower overall levels of performance.

Figure 2 shows the predicted position error gradients from the same simulations used to produce the bottom half of Table 1. All five aspects of the data in Fig. 1 noted earlier are apparent in the simulation results. The most likely incorrect position is adjacent to the correct position; the gradients are asymmetrical; the gradients for long words are slightly flatter than for short words in the quiet condition; and the gradients in the articulatory suppression condition are flatter than in the irrelevant speech condition. Of particular interest is the "interaction" between the implementations of order and item information: the error gradients for short and long words differ in the quiet condition, but are essentially identical in the irrelevant speech and articulatory suppression conditions.

The feature model produces a word length effect in the quiet condition because the probability of making an error during the output-planning stage is held constant at .10 for each segment in an item. Long words, however, have more segments than short words and so are more likely to have an error. When an error occurs, half of the modality-independent features are set to 0, which reflects the idea that some of the critical information about the word has been lost. This loss decreases the probability of correctly sampling the appropriate secondary memory item given a particular primary memory cue. It has been shown (Neath & Nairne, 1995) that this process can simulate most of the findings involving word length in the literature, including the linear relationship between proportion recalled and pronunciation time, the larger word length effect for visual than for auditory items, and the larger word length effect at the later serial positions than at the earlier serial positions.

Articulatory suppression is seen as adding noise to the modality-independent features through the feature adoption process. Articulatory suppression is implemented by setting half of the modality-independent features to a constant value, reflecting the experimental procedure of having the subject repeatedly say the word "teatime" over and over. This has the net effect of reducing the probability of sampling the correct secondary memory item. Articulatory suppression eliminates the word length effect because the noise that is added through feature adoption affects the same features as the word length manipulation. Articulatory suppression will cause some of the modality-independent features to be altered. If a segment assembly error occurs, there is no observable effect because changing an already altered feature does not make it any more different.

Irrelevant speech, in the feature model, is implemented in almost the same way as articulatory suppression. The major difference is that it is assumed that articulatory suppression is more distracting—diverts more resources or reduces available attention more—than irrelevant speech. The idea is that it takes more resources to articulate constantly than it does to listen passively. Thus, irrelevant speech eliminates the word length effect for the same reasons as articulatory suppression, but overall performance will be slightly higher.

The error gradients are due to perturbation, which is implemented as a probabilistic drifting process. Each cue in primary memory includes information about the original serial position. At recall, this information is used to compute a positional uncertainty gradient that indicates the probability that the cue originally encoded an item from position 1, position 2, and so on. The cue that has the highest probability of originally being in position 1 will be used to sample from secondary memory first. When an item is recalled out of order, it is most likely to be recalled in an adjacent position and the probability decreases for positions further away from the original. Because perturbation is allowed in both directions, it is possible for a representation to drift away from the original value and for it to drift back to the original value. The gradients are asymmetric because recall always proceeds from the item with the largest probability of being the first item. The reason that the error gradients become flattened is that when the proportion of match-

Model

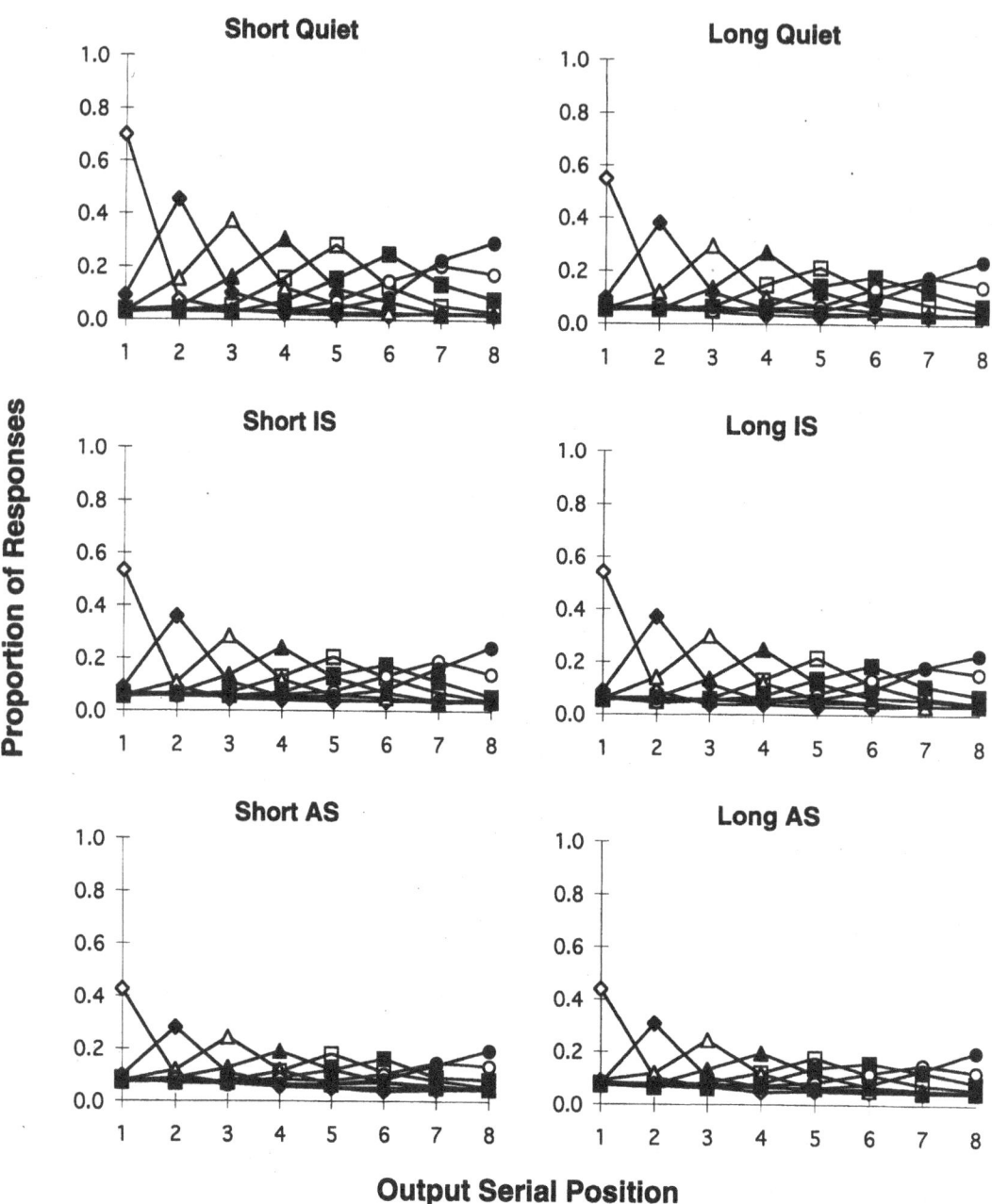

FIG. 2. The predictions of the feature model for the data shown in Fig. 1.

ing features decreases, the probability of sampling an incorrect item increases.

One interesting finding from the simulation is that a manipulation that affects only item information can produce an increase in order errors. Neither articulatory suppression nor irrelevant speech affect the information coding position or order information; however, both articulatory suppression and irrelevant speech produce an increase in order errors. The reason is that the cues are less likely to sample the correct item when a larger proportion of features have been affected by feature adoption. When such an item error occurs—the wrong item was selected as a match for the cue—an order error can result. One implication of this is that item errors and order errors can be distinguished only within the framework of a particular theory or model.

GENERAL DISCUSSION

When people are asked to recall a list of items in order, they usually recall some items out of order. These order errors are systematic and, as Fig. 1 shows, are affected by manipulations such as word length, irrelevant speech, and articulatory suppression. The feature model (Nairne, 1990; Neath & Nairne, 1995) was originally neutral on how order information was represented and did not address order errors[4]. An extension of the feature model that includes aspects of Estes' (1972, 1997) perturbation theory produces the appropriate pattern of errors.

Order errors occur due to a gradual loss of precision in the information that encodes position. The loss of precision described by the perturbation equations produces the same pattern of position error gradients as observed in empirical data (e.g. Estes, 1972, 1997; Nairne, 1991). The reduction in performance seen when list presentation is accompanied by either articulatory suppression or irrelevant speech is due, according to the model, to the process of feature adoption. The cues that encode item information adopt some of the features from the irrelevant speech items, which reduces the probability that the correct item in secondary memory will be sampled when probed with a cue from primary memory. The feature adoption process does not interfere directly with either rehearsal, phonological information, or order information. Rather, order information is encoded and preserved by a separate process, perturbation of the encoded cues in primary memory. Even though item and order information are separate in the model, they interact in appropriate ways.

One potential weakness of the current version of the feature model is the incomplete specification of when a perturbation will occur and what causes it. The current implementation is neutral, assuming for simplicity only that there are an equal number of opportunities for perturbations to occur for each list item. In an extended discussion of these issues, Estes (1997) suggested that perturbations are not directly related to the passage of time. Rather, opportunities for perturbations arise when an item is brought back to conscious awareness through intentional rehearsal or when some cue causes temporary recollection of the item. Although this incompleteness may be a weakness, it is relatively minor: Even large variations in the number of opportunities to perturb do not change the basic predictions.

The feature model (Nairne, 1990) originally offered an integrated explanation for the modality effect, the suffix effect, the phonological similarity effect, the serial position effect, temporal grouping effects, and the effects of articulatory suppression. It has since been extended to include the word length effect (Neath & Nairne, 1995) and the irrelevant speech effect (Neath, in press). The current paper demonstrates how the feature model can be extended to explain the pattern of errors in order information. The most important contribution, however, is that the model offers a framework in which interactions between all of these effects can be systematically explored. For example, it predicted that suffix effects should obtain under articulatory suppression (Surprenant, LeCompte, & Neath, in press), that irrelevant speech should eliminate the word length effect for both visual and auditory presentation (Neath et al., 1998), and that irrelevant speech should eliminate the phonological similarity effect only for visually presented items (Surprenant et al., 1999). It can also simulate such complex interactions as what occurs when presentation modality, phonological similarity, word length, articulatory suppression, and irrelevant speech are simultaneously manipulated. As shown here, the model is now capable of tossing order errors into the mix.

REFERENCES

Baddeley, A.D., Lewis, V.J., & Vallar, G. (1984). Exploring the articulatory loop. *Quarterly Journal of Experimental Psychology, 36*, 233–252.

Baddeley, A.D., Thomson, N., & Buchanan, M. (1975). Word length and the structure of short-term memory. *Journal of Verbal Learning and Verbal Behavior, 14*, 575–589.

Brown, G.D.A., & Hulme, C. (1995). Modelling item length effects in memory span: No rehearsal needed? *Journal of Memory and Language, 34*, 594–621.

Caplan, D., Rochon, E., & Waters, G.S. (1992). Articulatory and phonological determinants of word-length effects in span tasks. *Quarterly Journal of Experimental Psychology, 45A*, 177–192.

Colle, H.A., & Welsh, A. (1976). Acoustic masking in primary memory. *Journal of Verbal Learning and Verbal Behavior, 15*, 17–31.

Coltheart, V., & Langdon, R. (1998). Recall of short word lists presented visually at fast rates: Effects of phonological similarity and word length. *Memory and Cognition, 26*, 330–342.

Conrad, R. (1964). Acoustic confusions in immediate memory. *British Journal of Psychology, 55*, 75–84.

Dosher, B.A., & Ma, J.-J. (1998). Output loss or rehearsal loop? Output-time versus pronunciation-time limits in immediate recall for forgetting-matched materials. *Journal of Experimental Psychology: Learning, Memory, and Cognition, 24*, 316–335.

Estes, W.K. (1972). An associative basis for coding and organization in memory. In A.W. Melton & E. Martin (Eds.), *Coding processes in human memory* (pp. 161–190). Washington, DC: Winston.

Estes, W.K. (1997). Processes of memory loss, recovery, and distortion. *Psychological Review, 104*, 148–169.

Hintzman, D.L. (1991). Why are formal models useful in psychology? In W.E. Hockley & S. Lewandowsky (Eds.), *Relating theory and data: Essays on human memory in honor of Bennet B. Murdock* (pp. 39–56). Hillsdale, NJ: Lawrence Erlbaum Associates Inc.

LaPointe, L.B., & Engle, R.W. (1990). Simple and complex word spans as measures of working memory capacity. *Journal of Experimental Psychology: Learning, Memory, and Cognition, 16*, 1118–1133.

Luce, R.D. (1963). Detection and recognition. In R.D. Luce, R.R. Bush, & E. Galanter (Eds.), *Handbook of mathematical psychology* (pp. 103–189). New York: Wiley.

Melton, A.W. (1963). Implications of short-term memory for a general theory of memory. *Journal of Verbal Learning and Verbal Behavior, 2*, 1–21.

Murray, D.J. (1968). Articulation and acoustic confusability in short-term memory. *Journal of Experimental Psychology, 78*, 679–684.

Murray, D.J., Rowan, A.J., & Smith, K.H. (1988). The effect of articulatory suppression on short-term recognition. *Canadian Journal of Psychology, 42*, 424–436.

Nairne, J.S. (1988). A framework for interpreting recency effects in immediate serial recall. *Memory and Cognition, 16*, 343–352.

Nairne, J.S. (1990). A feature model of immediate memory. *Memory and Cognition, 18*, 251–269.

---

[4] It should be noted that Nairne (1990, p. 264) suggested the basic idea used in this paper.

Nairne, J.S. (1991). Positional uncertainty in long-term memory. *Memory and Cognition, 19*, 332–340.

Neath, I. (1998). *Human memory: An introduction to research, data, and theory*. Pacific Grove, CA: Brooks/Cole.

Neath, I. (in press). Modelling the effects of irrelevant speech on memory. *Psychonomic Bulletin and Review*.

Neath, I., & Nairne, J.S. (1995). Word-length effects in immediate memory: Overwriting trace decay theory. *Psychonomic Bulletin and Review, 2*, 429–441.

Neath, I., Surprenant, A.M., & LeCompte, D.C. (1998). Irrelevant speech eliminates the word length effect. *Memory and Cognition, 26*, 343–354.

Parkin, A.J. (1993). *Memory: Phenomena, experiment, and theory*. Oxford: Blackwell.

Raaijmakers, J.G., & Shiffrin, R.M. (1981). Search of associative memory. *Psychological Review, 88*, 93–134.

Surprenant, A.M., LeCompte, D.C., & Neath, I. (in press). Manipulations of irrelevant information: Suffix effects under articulatory suppression and irrelevant speech. *Quarterly Journal of Experimental Psychology*.

Surprenant, A.M., & Neath, I. (1996). The relation between discriminability and memory for vowels, consonants, and silent-centre syllables. *Memory and Cognition, 24*, 356–366.

Surprenant, A.M., Neath, I., & LeCompte, D.C. (1999). Irrelevant speech, phonological similarity, and presentation modality. *Memory, 7*, 405–420.

APPENDIX
Parameter settings for the simulations

Parameter	Setting
Comparison weighting factor [b]	1.0
Response bias [w_{ij}]	1.0
Response bias [w_{ik}]	1.0
Probability of encoding [L]	1.0
Recovery scaling constant [c]	2.0
Number of recovery attempts	2
Number of simulations	2000
Probability of overwriting [F]	0.5
Overall attention [a]	10
Attentional adjustment [δ]	+4
Number of modality-independent features	20
Number of modality-dependent features	2
List length	8
Number of segments	
Short	1
Long	10
Probability of segment error	0.10
Probability of a perturbation [θ]	0.05
Number of perturbation opportunities [π]	5

Testing the Idea of Distinct Storage Mechanisms in Memory

Donald Laming
University of Cambridge, UK

This paper sets out quantitative foundations for testing the idea that memory is served by two distinct storage mechanisms, a short-term and a separate long-term store, using data from the single-trial free-recall experiment by Murdock and Okada (1970). In single-trial free recall one can observe *which* word is recalled next and *how long* that recall takes, but that is all. So justification for two separate stores must turn either on the probabilities of recall, or on the latencies, for particular serial positions in the stimulus list.

(a) Nearly one-third of all recalls after the first are *successors* (Word n+1 immediately following recall of Word n). So recall is dominated, not by absolute serial position (as a short-term store would require), but by position relative to the preceding recall.

(b) To a first approximation, all first recalls have the same latency distribution except for Word 1. A common latency distribution is compatible with a single store. An explanation is offered why Word 1 should take longer, in which Word 1 is the *second retrieval* from a common store.

The idea of two separate stores appears to lack experimental support.

Cet article propose un test quantitatif de l'idée selon laquelle la mémoire comprendrait deux mécanismes distincts d'emmagasinage, un mécanisme à court terme et un mécanisme à long terme. Les données d'une expérience de Murdock et Okada (1970), dans laquelle un seul essai de rappel libre était présenté, sont utilisées. Dans cette tâche, il est possible de vérifier quel mot est rappelé après un autre mot et combien de temps prend ce rappel, mais ce sont là les deux seules mesures disponibles. Dans ces conditions, la justification de l'existence de deux systèmes séparés doit être basée soit sur les probabilités de rappel ou sur le temps de latence pour des positions sérielles spécifiques.

(a) Près d'un tiers de tous les mots rappelés après le premier sont des successeurs (Mot n+1 suit immédiatement le rappel du Mot n). Le rappel est donc dominé par la position relative de l'item rappelé précédemment et non pas par la position sérielle absolue (comme l'exigerait l'hypothèse d'un système à court terme).

(b) Tous les premiers rappels ont approximativement la même distribution de latence, excepté le Mot 1. Cette distribution de latence est compatible avec un système unitaire de mémoire. Le temps de latence plus long pour le Mot 1 serait attribuable au fait que celui-ci est le second à être récupéré d'un système commun.

L'idée de deux systèmes séparés de mémoire semble manquer de appui empirique.

The idea about which cognitive psychologists seem the most confident of all is that memory is served by two distinct storage mechanisms, a short-term and a separate long-term store. That idea is found in nearly all textbooks. But what the textbooks (e.g. Baddeley, 1997, pp. 38–44) omit to point out is that the supporting evidence, so carefully laid out, is equally compatible with a single store only, and so does not speak to the issue at all.

To examine one example, if there is sufficient delay between the end of the stimulus list and the beginning of recall, the recency effect disappears (Glanzer & Cunitz, 1966; Postman & Phillips, 1965). During that delay, it is claimed, the content of the short-term store decays. But the mental arithmetic that is commonly used to prevent rehearsal during that delay appends a series of three-digit numbers to the end of the list in memory, and the recency effect then attaches to the end of that list of numbers, which the subject is not asked to recall. Certainly, the accessibility of an item to recall decreases with the lapse of time since presentation; and analysis of Brown-Peterson data suggests that accessibility decreases as a reciprocal function of time, while a negative exponential decay is contraindicated (Laming, 1992). But there is nothing in the data to tell us whether that decreasing function of time is mediated by two separate stores or only one.

The principal experimental source of support claimed for the two-store idea has long been single-trial free recall. In what follows I use the data from Murdock and Okada (1970) to illustrate how the idea might be

---

Requests for reprints should be addressed to Donald Laming, University of Cambridge, Department of Experimental Psychology, Downing Street, Cambridge, England CB2 3EB (E-mail: drjl@cus.cam.ac.uk).

I thank Ben Murdock for making his raw data available to me for further analysis; without that data, this paper could never have been written. I also thank Gordon Brown for some particularly incisive criticism of the original MS.

© 1999 International Union of Psychological Science

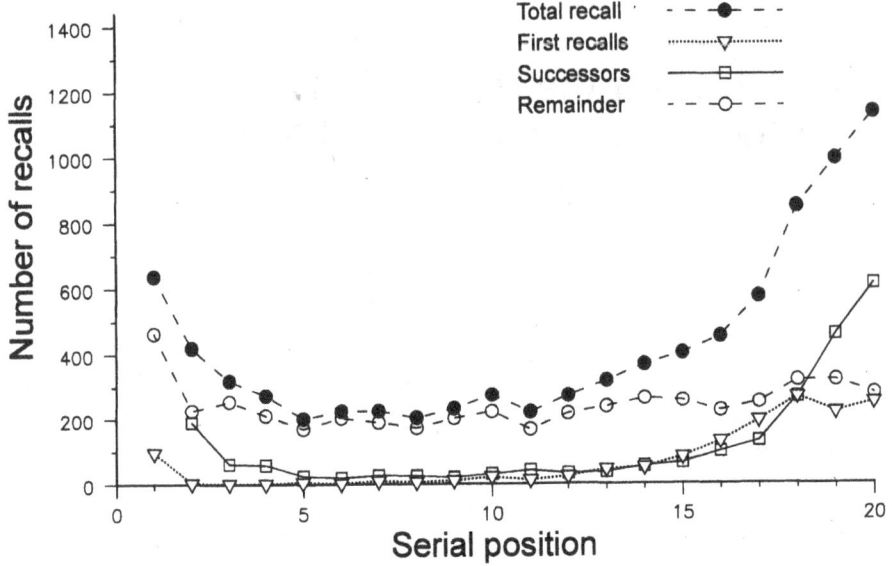

FIG. 1. Serial position curve from Murdock and Okada (1970) with the same data decomposed into first recalls, successors, and a remainder.

rigorously tested. Murdock and Okada showed their subjects a list of 20 words at a rate of either 1 or 2 word/s on successive frames of a cine film. Each subject's spoken recall was recorded on audio tape so that inter-recall latencies could be measured. Suppose, now, that a subject has recalled three words; what next? One can record the (4th) word spoken next and the time that elapses until its recall begins. Justification for assuming two stores in memory must therefore depend either on the response frequencies or on their latencies.

FREQUENCIES OF RECALL

Words are assigned to lists at random, so only the serial position of the word recalled is material. Figure 1 (filled circles) shows the serial position curve with the end of the list showing enhanced recall. This is the *recency effect*. Most subjects (though not all) attempt to recall the last few words first, and on that basis it is suggested that the last few words come from a separate short-term store of high accessibility, but a store in which material decays rapidly.

Figure 1 (open symbols) also shows the same data decomposed into first recalls, successors, and a remainder. A *successor recall* is Word $n+1$ recalled immediately after Word n. Successors comprise nearly one third of all recalls after the first. They occur at all serial positions in the list, though with somewhat greater relative frequency towards the end (exceeding .8 early in recall; see Fig. 2c below). The chance level in Murdock and Okada's (1970) experiment is 1/20 and the frequency of successors highly significant. This finding is robust. Murdock (1962) read lists of 10–40 words at 1 or 2 sec/word, with written recall. The proportions of successors in recall of the 8 different lists in Table 1 all exceed .25.

Some Consequences of Successor Recalls

If a separate short-term store is to be justified on the basis of *different* frequencies of recall, that justification must rest on an *enhanced* probability of recall for the last few words, above the level obtainable from the long-term store alone. What might that enhanced level be?

TABLE 1
Total Numbers of Successors from Murdock (1962, roman type) and Murdock and Okada (1970, italic)

Experimental Condition	Total No. of Cases	Number of Successors	Proportion
10 words @ 2sec each	6529	2163	.331
15 words @ 2sec each	8666	2469	.285
20 words @ 2sec each	8929	2645	.296
20 words @ 1sec each	7052	2106	.299
20 words @ 1sec each	*4218*	*1383*	*.328*
20 words @ ½ sec each	*3373*	*869*	*.258*
30 words @ 1sec each	9073	2428	.268
40 words @ 1sec each	8595	2222	.259

Figure 2(a) shows the serial position curve for first recalls only. Word 1 is generally agreed to be available only from long-term store. So the enhanced probability afforded by the short-term store cannot be less than .067, and Word 2 (prob. .003) is most certainly *not* in the short-term store. Word 20 is generally agreed to be available from the short-term store. So the unenhanced probability (from long-term store only) cannot be greater than .173. That is to say, the critical probability for the Murdock and Okada (1970) data lies somewhere between .067 and .173.

Now look at second recalls following Word 1 as first recall (Fig. 2b). The probability of Word 2 following Word 1 as first recall is .552—so Word 1 as first recall must somehow rewrite Word 2 in short-term store. At the same time, everything else (except possibly Words 3 and 4) is available only from long-term store (the conditional probability of Word 18, for example, is .031). Word 1 as first recall is by no means an "exception to the rule". There are many other results of similar kind; Fig. 2c shows some of them. Words 15 and 17 demonstrably tip Word 20 out of the short-term store; Words 14, 16, and 18 are not much different.

It is clear that recall probabilities after the first recall are dominated, not by absolute position in the list, but by proximity to the preceding recall. The theoretical problem posed by free recall is to describe that process succinctly. Assigning the last few words (absolute position) in the list to a short-term store with privileged access is simply starting off on the wrong foot. So, if there is empirical justification for two separate memory stores, it must depend on the inter-recall latencies.

INTER-RECALL LATENCIES

The analysis of recall latencies turns on a comparison between two generic models.

Two-store Model

Suppose the last few words in the list are in a separate short-term store that is distinguished by a distinct distribution of recall latency [i.e. $F_S(t)$ instead of $F_L(t)$ in Fig. 3]. There are two recall strategies to be distinguished:

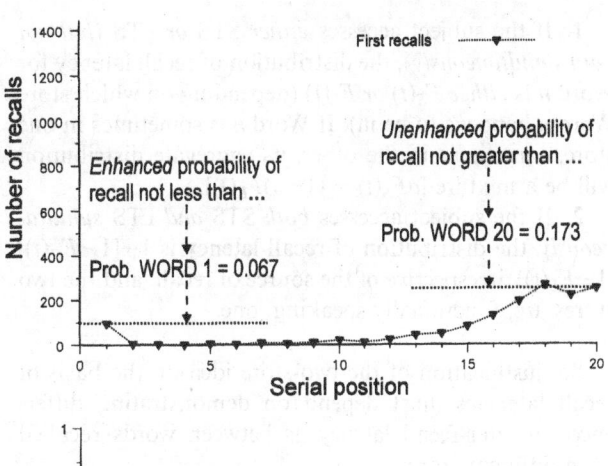
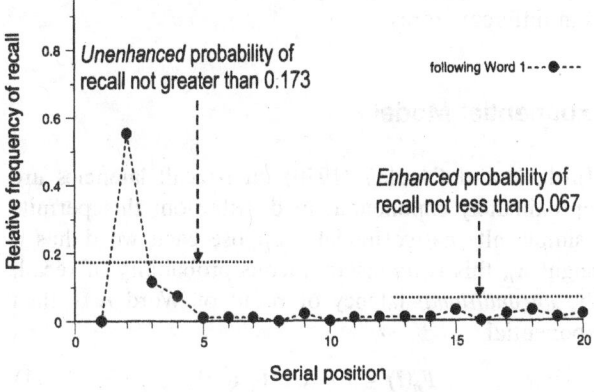
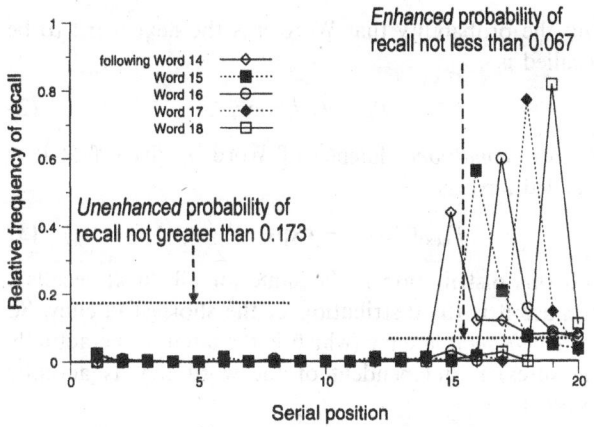

FIG. 2. (a) Serial position curve of first recalls from Murdock and Okada (1970); (b) serial position curve of second recalls following Word 1 as first recall; (c) serial position curves of second recalls following Words 14–18 as first recall.

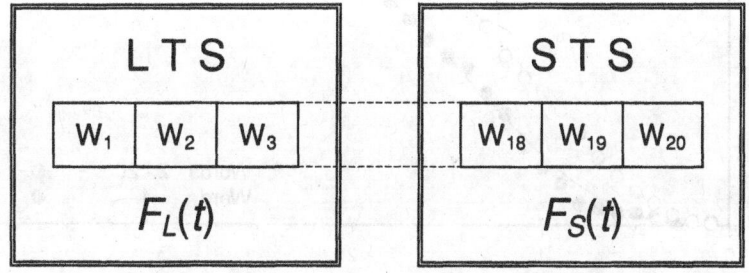

FIG. 3. Latency model for distinguishing two separate stores.

1. If the subject accesses *either* STS *or* LTS (*but not both simultaneously*), the distribution of recall latency for Word n is *either* $F_S(t)$ or $F_L(t)$ (depending on which store Word n happens to be in). If Word n is sometimes in one store, sometimes in the other, its aggregate distribution will be a mixture $[aF_S(t) + (1-a)F_L(t)]$.

2. If the subject accesses *both* STS *and* LTS *simultaneously*, the distribution of recall latency is $1-[1-F_S(t)][1-F_L(t)]$, irrespective of the source of recall, and the two stores are, functionally speaking, one.

So, justification of the two-store idea on the basis of recall latencies must depend on demonstrating differences in inter-recall latency as between words recalled from different stores.

Exponential Model

Murdock and Okada's (1970) inter-recall latencies are approximately exponential in distribution; this permits a simple alternative model. Suppose each word has a weight w_i; this is its instantaneous probability of recall. The *unconditional* latency of recall of Word n is then exponential

$$F_n(t) = 1 - \exp\{-w_n t\}, \quad (1)$$

and the probability that Word n is the next word to be recalled is

$$P_n = w_n / \Sigma_i w_i. \quad (2)$$

But the *conditional* latency of Word n, given that it is recalled next, is

$$F_{\text{next}}(t) = 1 - \exp\{-(\Sigma_i w_i)t\}; \quad (3)$$

and this distribution is the same for all "next recalls", because it is the distribution of the shortest latency. So the *conditional* latency (which is the latency one actually measures) is independent of the word that is actually recalled.

First-recall Latencies

Equation (3) implies that inter-recall latency depends on the pool of words available for recall and words once recalled are seldom repeated (the probability of repetition conditional on a previous recall is typically about .025 in Murdock & Okada's data). I shall look chiefly at first recalls because they are always drawn from a common pool. Figure 4 displays the distributions of first-recall latencies from Murdock and Okada (1970), and it is clear that Word 1 has longer latencies than the other words taken together [Kruskal-Wallis analysis of variance: χ^2 (1,1440) = 22.592]. Does this mean that Word 1 resides in a special long-term store?

The cumulative distribution functions fitted to the data in Fig. 4 are based on this model:

1. The distribution for Words 2–20 is the convolution of a RT distribution and an exponential. The reaction time is the time taken to respond to the "recall" signal at the end of the list; it is modelled as a gamma distribution of arbitrary parameter ν multiplied by a scale constant β. The exponential component is the time actually taken to retrieve a word, any word, from memory and is multiplied by the same scale constant β.

2. The distribution for Word 1 is the distribution for Words 2–20 convolved with a second exponential component, again multiplied by the scale constant β. That is to say, recall of Word 1 involves *two* retrievals, of which Word 1 is the *second*.

3. Both distributions are advanced by the same interval (186msec) ahead of the actual origin from which the inter-recall latencies were measured.

With only three free parameters this model is significant at .01 [χ^2 (51,1440) = 84.515], but nevertheless fits well enough to support the idea that the latency to recall Word 1 differs by the incorporation of an extra exponential component. What might that extra component signify?

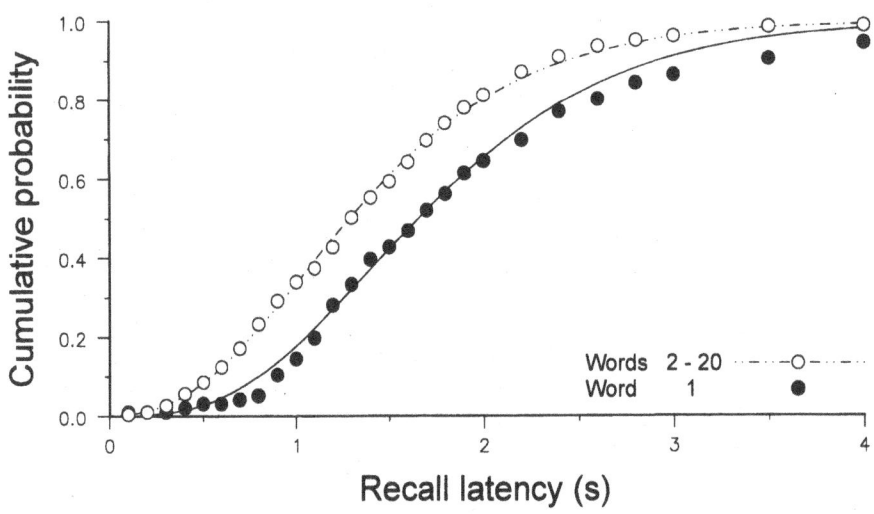

FIG. 4. Distributions of first-recall latencies from Murdock and Okada (1970).

Before presenting a list of stimuli any experimenter worth his salt will make sure his subject is ready. That amounts to the provision of an informal "GET READY" signal. Such a "start signal" has previously been employed by Shiffrin and Cook (1978) and by Lewandowsky and Murdock (1989), but in models for the recall of items in serial order. "GET READY" is a very clear, salient, stimulus; the subject is not allowed to miss it. It is also a von Restorff stimulus—it is not a word—and is easily recalled on that account. So Word 1 is accessed by first retrieving "GET READY" (which is not itself uttered as a response) and then Word 1 as its successor. That requires two retrievals from the same store and increases the latency by one exponential delay.

There is a simple check on this story. Figure 5 compares the latencies of Word 1 as first recall with the *sums* of the first recall latency of Word n and the second recall latency of Word $(n+1)$ where Word $(n+1)$ follows Word n immediately as successor. The distribution for Word 1 (filled circles) lies in the middle of the cluster.

Words 2–20

The first-recall latencies of Words 2–20 comprise the critical comparison. Figure 6 displays the cumulative distributions for every word for which the sample size is at least 40. There are no significant differences between Words 14–20 (where the short-term idea would lead us to expect them), but Word 13 (and also Word 10, but not Word 12) shows some long latencies like Word 1.

Figure 7 shows the primacy effect at the *beginning* of recall in Murdock and Okada (1970). There were 96 first

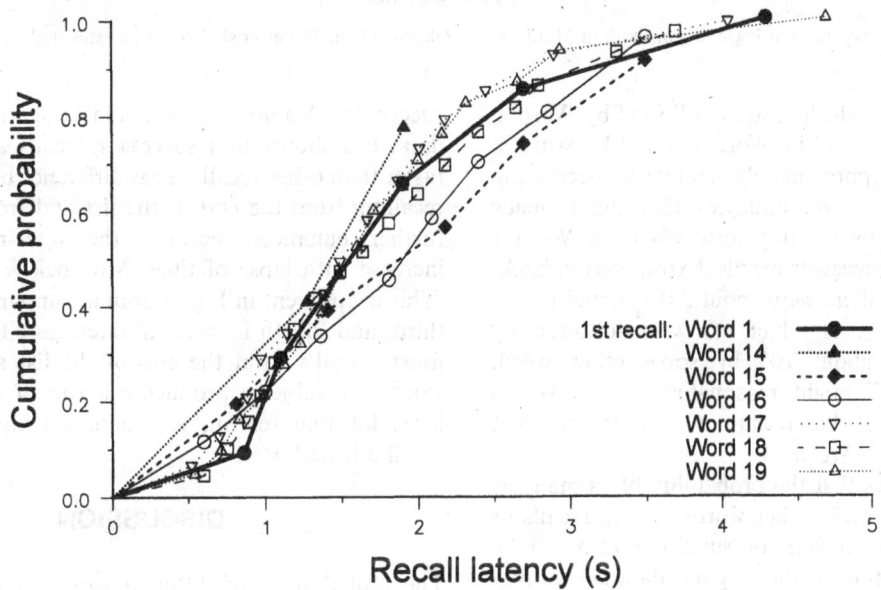

FIG. 5. Cumulative distributions of Word n + successor compared with Word 1 (filled circles) from Murdock and Okada (1970).

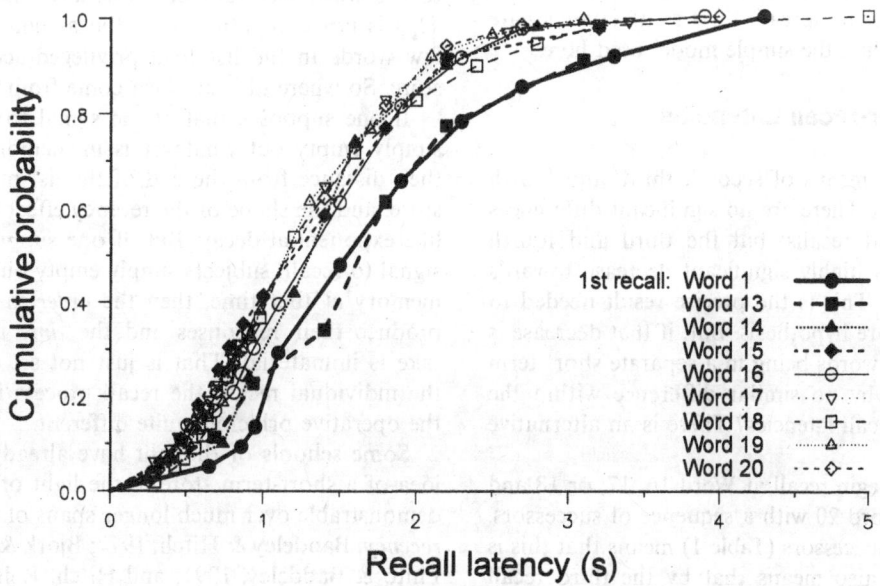

FIG. 6. Cumulative distributions of first recall latencies from Murdock and Okada (1970).

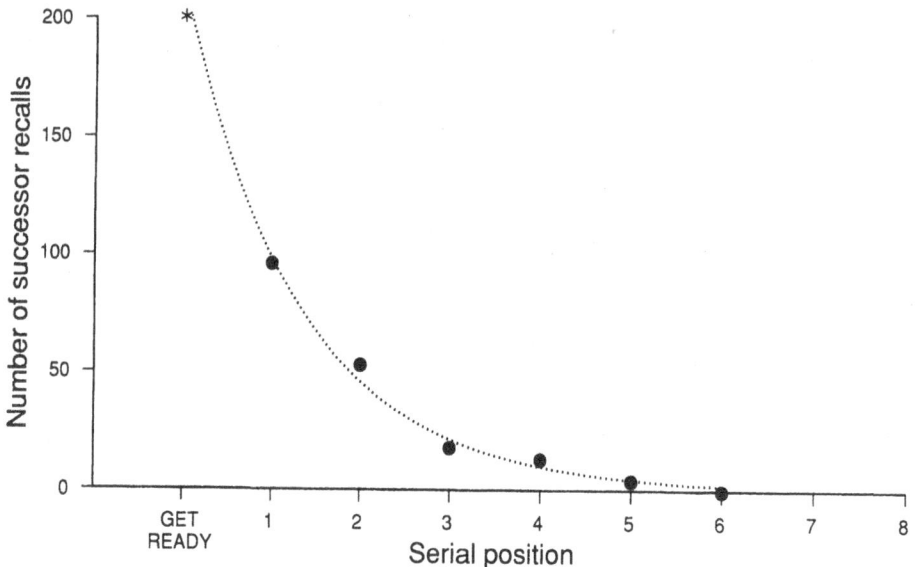

FIG. 7. Primacy effect at beginning of recall in Murdock and Okada (1970). The asterisk denotes an estimated frequency.

recalls of Word 1, of which 53 were followed by Word 2, 18 of those by Word 3, 13 by Word 4, and 4 by Word 5. That sequence is approximately geometric decreasing with probability .478 and indicates that the primacy effect is generated by running forwards from Word 1 with a sequence of successor recalls. Extrapolation backwards suggests that there were about 201 original recalls of "GET READY", of which 96 were followed by Word 1 etc. and about 105 by some other word. "Some other word" might reasonably include Words 2 and 3 (6 instances), but it cannot also include most of the 44 instances of Word 13.

Calculation shows that the probability of as many as 20 of the estimated 105 "other words" being recalls of the same word (any word) is too small (about 5×10^{-6}). Moreover, examination of the original data shows that Word 1 as first recall is principally due to a rather small proportion of subjects, whereas the first recalls of Word 13 are widely and evenly spread. First-recall latencies are more complicated than the simple model used here.

Subsequent Inter-recall Latencies

Figure 8 shows the means of second, third, and fourth inter-recall latencies. There are no significant differences amongst the second recalls; but the third and fourth recalls both show a highly significant decrease towards the end of the list. This is the precise result needed to support the two-store hypothesis. But, if that decrease is due to the last few words being in a separate short-term fast-access store, why no similar difference within the first- and second-recall latencies? There is an alternative explanation.

Many subjects begin recall at Word 16, 17, or 18 and try to run on to Word 20 with a sequence of successors. The prevalence of successors (Table 1) means that this is rather efficient. It also means that by the third recall those words recalled from the end of the list are chiefly successors. Kahana (1996), analyzing these very same data, has shown that successor recalls are intrinsically faster than other recalls. That difference between subjects recalling from the end of the list and from elsewhere is further enhanced because the inter-recall latencies increase with lapse of time (Murdock & Okada, 1970). (This is apparent in Fig. 8 from a comparison of second, third, and fourth inter-recall latencies.) Those third and fourth recalls from the end of the list are contributed chiefly by subjects producing a run of successors who have, for that reason, got there quickly and therefore recall a little faster.

DISCUSSION

The probabilities of different words in single-trial free recall are dominated by proximity in the stimulus list to the word just recalled (whichever one it might be). This is not compatible with the assignment of the last few words in the list to a privileged-access short-term store. So where did that idea come from?

If one supposes that at the signal to recall, subjects simply empty out whatever is in memory at that time, then distance from the end of the list measures time in store, and the shape of the recency effect looks (roughly) like exponential decay. But, if one supposes that at the signal to recall, subjects simply empty out whatever is in memory at that time, then the *order* in which subjects produce their responses and the *time* those responses take is immaterial. That is just not so. At the level of the individual recall, the recall process is dynamic and the operative principle quite different.

Some schools of thought have already discarded the idea of a short-term store in the light of recency effects demonstrable over much longer spans of time (*long-term recency*: Baddeley & Hitch, 1977; Bjork & Whitten, 1974; Pinto & Baddeley, 1991; and Hitch, Rejman, & Turner, 1980 [cited in Baddeley, 1986, pp. 156–160]). The popular

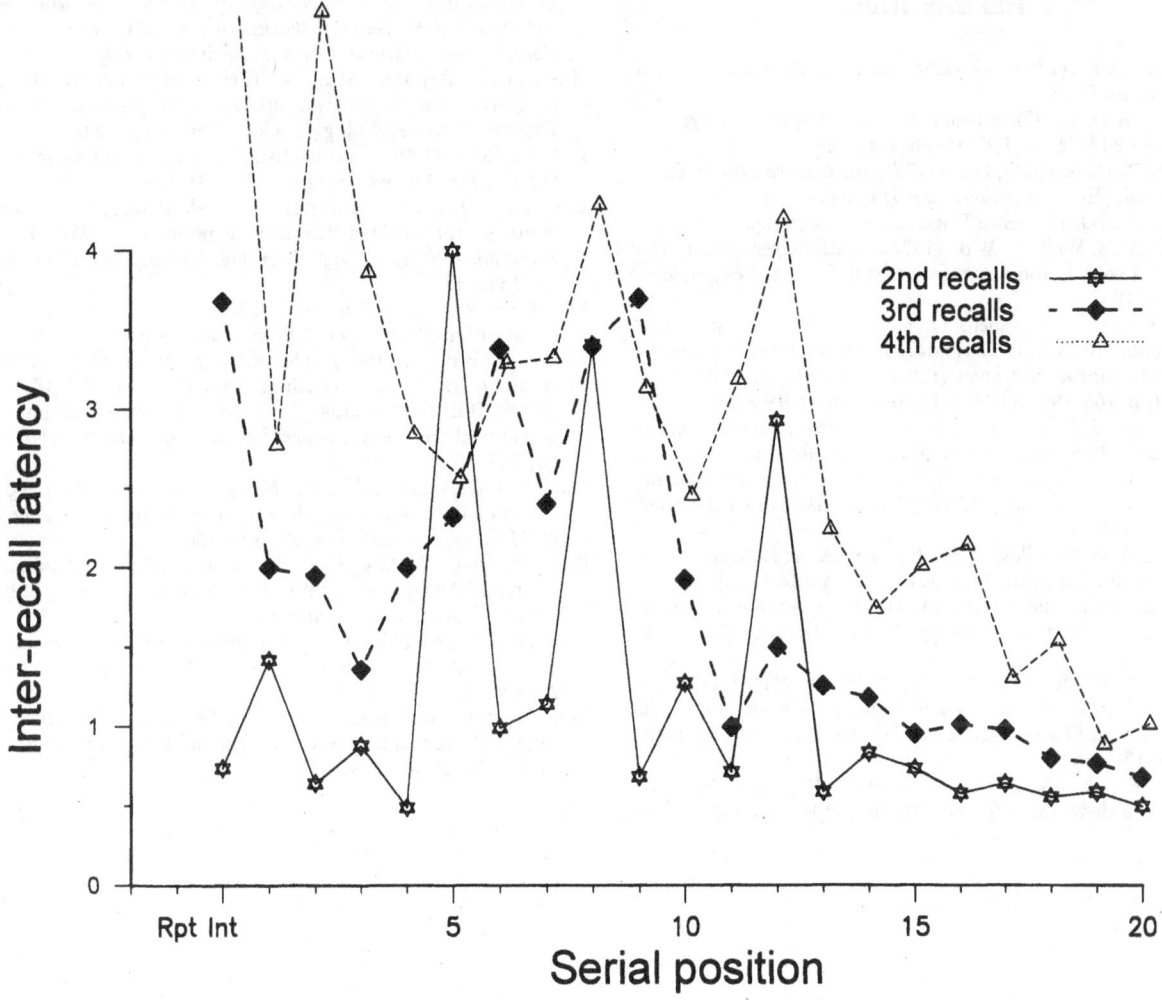

FIG. 8. Mean inter-recall latencies for second, third and fourth recalls from Murdock and Okada (1970).

alternative idea has been recall according to temporal cues whose discriminability depends, with a nod in the direction of Weber's Law, on the ratio *temporal separation between items/retention interval* (Bjork & Whitten, 1974; Crowder, 1976, pp. 461–462; Glenberg, Bradley, Kraus, & Renzaglia, 1983) and is therefore independent of the absolute scale of time. But those temporal cues cannot be elements of the original memories (because it is not known at the time of presentation when recall will be required) and they cannot be relevant to free recall (because any word will do in free recall, provided only that it has not been recalled previously, and there is no need for any temporal discrimination at all).

Suppose, instead, that the accessibility of items in memory decreases as the reciprocal of the lapse of time; this idea affords an accurate account of Brown-Peterson data (Laming, 1992). Then, as at the beginning of recall, items presented at regular intervals (every k sec) have accessibilities (a/nk for the nth word from the end of the list), and their *relative* accessibilities are independent of their spacing (k). On this reciprocal assumption, recency should be equally observable over any and every span of time. Moreover, if the items are spaced out simply by presenting a list at a slower rate (each item occupying k sec), then the *absolute* accessibilities are unchanged (because $k \times a/nk = a/n$). Glanzer and Cunitz (1966, p. 354, Fig. 1) display a striking example of this relationship. Until there are other different findings to be accommodated simultaneously, no more elaborate model (e.g. Glenberg & Swanson, 1986; Henson & Burgess, 1998; Nairne, Neath, Serra, & Byun, 1997) is either needed or justified. But the reciprocal idea does, of course, dispense with the short-term store.

The recency effect in the serial position curve results from a three-way interaction between (a) memory, (b) the experimental design, and (c) a particular way (Fig. 1) of summarizing the data. The short-term fast-decay store is no more than a *rule of thumb* that characterizes the end of the serial position curve when the data are summarized in that way.

If there is to be a scientific theory of memory, it must, at the very least, be independent of the way in which psychologists choose to analyze their data! It must also apply at the level of the individual recall. As a component of such a theory, a separate short-term store is no better than make-believe.

REFERENCES

Baddeley, A.D. (1986). *Working memory*. Oxford: Oxford University Press.

Baddeley, A.D. (1997). *Human memory: Theory and practice* (revised ed.). Hove, UK: Psychology Press.

Baddeley, A.D., & Hitch, G.J. (1977). Recency re-examined. In S. Dornic (Ed.), *Attention and performance VI* (pp. 647–667). Hillsdale, NJ: Lawrence Erlbaum Associates Inc.

Bjork, R.A., & Whitten, W.B. (1974). Recency-sensitive retrieval processes in long-term free recall. *Cognitive Psychology, 6*, 173–189.

Brown, G.D.A., & Vousden, J.I. (1998). Adaptive analysis of sequential behaviour: Oscillators as rational mechanisms. In M. Oaksford & N. Chater (Eds.), *Rational models of cognition* (pp. 165–193). Oxford: Oxford University Press.

Crowder, R.G. (1976). *Principles of learning and memory*. Hillsdale, NJ: Lawrence Erlbaum Associates Inc.

Glanzer, M., & Cunitz, A.R. (1966). Two storage mechanisms in free recall. *Journal of Verbal Learning and Verbal Behavior, 5*, 351–360.

Glenberg, A.M., Bradley, M.M., Kraus, T.A., & Renzaglia, G.J. (1983). Studies of the long-term recency effect: Support for a contextually guided retrieval hypothesis. *Journal of Experimental Psychology: Learning, Memory, and Cognition, 9*, 231–255.

Glenberg, A.M., & Swanson, N.C. (1986). A temporal distinctiveness theory of recency and modality effects. *Journal of Experimental Psychology: Learning, Memory, and Cognition, 12*, 3–15.

Henson, R.N.A., & Burgess, N. (1998). Representations of serial order. In J.A. Bullinaria, D.W. Glasspool, & G. Houghton (Eds.), *Proceedings of the Fourth Neural Computation and Psychology Workshop* (pp. 283–300): *Connectionist representations*. London: Springer-Verlag.

Hitch, G.J., Rejman, M.J., & Turner, N.C. (1980). *A new perspective on the recency effect*. Paper presented to the Experimental Psychology Society, Cambridge, July.

Kahana, M.J. (1996). Associative retrieval processes in free-recall. *Memory and Cognition, 24*, 103–109.

Laming, D. (1992). Analysis of short-term retention: Models for Brown-Peterson experiments. *Journal of Experimental Psychology: Learning, Memory, and Cognition, 18*, 1342–1365.

Lewandowsky, S., & Murdock, B.B. Jr. (1989). Memory for serial order. *Psychological Review, 96*, 25–57.

Murdock, B.B. Jr. (1962). The serial position effect of free recall. *Journal of Experimental Psychology, 64*, 482–488.

Murdock, B.B. Jr. & Okada, R. (1970). Interresponse times in single-trial free recall. *Journal of Experimental Psychology, 86*, 263–267.

Nairne, J.S., Neath, I., Serra, M., & Byun, E. (1997). Positional distinctiveness and the ratio rule in free recall. *Journal of Memory and Language, 37*, 155–166.

Pinto, A. Da C., & Baddeley, A.D. (1991). Where did you park your car? Analysis of a naturalistic long-term recency effect. *European Journal of Cognitive Psychology, 3*, 297–313.

Postman, L., & Phillips, L.W. (1965). Short-term temporal changes in free recall. *Quarterly Journal of Experimental Psychology, 17*, 132–138.

Shiffrin, R.M., & Cook, J.R. (1978). Short-term forgetting of item and order information. *Journal of Verbal Learning and Verbal Behavior, 17*, 189–218.

Item and Associative Interactions in Short-term Memory: Multiple Memory Systems?

Bennet Murdock
University of Toronto, Canada

Three interactions of item and associative information are discussed: differential forgetting (item recognition declines over lag ranges where pair recognition does not; Hockley, 1991); differential emphasis (instructions to attend to items degrade later pair recognition but instructions to attend to pairs does not degrade later item recognition; Hockley & Cristi, 1996a), and multiple presentations of pairs or items from pairs has little effect on judgements of frequency of items and pairs (Hockley & Cristi, 1996b). Taken as a whole, these results seem to be inconsistent with a separate memory-systems view of memory. TODAM, a global-matching model, has always assumed a single memory system for the storage and retrieval of item and associative information and, with the addition of context and mediators, it can generate the whole pattern of data.

Trois interactions entre l'information d'item et l'information associative sont discutées: l'oubli différentiel (la reconnaissance d'items décline sur certaines distances contrairement à la reconnaissance de paires; Hockley, 1991), l'emphase différentielle (des instructions de porter attention aux items diminuent la reconnaissance de paires mais des instructions de porter attention aux paires d'items ne diminuent pas la reconnaissance des items; Hockley & Cristi, 1996a) et la présentation répétée de paires, ou d'items provenant de paires, ont peu d'effet sur les jugements de fréquence pour les items et les paires (Hockley & Christi, 1996b). Dans l'ensemble, ces résultats semblent être incompatibles avec une vision de systèmes de mémoires multiples. TODAM, un modèle d'appariement global, nécessite un seul système de mémoire pour l'encodage et la récupération des items et de l'information associative. De plus, avec l'ajout de contextes et de médiateurs, TODAM est en mesure de générer l'ensemble des résultats.

Item information is that information in memory which allows us to assess the familiarity of single items or events whereas associative information connects or relates two separate items or events (e.g. names and faces, tastes and smells, words and their meanings). A third type of information (serial-order information) is also important, but it will not be discussed here. There have been some recent developments in the interactions of item and associative information, and they will be the focus of the present paper.

Interactions between item and associative information (or recognition and cued recall; e.g. the Tulving-Wiseman function; Tulving & Wiseman, 1975) have provided a major impetus to the development of the multiple-memory system view. Given experimental separations (independence or near-independence) it is certainly a reasonable first try for an explanation. Here we summarize some recent data on three such interactions between item and associative information, point out some problems they pose for multiple memory systems, and show how a single-system model (TODAM) can explain them.

EXPERIMENTAL INTERACTIONS

The three interactions are differential forgetting of item and associative information, the differential results of attentional instructions, and the effect of repetition of items and pairs on judgments of frequency of pairs and items.

Differential Forgetting

Using a continuous task, Hockley (1991) presented pairs but tested either items or pairs at comparable lags. For item recognition, the items were either old or new; for tests of associative recognition, the pairs were either intact or rearranged. Item information was controlled in tests of associative recognition because all items in both intact and rearranged pairs were old. Either the item (A or B) or the pair (A–B) was tested, never both.

The results are shown in Fig. 1. There was no forgetting of associative information (this replicated results reported in Murdock & Hockley, 1989); in fact, visually

---

Requests for reprints should be addressed to Bennet Murdock, Department of Psychology, University of Toronto, Toronto, ON M5S 3G3, Canada (Phone: (416) 978-3175; Fax: (416) 978-4811; E-mail: murdock@psych.utoronto.ca).

This research was supportd by NSERC Grant #146 from the Natural Sciences and Engineering Research Council of Canada. I thank Bill Hockley for many useful comments on the manuscript.

© 1999 International Union of Psychological Science

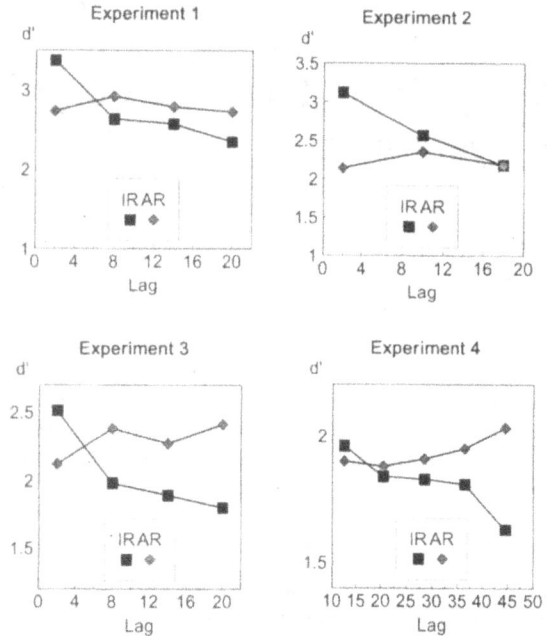

FIG. 1. d' as a function of lag for item recognition (IR) and associative recognition (AR) for four experiments adapted from Hockley (1991).

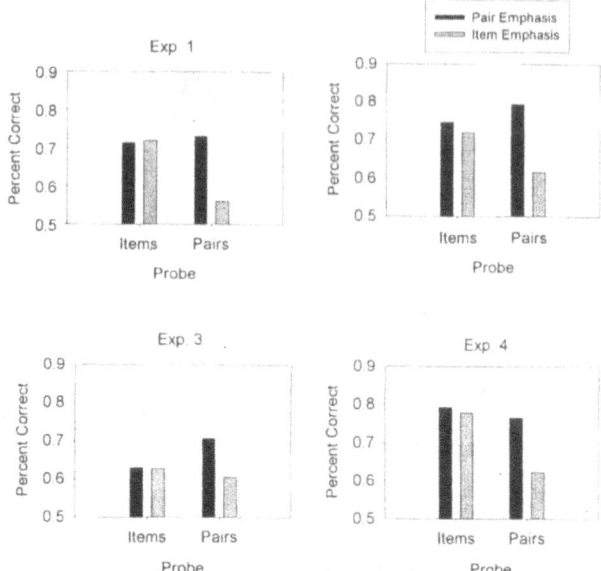

FIG. 2. Percentage correct on final recognition for item and pair probes following item and pair emphasis instructions for four experiments adapted from Hockley and Cristi (1996a).

(but not statistically), recognition accuracy for associative information improved with lag in Expts. 3 and 4. However, in all four experiments, the d' value for item information decreased with lag. Thus, under comparable conditions, in a within-study comparison, item information was forgotten while associative information was not forgotten. These results were replicated and generalized in Hockley (1992).

Differential Attention

The differential attention studies were an attempt to assess the effect of instructions to attend to item or pairs on the retention of pairs and items, respectively. The experiments (Hockley & Cristi, 1996a) used a study-test procedure, and lists of paired associates were presented. One group of subjects was given item-emphasis instructions ("Remember the items") whereas the other group was given associative-emphasis instructions ("Remember the association"). Each list was followed by appropriate recognition tests (old and new items for the item-emphasis group, intact and rearranged pairs for the associative-emphasis group), and neither group was tested for the other kind of information. However, there was a final recognition test for both groups that involved both types of information, and these data constituted the main findings of the experiment.

The results of the final recognition test are shown in Fig. 2. Performance on pair recognition dropped considerably when associative emphasis was changed to item emphasis. However, the converse was not true; performance on item tests was statistically not different for the two emphasis groups. Thus, it would seem that little or no associative information is available when subjects focus on the items, but item information is essentially the same regardless of whether subjects focus on the items or the pairs.

Judgements of Frequency

The third item-associative interaction deals with judgements of frequency (JOF). In studies of absolute JOF, subjects estimate how often the probe item or pair had been presented in the study list. It seems to be generally accepted that JOF are based on strength (see Hockley & Cristi, 1996b, footnote 2), and studies of yes-no recognition are the special case (one presentation vs. no presentation). Here we shall be concerned with the effect of number of item presentations on JOF for pairs, and the number of pair presentations on JOF for items.

Such an experiment has been reported by Hockley and Cristi (1996b). Pairs and single items from these pairs were presented one, two, or four times and the presentation frequencies were crossed (3 × 3). Only one item from each pair was presented in the item conditions, and subjects were instructed to keep the item frequency and the pair frequency separate. There were separate JOF tests for items and pairs, and the instructions were to judge the presentation frequencies of the items and the pairs independently.

The results are presented in Fig. 3, separately for the item and the pair probes. In both cases, mean JOF is plotted as a function of the irrelevant presentation frequency and the parameter is the relevant presentation frequency. In all cases the curves are quite flat but the intercepts are ordered appropriately. Thus, to a good approximation, subjects were able to judge the item presentation frequencies independently of the pair presentation frequencies and vice versa.

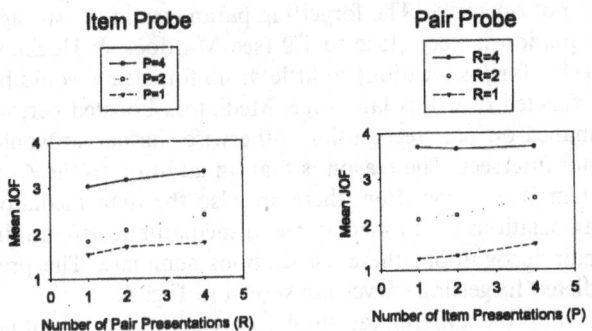

FIG. 3. Judgements of frequency (JOF) for item and pair probes. The data are plotted as a function of the number of irrelevant presentations of the pairs (R) or items (P), and the parameter is the number of relevant presentations of the items (P) or pairs (R). Data taken from Hockley and Cristi (1996b).

MULTIPLE MEMORY SYSTEMS

Are these data consistent with a multiple-memory systems view? Differential forgetting (Fig. 1) certainly is. We have two memory systems, they have different forgetting rates, the forgetting rate for item information is greater than the forgetting rate for associative information. The fact that the curves intersect just happens to be the way that the data come out.

The slopes of the JOF curves in Fig. 3 are also consistent with a multiple memory systems view. If items and associations are stored in different systems, neither should have any effect on the JOF for the other. The slight interaction is not a big problem; some spillover might be expected. However, the fact that, overall, the intercept differences of the JOF functions for items and pair probes are about the same doesn't fit with the differential forgetting. While in fact the R2–R1 difference for pair probes is actually greater than the P2–P1 difference for item probes, the R4–R2 and P4–P2 differences are about the same. Because of the steeper forgetting curve for item than associative information, the effect of repetition should be greater for pairs than items because the forgetting of items is greater than pairs and the intercept differences are a measure of the learning rate. This intercept effect seems to be contrary to the differential forgetting rate.

The biggest problem is to account for the differential emphasis results. If one assumes multiple memory systems, when subjects attend to the items the items should be stored in the item system and when they attend to the pairs the pairs should be stored in the pair system. Instructions to attend to the pairs should have as much deleterious effect on the items as instructions to attend to the items should have on the pairs. This is clearly not the case. Perhaps subjects need to encode some item information before they can encode associative information, whereas the reverse is not true. They do not need to encode associative information in order to encode item information. If this is the case, then the real problem is to explain why associative information has no effect on item information.

Can we argue that the item information also goes into the pair system but the item system only has items? If that is so, you should not get the differential forgetting of Fig. 1. In fact the items should show less forgetting than the pairs because they are stored in both systems.

Even if it could be explained this way, the effect of item repetition on pair JOF should be greater than it is. If subjects just checked the pair system for pair JOF there would also be item information there, and how do subjects disregard that? Perhaps there are two subsystems in the pair system, one for items and one for pairs. What sense does this make? The point of having two systems is to keep item and associative information separate yet the two subsystems mean that the item subsystem is redundant. And of course the item system and subsystem together still show much more forgetting than the single pair subsystem.

Perhaps all this is possible; after all, ad hoc speculation sometimes turns out to be correct. I think the major problem is that advocates of multiple memory systems have not told us how the multiple systems work, or provided us with a model that leads to quantitative predictions and can be tested (see also McKoon, Ratcliff, & Dell, 1986). Until they do, and if they want to explain behavioral data, the notion of separate memory systems for item and associative information seems to be inconsistent with these data.

GLOBAL MATCHING MODELS

Global matching models (e.g. the SAM model of Shiffrin & Raaijmakers, 1992; the MINERVA2 model of Hintzman, 1986, 1988; the matrix model of Humphreys, Bain, & Pike, 1989; the CHARM model of Metcalfe-Eich, 1985; the TODAM model of Murdock, 1996; and the resonance-retrieval theory of Ratcliff, 1978) are recent developments in the short-term memory area. They assume that the matching of a probe item to memory is a global not a local process. In a recognition task, one way or another, the response to the probe is affected by all the list items, not just by the target item itself.

These global matching models have done an impressive job of accounting for much of the short-term memory data on item and associative information (exceptions would be the mirror effect of Glanzer and his colleagues; see Glanzer, Adams, Iverson, & Kim, 1993, and the slopes of ROC curves; see Ratcliff, Sheu, & Gronlund, 1992) and they represent an important development in the understanding of short-term memory. However, these results on the interactions of item and associative information reported by Hockley and his colleagues seem to pose problems for these models. This paper will focus on the attempt of one model (TODAM) to explain these data.

TODAM

TODAM, a theory of distributed associative memory, is a global matching model that deals with the storage and retrieval of item and associative information. TODAM developed from the holographic memory models of the 1970s (see Murdock, 1979, for references) and is also related to the multidimensional evidence models such as those proposed by Ashby and Townsend (1986) and Wickens and Olzak (1992). Items are represented by random vectors (lists of features), associations are represented by the convolution of these item vectors, and item and associative information is stored by superposition in a common memory system. For recognition, the decision (old-new or intact-rearranged) is based on the dot product of the probe (item or pair) with the memory vector. For further details see Murdock (1996).

These three sets of results also pose problems for TODAM, but the problems are almost the exact opposite of the multiple memory systems view. Since items and pairs are stored in a common memory system, they should be forgotten at the same rate, and the differential forgetting results shows that this is not true. There is a limited-capacity assumption so the more attention paid to items the less attention is available for associations and vice versa, and the differential emphasis results show that this is not true either. The JOF results, however, are quite consistent with TODAM since items and associations are independent. However, modifications to TODAM were required to explain these first two sets of results, and this lead to TODAM2 (Murdock, 1997).

TODAM2

In TODAM2, items are embedded in context and the item-plus-context vector is auto-associated to bind the item to context. The context is assumed to change slightly as each new item or pair is presented, and this context drift means that the context difference between study and test would increase with lag. We assume that subjects in the Hockley experiments used context for item recognition; after all, the main difference between old and new items (which were words) was the context of the most recent presentation. We also assume subjects did not use context for pair recognition because it was extraneous information; the items in both intact and rearranged pairs on average had the same context, so context was neither necessary nor useful. In addition, we assume that, when possible, subjects use mediators to remember the pairs. With these assumptions, TODAM2 can explain the differential forgetting and differential emphasis results shown in Figs. 1 and 2.

How does TODAM2 explain these two sets of results? For the differential forgetting, the forgetting of item information occurs because of the context change between study and test, and the greater the lag the greater the context change. For the associative information, we assume subjects do not use context so this factor is not operative. The forgetting parameter in the storage equation is very close to 1.0 (see Murdock & Hockley, 1989, for justification) so little or no forgetting would be expected over this lag range. Mediators boosted performance on pair recognition; otherwise the curves would not intersect. The reason is that, in addition to the A–B item–item association, there are also the item–mediator associations (A to mediator and mediator to B) and, in pair recognition, these associations summate. The predicted forgetting curves are shown in Fig. 4.

For the differential emphasis result there is a dual basis for item information. According to the TODAM2 storage equation, subjects add the autoconvolution of the item vectors and the autoconvolution of the sum of the item vectors, and the latter constitutes both the associative information and a second (or dual) basis for the item information. It can be shown (Murdock, 1997) that item information in memory is almost independent of the attentional weighting, but associative information is clearly not. Consequently a dissociation would be expected, and the predicted results are shown in Fig. 5.

What about the JOF results? Given the differential emphasis results, the JOF results are quite surprising. The differential emphasis results showed that item recognition was independent of the emphasis condition but pair recognition showed a marked effect of the emphasis condition. Suppose in the JOF study, when subjects studied pairs, they gave no weight to the separate A and B members of the pair. However, since item information is included in the pairs (this is the dual basis), item frequency would still be expected to have some effect on JOF for pairs. On the other hand, when items were presented subjects could not store any associative information so pair frequency should have no effect on JOF for items. In fact the data showed little effect either way.

The question, then, is why item frequency had so little effect on pairs. One possible reason is that repetitions of

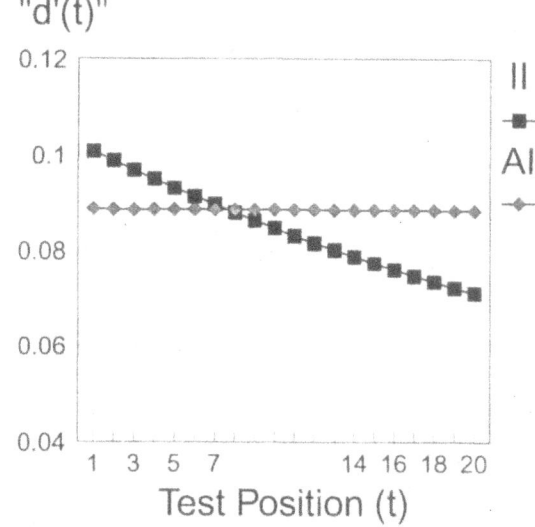

FIG. 4. TODAM2 fits to the differential forgetting data shown in Fig. 1. Adapted from fig. 10 from Murdock (1997). See Appendix for parameter values.

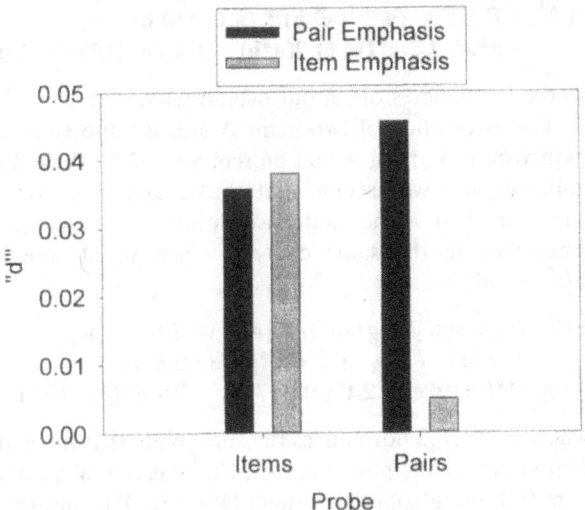

FIG. 5. TODAM2 fits to the differential-emphasis data shown in Fig. 2. Redrawn from Fig. 11 in Murdock (1997). See Appendix for parameter values.

both items and pairs are attenuated. This topic is beyond the scope of the present paper, but see Murdock (1999). Another possible explanation, ad hoc but not unreasonable, is that, at test subjects do not sum the items in the pairs but, as in the original version of TODAM, simply convolve the two items and then compute the dot product of the convolution with the memory vector. If so, then item frequency would have no effect on JOF for pairs; the item information would be filtered out by using a simpler probe because $E[(f*g) \cdot (f*f)] = E[(f*g) \cdot (g*g)] = 0$ (see Appendix). It does, of course, predict that all the functions should be flat, which is not completely true. However, the slight dependence might result from inter-item similarity, not considered in this paper.

These two possible explanations need to be tested, perhaps by combining the differential emphasis procedure and the JOF manipulations in a single experiment. However, it is worth noting that our explanations of the differential-emphasis and JOF results both assume that subjects use encoding and retrieval strategies that are appropriate given the task demands. The TODAM2 model is admittedly rather complex but, as it should, it allows for some flexibility in short-term memory processing.

DISCUSSION

Interactions are the bread-and-butter of cognitive psychology, and they have spawned many useful and interesting ideas. However, if we are ever to become a mature scientific discipline, we must go beyond metaphors and take our data seriously. We must develop models and theories that can explain the data (both main effects and interactions) at a quantitative level.

The three interactions considered in this paper have been singled out because they are particularly difficult to explain in a parsimonious fashion. Any one of them, by itself, would probably be easy to explain, but explaining them all in a consistent manner is a more difficult problem. A view of memory based simply on the notion of separate memory stores for item and associative information seems to be inconsistent with the data. TODAM has always assumed a single memory system for the storage of item and associative information. Using context and mediators, an elaborated version of TODAM is able to provide a reasonable account of the data. It can fit the differential-forgetting and differential emphasis results using the same parameter values and the judgements of frequency (JOF) results are essentially independent of parameter values if subjects use an appropriate retrieval strategy.

REFERENCES

Adams, J.A. (1967). *Human memory.* New York: McGraw-Hill.
Anderson, J.A. (1973). A theory for the recognition of items from short memorized lists. *Psychological Review, 80,* 417–438.
Ashby, F.G., & Townsend, J.T. (1986). Varieties of perceptual independence. *Psychological Review, 93,* 154–179.
Cooper, L.N. (1973). *A possible organization of animal memory and learning.* Paper presented at the Proceedigns of the Nobel Symposium on Collective Properties of Physical Systems, New York.
Estes, W.K. (1955). Statistical theory of spontaneous recovery and regression. *Psychological Review, 62,* 145–154.
Glanzer, M., Adams, J.K., Iverson, G.J., & Kim, K. (1993). The regularities of recognition memory. *Psychological Review, 100,* 546–567.
Hintzman, D.L. (1986). "Schema abstraction" in a multiple-trace memory model. *Psychological Review, 93,* 411–428.
Hintzman, D.L. (1988). Judgements of frequency and recognition memory in a multiple-trace memory model. *Psychological Review, 95,* 528–551.
Hockley, W.E. (1991). Recognition memory for item and associative information: A comparison of forgetting rates. In W.E. Hockley & S. Lewandowsky (Ed.), *Relating theory and data: Essays on human memory in honor of B.B. Murdock* (pp. 227–248). Hillsdale, NJ: Lawrence Erlbaum Associates Inc.
Hockley, W.E. (1992). Item versus associative information: Further comparisons of forgetting rates. *Journal of Experimental Psychology: Learning, Memory, and Cognition, 18,* 1321–1330.
Hockley, W.E., & Cristi, C. (1996a). Tests of encoding trade-offs between item and associative information. *Memory and Cognition, 24,* 202–216.
Hockley, W.E., & Cristi, C. (1996b). Tests of the separate retrieval of item and associative information using a frequency judgment task. *Memory and Cognition, 24,* 796–811.
Humphreys, M.S., Bain, J.D., & Pike, R. (1989). Different ways to cue a coherent memory system: A theory for episodic, semantic, and procedural tasks. *Psychological Review, 96,* 208–233.
Macmillan, N.A., & Creelman, C.D. (1991). *Detection theory: A user's guide.* Cambridge: Cambridge University Press.
McKoon, G., Ratcliff, R., & Dell, G.S. (1986). A critical evaluation of trhe semantic-episodic distinction. *Journal of Experimental Psychology: Learning, Memory, and Cognition, 12,* 295–306.
Metcalfe-Eich, J.M. (1985). Levels of processing, encoding specificity, elaboration, and CHARM. *Psychological Review, 92,* 1–38.
Murdock, B.B. (1979). Convolution and correlation in perception and memory. In L.G. Nilsson (Ed.), *Perspectives in memory research: Essays in honor of Uppsala University's 500th Anniversary.* Hillsdale, NJ: Lawrence Erlbaum Associates Inc.

Murdock, B.B. (1982). A theory for the storage and retrieval of item and associative information. *Psychological Review, 89*, 609–626.

Murdock, B.B. (1993). TODAM2: A model for the storage and retrieval of item, associative, and serial-order information. *Psychological Review, 100*, 183–203.

Murdock, B.B. (1996). Item, associative, and serial-order information in TODAM. In S. Gathercole (Ed.), *Models of short-term memory* (pp. 239–266). Hove, UK: Psychology Press.

Murdock, B.B. (1997). Context and mediators in a theory of distributed associative memory (TODAM2). *Psychological Review, 104*, 839–862.

Murdock, B.B. (1999). *Judgements of frequency and judgments of recency in a distributed-memory model*. Manuscript under revision.

Murdock, B.B., & Hockley, W.E. (1989). Short-term memory for associations. In G.H. Bower (Ed.), *The psychology of learning and motivation: Advances in research and theory, Vol. 24* (pp. 71–108). New York: Academic Press.

Murdock, B.B., & Kahana, M.J. (1993). An analysis of the list-strength effect. *Journal of Experimental Psychology: Learning, Memory, and Cognition, 19*, 689–697.

Murdock, B.B., & Lamon, M. (1988). The replacement effect: Repeating some items while replacing others. *Memory and Cognition, 16*, 91–101.

Ratcliff, R. (1978). A theory of memory retrieval. *Psychological Review, 85*, 59–108.

Ratcliff, R., Sheu, C.-F, & Gronlund, S.D. (1992). Testing global memory models using ROC curves. *Psychological Review, 99*, 518–535.

Shiffrin, R.M., & Raaijmakers, J. (1992). The SAM retrieval model: A retrospective and prospective. In A.F. Healy, S.M. Kosslyn, & R.M. Shiffrin (Eds.), *From learning theory to connectionist theory: Essays in honor of William K. Estes*, (Vol. 2, pp. 69–86). Hillsdale, NJ: Lawrence Erlbaum Associates Inc.

Tulving, E., & Wiseman, S. (1975). Relation between recognition and recognition failure of recallable words. *Bulletin of the Psychonomics Society, 6*, 79–82.

Wickens, T.D., & Olzak, L.A. (1992). Three views of association in concurrent detection ratings. In F.G. Ashby (Ed.), *Multidimensional models of perception and cognition*. (pp. 229–252). Hillsdale, NJ: Lawrence Erlbaum Associates Inc.

APPENDIX

In TODAM2 we assume that items are represented by N-dimensional random vectors, vectors whose elements are random variables from a normally distributed feature distribution with mean zero and variance $1/N$. Context is represented by three-way partitioned random vectors with dimension N_x, $N_x > N$. Call the left-hand vector **a** (with dimension N_a) and the right-hand vector **b** (with dimension N_b). Then an item **f** embedded in context denoted **F** is the concatenation ($\oplus$) of **a**, **f**, and **b**, so **F** = (**a** $\oplus$ **f** $\oplus$ **b**) (Murdock, 1997).

Associations are represented by convolution (*) where the v-th element of the convolution of two item vectors **f** and **g** is defined as

$$(\mathbf{f} * \mathbf{g})_v = \Sigma_i \mathbf{f}(i)\mathbf{g}(v-i).$$

Autoconvolution (the convolution of a vector with itself) is used to bind items to context, and the autoconvolution of an item embedded in context, denoted $\mathbf{F}^{*2}$, is

$$\mathbf{F}^{*2} = \mathbf{F} * \mathbf{F} = (\mathbf{a} \oplus \mathbf{f} \oplus \mathbf{b}) * (\mathbf{a} \oplus \mathbf{f} \oplus \mathbf{b})$$
$$= \mathbf{a}*\mathbf{a} /+/ 2(\mathbf{a}*\mathbf{f}) /+/ 2(\mathbf{a}*\mathbf{b}) + \mathbf{f}*\mathbf{f} /+/ 2(\mathbf{f}*\mathbf{b}) /+/ \mathbf{b}*\mathbf{b}$$

where /+/ denotes offset but overlapping.

The association of two items A and B represented by item vectors **f** and **g** would be represented by their convolution, but we assume that the A and B items are summed first. The autoassociation of two items embedded in the same context which we denote by $\mathbf{FG}^{*2}$ would be

$$\mathbf{FG}^{*2} = (\mathbf{a} \oplus w_2(\mathbf{f}+\mathbf{g}) \oplus \mathbf{b}) * (\mathbf{a} \oplus w_2(\mathbf{f}+\mathbf{g}) \oplus \mathbf{b})$$
$$= \mathbf{a}*\mathbf{a} /+/ 2w_2(\mathbf{a}*\mathbf{f} + \mathbf{a}*\mathbf{g}) /+/ 2(\mathbf{a}*\mathbf{b}) +$$
$$w_2^2\{\mathbf{f}*\mathbf{f} + \mathbf{g}*\mathbf{g} + 2(\mathbf{f}*\mathbf{g})\} /+/ 2w_2 (\mathbf{f}*\mathbf{b} + \mathbf{g}*\mathbf{b}) /+/ \mathbf{b}*\mathbf{b}$$

where $w_2 = 1/\sqrt{2}$ normalizes the sum. Note that there are four components: pure context ($\mathbf{a}*\mathbf{a}$, $\mathbf{a}*\mathbf{b}$, and $\mathbf{b}*\mathbf{b}$), pure item ($\mathbf{f}*\mathbf{f}$ and $\mathbf{g}*\mathbf{g}$), context-item ($\mathbf{a}*\mathbf{f}$, $\mathbf{a}*\mathbf{g}$, $\mathbf{f}*\mathbf{b}$, and $\mathbf{g}*\mathbf{b}$), and pure associative ($\mathbf{f}*\mathbf{g}$). This is similar to the SAM model except that here the components fell out of the underlying assumptions of the model.

As in the original TODAM we assume an attentional coefficient (γ) to control the relative weightings of item and associative information so, with a forgetting parameter (α), the memory vector (**M**) after the presentation of the j-th pair in a list is

$$\mathbf{M}_j = \alpha \mathbf{M}_{j-1} + \gamma \mathbf{F}_j^{*2} + \gamma \mathbf{G}_j^{*2} + (1-2\gamma) \mathbf{FG}_j^{*2}, \quad 0 \leq \gamma \leq 0.5. \quad (A1)$$

We also assume that, with probability σ, subjects come up with a mediator (**m**) to facilitate pair memory, and a mediated pair denoted **FMG** would be (**a** $\oplus$ $w_3(\mathbf{f}+\mathbf{m}+\mathbf{g})$ $\oplus$ **b**) where w_3 (=$1/\sqrt{3}$) is the normalization constant. Thus, the last term in Equation (A1) is $\mathbf{FMG}^{*2}$ with probability σ or $\mathbf{FG}^{*2}$ with probability $1-\sigma$.

Recognition involves the dot product of the probe with the memory vector where the probe can be an item or a pair. For context drift, with noise vectors ζ_j and ζ'_j the context vectors **a** and **b** are

$$\mathbf{a}_j = \rho \mathbf{a}_{j-1} + \sqrt{1-\rho^2}\, \zeta_j, \quad \mathbf{b}_j = \rho \mathbf{b}_j + \sqrt{1-\rho^2}\, \zeta'_j$$

where ρ is the context-drift parameter.

There are study and test parameters for attention (γ for study, κ for test), mediator probability (σ for study, τ for test), and encoding probability parameters (p_s for study, p_r for test or retrieval, and p_m for mediator). For encoding probability, we assume that only some of the features in the item vectors are added to memory. With probability p_s or p_r the feature will be added, and with probability $1-p_s$ or $1-p_r$ nothing will be added. For the mediator, it is assumed that this probability (p_m) is the same for study and test since a mediator comes from semantic memory.

We need the expected values of the dot products of the probe and memory vector to fit the data. We assume the variance is the same for all conditions (Murdock & Kahana, 1993) so this expected value is equivalent to d'. The necessary equations are shown in the Appendix of Murdock (1997) except that there are several typographical errors; Eq. s1 in Table A1 should be the product of

N_a/N_x and N_b/N_x, not the sum, s2 should be 2 {...}, and t4I assumes that τ is an unconditional not a conditional probability.

We used a study-test procedure to fit both sets of data with L (list length) of 20 and, for the final-recognition test of Fig. 5, a lag of 100. The parameter values used were $\alpha = .9998$, $\rho = .97$, $\gamma = .2$ (or $\gamma = .45$ for item emphasis, $\gamma = .1$ for pair emphasis), $\kappa = 0$, $p_s = .2$, $p_m = 1.0$, $p_r = .95$, $\sigma = .35$, $\tau = .9$ (or for the final recognition $\tau = .2$), $N_a = N_b = 10$, and $N_x = 100$. We now use N_x not N_c for the number of context features. The absolute N values do not matter; only the ratio N_a/Nx (= N_b/N_x).

Redintegration and Response Suppression in Serial Recall: A Dynamic Network Model

Stephan Lewandowsky
University of Western Australia, Nedlands, Australia

This article presents a dynamic network model of redintegration and response suppression. Redintegration is the process that disambiguates partially retrieved memorial information into an overt response, and response suppression renders retrieved items temporarily unavailable for further report. Most models of serial recall assume the presence of both processes, but few explain how they are performed. Exploration of the network revealed that it can predict recency in serial recall of lists of varying lengths, the pattern of the associated transposition, omission, intrusion, and repetition errors, and the temporal dynamics of retrieval. The network thus augments any existing model of serial recall that assumes a distributed vector representation but does not specify the processes underlying redintegration and response suppression.

Cet article présente un modèle de réseau dynamique de reconstruction et de suppression de réponse. La reconstruction est le processus qui convertit les informations partiellement récupérées en réponses et la suppression de réponse rend les items récupérés temporairement non disponibles au rappel. La majorité des modèles de rappel sériel présupposent l'existence de ces deux processus, mais peu d'entre eux expliquent l'éxécution effectuée. L'exploration du réseau révèle qu'il peut prédire l'effet de récence pour le rappel sériel de listes de différentes longueurs, les différents patrons d'erreurs et la dynamique temporelle de récupération. Le réseau peut être incorporé aux modèles existants de rappel sériel en spécifiant les processus sous-jacents à la reconstruction et à la suppression de réponse.

There is widespread agreement among memory theorists that serial recall involves not one but two distinct stages of processing. The first stage, called the *associative* stage in this article, is conceptualized as providing access to a memory trace and retrieval of at least partial information about the desired item and its ordinal position. The second stage, called here *redintegration*, refers to the disambiguation of that partial memorial information into a unique item and selection of an overt response. Most theorists also agree that redintegration is followed by response suppression, which renders recalled items temporarily unavailable for further retrieval.

Current theories of serial order memory that encompass those two stages fall into three broad classes, differentiated by their representational assumptions and explanatory emphasis: first, there are purely descriptive models that seek to identify the relative contributions of the associative and redintegrative stages through estimation of parameters (e.g. Brown & Hulme, 1995; Schweickert, 1993). These models do not specify any underlying cognitive processes, but by comparing parameter estimates across conditions, they can isolate the effect of experimental variables on the two stages. For example, redintegration has been consistently identified as the sole locus of word frequency and word lexicality effects in serial recall (e.g. Brown & Hulme, 1995; Hulme et al., 1997). However, these models do not predict the shape of the serial position curve (although Hulme et al. predicted the magnitude of the word frequency effect across serial positions), and they cannot capture the distribution of errors and the delicate balance among transpositions, omissions, and intrusions that are observed in serial recall (see Brown & Hulme, 1995, p. 617).

The second class of theories includes localist models that are specified at a process level. These models assume that each item is stored in a different location in memory and is represented by a distinct identifiable entity (e.g. Burgess & Hitch, in press; Henson, 1998; Page & Norris, in press a, b). Localist theories have much in common: all provide a process account of the associative and redintegration stages, all assume the presence of response suppression, and all handle a broad range of data, including the exact shapes of the serial position curve and underlying error gradients. These theories are,

---

Requests for reprints should be addressed to Stephan Lewandowsky, Department of Psychology, University of Western Australia, Nedlands, WA 6907, Australia (E-mail: lewan@psy.uwa.edu.au) (personal home page at URL: http://www.psy.uwa.edu.au/user/lewan/).

I wish to thank James S. Nairne for providing the data of his 1992 study in electronic form. Thanks are also due to Rik Henson, Ben Murdock, and Klaus Oberauer for their comments on an earlier draft of this paper. Simon Farrell and Mike Mundy assisted with manuscript preparation and their help is gratefully acknowledged.

This article was written while the author held a position as a Visiting Professor at the University of Potsdam, Germany, financed by funds from the Deutsche Forschungsgemeinschaft (German Research Foundation; Grant INK 12/A1, Project C).

© 1999 International Union of Psychological Science

however, limited to immediate serial recall of typically short lists.

Finally, distributed memory models represent items as vectors of features that, in contrast to localist models, are assumed to share a single storage location in memory (Brown, Preece, & Hulme, in press; Lewandowsky & Murdock, 1989; Murdock, 1982, 1983, 1993). Like their localist counterparts, these models specify the associative stage in quantitative detail and with conceptual precision. Like localist models, they assume that recalled items are suppressed. Distributed memory models also successfully account for benchmark data on serial recall; for example, the explanatory power of the recent model by Brown et al. (in press) rivals that of any localist theory. However, distributed theories have so far employed descriptive surrogates for redintegration rather than complete process implementations[1].

This article seeks to redress that potential shortcoming by presenting a stand-alone dynamic network model of redintegration that makes minimal assumptions about the associative stage. By remaining uncommitted to an associative stage, the network can potentially augment any model of memory in which a vector containing partial memorial information must be redintegrated (e.g. Brown et al., in press; Lewandowsky & Murdock, 1989; Murdock, 1993). In related precedents, stand-alone models that implement parts of a sequence of cognitive processes have been successfully used to constrain recognition models (e.g. Hockley & Murdock, 1987).

The article first reviews the evidence and theoretical considerations in support of a separate redintegration stage. I then examine the empirical and theoretical grounds for response suppression and outline how it can account for recency. Next, the redintegration network is applied to several benchmark findings. The model is shown to handle serial position effects across a range of list lengths and retention intervals. It also predicts the underlying pattern of transposition, intrusion, omission, and repetition errors. Finally, the model is shown to provide a natural account of retrieval latencies in serial recall. To conform to space constraints, the present article is restricted to single-trial effects in experiments involving visual presentation of phonologically nonconfusable items. Lewandowsky and Farrell (in press) applied the model to a variety of other paradigms, including the effects of articulation rate and word frequency.

THE NEED FOR REDINTEGRATION

The need for a separate redintegration process is obvious and most pressing in distributed models of memory, such as TODAM (e.g. Lewandowsky & Murdock, 1989), TODAM2 (Murdock, 1993), or OSCAR (Brown et al., in press). Central to these models is the assumption that the to-be-studied vectors are superimposed, by some mathematical process, in a common memory trace. This superimposed storage implies that the memorial information retrieved by the associative stage is, typically, a fuzzy approximation of the target that requires redintegration.

In TODAM, the early version of the theory (Lewandowsky & Murdock, 1989; Murdock, 1983) represented seriation by pairwise associations between adjacent items on the list. Items are associated by a process known as convolution, whereby the two constituent vectors are combined into another vector containing their symmetric association (for details, see Murdock, 1982). The convolved vector, and the constituent items, are then added to a common memory vector. At retrieval, cueing with one member of an association retrieves an approximation of the other item. Thus, in serial recall, the pairwise associations are consecutively probed to retrieve one item after the other. This chaining view of seriation has been repeatedly criticized (e.g. Henson, Norris, Page, & Baddeley, 1996; Mewhort, Popham, & James, 1994; Nairne & Neath, 1994), and in a major revision of the theory (TODAM2: Murdock, 1993), simple chaining was abandoned in favour of several other ways of representing serial order information (Murdock, 1995).

In OSCAR, by contrast, list items are associated not with each other but to a dynamically advancing timing signal provided by a set of oscillators. Unlike TODAM, associations are formed by computation of the outer product of the constituent vectors, which is then added to a common memory matrix. After study, the matrix contains the associations between each list item and the state of the timing signal at the time of its presentation. At retrieval, the dynamic timing signal is rewound to its initial state, and items are retrieved from the memory matrix in response to successive cueing with the advancing timing signal.

In both models, the output obtained in response to a cue is never exactly identical to any of the studied items or any other possible response. The model's performance therefore cannot be scored without some further mechanism to select a response[2]. The early TODAM (Lewandowsky & Murdock, 1989) and the current version of OSCAR (Brown et al., in press) sequentially compare the model's output to a set of available response candidates. The candidate that provides the best match is selected. One conceptual drawback of this scheme is that it assumes the existence of a lexicon of items, in which each response candidate has an identifiable and separate representation. This negates one of the basic premises of distributed memory models, that all information is stored in a common trace. In addition, the particular version of sequential comparison in the early TODAM (Lewandowsky & Murdock, 1989) has been the subject

---

[1] Chappell and Humphreys (1994) presented a model of memory that included a redintegration component. However, their emphasis was on recognition memory and they only reported a single simulation of recall involving paired associates. It is unclear whether their model could be extended to handle serial recall.

[2] This comment does not apply to the analytic version of TODAM that computes predicted recall probabilities without simulating individual study and test trials.

of critical attention (Mewhort et al., 1994; Nairne & Neath, 1994).

The need for redintegration following noisy selection of a response candidate arises also with localist models. For example, the Primacy Model (Page & Norris, in press a), which relies on differentially activated item nodes, relies on a second response stage to model the detrimental effects of phonological similarity. One critical attribute of phonological similarity is that, when lists contain a mix of similar and dissimilar items, recall of the dissimilar items is not impaired relative to a list containing only dissimilar items. Instead, the detrimental effect of similarity is limited to transpositions among the phonologically confusable items (e.g. Henson et al., 1996). Page and Norris (in press b, p. 13) reported that explorations of several single-stage models to handle those data were unsuccessful, concluding that ". . . the data alone appear to force us to accept a two-stage model. . . ." The same conclusion was reached for similar reasons by Henson (1998) during development of his Start-End Model (SEM). As in the Primacy Model, SEM postulates a second output competition that follows initial retrieval of a response candidate and that affects phonologically similar items[3].

Notwithstanding their explanatory diversity, most models thus agree on the need for a separate redintegration process. The models additionally agree that a recalled item is in most cases (at least temporarily) suppressed.

THE NEED FOR RESPONSE SUPPRESSION

Response suppression is required for a variety of empirical and theoretical reasons, predominant among them the frequent occurrence of pairwise transposition errors during recall. To illustrate with an example provided by Houghton and Hartley (1996), suppose a list of letters, such as T R A P, is actually recalled as T A R P, as is common in immediate serial recall. For this error to occur, A must be produced instead of R on the second retrieval. The further fact that A is then *not* produced in its correct third position suggests that its first recall was followed by suppression. If A had not been suppressed, errors such as T A A R P or T A A P should be quite common. In fact, however, these erroneous repetitions are rarely observed in serial recall (e.g. Henson et al., 1996; Vousden & Brown, 1998). Moreover, when erroneous repetitions do occur, they are most often separated by three or four intervening retrievals. Immediate repetitions are exceedingly rare (Vousden & Brown, 1998). This is compatible with the contention that an item, once recalled, is suppressed, and that the suppression gradually wears off while other items are recalled.

Turning to theoretical considerations, there is a pressing need for suppression in localist models that use a competitive cueing mechanism (e.g. Burgess & Hitch, in press; Houghton & Hartley, 1996; Page & Norris, in press a, b). In those models, the strongest or most active item is reported at each recall attempt. On the further assumption that activity is maximal for the first item and then decreases across list position, this mechanism will inevitably commence recall with the first item. However, to proceed through the list to progressively less active items, each retrieval must be followed by response suppression. A similar consideration applies to TODAM (Lewandowsky & Murdock, 1989) with its symmetric pairwise associations. Without suppression of previously recalled items, cueing with a list item would elicit not only the desired next item in the sequence but also the previous one. A final pragmatic reason for inclusion of response suppression is that it can provide a means of explaining recency.

VARIETIES OF RECENCY

Process explanations of recency in serial recall[4] tend to fall into two broad classes, referred to here as edge effects and response suppression. Edge effects refer to the inability of the terminal item to be involved in a transposition in more than one way because there are no adjacent items beyond the end of the list. The reduced frequency of transpositions necessarily results in recency. This mechanism principally contributes to recency in the Primacy Model (Page & Norris, in press a) and OSCAR (Brown et al., 1998). By themselves, edge effect explanations have two limitations. First, because items can exhibit recency only to the extent that the list boundary curtails their ability to transpose, the finding that relatively few transpositions involve nonadjacent items implies that edge effects cannot predict much recency beyond the terminal item. This runs counter to the observation that, even with visual presentation, recency often extends to the penultimate and even antepenultimate item (Madigan, 1971; Watkins & Watkins, 1977). Second, edge effects predict that recency should occur regardless of list length, which also appears to run counter to the data (e.g. Farrell, 1997).

Explanations based on response suppression, on the other hand, exploit the fact that as more and more items are recalled—and hence suppressed—fewer response

---

[3] Technically, Henson (1998, Appendix B) postulates five stages in his model. However, these stages can be subsumed under two umbrella processes corresponding to associative retrieval (Henson's Stages 1 and 2) and redintegration (Stages 3 through 5).

[4] It is critically important to differentiate between two classes of recency. On the one hand, the recency observed in free recall, backward recall, and probed recall is associated with items that are recalled *first*. In these situations it is conceivable that recency reflects a contribution from some type of "short-term memory" or "rehearsal buffer". In forward serial recall, on the other hand, the terminal list items are necessarily recalled *last*. Moreover, ignoring omissions, the lag (i.e. the combined number of study and recall events) between study and report of an item is constant across all serial positions. This rules out any contribution of short-term memory to recency in forward recall, which renders it particularly theoretically interesting. This article focuses exclusively on forward recall.

alternatives remain, thus facilitating choice of the correct item. Henson (1998) acknowledged the contribution of response suppression to recency in his SEM model. Brown (personal communication, 18 August, 1998) suggested that suppression may likewise contribute to recency in OSCAR, although the contribution is difficult to differentiate from edge effects: Because suppression in OSCAR is all or none, removal of suppression would inevitably lead to an unreasonable increase in erroneous repetitions. Finally, Lewandowsky and Murdock (1989) relied entirely on response suppression to produce recency (see Mewhort et al., 1994; Nairne & Neath, 1994, for a cogent critique of that mechanism). Unlike edge effects, response suppression can handle recency that extends further into the list because the size of the response set continually decreases across serial position.

A DYNAMIC CONNECTIONIST MODEL OF REDINTEGRATION AND RESPONSE SUPPRESSION

The discussion thus far permits the following conclusions. First, redintegration plays a major theoretical role in serial recall, with a process implementation being particularly indispensable for distributed memory models. Second, most models of serial recall assume that redintegration is followed by response suppression, primarily to accommodate the observed pattern of transpositions. Third, response suppression has been linked to the occurrence of recency, and may present a more powerful explanation than edge effects. The remainder of this article therefore presents a dynamic nonlinear auto-associative network that implements redintegration and response suppression (see Lewandowsky & Li, 1994, for an early sketch of this model).

Overview

The redintegration model was instantiated as a dynamic auto-associative network known as the "brain-state-in-a-box" (BSB) model (Anderson, Silverstein, Ritz, & Jones, 1977). The BSB has the key property that when cued with an arbitrary starting vector, the obtained output is iteratively fed back into the network until a stable state, known as an attractor, is reached. Attractors comprise all previously studied items (under the conditions of orthogonality assumed here) plus a number of additional "spurious" attractors.

To model redintegration, possible response candidates are first encoded in the BSB. In the present simulations, response candidates comprised the list items for a given trial. At the time of recall, it is assumed that the associative stage provides a partial response vector (call that $\mathbf{f}'$) that serves as starting vector for the BSB. If $\mathbf{f}'$ is sufficiently similar to the correct response, and it falls within the basin of attraction that surrounds the correct item, an exact copy of the target ($\mathbf{f}$) will be recovered. If $\mathbf{f}'$ falls into a different basin of attraction, it will reach another attractor representing either a different list item or, in the case of a spurious attractor, an extra-list intrusion. In all cases, once an attractor is reached, there is no longer any ambiguity about the identity of the network's response.

Because all attractors consist of symmetric binary vectors (i.e. sequences of $-1, +1, \ldots$), they can be thought of as vertices in hyperspace. Moreover, because all activations are restricted to the range -1 through $+1$, the state of the network at any given time is confined to lie within the box formed by the attractors at the vertices—hence the name "brain-state-in-a-box." The presence of the box in conjunction with the iterative update dynamics guarantees that an attractor is eventually reached from any (nonpathological) starting point.

The BSB provides a natural way to implement response suppression through a mechanism known as anti-learning. Anti-learning refers to a selective *reduction* of the strength (through a negative learning rate) of an attractor. In previous applications, anti-learning has been used to model the multi-stable perception of the Necker cube (Anderson, 1991) or the change in perceived meaning of ambiguous words (Kawamoto, 1993). In the present context, whenever an attractor is reached and redintegration is complete, its strength is reduced through anti-learning.

Unlike response suppression in existing distributed memory models, the extent of anti-learning is determined by a parameter, thus allowing for *partial* suppression of recalled items. Partial suppression, in turn, can subsequently be reversed (e.g. Anderson, 1991). Although not relevant to the present set of single-trial simulations, this "release from suppression" is assumed to follow completion of recall and occurs through amplification of the weight matrix. Thus, release from suppression affects the entire response set rather than individual items. The implications of this mechanism were explored elsewhere (Farrell, 1997).

Associative Component: Assumptions

The redintegration model is known to function in conjunction with the early TODAM (Lewandowsky & Li, 1994). Here, emphasis was on extending the generality of the BSB by designing a stand-alone model that made only minimal assumptions about the associative stage. In line with virtually all models of serial recall, it was assumed that the quality of the information available in the associative stage decreased across serial position. This decreasing function has been variously described as a gradient of activation (Page & Norris, in press a), a decline in attention (Brown et al., in press), or a decreasing effectiveness of rehearsal (Lewandowsky & Murdock, 1989). For the present simulations, this assumption was embodied by:

$$s_j = c \times j^{-\lambda} \qquad (1)$$

where s represented the similarity between the output provided by the associative stage and the correct response. The constants c and λ were two free parameters representing, respectively, a starting value and the rate of decline of the similarity (s) across serial positions (j). Equation 1 represents only one possible form of the decreasing effectiveness assumption; see Lewandowsky and Li (1994) for an alternative. The similarity value, s, was used to create a random starting vector ($\mathbf{f}'$), by Monte Carlo means, with that specified similarity to the correct response ($\mathbf{f}$). The starting vector was then redintegrated using the following BSB dynamics.

BSB Dynamics

Study

During study, the weight matrix for the BSB, $\mathbf{A}$, was formed by superimposition of auto-associations of all list items using standard Hebbian learning:

$$\mathbf{A}_j = \mathbf{A}_{j-1} + w_j\, \mathbf{f}_j \mathbf{f}_j^T, \qquad (2)$$

where $\mathbf{f}_j \mathbf{f}_j^T$ represents the outer product of the jth item with itself. For parsimony, the w_js were related to the similarity values in Equation (1) by the function $s_j = f^s\, w_j$, where f^s is a parameter that remained fixed at .15 for most simulations.

$\mathbf{A}$ was of constant dimensionality 128 and initialized to zero at the outset. For each simulated list, study items were randomly sampled without replacement from a vocabulary formed by the complete set of Walsh vectors. Walsh vectors are symmetric binary vectors (i.e. -1, $+1$, ...) that are mutually orthogonal (e.g. Golubov, Efimov, & Skvortsov, 1987). The size of the vocabulary was therefore equal to the dimensionality (128) of the weight matrix.

Recall and redintegration

At retrieval, for each serial position j, the starting vector $\mathbf{f}'_j$ was derived from the correct item $\mathbf{f}_j$ according to the similarity specified by Equation (1), such that the dot product between $\mathbf{f}'_j$ and $\mathbf{f}_j$ was equal to s_j. The length of $\mathbf{f}'_j$ was set to .001.[5] Creation of this vector modeled retrieval from the associative stage. The starting vector $\mathbf{f}'_j$ then migrated towards an attractor using standard BSB dynamics, with the "state" vector $\mathbf{x}$ at any time t given by:

$$\mathbf{x}(t) = g(\beta\, \mathbf{x}(t-1) + \varepsilon\, \mathbf{A}\, \mathbf{x}(t-1) + \delta\, \mathbf{f}'_j), \qquad (3)$$

where $\mathbf{x}(t-1)$ is the preceding state at time $t-1$, $\mathbf{f}'_j$ is $\mathbf{x}$ at time $t=0$, and β, ε, and δ are fixed parameters. The function g truncates all activations to the range -1 to 1, thus constraining the network state to lie within the box formed by the attractor vertices. Given a non-zero initial input, the system is guaranteed to converge to some attractor, located in a vertex (i.e. all elements of $\mathbf{x}$ either -1 or $+1$), in a finite number of steps.

In the simulations, a response was scored as correct when the state vector reached the correct item. Additionally, the number of steps taken to reach an attractor provided a natural account of predicted response latency (Anderson, 1991; Ratcliff, Van Zandt, & McKoon, 1999).

Response suppression

To implement response suppression, once the system had redintegrated $\mathbf{f}'_j$ to some vector $\mathbf{x}$, that attractor was removed from $\mathbf{A}$ using:

$$\mathbf{A}_j = \mathbf{A}_{j-1} - \eta\, w_j\, \mathbf{x}\, \mathbf{x}^T, \qquad (4)$$

where η was a parameter and the w_js were as in Equation (2), except that j here indexed output position not (input) serial position.

Parameters

Fixed parameters comprised ε, β, and δ, set to .2, .9, and 1.0, respectively. There were three *free* parameters: c, the starting value for the similarity, λ, the rate of decline of similarity across serial positions, and η, the anti-learning fraction. Additionally, f^s, the scaling constant relating encoding weights and associative retrieval similarity, was increased for two of the simulations in order to capture the particularly high level of accuracy shown by subjects. For the demonstrations reported here, all parameter values (summarized in Table 1) were obtained by manual adjustment. All results were based on 1000 replications, each using a different random sample of list items drawn from the vocabulary of Walsh vectors.

Summary

To clarify the operation of the network, it is helpful to contrast the two time scales at which events occur. First, each presentation of an item for study corresponds to an update of the weight matrix $\mathbf{A}$ according to Equation (1) (although not modeled here, a parallel update would occur in the associative stage). Similarly, each completed redintegration is followed by a modification of $\mathbf{A}$ according to Equation (4) (without a necessary parallel in the associative stage). Both events are indexed by the positional index j, and both correspond to study or retrieval events in models such as OSCAR or TODAM. Within this coarse time scale, a second type of iteration takes place while a given item j is being redintegrated. The matrix $\mathbf{A}$ remains static across iterations within this finer time scale. At each time t at this finer scale, the state vector $\mathbf{x}$ is updated by renewed probing of $\mathbf{A}$ until an attractor is reached. This dynamic redintegration does not have a parallel in existing models of serial recall.

---

[5] In most studies, list items are drawn from the same class (e.g. digits, letters) and thus share defining features. To represent this residual similarity among list items, $\mathbf{f}'_j$ was derived from a linear combination of all list items, with unit weight for the correct item ($\mathbf{f}_j$) and a weight of .2 for the others. The simulation results remained qualitatively unchanged if $\mathbf{f}'_j$ was derived from the correct item only.

TABLE 1
Summary of Parameter Values Used across All Simulations

Simulation	List Length	Condition	c	λ	η	Comments
1.1	6		.6	.4	.999	$f^s = .4$
1.2	9		.8	.8	.999	
1.3	24		1.0	.5	.999	
1.4	6		1.0	.6	.900	
1.5	6		1.0	.6	.750	
1.6	6		1.0	.6	.500	
2.1	6		1.0	.6	.999	
2.2	5	Immediate	1.0	.3	.900	
		4 hours	.5	.3	.900	
		24 hours	.3	.3	.900	
3.1	4 to 9		1.0	.6	.999	$f^s = .4$

SIMULATIONS

Simulation 1: Recency and List Length

Lewandowsky and Li (1994) showed that the BSB, when combined with the early TODAM, can produce recency through response suppression. The first simulation sought to extend this finding to lists of varying lengths. The results (Simulations 1.1–1.3 for list lengths 6, 9, and 24) are shown in the left panel of Fig. 1.

The figure shows representative data in its right panel. The data for list lengths six and nine were taken from Henson et al. (1996) and Hitch, Burgess, Towse, and Culpin (1996), respectively. Data for the longest list were taken from Farrell (1997). The redintegration model handled the recency that was observed with short and intermediate lists and, simultaneously, the observed elimination of recency with longer lists. This effect emerged without manipulation of parameters because anti-learning was identical in all cases. The elimination of recency resulted from the fact that with longer lists, there was a greater likelihood of intrusion errors occurring before terminal list items had to be recalled. Suppression of intrusions does not affect the strength of nonrecalled items; by implication, for longer lists, there is a relatively

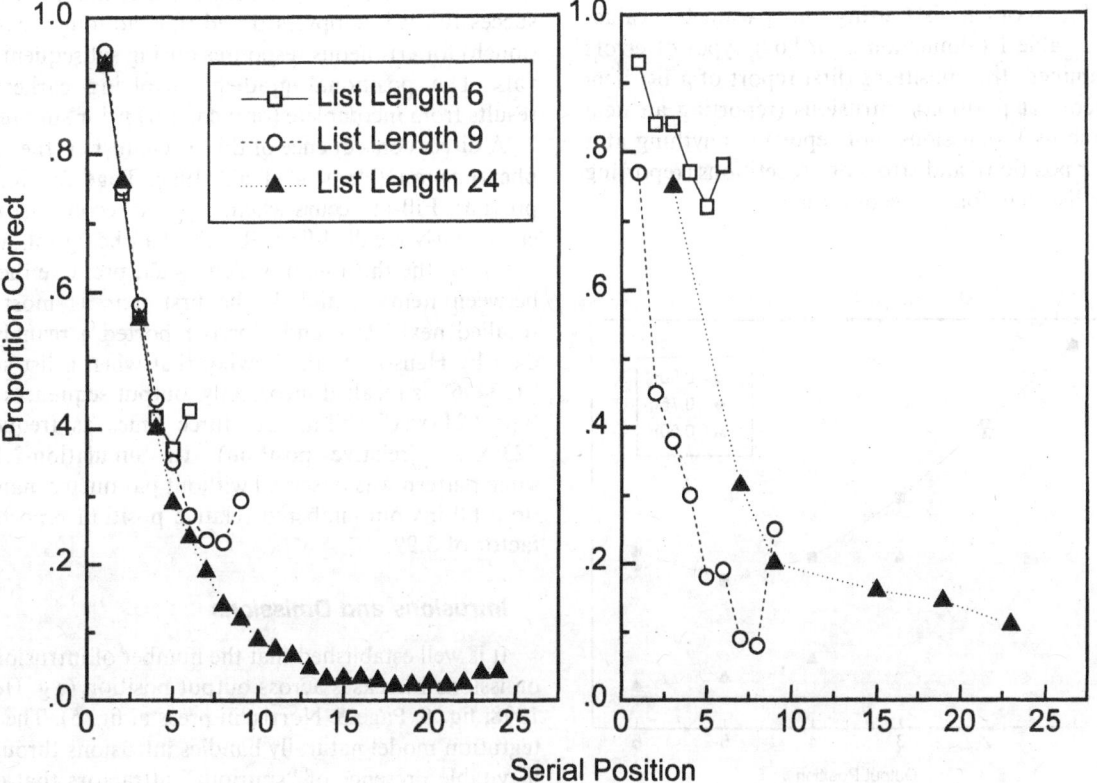

FIG. 1. Serial position curves for various list lengths. The left panel shows predictions of the redintegration model and the right panel shows the corresponding data.

greater number of strong attractors that compete for responses even towards the end of recall.

To confirm that response suppression was responsible for the occurrence of recency, another set of simulations using six-item lists was conducted that manipulated the value of the anti-learning parameter (η). To accentuate the effects of η, the other parameters were chosen to ensure steep primacy. The results (Simulations 1.4–1.6) are shown in Fig. 2 for values of η of .9, .75, and .5.

It is clear that the extent of recency in the redintegration model is tied to the magnitude of response suppression. Comparison of the serial position curves for $\eta = .5$ and $\eta = .9$ reveals that when response suppression is greatest, it exerts its effects on the last three to four list positions, despite the fact that proper recency (defined as an increase in performance from item n to item $n+1$) may not emerge until the last or penultimate position. By implication, models that explain recency primarily through edge effects, but which also include response suppression, may not in fact yield recency for the primary reasons cited (e.g. Brown et al., in press; Page & Norris, in press a).

Simulation 2: Errors in Serial Recall

There has been much recent emphasis on errors, owing to their presumed diagnostic value in differentiating between rival models of serial recall (Henson et al., 1996), in particular between chaining models and their alternatives. The second simulation analyzed the error pattern for six-item lists using the parameter values shown in Table 1 (Simulation 2.1). Four types of errors were examined: transpositions (first report of a list item in an incorrect position), intrusions (reporting an item not on the list), omissions (not reporting anything at a particular position), and erroneous repetitions (reporting a unique list item for the second time).

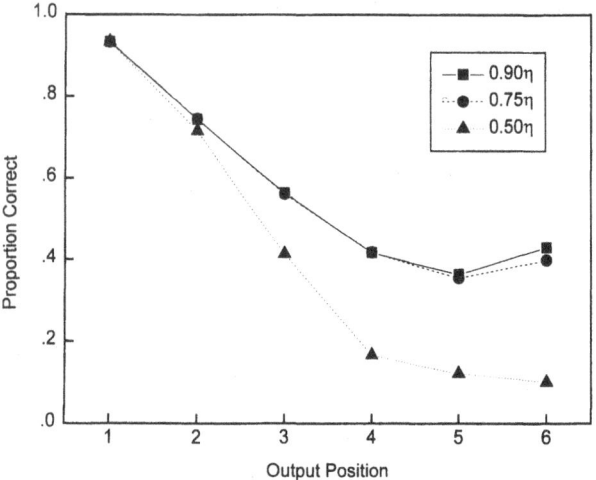

FIG. 2. The effect of reducing anti-learning (captured by the parameter η) on recency. All parameters other than η remain unchanged.

Transpositions

Figure 3 shows the predicted transposition gradients. Each plotted parameter refers to an output position and shows the proportion of items reported from each serial position. The peaks of each function represent correctly recalled items and, when connected, exhibit the typical serial position curve.

The model captured the pervasive finding that output positions tend to cluster around the items' serial positions. That is, items may erroneously migrate to adjacent positions but they are unlikely to be reported far from their true list position. Henson et al. (1996) called this the *locality constraint*.

The redintegration model satisfied the locality constraint without any item-to-item or item-to-position associations, but as a direct result of the differential strength of encoding at study. In the BSB, the size of the basins of attraction surrounding the list items is a function of the weighting received at study [see Equations (1) and (2)]. Thus, the first item has the largest basin of attraction and the last item the smallest. If the starting vector ($\mathbf{f}'_j$) is sufficiently different from the target ($\mathbf{f}_j$) to fall outside its basin of attraction, then the likelihood of $\mathbf{f}'_j$ reaching any of the remaining attractors is a sole function of their strength (ignoring for now the role of inter-item similarity). For example, if on the first retrieval the starting vector falls outside the correct basin of attraction, the second and third items are the most likely candidates for redintegration, thus giving rise to the observed positional gradient involving later list items. If, on the other hand, redintegration of the first item was successful, it is suppressed and thus no longer competes (much) for erroneous responses during subsequent retrievals. The positional gradient involving earlier items results from incomplete (or incorrect) prior suppressions.

A direct consequence of this mechanism is the "fill-in" phenomenon (Henson et al., 1996; Page & Norris, in press a). Fill-in occurs when, say, the second list item is erroneously recalled first. Rather than being followed by report of the third item, which would preserve the order between items 2 and 3, the first item is most likely recalled next. Page and Norris reported a reanalysis of data by Henson et al. showing that when a list such as "123456" is recalled incorrectly, output sequences of the type "21xxxx" (fill-in) are three times as frequent as "23xxxx" (relative position). In Simulation 2.1, the same pattern was observed without parameter manipulation: fill-ins outnumbered relative position reports by a factor of 3.99.

Intrusions and Omissions

It is well established that the number of intrusions and omissions increases across output position (e.g. Henson, 1998, fig. 6; Page & Norris, in press a, fig. 5). The redintegration model naturally handles intrusions through the inevitable presence of "spurious" attractors that do not represent studied items. Modeling of omissions is less straightforward because any starting vector will reach

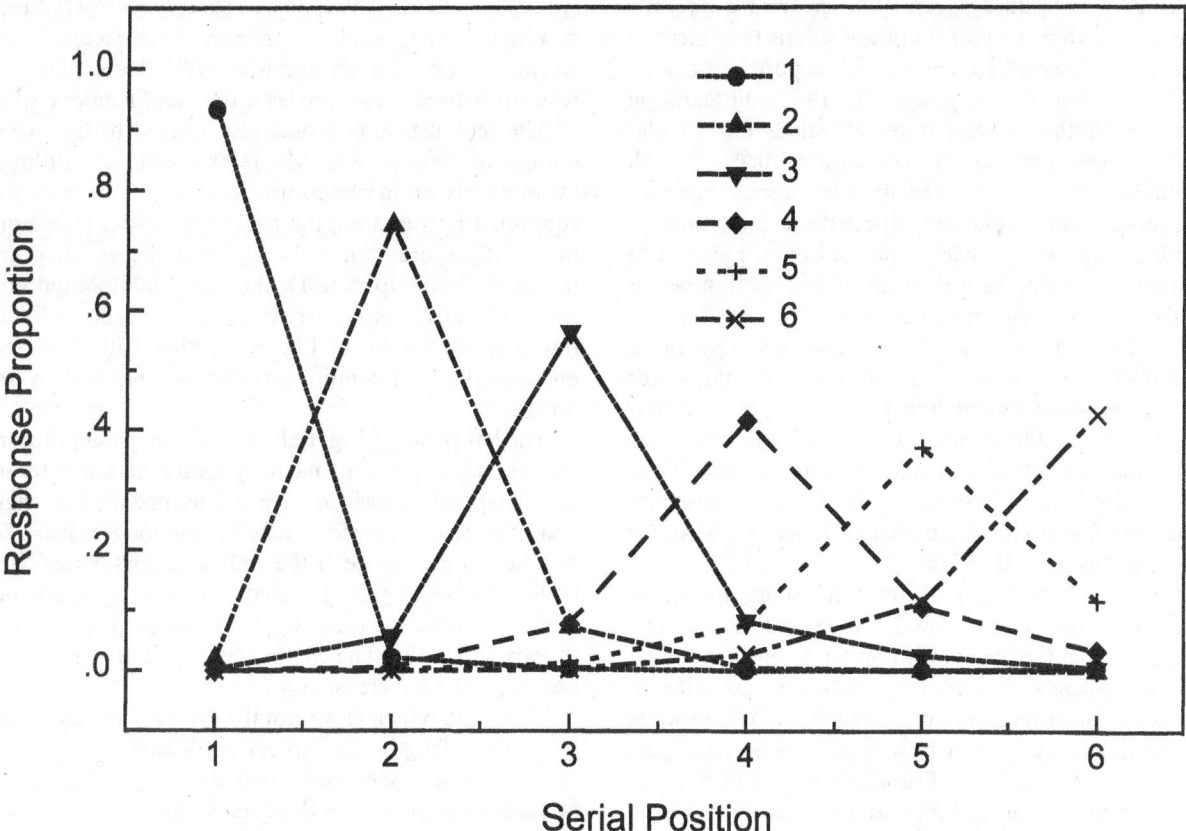

FIG. 3. Transposition gradients predicted by the redintegration model. Each parameter represents a unique output position and shows the proportion of responses from each original serial position.

an attractor in a finite number of steps. Given the implausibility of arbitrarily designating some attractors to represent nonresponses, omissions were instead classified as any response that exceeded a maximum number of iterations (set here to 10) before reaching a vertex. Figure 4 shows the predicted number of intrusions and omissions as a function of output position (note the different scales for the two types of errors).

The model captured the basic empirical pattern of omissions and intrusions: The steep increase in the number of omissions across output position corresponded to the functional relationship observed in the data (e.g. Henson et al., 1996). Likewise, the predicted negatively accelerated function for intrusions resembled the data reported by Page and Norris (in press a, fig. 5)[6]. Finally, predicted intrusions outnumbered omissions by a factor of about 10: This is identical to the ratio predicted by Henson's (1998, fig. 12) SEM model for an immediate test.

Repetition Errors

Erroneous repetitions of an item occur very infrequently—indeed, their low incidence was cited earlier in support of response suppression. For example, Henson (1996) reported that erroneous repetitions constituted 2% of all responses, and Vousden and Brown (1998) cited a figure of 5%. Nonetheless, repetition errors have a distinct distribution, with most repetitions involving early list items that are reported a second time late

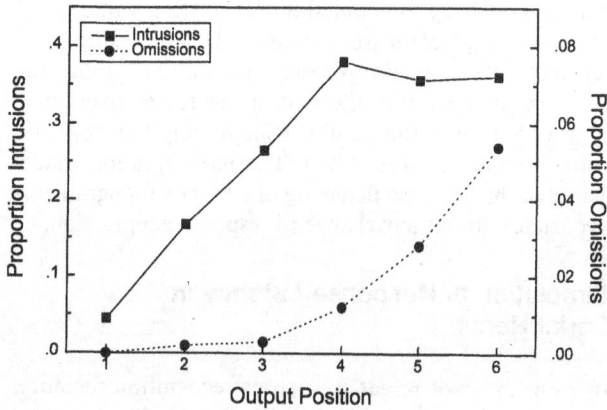

FIG. 4. Proportion of intrusions (scale on the left ordinate axis) and omissions (scale on the right) predicted by the redintegration model as a function of output position.

---

[6] Their figure reported data from an unpublished experiment in which omissions, intrusions, and repetition errors were summed together. The net contribution of intrusions is therefore not discernible from their data. However, Lewandowsky, Neely, Amos, and Ver Wys (1998) reported similar output position functions for intrusions in experiments in which subjects were not permitted to omit responses.

in recall. In consequence, repetition errors are typically separated by three or four output positions (e.g. Henson et al., 1996, observed an average of 3.34 positions apart).

This pattern was captured by the redintegration model. With the set of parameter values for Simulation 2.1, repetition errors constituted 0.7% of all responses and were separated by 3.57 output positions on average. As would be expected, a reduction of response suppression while keeping all other parameters constant was accompanied by an increased number of repetition errors, with η values of .8, .75, and .7 giving rise to 1.4%, 4.6%, and 11.1% erroneous repetitions, respectively. Remarkably, at a finer grain of analysis for one of those cases (Simulation 1.5; η=.75), the last output position included more reports of the first item (3.9%) than of the second and third (0.4% and 0.5%, respectively). This violation of the locality constraint occurs when a moderate number of repetition errors is present (Henson et al., 1996).

Overall, as with transpositions, intrusions, and omissions, the redintegration model predicted the correct pattern of repetition errors without parameter manipulation. Interestingly, the correctly predicted separation of repetitions occurred without a reduction of response suppression across output positions. This account goes beyond that offered by the Primacy Model, which lumps omissions, intrusions, and repetitions together as "item" errors (Page & Norris, in press a, b).

Retention Intervals

Many of the more recent models of serial order have been explicitly restricted to immediate recall from short-term memory (Burgess & Hitch, in press; Henson, 1998; Page & Norris, in press a, b). In some cases, this limitation was mandated by intrinsic problems, for example the properties of the context signal in the model by Burgess and Hitch (Brown et al., in press, p. 23). This limited scope presents a problem in the light of data showing the qualitative uniformity of serial recall performance across retention intervals (Nairne, 1992).

The redintegration model was applied to the data by Nairne (1992) by manipulating the starting value (c) of the primacy gradient [see Equation 1]. The change in c reflected the uncontroversial assumption that the strength of memorial information decreases over time. Figure 5 shows the results (Simulation 2.2) together with the data (Nairne, 1992). The redintegration model captured the observed flattening of transposition gradients over time without any change to response suppression.

Simulation 3: Response Latency in Serial Recall

In some areas of research, such as recognition memory, response latency has played a significant role in guiding and constraining theories for several decades. Accordingly, recognition memory is characterized by a large database of latency measurements (e.g. Murdock & Anderson, 1975). This contrasts sharply with serial recall in which latency analyses are rare. One exception is a recent paper by Dosher and Ma (1998) that explored the relation between total retrieval time and memory span.

The redintegration model was applied to the methodology of Dosher and Ma (1998) without additional assumptions or mechanisms. Total retrieval times were computed by summing the number of cycles [t in Equation (3)] required for redintegration across all output positions. To conform to Dosher and Ma's methodology, no omissions were permitted. The results (Simulation 3.1) are shown in Fig. 6 together with data from one experimental condition (word lists recalled by keypress).

The left panel of Fig. 6 shows that the model captured the general shape of the memory span function, although it under-predicts performance at intermediate list lengths and over-predicts performance for the longest lists. This may be a consequence of the unusually high performance levels observed by Dosher and Ma; memory span functions for words are typically much steeper (e.g. Crannell & Parrish, 1957). The high accuracy in the data again necessitated an increase in f^s.

The right panel shows total retrieval time as a function of list length. To express predictions in real time, redintegration cycles were divided by eight. The slightly quadratic component in the data is significant (Dosher & Ma, 1998, p. 322), and it was at least qualitatively captured by the model: The predicted retrieval time *per item* increased across list lengths from 691msec (length 4) to 858msec (length 9).

One implication of the latter result is that all changes in latency are assumed to arise during redintegration, and that processing at the associative stage must take a constant amount of time. (Because if list length additionally affected the associative stage, the predictions shown in Fig. 6 would necessarily diverge from the data.) This constant-duration assumption is compatible with models such as TODAM or OSCAR, in which retrieval is based on a single operation (convolution or matrix post-multiplication) whose duration is unaffected by experimental manipulations.

GENERAL DISCUSSION

Potential Criticisms

At least two major criticisms can be leveled against the redintegration model. First, the model may be seen to beg the entire question of seriation because it relegates the—arguably—most crucial component of memory retrieval to an hypothetical associative stage that is characterized by assumptions that are conveniently compatible with the redintegration architecture. Despite that, the redintegration model required three or four free parameters. Second, although the scope of the redintegration model extends beyond the current simulations (cf. Lewandowsky & Farrell, in press), the field already has

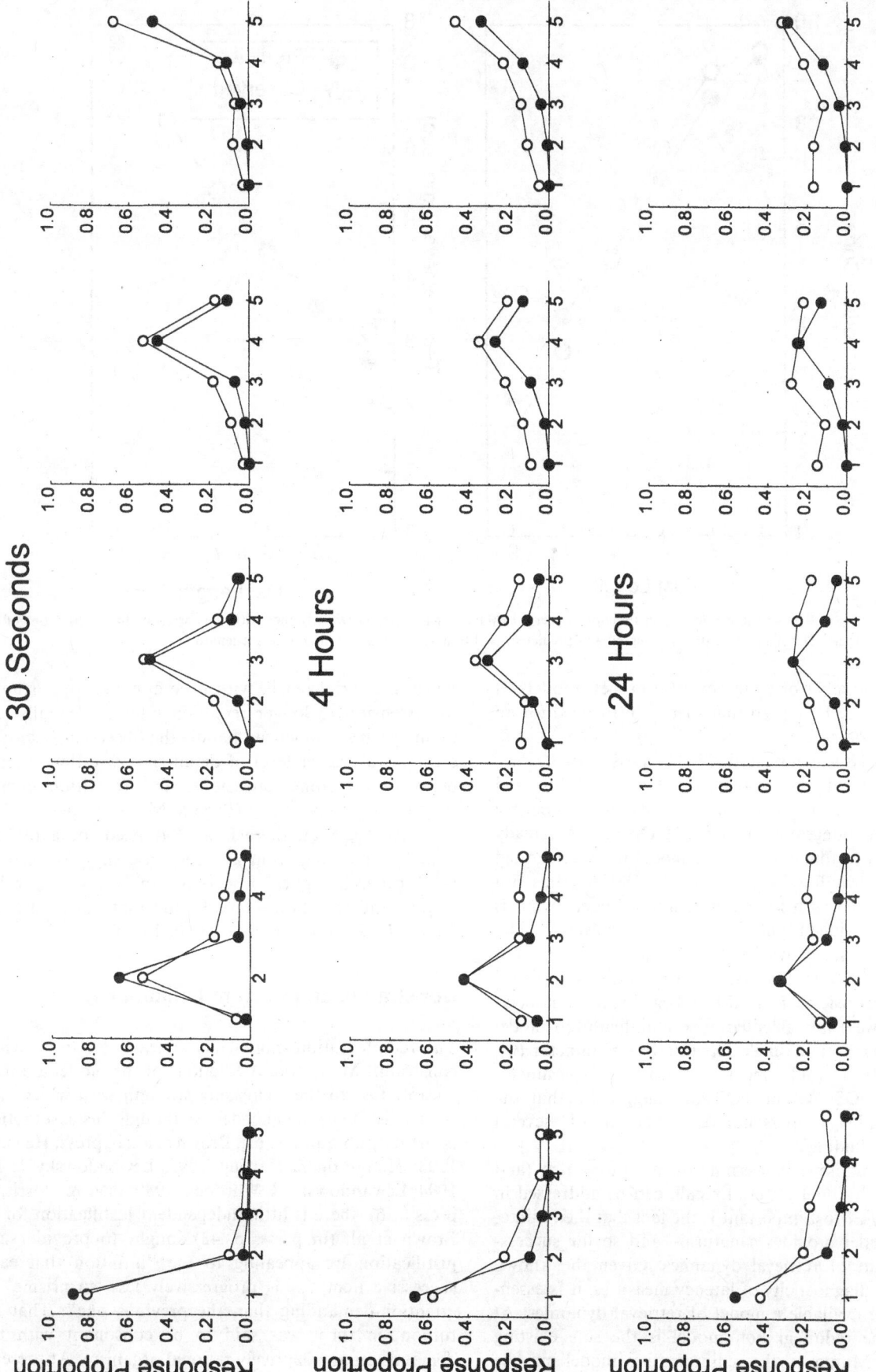

FIG. 5. The effects of retention interval on transposition gradients. The observed data (Nairne, 1992) are represented by open circles and the predictions of the redintegration model by filled circles.

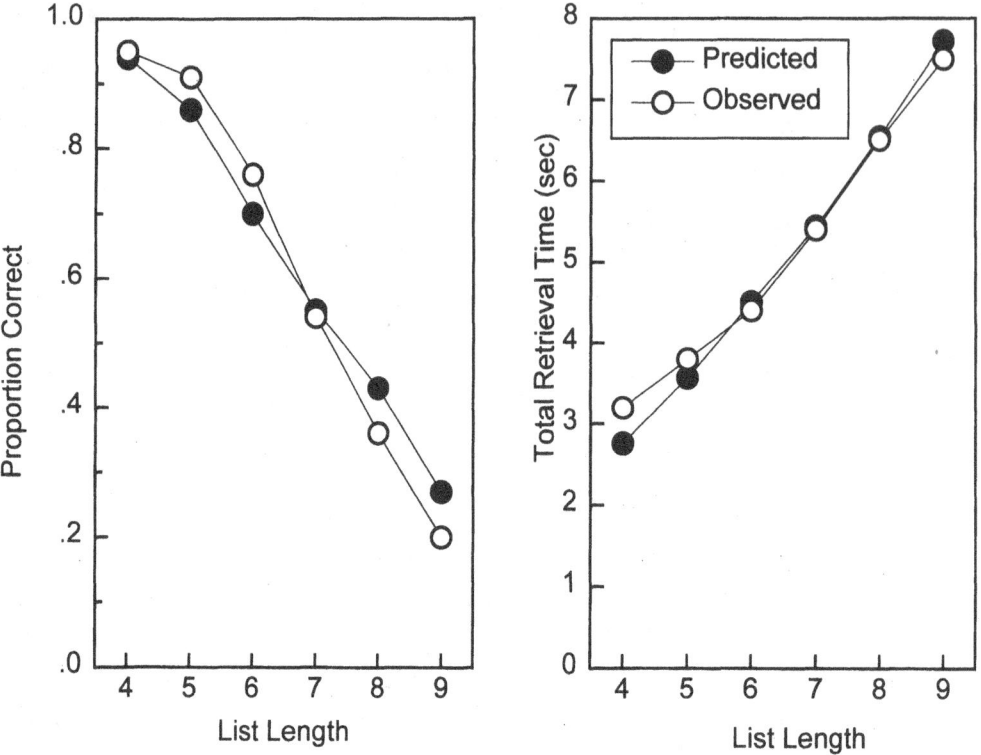

FIG. 6. The left panel shows the memory span functions observed by Dosher and Ma (1998) together with the corresponding predictions of the redintegration model. The right panel shows observed and predicted total time to recall as a function of list length.

access to a number of quite powerful process models. It might therefore be argued that there is little need for an additional contender.

The first issue can be settled by analysis of two candidate models of the associative stage, OSCAR and TODAM, both of which are demonstrably compatible with the redintegration model. TODAM has already been shown to function with the model in an integrated manner (Lewandowsky & Li, 1994). OSCAR has not been integrated with the redintegration model, but it is known to provide output of the general form specified by Equation (1) (see Brown et al., in press, fig. 11c). Two of the current BSB parameters, c and λ, would be replaced by those intrinsic to TODAM or OSCAR if an associative stage were implemented. The redintegration model therefore has only a single intrinsic free parameter (η), which in turn would replace at least one parameter intrinsic to OSCAR or TODAM, suggesting that the BSB provides a parsimonious account of several benchmark findings.

The second issue, concerning the need for a new (and only partial) model of serial recall, can be addressed in several ways. Most important is the fact that the redintegration model provides a natural—and so far successful—account of retrieval dynamics. Given the known theoretical diagnosticity of latency measures, it is essential to have available a model of retrieval dynamics: At present, the redintegration model is the sole existing candidate. Moreover, the redintegration model may be more general than some current localist theories. For example, Henson's (1998) SEM and the model by Burgess and Hitch (in press) are explicitly restricted to *immediate* serial recall, with little apparent opportunity for extension to longer retention intervals. Finally, the redintegration model can handle the observed pattern of errors at a greater level of detail (i.e. by differentiating between intrusions, omissions, and repetition errors) than the Primacy Model (Page & Norris, in press a).

Taken together, there is a clear need for a process model of redintegration and response suppression that is of general applicability, that can handle many list lengths and retention intervals, and that can model different classes of errors at a detailed level.

Constraints and Current Limitations

The redintegration model has at least one in-principle constraint. Many core predictions of the model are irrevocably tied to the decreasing strength with which successive list items are encoded. Although this assumption is virtually ubiquitous (e.g. Brown et al., in press; Henson, 1998; Houghton & Hartley, 1996; Lewandowsky & Li, 1994; Lewandowsky & Murdock, 1989; Page & Norris, in press a, b), there is little independent justification for it. Brown et al. (in press, p. 43) sought to provide such justification by appealing to the "intuition that each successive item . . . is progressively less 'surprising' or attention-demanding than the previous one". That intuition, in turn, was said to be consonant with the demands on an adaptively rational organism. At present, this reasoning must suffice to accept the decreasing-strength constraint as a necessary assumption of the redintegration model.

The redintegration model presently also has limited scope. It has not been applied to lists with repeated items; it does not account for any similarity effects, phonological or semantic; and it does not account for any of the variables surrounding phonology (e.g. modality effects and the effects of articulatory suppression). It is unclear how many of those effects will remain beyond the scope of the model, and thus need to be addressed by the associative stage, versus how many can be explained with further development work.

Relationship to Other Models

On the one hand, the redintegration model provides a process implementation of the descriptive approaches to redintegration pursued by Brown and Hulme (1995), Hulme et al. (1997), and Schweickert (1993). Those models estimated the relative contributions of memory retrieval and redintegration in a variety of situations, concluding that the effects of lexicality (word vs. nonword lists) and word type (e.g. word length and word frequency) primarily involved redintegration. By implication, the redintegration model should accommodate lexicality and word type effects: This was shown to be the case by Lewandowsky and Farrell (in press).

On the other hand, the redintegration model could also be modified to subsume a fairly simple associative stage, in which case it would resemble the Primacy Model (Page & Norris, in press a, b). There already are a number of similarities between the Primacy Model and the redintegration model: both postulate that item strengths decrease with serial position, both assume that item strength contributes to the likelihood of recall, both postulate response suppression as an integral part of retrieval, and neither contains any item-to-item or item-to-position associations. The principal difference between the models is that in the Primacy Model localist representations compete for output of the strongest item, whereas in the distributed redintegration model a retrieval cue is required to elicit, typically, the strongest item. By implication, if the redintegration model could recall items in their order of strength without external cues, it would represent a distributed implementation of the Primacy Model with the added capability of modeling retrieval dynamics. It turns out that, in principle, the redintegration model can "cue itself" by using a completely random vector as the starting state. Anderson (1995) illustrated the process by which a random cue moves to the attractor representing the strongest item (for a related idea, see Murdock, 1983, p. 320). This possibility would deserve exploration if one sought to incorporate the associative stage into the redintegration model.

CONCLUSION

The redintegration model was shown to account for several benchmark findings in memory for serial order: recency across a wide range of list lengths; transposition gradients across a wide range of retention intervals; the pattern of intrusions, omissions, and repetition errors in immediate recall; and the temporal dynamics of retrieval. It follows that these phenomena need no longer be addressed by a model of the associative stage. Indeed, this article showed that the single necessary contribution of such a model is to retrieve information with decreasing accuracy across serial positions.

REFERENCES

Anderson, J.A. (1991). Why, having so many neurons, do we have so few thoughts? In W.E. Hockley & S. Lewandowsky (Eds.), *Relating theory and data: Essays on human memory in honor of Bennet B. Murdock* (pp. 477–507). Hillsdale, NJ: Lawrence Erlbaum Associates Inc.

Anderson, J.A. (1995). *An introduction to neural networks.* Cambridge, MA: MIT Press.

Anderson, J.A., Silverstein, J.W., Ritz, S.A., & Jones, R.S. (1977). Distinctive features, categorical perception, and probability learning: Some applications of a neural model. *Psychological Review, 84,* 413–451.

Brown, G.D.A., & Hulme, C. (1995). Modeling item length effects in memory span: No rehearsal needed? *Journal of Memory and Language, 34,* 594–621.

Brown, G.D.A., Preece, T., & Hulme, C. (in press). Oscillator-based memory for serial order. *Psychological Review.*

Burgess, N., & Hitch, G. (in press). Memory for serial order: A network model of the phonological loop and its timing. *Psychological Review.*

Chappell, M., & Humphreys, M.S. (1994). An auto-associative neural network for sparse representations: Analysis and application to models of recognition and cued recall. *Psychological Review, 101,* 103–128.

Crannell, C.W., & Parish, J.M. (1957). A comparison of immediate memory span for digits, letters, and words. *Journal of Psychology, 44,* 319–327.

Dosher, B.A., & Ma, J.-J. (1998). Output loss or rehearsal loop? Output-time versus pronunciation-time limits in immediate recall for forgetting-matched materials. *Journal of Experimental Psychology: Learning, Memory, and Cognition, 24,* 316–335.

Farrell, S. (1997). *Serial and associative recall: Dissociating the effects of repeated testing.* Unpublished honours thesis, University of Western Australia.

Golubov, B., Efimov, A., & Skvortsov, V. (1987). *Walsh series and transforms: Theory and applications.* Dordrecht, The Netherlands: Kluwer Academic Press.

Henson, R.N.A. (1998). Short-term memory for serial order: The Start-End Model. *Cognitive Psychology, 36,* 73–137.

Henson, R.N.A., Norris, D.G., Page, M.P.A., & Baddeley, A.D. (1996). Unchained memory: Error patterns rule out chaining models of immediate serial recall. *Quarterly Journal of Experimental Psychology, 49A,* 80–115.

Hitch, G., Burgess, N., Towse, J., & Culpin, V. (1996). Grouping and immediate recall: A working memory analysis. *Quarterly Journal of Experimental Psychology, 49A,* 116–139.

Hockley, W.E., & Murdock, B.B. Jr. (1987). A decision model for accuracy and response latency in recognition memory. *Psychological Review, 94,* 341–358.

Houghton, G., & Hartley, T. (1996). Parallel models of serial behaviour: Lashley revisited. *Psyche, 2(25).* Symposium on implicit learning and memory (http://psyche.cs.monash.edu.au).

Hulme, C., Roodenrys, S., Schweickert, R., Brown, G.D.A., Martin, S., & Stuart, G. (1997). Word-frequency effects on short-term memory tasks: Evidence for a redintegration process in immediate serial recall. *Journal of Experimental Psychology: Learning, Memory, and Cognition, 23,* 1217–1232.

Kawamoto, A.H. (1993). Nonlinear dynamics in the resolution of lexical ambiguity: A parallel distributed processing account. *Journal of Memory and Language, 32,* 474–516.

Lewandowsky, S., & Farrell, S. (in press). A redintegration account of word-length, lexicality, and articulatory suppression effects in short-term serial memory. *Psychological Research.*

Lewandowsky, S., & Li, S-C. (1994). Memory for serial order revisited. *Psychological Review, 101,* 539–543.

Lewandowsky, S., & Murdock, B.B. Jr. (1989) Memory for serial order. *Psychological Review, 96,* 25–57.

Lewandowsky, S., Neely, J. H., Amos, A., & Ver Wys, C. (1998). *Failures to see repetition blindness in RSVP.* Manuscript in preparation.

Madigan, S.A. (1971). Modality and recall order interactions in short-term memory for serial order. *Journal of Experimental Psychology, 87,* 294–296.

Mewhort, D.J.K., Popham, D., & James, G. (1994). On serial recall: A critique of chaining in the theory of distributed associative memory. *Psychological Review, 101,* 534–538.

Murdock, B.B. Jr. (1982). A theory for the storage and retrieval of item and associative information. *Psychological Review, 89,* 609–626.

Murdock, B.B. Jr. (1983). A distributed memory model for serial-order information. *Psychological Review, 90,* 316–338.

Murdock, B.B. Jr. (1993). TODAM2: A model for the storage and retrieval of item, associative, and serial-order information. *Psychological Review, 100,* 183–203.

Murdock, B.B. Jr. (1995). Developing TODAM: Three models for serial-order information. *Memory & Cognition, 23,* 631–645.

Murdock, B.B. Jr., & Anderson, R.E. (1975). Encoding, storage, and retrieval of item information. In R.L. Solso (Ed.), *Information processing and cognition: The Loyola Symposium* (pp. 145–194). Hillsdale, NJ: Lawrence Erlbaum Associates Inc.

Nairne, J.S. (1992). The loss of positional certainty in long-term memory. *Psychological Science, 3,* 199–202.

Nairne, J.S., & Neath, I. (1994). A critique of the retrieval/deblurring assumptions of the theory of distributed associative memory. *Psychological Review, 101,* 528–533.

Page, M.P.A., & Norris, D. (in press a). The Primacy Model: A new model of immediate serial recall. *Psychological Review.*

Page, M.P.A., & Norris, D. (in press b). Modeling immediate serial recall with a localist implementation of the Primacy Model. In J. Grainger & A.M. Jacobs (Eds.), *Localist connectionist approaches to human cognition.* Hillsdale, NJ: Lawrence Erlbaum Associates Inc.

Ratcliff, R., Van Zandt, T., & McKoon, G. (1999). Connectionist and diffusion models of reaction time. *Psychological Review, 106,* 261–300.

Schweickert, R. (1993). A multinomial processing tree model for degradation and redintegration in immediate recall. *Memory & Cognition, 21,* 168–175.

Vousden, J.I., & Brown, G.D.A. (1998). To repeat or not to repeat: The time course of response suppression in sequential behaviour. In J.A. Bullinaria, D.W. Glasspool, & G. Houghton (Eds.), *Proceedings of the Fourth Neural Computation and Psychology Workshop: Connectionist representations* (pp. 301–315). London: Springer Verlag.

Watkins, O.C., & Watkins, M.J. (1977). Serial recall and the modality effect: Effects of word frequency. *Journal of Experimental Psychology: Human Learning and Memory, 3,* 712–718.

Redintegration and the Useful Lifetime of the Verbal Memory Representation

Richard Schweickert and Shengbao Chen
Purdue University, West Lafayette, IN, USA

Marie Poirier
Laval University, Ste-Foy, Québec, Canada

Factors affecting immediate serial recall of individual items can be classified according to whether they influence the degradation of the representation, or influence the ability to redintegrate a degraded representation. For recall of entire lists, factors can be classified according to whether or not they influence the rate at which items are recalled. We review experiments in order to classify the factors of serial position, word length, word frequency, and lexicality. We propose that the two classification systems coincide, at least for those factors whose classification is known for both schemes. We end by considering whether probability of recall of an entire list might be predicted from probability of recall of individual items.

Les facteurs qui affectent le rappel sériel immédiat d'items peuvent être classifiés selon qu'ils influencent la dégradation des représentations ou selon qu'ils influencent la reconstruction d'une représentation dégradée. Pour le rappel de listes entières, ces facteurs peuvent être classifiés selon qu'ils influencent ou non le taux de rappel des items. Un certain nombre d'expériences sont examinées dans le but de classifier les facteurs de position sérielle, longueur du mot, fréquence et lexicalité. Il est proposé que les deux systèmes de classification concordent, du moins pour les facteurs dont la classification est connue pour les deux systèmes. Nous terminons en considérant la possibilité que la probabilité de rappel pour une liste entière puisse être prédite par la probabilité de rappeler chaque item séparément.

It is commonly assumed in immediate serial recall that when items are presented, a speech-like representation is formed, which soon becomes degraded through decay or interference (Baddeley & Hitch, 1974; Baddeley, Thomson, & Buchanan, 1975; Schweickert & Boruff, 1986). When an individual item is ready to be recalled, its representation may be intact or degraded. If the representation is degraded, the subject may nonetheless be able to use it to reconstruct the item and recall it correctly, a process known as redintegration (e.g. Brown & Hulme, 1995; Cowan, 1992; Nairne, 1990; Schweickert, 1993). Intuitively, the difference between the two ways of recalling an item is analogous to the difference between reading a word aloud from legible handwriting and from illegible handwriting.

Schweickert (1993) expressed this idea in a multinomial processing tree model for the recall of an individual item (Fig. 1). (Batchelder and Riefer, 1999, provide a recent review of multinomial processing tree models.) Let I be the probability the representation of the item is intact, and let R be the probability the item can be successfully redintegrated, given that its representation is not intact. Then the probability the item is recalled correctly is

$$I + (1-I)R.$$

In this paper we show how the model accounts for effects of several factors affecting immediate recall in recent experiments. We then compare the effects of factors on recall of individual items and on recall of entire lists. In the final section, we discuss the problem of predicting the probability of recall of an entire list from the probabilities of recalling the individual items.

DEGRADATION AND REDINTEGRATION

We begin by discussing experimental factors that appear to selectively influence either degradation or redintegration. In other words, these factors can be classified according to whether they change only the parameter I or only the parameter R.

Requests for reprints should be addressed to Richard Schweickert, Department of Psychological Sciences, Purdue University, West Lafayette, IN 47907-1364, USA (E-mail: swike@psych.purdue.edu).

This research was supported in part by an NSF grant SBR-9601465 to the first author. We thank Xiangen Hu, Charles Hulme, Xiaojain Li, Bennet B. Murdock, Jr, Steven Roodenrys, and Jean Saint-Aubin for helpful discussions. We are especially grateful to Charles Hulme, Steven Roodenrys, and Jean Saint-Aubin for kindly providing their data.

© 1999 International Union of Psychological Science

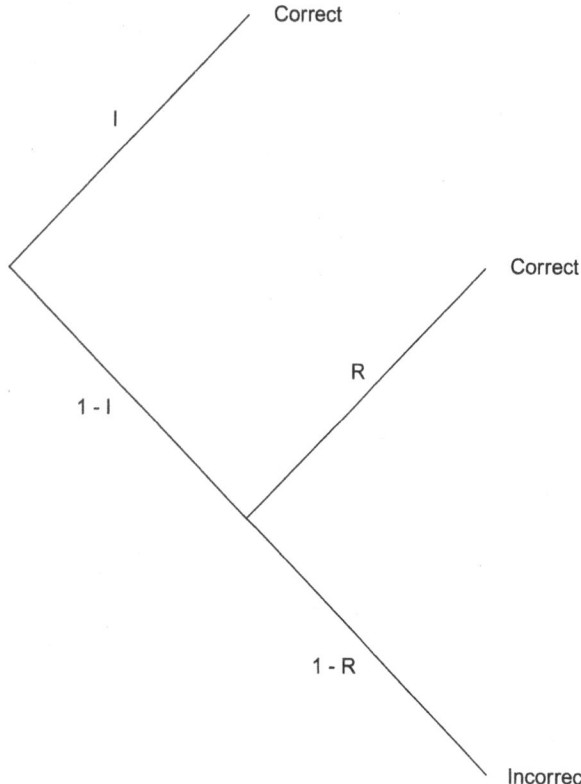

FIG. 1. A multinomial processing tree. An item is recalled correctly if its representation is intact, or if its representation is not intact, but is redintegrated.

Word Frequency and Serial Position

One would expect representations of items in the middle serial positions to be more degraded than representations of items at the beginning. One might also expect redintegration to be more likely to succeed for high-frequency words than low-frequency words. These expectations were supported in a series of experiments reported in Hulme et al. (1997). Data from a similar experiment by Roodenrys and Hulme are in Tables 1 and 2.

The words were high- and low-frequency words. (For the stimuli, see the long words of Experiment 1 in Hulme, et al., 1997.) Apparatus, software, and general procedures are as in that experiment. Each pool had eight words. Each of 24 subjects received a block of 15 lists of high-frequency words and a block of 15 lists of low-frequency words. Each list consisted of five words presented visually at 2/3 items per second. Subjects attempted to recall the words in order, saying "blank" for items they could not recall.

TABLE 1
Probability of Correct Recall for the Experiment of Roodenrys and Hulme

	Serial Position				
	1	2	5	3	4
High frequency	.93	.75	.58	.58	.44
Low frequency	.84	.59	.43	.36	.27
Difference	.09	.16	.15	.22	.17

Operations were performed before rounding.

Two qualitative patterns are evident in Table 1. (a) When probability of correct recall is ordered from highest to lowest, the order over serial positions is the same for high- and low-frequency words. At each serial position, probability of correct recall is higher for high-frequency words. (b) As probability decreases from one serial position to another, the effect of word frequency tends to increase.

These patterns are predicted by the model, if we assume that serial position selectively influences degradation and word frequency selectively influences redintegration. For serial position i, let the probability the item is intact be I_i. When word frequency is at level j, let the probability of successful redintegration, given the representation is not intact, be R_j. Finally, let the probability of correct recall of the item in serial position i, with word-frequency level j be P_{ij}. Then

$$P_{ij} = I_i + (1-I_i)R_j. \quad (1)$$

By constructing numerical examples, it is easy to check that patterns (a) and (b) are predicted, for example, that as the value of I_i goes down, the effect of a change in R_j goes up. The more degraded the representation is, the

TABLE 2
Frequencies of Correct Recall and Parameter Estimates for the Experiment of Roodenrys and Hulme

	Serial Position					
	1	2	3	4	5	Parameter R
Parameter I	.816	.493	.186	.028	.240	
High frequency						
Observed	333	271	210	159	207	
Predicted	324	262	202	172	213	.462
Low frequency						
Observed	301	212	130	98	154	
Predicted	309	220	135	91	150	.232

Total possible correct is 360. $G^2 = 9.887$, 3 df over correct and incorrect frequencies. For correct frequencies, $r^2 = .988$. Data from S. Roodenrys and C. Hulme (personal communication, January 28, 1993).

greater the role of redintegration. For more on qualitative predictions made by tree models, see Schweickert (1993).

In Table 1, the ordering of the differences is not as tidy as the ordering of the probabilities themselves. Differences truly out of order imply the model is false. The discrepancies appear small enough that they might be explained by noting that the differences have greater variability than the probabilities themselves, so we will proceed.

The model can be evaluated quantitatively by estimating parameters and examining goodness of fit. The computer program by Hu (1991) was used to estimate the parameters; results are in Table 2. Two measures of goodness of fit are reported. Parameters were estimated to minimize G^2, a quantity approximately equal to the usual chi-square goodness of fit statistic. It is difficult to know how large a value of G^2 to expect, because the repeated measurements on each subject are not independent. The value obtained is not large. The large value of r^2 indicates that the model accounts for a large percentage of the variance. The data support the conclusion that serial position selectively influences degradation and word frequency selectively influences redintegration.

We caution that the model only explains effects in terms of item information. Primacy and recency effects due to item information can be expressed in the model through the parameter I. Effects due to other sources, e.g. order errors, are not included in the model. The model fitting attempts to use the available parameters, hence sources of errors not included in the model may produce distortions in the parameter estimates.

The next section discusses an experiment on word length (Hulme et al., 1997, Experiment 3). One of the factors was word frequency, and the reader is referred to the paper for the goodness of fit calculations supporting the conclusion again that word frequency selectively influences redintegration whereas serial position selectively influences degradation. The qualitative predictions can be assessed in Table 3. (a) When probability of correct recall is ordered, the order over serial positions is the same for high- and low-frequency words. Probability is higher for high- than for low-frequency words. (b) As probability of correct recall decreases, the effect of word frequency increases. There are places where the predictions do not hold. These seem to be minor, and the discrepancies are greater for the differences than for the probabilities themselves.

Word Length

It is well known that immediate recall is worse for long words than for short ones (Baddeley et al., 1975; Mackworth, 1963; Schweickert & Boruff, 1986). The usual explanation is that there is more decay or interference for longer words. Suppose that word frequency selectively influences redintegration (the conclusion from the experiment reported above), and further, that word length selectively influences degradation. Then Equation (1) predicts qualitatively that the effect of word frequency will be bigger for longer words. [To apply Equation (1) here, subscript i stands for levels of word-length, and not for serial position as before.] At each serial position, the representation of a long word is expected to be more degraded than the representation of a short word.

Relevant data are in Experiment 3 of Hulme et al. (1997). The words were of short and medium length. The model predicts an interaction between word length and word frequency. The interaction was not significant, but it has the numerical form predicted by the model. This is seen in the frequencies of correct recall from table B3 of Hulme et al. (1997). When the effect of frequency for medium length words is subtracted from that for short words, the model predicts the resulting difference of differences to be negative. Each serial position provides a separate test. From serial positions 1 to 7, the results are $-25, -16, -35, -19, -3, -16$, and 6. Except for the last serial position, the quantity is negative, as predicted.

It is natural to ask what the relation between serial position and word length is. The data are not informative, however, because there does not appear to be any pattern in the way these negative numbers change with serial position.

Qualitatively, the data support the hypothesis that word length and word frequency selectively influence degradation and redintegration, respectively. The last serial position may be an exception, where a recency mechanism not included in the model may be at work. We should note that there is little effect of word frequency on short words in serial positions 1 and 2, although this does not imply the prediction should not hold there.

The hypothesis of selective influence can also be tested quantitatively. Overall, Hulme et al. (1997) reported $G^2 = 8.46$, 5 df, $r^2 = .992$ for short words, and $G^2 = 3.33$, 5 df, $r^2 = .997$ for long words. Of more specific interest here, let R_1 be the probability of redintegrating a

TABLE 3
Probability of Correct Recall
from Hulme et al. (1997, Experiment 3)

Short Words	Serial Position						
	1	2	7	3	4	6	5
High frequency	.92	.82	.81	.74	.67	.56	.57
Low frequency	.93	.82	.73	.72	.56	.45	.44
Difference	−.01	.00	.08	.03	.12	.10	.13

Medium Words	Serial Position						
	1	7	2	3	4	6	5
High frequency	.90	.78	.73	.61	.54	.47	.40
Low frequency	.86	.71	.70	.51	.39	.34	.26
Difference	.04	.07	.03	.10	.16	.14	.13

Operations were performed before rounding.

degraded representation for high-frequency words, and let R_2 be that for low-frequency words. If word length selectively influences degradation, it should have no effect on redintegration. Then the value of R_1 should be the same for short and medium length words, and so should the value of R_2. Parameters were estimated separately for the short and medium words. For short and medium words the values of R_1 were .43 and .41, respectively, and the values of R_2 were .28 and .25, respectively (Hulme et al., 1997, table B3). There is remarkable agreement between the estimated values, indicating that word length has little or no effect on R.

Effects of word length are not always so straightforward. Word length may have more than one effect (Cowan, Wood, Nugent, & Treisman, 1997; Service, 1998). Sometimes there appears to be an advantage for longer words in redintegration (Schweickert, Hayt, Hersberger, & Guentert, 1996), probably because longer words leave more cues in degraded representations. Nonetheless, for this experiment, the data support the conclusion that word length selectively influences degradation and word frequency selectively influences redintegration.

Lexicality

We concluded earlier that word frequency selectively influences the probability of redintegrating a degraded item. One could argue that nonwords are like words of extremely low frequency, so the effects of lexicality should be analogous to the effects of word frequency. Relevant data are in an experiment by Saint-Aubin and Poirier (in press), on immediate ordered recall of lists of words and nonwords.

If the effect of lexicality is analogous to the effect of word frequency, the multinomial tree model makes the qualitative predictions stated earlier. (a) For each serial position, probability of correct recall is higher for words than for nonwords. Moreover, serial positions can be permuted so the probability of correct recall is decreasing for both words and nonwords. These predictions are satisfied (see Table 4).

There was a significant interaction between serial position and lexicality. The second qualitative prediction is about the interaction. (b) When the serial positions are permuted as before, the effect of word frequency increases as the probability of correct recall decreases. This prediction is satisfied, with the exception of serial position 3 (see Table 4).

The model can also be tested quantitatively. We estimated parameters using the program by Hu (1991) assuming serial position changes I and lexicality changes R. Parameter estimates and predicted and observed probabilities of correct recall are in Table 5. Although there is room for improvement, agreement between predicted and observed values is good, and 97% of the variance is accounted for. We conclude that lexicality selectively influences redintegration and that the effect of lexicality is analogous to that of word frequency.

TABLE 4
Probability of Correct Recall from Saint-Aubin and Poirier (in press)

	Serial Position				
	1	5	2	4	3
Words	.93	.90	.79	.74	.66
Nonwords	.58	.51	.38	.27	.26
Difference	.36	.39	.40	.46	.39

Phonological Similarity

Li and Schweickert (1999) presented lists of phonologically similar words and lists of phonologically dissimilar words for immediate ordered recall. Word pools were equated for mean pronunciation time, and approximately equated for mean word frequency. The multinomial tree model in Equation 1 fit the data well, under the assumption that serial position selectively influences degradation whereas phonological similarity selectively influences redintegration. Briefly, for list length 5, $G^2 = 9.28$, 11 df, $r^2 = .992$, and for list length 6, $G^2 = 21.38$, 14 df, $r^2 = .997$. When a representation is noisy or has missing parts, it is less likely that redintegration will succeed when more items in the pool share phonemes with the remnant of the representation. Incidentally, this account is contrary to the acid bath hypothesis of Posner and Konick (1966), which says that phonological similarity makes forgetting of representations quicker.

RECALL OF INDIVIDUAL ITEMS AND OF ENTIRE LISTS

To summarize so far, for recall of individual items, serial position and word length appear to affect the probability that the representation of an item is intact at the time of recall. Word frequency, lexicality, and phonological similarity appear to affect the probability a degraded representation of an item can be successfully redintegrated. It is instructive to consider the effects of these factors on recall of entire lists.

TABLE 5
Frequency of Correct Recall and Parameter Estimates for Data of Saint-Aubin and Poirier (in press)

	Serial Position					
	1	2	3	4	5	Parameter R
Parameter I	.55	.27	.09	.13	.46	
Words						
Observed	223	188	157	176	215	
Predicted	208	189	177	179	202	.71
Nonwords						
Observed	138	92	63	65	122	
Predicted	149	92	57	64	130	.16

Total possible correct is 239 for words, 240 for nonwords. $G^2 = 28.44$, 3 df, over all cells. For correct recall, $r^2 = .97$. Operations are performed before rounding. Data from J. Saint-Aubin (personal communication, August 3, 1998).

We began with the widely accepted idea that when items in a list are presented, a speech-like representation is formed, and this soon becomes degraded through decay or interference. Correct recall based on this representation proceeds until it is no longer useful.

For recall of entire lists, the most important quantity is memory span, the length of a list that can be correctly recalled immediately in order, half the time. Memory span is smaller for items pronounced at a slower rate (Baddeley et al., 1975; Mackworth, 1963; Schweickert & Boruff, 1986). Baddeley et al. (1975) proposed that span is a linear function of the rate at which the items can be pronounced,

$$s = rt + c,$$

where s is the memory span (in items) for a given type of item, and r is the rate at which the items can be pronounced (in items/second). The time t (in seconds) may be interpreted as the useful lifetime of the short-term memory representation, and c is the number of items recalled in some other way. Hulme, Maughan, and Brown (1991), for example, say c indexes a contribution to span via long-term memory. The basic idea is that the short-term representation endures for t seconds, and while it endures items are recalled at the rate of r items per second.

Despite the simplicity of the equation, there are a few complications. Sometimes s is a nonlinear function of r (Hulme et al., 1997) Sometimes c is significantly different from zero (Baddeley et al., 1975; Hulme et al., 1991) but sometimes it is not (Li & Schweickert, 1999). Some portion of c, when it is not zero, may be an artefact (Poirier, Schweickert, & Oliver, 1996; Schweickert, Guentert, & Hersberger, 1990). The time t is usually reported to be about 2sec, but recently Dosher and Ma (1998) reported that if time to pronounce items during recall is considered, the time available is considerably longer.

Although these complications must some day be resolved, the equation has already proven useful for classifying factors that affect memory span. According to the equation, an experimental factor changing memory span must change the value of at least one of the variables t, r, or c. The key classification is whether or not a factor produces an effect on span by changing r. When stimuli are controlled for nuisance factors, word length has been found to change only r (longer words are pronounced at a slower rate), leaving t and c unchanged (Baddeley et al., 1975; Hulme et al., 1991). Lexicality has been found to change span, without changing r (Hulme et al., 1991; Schweickert, Ansel, & McDaniel, 1991). Finally, phonological similarity has been found to change span with little or no change in r (Hulme & Tordoff, 1989, pp. 77 & 82; Li & Schweickert, 1999; Schweickert et al., 1990).

There is striking agreement between the classification for recall of individual items, and the classification for recall of entire lists. The factor changing I (word length) also changes r. The factors changing R (lexicality and phonological similarity) do not change r. Our interpretation is that factors improving redintegration increase the useful lifetime of the representation. (Earlier, serial position was said to change I. It is not clear what it means to consider the effect of this factor on recall of entire lists.)

It is natural to ask whether factors that do not change r can be further classified according to whether they change t or change c. On this point there is little data. Note that a change in lexicality could not be detected by a subject who did not know the language, whereas a change in phonological similarity could be. We are led to conjecture that when a factor changes the verbal stimuli in a way that can be discriminated only with knowledge of the language, the factor changes c. When a factor changes the verbal stimuli in a way that can be discriminated without prior knowledge of the language, the factor changes t.

Probability of Recalling a List

For the factors we have considered, there is good correspondence between effects on recall of individual items and effects on recall of entire lists. This encourages investigation of other factors. But to compare results on the two measures of recall, one must have some way to compare recall of an entire list to recall of the individual items.

If recall of items were stochastically independent, then the probability of recall of an entire list would simply be the product of the probabilities of recalling the individual items according to the formula

$$p(1)p(2) \ldots p(n),$$

where $p(i)$ is the probability of correctly recalling the item in serial position i. But recall from individual positions is known to be not independent (Henson, Norris, Page, & Baddeley, 1996; Johnson, 1972; Murdock, 1968). In particular, the probability of recalling an item correctly is much higher if the preceding item was recalled correctly than if it was not, although the item in the last serial position is an exception, likely to be recalled correctly regardless of the recall of the preceding item (Murdock, 1968).

Often the most important dependencies are those between adjacent items. When that is so, a good approximation to the probability of recall of an entire list of length n might be obtained from the formula

$$p(1)p(2|1)p(3|2) \ldots p(n|n-1).$$

Here, $p(1)$ is the probability item 1 is recalled correctly, and $p(i|i-1)$ is the probability item i is correctly recalled, given that item $i - 1$ was correctly recalled. An experiment was carried out to see whether the product of conditional probabilities is a reasonable estimator. The experiment was not designed to test whether the formula is theoretically true, because we know that the formula will be false whenever dependencies across long lags are produced. The question is whether the formula is close enough to be a useful approximation, for more or less typical list lengths, under more or less ordinary circumstances.

EXPERIMENT

Method

Stimuli. The stimuli were lists of 8, 9, or 10 digits presented on a computer monitor. To start each trial, a + appeared for 1000msec. In one condition, digits were presented successively, in the same position. Each was displayed for 100msec. The last was followed by "?" to prompt immediate ordered recall via the numeric keypad. In another condition, more conducive to forming associations, digits were presented simultaneously. The subject rehearsed them by typing; 2000msec per item were available for rehearsal. As each digit was typed, it appeared on the screen, one line below the corresponding stimulus digit, and remained on the screen. When the last was entered, a mask appeared covering the positions where the digits had appeared, and prompted immediate ordered recall by typing.

Subjects. Two subjects were tested for each list length and condition.

Procedure. Each of the 12 subjects came for 3 sessions. In each session, there were 5 blocks of 35 trials. The first block of the first session, and the first 3 trials of each block, were not analyzed.

Results

Results are in Table 6. The probability of correctly recalling the entire list covers a wide range, from .01 to .89. The condition with successive presentation and no rehearsal is not conducive to forming associations between items. Nonetheless, recall of individual items is not independent, because the product of the marginal probabilities of recalling individual items falls short of the probability of recalling the entire list. The estimate based on conditional probabilities is also an underestimate, indicating that dependencies are not formed only between adjacent items; however the amount of underestimation is small, only .05 in the worst cases.

The condition with simultaneous presentation and rehearsal was designed to allow more associations to develop. The assumption of independence leads to a large underestimation of the probability of recall of the entire list; an error of .31 in the worst case. The estimate based on conditional probabilities is also an underestimation, not as good as in the other condition, but nonetheless only in error by .11 in the worst case.

Whether an approximation is good depends on its use, of course. For many purposes the estimate based on the product of conditional probabilities would be close enough. The fact that this estimate is reasonably close indicates that for understanding recall of an entire list, an important quantity to focus on, after recall of the individual items themselves, is the degree of statistical dependence between adjacent items. Note that statistical dependence does not imply chaining (although chaining is an obvious way to account for dependence). Two items not directly associated could become dependent by being individually associated with something else, e.g. position cues. In a multinomial tree, one way to represent dependence would be to allow parameter values for item i to depend on whether item $i-1$ was recalled correctly or not.

SUMMARY AND CONCLUSIONS

In a widely held framework for immediate serial recall, after items are presented a representation is formed and correct recall continues until the representation is no longer useful. Factors affecting immediate serial recall can be classified in two ways. For recall of entire lists, a factor can be classified according to whether or not it affects the rate at which items are pronounced. For recall of individual items, a factor can be classified according to whether it affects degradation of the representation, or redintegration. We propose that the two classification schemes coincide, because they coincide for those factors reviewed here, whose classification is known for both schemes. A factor increasing the time required to pronounce a list of span length does so by increasing the probability with which degraded representations can be redintegrated. The final section of the paper presents an experiment demonstrating that recall of an entire list can be well approximated by a product of conditional recall probabilities for the individual items.

REFERENCES

Baddeley, A.D., & Hitch, G. (1974). Working memory. In G.H. Bower (Ed.), *The psychology of learning and motivation.* New York: Academic Press.

TABLE 6
Estimates of the Probability of Recalling an Entire List

	List Length					
	8		9		10	
	Subject		Subject		Subject	
	1	2	1	2	1	2
Successive Presentation, No Rehearsal						
Observed probability	.79	.78	.61	.89	.10	.01
Product of conditionals	.75	.74	.56	.85	.05	.00
Product of marginals	.63	.62	.43	.78	.02	.00
Simultaneous Presentation, with Rehearsal						
Observed probability	.73	.77	.64	.71	.88	.19
Product of conditionals	.66	.71	.53	.62	.87	.09
Product of marginals	.48	.60	.33	.47	.78	.02

Baddeley, A.D., Thomson, A., & Buchanan, M. (1975). Word length and the structure of short-term memory. *Journal of Verbal Learning and Verbal Behavior, 14*, 575–589.

Batchelder, W.H., & Riefer, D.M. (1999). Theoretical and empirical review of multinomial process tree modeling. *Psychonomic Bulletin and Review, 6*, 57–86.

Brown, G.D.A., & Hulme, C. (1995). Modeling item length effects in memory span: No rehearsal needed? *Journal of Memory and Language, 34*, 594–621.

Cowan, N. (1992). Verbal memory span and the timing of spoken recall. *Journal of Memory and Language, 31*, 269–295.

Cowan, N., Wood, N.L., Nugent, L.D., & Treisman, M. (1997). There are two word-length effects in verbal short-term memory: Opposed effects of duration and complexity. *Psychological Science, 8*, 290–295.

Dosher, B.A., & Ma, J.J. (1998). Output loss or rehearsal loop? Output time versus pronunciation-time limits in immediate recall for forgetting matched materials. *Journal of Experimental Psychology: Learning, Memory, and Cognition, 24*, 316–335.

Henson, R.N.A., Norris, D.G., Page, M.P.A., & Baddeley, A.D. (1996). Unchained memory: Error patterns rule out chaining models of immediate serial recall. *The Quarterly Journal of Experimental Psychology, 49A*, 80–115.

Hu, X. (1991). *General program for processing tree models* [Computer program]. Irvine, CA: University of California, School of Behavioral Sciences.

Hulme, C., Maughan, S., & Brown, G.D.A. (1991). Memory for familiar and unfamiliar words: Evidence for a long-term memory contribution to short-term memory span. *Journal of Memory and Language, 30*, 685–701.

Hulme, C., Roodenrys, S., Schweickert, R., Brown, G.D.A., Martin, S., & Stuart, G. (1997). Word-frequency effects on short-term memory tasks: Evidence for a redintegration process in immediate serial recall. *Journal of Experimental Psychology: Learning, Memory, and Cognition, 23*, 1217–1232.

Hulme, C., & Tordoff, V. (1989). Working memory development: The effects of speech rate, word length, and acoustic similarity on serial recall. *Journal of Experimental Child Psychology, 47*, 72–87.

Johnson, N. (1972). Organization and the concept of a memory code. In A.W. Melton & E. Martin (Eds.), *Coding processes in human memory* (pp. 125–160). Washington, DC: V. H. Winston & Sons.

Li, X., & Schweickert, R. (1999). *The phonological similarity effect in immediate recall: Positions of shared phonemes.* Manuscript in preparation.

Mackworth, J.F. (1963). The duration of the visual image. *Canadian Journal of Psychology, 17*, 62–81.

Murdock, B.B., Jr. (1968). Serial order effects in short-term memory. *Journal of Experimental Psychology Monograph Supplement, 76*, 1–15.

Nairne, J.S. (1990). A feature model of immediate memory. *Memory and Cognition, 18*, 251–269.

Poirier, M., Schweickert, R., & Oliver, J. (1996). *Lexicality and the relationship between memory span and speaking rate.* Paper presented at the International Conference on Memory, Abano Terme (Padova), Italy, July.

Posner, M.I., & Konick, A.F. (1966). On the role of interference in short-term retention. *Journal of Experimental Psychology, 72*, 221–231.

Saint-Aubin, J., & Poirier, M. (in press). Immediate serial recall of words and nonwords: Tests of the retrieval based hypothesis. *Psychonomic Bulletin & Review.*

Schweickert, R. (1993). A multinomial processing tree model for degradation and redintegration in immediate recall. *Memory and Cognition, 21*, 168–175.

Schweickert, R., Ansel, B., & McDaniel, M. (1991). *Lexicality and generation effects on memory span.* Paper presented at the Psychonomic Society Meeting, November.

Schweickert, R., & Boruff, B. (1986). Short-term memory capacity: Magic number or magic spell? *Journal of Experimental Psychology: Learning, Memory, and Cognition, 12*, 419–425.

Schweickert, R., Guentert, L., & Hersberger, L. (1990). Phonological similarity, pronunciation rate, and memory span. *Psychological Science, 1*, 74–77.

Schweickert, R., Hayt, C., Hersberger, L., & Guentert, L. (1996). How many words can be held in working memory? A model and a method. In S. Gathercole (Ed.), *Models of short-term memory.* Hove, UK: Lawrence Erlbaum Associates Ltd.

Service, E. (1998). The effect of word length on immediate serial recall depends on phonological complexity, not articulatory duration. *The Quarterly Journal of Experimental Psychology, 51A*, 283–304.

The Dimensionality of Memory Strength Between Levels of Both Serial Position and Word Frequency Category

Matthew Duncan
University of Toronto, Canada

In recognition tasks where Signal Detection Theory (SDT) is applied, a suitable decision variable is required. This variable is typically assumed to be a global assessment of memory strength. A further assumption is that factors such as old-new, serial position (SP), and word frequency (WF) simply act to change the value of strength across levels within the factor. In terms of SDT, the decision variable is assumed to be uni-dimensional. Four experiments are reported that provide a direct empirical assessment of this assumption for SP and WF. Judgements of items (JOI), recency (JOR), and primacy (JOP) were measured for SP; and subjective frequency (JOF) was measured for WF. Multiple dimensions imply non-additive effects across factor levels and different retrieval processes or the influence of an extra process. A single dimension is consistent with an additive effect of factor levels and current theorizing. The data are in fairly good agreement with the uni-dimensional assumption across all four factors with the exception of JOR and JOP. These showed less uni-dimensionality for comparisons between beginning vs. end list items. The implications of this are discussed.

Dans des tâches de reconnaissance où la théorie de détection de signal est appliquée, une variable décisionnelle convenable est nécessaire. On considère typiquement que cette variable est une évaluation globale de la force de la trace mnésique et qu'elle est unidimensionnelle. Une hypothèse supplémentaire veut que des facteurs comme anciens/nouveaux, la position sérielle et la fréquence des mots modifient la force de la trace. Quatre expériences vérifient empiriquement cette hypothèse pour la position sérielle et la fréquence des mots. Des jugements d'items, de récence et de primauté sont mesurés pour la position sérielle et des jugements de fréquence subjective sont mesurés pour la fréquence des mots. Des effets non additifs appuieraient une hypothèse de dimensions multiples, de processus de récupération différents ou encore l'influence d'un processus supplémentaire. Des effets additifs appuieraient l'hypothèse d'une trace unidimensionnelle et les conceptions théoriques actuelles. De façon générale, les données appuient l'hypothèse d'unidimensionnalité.

The application of Signal Detection Theory (SDT) in the analysis of recognition memory data has a long history. Although the procedures used in yes-no and m-alternative forced-choice recognition tasks make it natural to apply a signal detection analysis to the data (see Macmillan & Creelman, 1991), simplifying assumptions are necessary. In the case of SDT and recognition memory, a suitable decision variable is needed that meets the requirements of both the model and the psychological theory.

The decision variable typically used in SDT applications of memory data is strength (but see Glanzer, Adams, Iverson, & Kim, 1993). In recognition memory tasks, strength of items is assumed to be a familiarity match between the probe and the contents of memory (e.g. Gillund & Shiffrin, 1984; Hintzman, 1986; Murdock, 1982). High-familiarity matches correspond to high strength; low-familiarity matches correspond to low strength. Because familiarity is assumed to be a direct measure of strength, the two are often used interchangeably.

There are numerous examples where SDT and notions of strength have been used to analyze data (Glanzer & Adams, 1990; Koppell, 1972; Murdock, 1965; Ratcliff, Sheu, & Gronlund, 1992; Shiffrin, Huber, & Marinelli, 1995; Yonelinas, 1994). When fitting this notion of strength to a SDT model, the following assumptions are usually implied or occasionally made explicit: (a) strength is a uni-dimensional random variable, (b) strength is distributed as normal, (c) the effect of factors is to shift strength distributions along the strength axis, and (d) factor levels are mapped onto individual distributions (e.g. items at each position in a list could be mapped onto separate strength distributions). The experiments reported here were designed to assess the assumption of uni-dimensionality. This assumption is a key part in a SDT analysis of recognition data because of the way in which distributions are assumed to shift along the strength axis, and how this constrains the interpretation of level mapping. A SDT model and analysis can be used to test this uni-dimensionality assumption.

ASSESSING UNI-DIMENSIONALITY

The model used was adopted from a theory initially proposed by Tanner (1956) as part of a general theory of recognition (see Fig. 1). Dimensions i and j refer to two different signals whose distributions are S_i and S_j. The N distribution refers to a null signal or noise distribution. The relationship between the three d' variables d'_{ij}, d'_i, and d'_j is defined as

$$d'^2_{ij} = d'^2_i + d'^2_j - 2d'_i d'_j \cos(\theta) \qquad (1)$$

where d'_{ij} is the difference between the two signal distributions, d'_i is the difference between the signal i and noise distributions, and d'_j is the difference between the signal j and noise distributions. The angle between the two signal dimensions is θ, which in this case happens to be 90°.[1] When the two dimensions are completely orthogonal $\cos(\theta) = 0$ and Equation (1) becomes

$$d'^2_{ij} = d'^2_i + d'^2_j \qquad (2)$$

When the dimensions are completely nonorthogonal $\cos(\theta) = 1$ and Equation (1) becomes

$$d'^2_{ij} = d'^2_i + d'^2_j - 2d'_i d'_j$$
$$d'^2_{ij} = (d'_i - d'_j)^2$$
$$d'_{ij} = |d'_i - d'_j| \qquad (3)$$

Equation (2) is the case where dimensions i and j are considered separate dimensions and corresponds to the well-known Pythagorean theorem for right triangles. This relationship is shown in Fig. 1. Equation (3) is the case where dimensions i and j are considered to be distributions with different means along a single dimensional axis. This uni-dimensional (or additive) case is shown in Fig. 2.

Determining orthogonality is simply a matter of obtaining empirical measures for the three d' variables. Equation (1) is then rearranged to isolate $\cos(\theta)$ on one side.[2]

$$\cos(\theta) = \left| \frac{d'^2_{ij} - d'^2_i - d'^2_j}{2d'_i d'_j} \right| \qquad (4)$$

Values of $\cos(\theta)$ near 0 imply separate dimensions whereas values close to 1 imply a single dimension.

---

[1] The distributions are assumed to be independent with equal variance and zero covariance.
[2] The absolute value was taken for the sake of convenience.

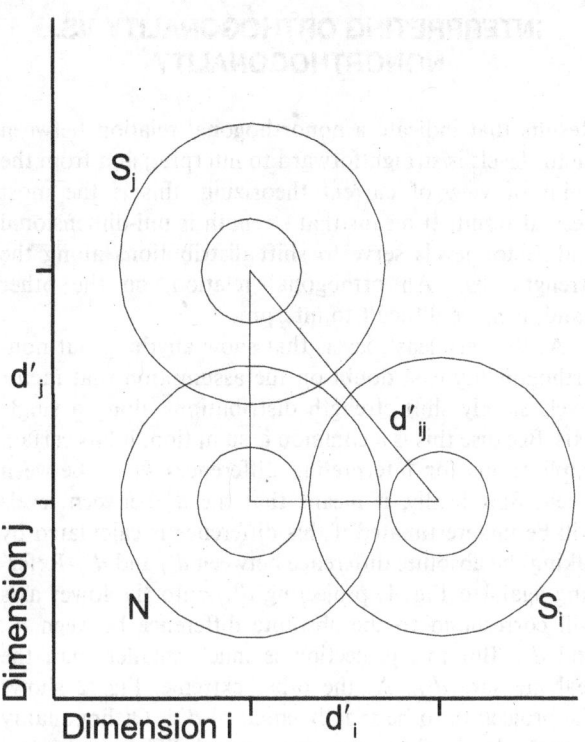

FIG. 1. Geometric interpretation of Tanner's (1956) recognition model showing differences between strength distributions as measured by d'. The figure is a top-down view of bivariate normal distributions. The circles represent contours of equal likelihood. This particular configuration also happens to represent the geometric interpretation of differences between strength distributions as measured by d' when factor levels are perfectly orthogonal.

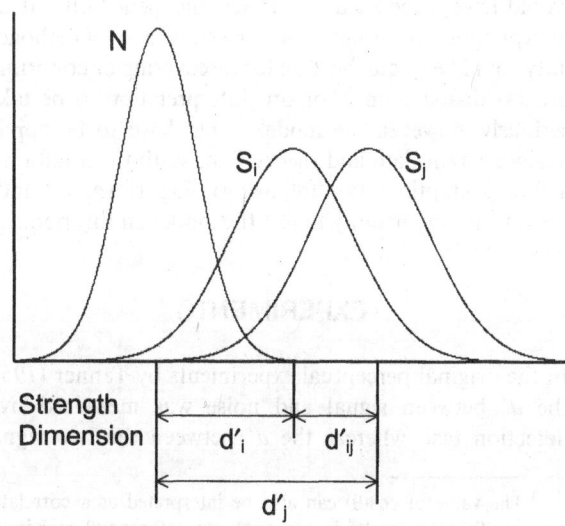

FIG. 2. Geometric interpretation of differences between strength distributions as measured by d' when factor levels are perfectly nonorthogonal (d' values are additive).

INTERPRETING ORTHOGONALITY VS. NONORTHOGONALITY

Results that indicate a nonorthogonal relation between factor levels is straightforward to interpret; and from the point of view of current theorizing, this is the most desired result. It means that strength is uni-dimensional and factor levels serve to shift distributions along the strength axis. An orthogonal relation, on the other hand, is more difficult to interpret.

At the very least, levels that show anything but non-orthogonality cast doubt on the assumption that factor levels simply shift strength distributions along a single axis. Because this is a common assumption, it has certain implications for interpreting differences in d' between levels. Specifically, it means that the d' between levels will be underestimated if this difference is calculated by taking the absolute difference between d'_i and d'_j. Referring again to Fig. 1, projecting d'_{ij} onto the lower axis will correspond to the absolute difference between d'_i and d'_j. But this projection is much smaller than the real measure d'_{ij}. At the other extreme, Fig. 2 shows the projection to be exactly equal to d'_{ij}. Orthogonality between levels, then, can obscure real differences unless those differences are measured directly.

One other interpretation relates orthogonality to processes dissociations. According to the model, strength between completely orthogonal levels is independent and uncorrelated allowing one dimension to change independently of the other.[3] This is consistent with the idea that separate processes are at work at each level (Jacoby, 1991). Requiring complete orthogonality does leave open the question of how to deal with intermediate values of $\cos(\theta)$. Values of $\cos(\theta)$ between 0 and 1 could be seen as the relative contribution of an extra process at one level compared to another which then carries with it the interpretation of independent processes as a special case [i.e., for $\cos(\theta)$ to be 0, the relative contribution of the extra process would have to be such that it acts independently]. If this interpretation turns out to be correct, degrees of orthogonality could be a valuable tool for discovering or confirming process dissociations. For this interpretation to be taken seriously, however, the model would have to be applied against extant data and theory first. With the addition of a few assumptions (see following), Experiments 2 and 3 provide an opportunity to test the model on this point.

EXPERIMENTS

In the original perceptual experiments by Tanner (1956), the d' between signal and noise was measured by a detection task whereas the d' between the two signals was obtained through a 2AFC identification task. In these experiments, all d' values were obtained through a 2AFC procedure. This was necessary for judgements of recency, primacy, and word frequency. A further advantage was that no scaling of d' values needed to be done to equate signal–signal and signal–noise comparisons. This also meant subjects made signal–noise and signal–signal comparisons all in the same experiment.

Experiments 1–3

These three experiments were conducted to measure the orthogonality of levels of serial position (SP) for judgements of items (JOI), recency (JOR), and primacy (JOP). The experiments were all identical except for the judgement subjects had to make.

Method

Subjects and Design. Sixty subjects participated for course credit in each experiment. A standard study-test procedure using a seven-item list was used. All possible permutations of comparisons between noise and SP were tested (e.g. SP_1 vs. Noise, SP_1 vs. SP_2, SP_1 vs. SP_3, ..., SP_6 vs. SP_7; where Noise = new items).

Materials. List items were sampled from the Toronto Word Pool.

Procedure. List generation and ordering of comparisons were determined randomly for each subject. Instructions for each experiment were as follows: for JOI, subjects chose the word they were most sure was on the list; for JOR, subjects chose the word nearest to the end of the list; for JOP, subjects chose the word nearest to the beginning of the list. Subjects were then told that some comparisons would be against items not from the list (i.e. signal–noise comparisons), but that it wasn't important they recognize this and they should always respond according to instructions on every trial. Each trial consisted of the presentation of seven words, one at a time, at a 500msec rate followed 1sec later by a 2AFC test.

Experiment 4

Assessment of orthogonality for judgements of word frequency (JOF).

Method

Subjects and Design. Sixty subjects participated for course credit. Six WF categories were constructed using the norms in Kuçera and Francis (1967). A continuous 2AFC task was used. All possible permutations of comparisons between noise and categories were tested (e.g. Cat_1 vs. Noise, Cat_1 vs. Cat_2, Cat_1 vs. Cat_3, ..., Cat_6 vs. Cat_7; where Cat means frequency category and Noise is either pronounceable nonwords, PNW, or pseudohomophones, PSH).

---

[3] The value of $\cos(\theta)$ can also be interpreted as a correlation because Tanner's model is a special case of general recognition theory (Ashby & Townsend, 1986). In this case, the value of $\cos(\theta)$ is the correlation between dimensions assuming independent equal variance distributions with zero covariance.

Materials. List items were sampled from the 6 WF categories. There was one category of zero-frequency items and five categories of items ranging from 1 to 600 in steps of approximately 100 with approximately equal standard deviations.

Procedure. Ordering of comparisons was determined randomly for each subject. Instructions for each experiment were as follows: choose the word you think occurs more frequently. Again subjects were informed about the signal–noise comparisons as in Experiments 1–3. Each subject did 6 blocks of 70 word pairs presented continuously at a 3sec rate between responses.

Results and Discussion for Experiments 1–4

Proportions for hits and false alarms were computed for each subject by collapsing across blocks of trials. Corresponding d' values were then calculated for each subject then averaged to produce a single value for each comparison.[4] The estimates of $\cos(\theta)$ for each experiment are given in Table 1. Corresponding values of d' for each comparison are given in Table 2. The data in Table 1 show that many of the comparisons are nonorthogonal for all four experiments. For JOR and JOP, levels are less orthogonal for beginning vs. end of the list comparisons. Both show strong orthogonality for most comparisons involving position 7. For JOI and both JOF these trends are nonexistent with estimates of $\cos(\theta)$ fairly homogenous and close to 1.

The earlier interpretation that an orthogonal relationship corresponds to different processes is consistent with at least one body of data. McElree and Dosher (1989, 1993) found that the terminal list item in a JOR speed–accuracy tradeoff (SAT) task showed differences in both the rate and asymptote parameters of the SAT function. Analysis of response time distributions showed less variability in comparisons with the terminal list item. This was interpreted to mean that the last item is not retrieved by the same processes as earlier list items because the terminal item had not been interfered with

---

[4] The value of d' in each case was calculated by dividing $[z(HR) - z(FA)]$ by $\sqrt{2}$ where $z(x)$ refers to the inverse normal function which returns a z-score for the proportion x below z. This calculation assumes a difference model where the decision variable is the difference in strength between the two alternatives. Scaling by $\sqrt{2}$ is required to normalize $[z(HR) - z(FA)]$ when assuming a difference model (see Macmillan & Creelman, 1991, p. 124).

Some subjects produced error-free responding for a few of the comparisons involving the easiest discriminations (e.g. SP_1 vs. SP_7 in JOI). This occurred because the large number of trials required to counter-balance the design prohibited testing subjects enough times to ensure reliable error rates. Consequently, estimates of d' for these comparisons could not be calculated for some subjects and so the sample sizes for most d' values are unequal and correlated with the value of d'. However, the difference in sample size was never larger than 30%. Considering the number of subjects run in each experiment, this should not present much of a problem except to make the larger d' values slightly more variable.

TABLE 1
Estimates of $\cos(\theta)$ for Experiments 1–4

SP_i	SP_j					
	2	3	4	5	6	7
JOI						
1	1.00	1.00	1.00	0.98	0.92	0.98
2		1.00	1.00	0.96	0.90	0.88
3			1.00	1.01	0.94	0.96
4				1.00	0.94	0.95
5					0.97	1.00
6						1.04

SP_i	SP_j					
	2	3	4	5	6	7
JOR						
1	1.02	0.98	0.98	0.68	0.80	0.38
2		1.01	0.95	0.82	0.81	0.48
3			1.02	0.86	0.99	0.31
4				0.92	0.87	0.55
5					0.96	0.69
6						0.76

SP_i	SP_j					
	2	3	4	5	6	7
JOP						
1	0.92	0.94	0.93	0.88	0.77	0.60
2		1.00	0.99	0.94	0.82	0.47
3			1.00	0.98	0.96	0.77
4				0.97	0.93	0.35
5					0.85	0.25
6						0.11

Cat_i	Cat_j					
	1	2	3	4	5	6
JOF: PNW						
Zero	1.00	1.00	0.98	0.94	0.99	0.97
1		0.96	0.97	0.92	0.91	0.92
2			1.00	1.00	1.00	0.97
3				1.00	1.00	1.00
4					1.00	0.99
5						1.00

Cat_i	Cat_j					
	1	2	3	4	5	6
JOF: PSH						
Zero	1.00	0.96	0.96	0.95	0.95	0.90
1		0.99	1.04	0.98	0.90	0.90
2			1.00	1.00	0.99	0.96
3				1.00	1.01	1.00
4					1.00	0.98
5						0.99

Entries are the $\cos(\theta)$ estimate for comparisons between SP_i and SP_j or WF Cat_i and Cat_j.

by subsequent items. Estimates of $\cos(\theta)$ for the JOR and JOP data of Experiments 2 and 3 are in line with this interpretation. Position 7 is more orthogonal to positions 1 through 6 than these positions are to themselves.

Deviations of $\cos(\theta)$ from 1 can also be interpreted in terms of dual process theory (Yonelinas, 1994).

TABLE 2
d' Values for Experiments 1–4

	SP_j						
SP_i	1	2	3	4	5	6	7
JOI							
New	1.66	1.62	1.58	1.66	2.02	1.95	2.83
1		0.01	0.03	0.10	0.48	0.78	1.25
2			0.08	0.11	0.68	0.87	1.61
3				0.36	0.38	0.71	1.37
4					0.36	0.68	1.35
5						0.46	0.84
6							0.59

	SP_j						
SP_i	1	2	3	4	5	6	7
JOR							
Noise	1.10	1.35	1.15	1.60	1.82	2.36	2.21
1		0.12	0.23	0.56	1.35	1.63	2.05
2			0.01	0.52	1.06	1.50	1.96
3				0.37	1.00	1.25	2.15
4					0.73	1.26	1.88
5						0.82	1.64
6							1.59

	SP_j						
SP_i	1	2	3	4	5	6	7
JOP							
Noise	1.60	1.48	1.71	1.46	1.30	1.09	0.56
1		0.61	0.58	0.58	0.77	1.04	1.34
2			0.21	0.20	0.51	0.85	1.32
3				0.23	0.51	0.73	1.33
4					0.39	0.61	1.37
5						0.70	1.29
6							1.29

	Cat_j						
Cat_i	Zero	1	2	3	4	5	6
JOF: PNW							
Noise	1.74	2.01	2.37	2.50	2.23	2.37	2.58
Zero		0.24	0.65	0.85	0.82	0.71	0.98
1			0.68	0.73	0.86	0.98	1.05
2				0.18	0.23	0.24	0.64
3					0.09	0.10	0.22
4						0.14	0.47
5							0.23

	Cat_j						
Cat_i	Zero	1	2	3	4	5	6
JOF: PSH							
Noise	1.59	1.39	2.02	2.28	2.17	2.02	2.12
Zero		0.24	0.65	0.85	0.82	0.71	0.98
1			0.68	0.73	0.86	0.98	1.05
2				0.18	0.23	0.24	0.60
3					0.09	0.10	0.22
4						0.14	0.47
5							0.23

Entries are the d' estimate for comparisons between words at SP_i and SP_j, or between WF Cat_i and Cat_j. "Noise" refers to comparisons to the noise stimulus which were new items for Experiments 1 to 3 and pronounceable nonwords or psuedohomophones in the case of Experiment 4.

According to this theory, recognition judgements are determined by a combination of recollection and familiarity-based retrieval processes. The overall observed hit rate (HR) is defined as $HR = R + F - (R * F)$, where R and F refer to the contribution of recollection and familiarity respectively. If familiarity is uni-dimensional and the amount of recollection varies across levels, then the model would predict deviations from $\cos(\theta)$ because the contribution of an extra process changes as a function of level. It is possible to explain the deviations of $\cos(\theta)$ from 1 given the following assumptions: (a) for the short-term memory task used here, the familiarity process is uni-dimensional with respect to strength across SP and WF category, (b) the amount of recollection contributing to recognition performance increases as a function of SP, and (c) subjects' responses are dependent on the most recent item.

Relative to Experiments 2 and 3, the data in Experiments 1 and 4 show strength to be uni-dimensional across SP and WF category. This could be the result of familiarity, but not recollection, determining subject performance. This implies values of $\cos(\theta)$ close to 1 reflect familiarity alone whereas deviations from 1 reflect a contribution of both recollection and familiarity. Because subjects in Experiments 2 and 3 had to learn both the list items *and* their positions, the extra encoding effort could have led to a higher probability of recollection than in Experiment 1 (Nelson, Bennet, & Xu, 1997; Toth, Reingold, & Jacoby, 1994). Furthermore, WF judgements do not require subjects to remember list items, which means familiarity, not recollection, is the factor determining performance. Both these results imply that values of $\cos(\theta)$ close to 1 represent familiarity alone determining performance.

Yonelinas (1994) also found that recollection increased with SP. Given similarities with the task used here, it seems reasonable to assume this is true in Experiments 2 and 3 as well. Finally, congruent with the data of McElree and Dosher (1989), discrimination performance in Experiments 1, 2, and 3 does indeed appear to depend on the most recent item. The data in Table 2 show changes in d' across rows (according to the most recent item) are much greater than down columns (according to the least recent item). This is less pronounced for JOP probably because subjects used a mixture of strategies (i.e. occasionally perform a JOR then give the opposite response). Given these assumptions, the model would predict increasing deviations of $\cos(\theta)$ from 1 as the contribution of recollection increases.

The data from Experiments 1 to 4 cannot support the model directly, but it is possible to simulate the effects of changing the contribution of recollection to see whether the model produces the correct change in $\cos(\theta)$. Figure 3 shows how $\cos(\theta)$ changes as the amount of recollection contributing to the HR is increased. It is clear from the figure the model produces a prediction in the correct direction. It is now a matter of testing if the model produces the correct amount. The procedures used in Yonelinas (1994) can be adapted to the current task

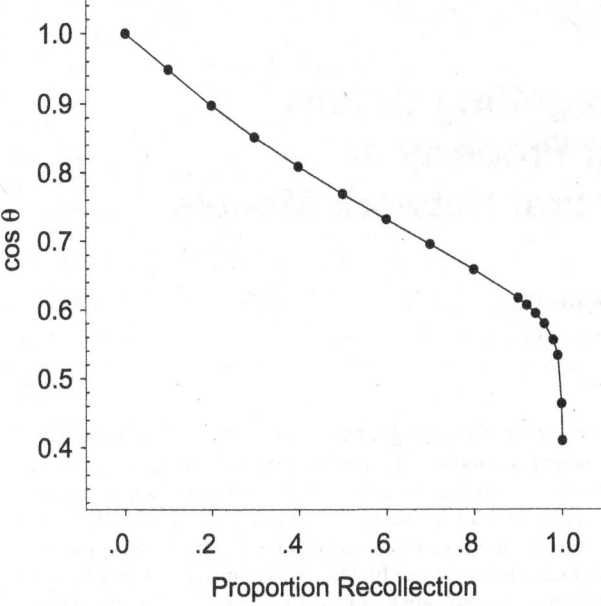

FIG. 3. Estimates of $\cos(\theta)$ as a function of the contribution of recollection to retrieval performance. For these simulated data, the hit rate for S_i vs. N was .80, the hit rate for S_j vs. N was .63, hit rate for S_i vs. S_j was .43, and the false alarm rate was .46 for all hit rates. These parameters were arbitrarily chosen so that $\cos(\theta)=1$ when $R=0$.

and the contribution of recollection measured. One can then predict $\cos(\theta)$ from recollection and test the model.

One final note about the noise distributions. Clearly, the calculation of $\cos(\theta)$ depends on the relationship between the choice of noise stimulus and factor levels. Because of this, any results either for or against orthogonality must be interpreted in the context of what constitutes noise[5]. One area of research where this may be relevant is word frequency. For example, it is possible that the nonorthogonal results in Experiments 1 to 3 are carried largely by the effects of high-frequency words because of the difference in recency effect compared to low-frequency words. As it stands, the model is not stuck on any specific kind of noise stimulus; only the interpretation of the data are.

CONCLUSIONS

The assumption that recognition tasks are based on a uni-dimensional strength variable turned out to be largely supported for a variety of judgement types across most level comparisons. The exception occurred with JOR and JOP, in which the terminal item showed a fairly strong orthogonal relationship to most of the other list items. This was taken as evidence that the last item in a list is processed differently. This interpretation was supported by previous research at least for this particular case. It was also shown that orthogonality can reflect the degree to which an extra process contributes to performance at one level as opposed to another. It still needs to be seen whether the model can stand up to further empirical tests, but it is reasonably consistent with the data so far.

REFERENCES

Ashby, F., & Townsend, J. (1986). Varieties of perceptual independence. *Psychological Review, 93*, 154–179.

Gillund, G., & Shiffrin, M. (1984). A retrieval model for both recognition and recall. *Psychological Review, 91*, 1–67.

Glanzer, M., & Adams, J. (1990). The mirror effect in recognition memory: Data and theory. *Journal of Experimental Psychology: Learning, Memory and Cognition, 16*, 5–16.

Glanzer, M., Adams, J.K., Iverson, G.J., & Kim, K. (1993). The regularities of recognition memory. *Psychological Review, 100*, 546–567.

Hintzman, D. (1986). "Schema abstraction" in a multiple-trace memory model. *Psychological Review, 93*, 411–428.

Jacoby, L.L. (1991). A process dissociation framework: Separating automatic from intentional uses of memory. *Journal of Memory and Language, 30*, 513–541.

Koppell, S. (1972). Decision latencies in recognition memory: A signal detection analysis. *Journal of Experimental Psychology: Human Learning and Memory, 3*, 445–457.

Kucera, F., & Francis, W. (1967). *Computational analysis of present-day American English*. Providence, RI: Brown University Press.

Macmillan, N.A., & Creelman, C.D. (1991). *Detection theory: A user's guide*. Cambridge: Cambridge University Press.

McElree, B., & Dosher, B.A. (1989). Serial position and set size in short-term memory: The time course of recognition. *Journal of Experimental Psychology: General, 118*, 346–373.

McElree, B., & Dosher, B.A. (1993). Serial retrieval processes in the recovery of order information. *Journal of Experimental Psychology: General, 122*, 291–315.

Murdock, B.B. (1965). Signal detection theory and short-term memory. *Journal of Experimental Psychology, 70*, 443–447.

Murdock, B.B. (1982). A theory for the storage and retrieval of item and associative information. *Psychological Review, 89*, 609–626.

Murdock, B.B. (1985). An analysis of the strength-latency relationship. *Memory and Cognition, 13*, 511–521.

Nelson, D., Bennet, D., & Xu, J. (1997). Recollective and automatic uses of memory. *Journal of Experimental Psychology: Learning, Memory and Cognition, 23*, 872–885.

Ratcliff, R., Sheu, C., & Gronlund, S. (1992). Testing global memory models using ROC curves. *Psychological Review, 99*, 518–535.

Shiffrin, R., Huber, D., & Marinelli, K. (1995). Effects of category length and strength on familiarity in recognition. *Journal of Experimental Psychology: Learning, Memory and Cognition, 21*, 267–287.

Tanner, W.P. (1956). Theory of recognition. *Journal of the Acoustical Society of America, 28*, 882–888.

Toth, J., Reingold, E., & Jacoby, L. (1994). Toward a redefinition of implicit memory: Process dissociations following elaborative processing and self-generation. *Journal of Experimental Psychology: Learning, Memory and Cognition, 20*, 290–303.

Yonelinas, A. (1994). Receiver-operating characteristics in recognition memory: Evidence for a dual process model. *Journal of Experimental Psychology: Learning, Memory and Cognition, 20*, 1341–1354.

---

[5] I thank an anonymous reviewer for bringing this issue to my attention.

Power Function Forgetting Curves as an Emergent Property of Biologically Plausible Neural Network Models

Sverker Sikström
University of Toronto, Canada

Empirical forgetting curve data have been shown to follow a power function. In contrast, many connectionist models predict either an exponential decay or flat forgetting curves. This paper simulates power function forgetting curves in a Hopfield network modified to incorporate the more biologically realistic assumptions of bounded weights and a distribution of learning rates. The modified model produces power function forgetting curves. The bounded weights introduce exponential decay for individual weights, and a power function forgetting curve when summing exponential decays with different learning rates. Because these assumptions are biologically reasonable, power function forgetting curves may be an emergent property of biological networks. The results fit empirical data and indicate that forgetting curves restrict possible implementation of models of memory.

Il a été démontré que les données associées à la courbe d'oubli suivent une fonction de puissance. Par ailleurs, plusieurs modèles connexionnistes prédisent soit un estompage exponentiel, soit des courbes d'oubli aplaties. Cet article simule les courbes d'oubli suivant une fonction de puissance dans un réseau Hopfield modifié afin d'incorporer les hypothèses les plus réalistes possibles au plan biologique. Le modèle modifié produit des fonctions de puissance comme courbes d'oubli. Les coefficients limites introduisent un estompage exponentiel pour les coefficient individuels et une fonction de puissance lorsque l'on fait la somme de ceux-ci avec des rythmes d'apprentissage différents. Parce que ces postulats sont raisonnables au plan biologique, les courbes d'oubli en fonctions de puissance pourraient être une propriété émergente des réseaux biologiques. Les résultats concordent avec les données empiriques et indiquent que les courbes d'oubli restreignent les modèles de mémoire possible.

Laboratory studies of recognition and autobiographical data show a linear relationship between the logarithm of a measurement of memory (e.g. d') and the logarithm of the time since the items were encoded, indicating a power function forgetting curve. Rubin and Wenzel (1996) gathered a database of 210 published data sets of forgetting curves, which had five or more datapoints, were smooth, and to which at least one function could be fitted with a correlation coefficient of .90. They fitted the database with 105 different functions and found that the power function accounted for more variance than the exponential function, or several other functions. However, on empirical grounds they found it difficult to distinguish between the power function and three other functions, namely the logarithm, the exponential in the square root of time, and the hyperbola in the square root of time. In accordance, this paper makes no strong claim whether the power function or one of the other three functions suggested by Rubin and Wenzel is the true function on empirical grounds.

Crovitz and Schiffman (1974) suggested that a memory measurement (M) could be summarized by a power function of time (t):

$$M = \beta t^{-\alpha} \qquad (1)$$

where α and β are positive constants. It follows from Equation (1) that the logarithm of a memory measurement [log(M)] is a linear relationship with the logarithm of the time passed since encoding. In autobiographical memory, M is the number of memories per time unit. In laboratory studies M is d', which is a measurement proportional to the underlying trace strength. To achieve a high degree of accounted variance a large range of performance seems to be necessary. For example, the power function in autobiographical memory, where the range typically is three or four magnitudes, has been found to account for .95 to 1.00 of the variance. Anderson and Tweney (1997) argued that the experimental power function curves may be an artefact due to averaging over subjects. However, Wixted and Ebbesen (1997) showed that the power function also fits better than the expo-

---

Requests for reprints should be addressed to Sverker Sikström, PhD, Department of Psychology, University of Toronto, 100 St George Street, Toronto, Ontario, Canada M5S 3G3 (Fax: ++1 416 978 4811; Tel: ++1 416 978 4518; E-mail: sverker@psych.utoronto.ca; Homepage: http://www.psych.utoronto.ca/~sverker/sikstrōm.html).

© 1999 International Union of Psychological Science

nential function when data from the individual subjects are fitted. This indicates that the power function is not an artefact due to averaging over subjects.

The purpose of this paper is to show that a Hopfield network modified in two aspects shows power function forgetting curves. The modifications are bounded weights and a variance in the distribution of learning rates. The bounded weights make the weights decay exponentially. Power function forgetting curves are found when the exponential decays are summed over a distribution of learning rates. Bounded weights and a distribution of learning rates are biologically reasonable assumptions. Therefore, it is argued that a power function forgetting curve may be an emergent property of a biological neural network. The model is consistent with TECO (Sikström, 1996a, b, 1998) that has been applied to a wide set of memory phenomena (a full summary of TECO is beyond the scope of the present paper).

A MODEL FOR POWER FUNCTION FORGETTING CURVES

First, the Hopfield network (Hopfield, 1982, 1984) is described. Activated nodes correspond to features in the represented information. Items are represented in patterns of activation. Each pattern consists of N nodes. The activation of node i at time t (ξ^t_i) can be in one of two states. The active state is represented as $+1$ and the inactive state as 0. The probability that a node is active is a ($0 < a < 1$). Each pattern is created by randomly setting exactly aN nodes to an active state and the other nodes to an inactive state.

All nodes are connected to all other nodes in the network and a weight is attached to each connection. The weight between node i and node j at time t is w^t_{ij}. The weight change (Δw^t_{ij}) for $i = j$ is zero, and for $i \neq j$ is calculated by:

$$\Delta w^t_{ij} = \frac{1}{N} (\xi^t_i - a)(\xi^t_j - a) \qquad (2)$$

Retrieval from the network is conducted by presenting a pattern to the network. The retrieved pattern can be found by calculating the net input for each node:

$$net^t_i = \sum_{j=1}^{N} w_{ij} \xi^t_j \qquad (3)$$

The encoded pattern can then be retrieved by synchronously activating the nodes to $+1$ if the argument is positive and otherwise to 0.

A standard Hopfield network produces flat forgetting curves because the probability of retrieval is independent of when the patterns are stored. To account for forgetting curves it is suggested that the weights should be bounded and that the learning rates should be different for each weight (η_{ij}). The boundaries are created by setting the weights to the maximum boundary (b) if the weight is above b. If the weight is below the minimum boundary ($-b$) then the weight is set to $-b$:

$$w^{t+1}_{ij} = \text{Max}[\text{ Min}[w^t_{ij} + \eta_{ij} \Delta w^t_{ij}, b], -b] \qquad (4)$$

where Min[ ] takes the minimum of the two arguments and Max[ ] takes the maximum of the two arguments.

The slope of the forgetting curves are zero as long as the weight does not reach the boundary. When the boundary is reached the slope of the forgetting curves become negative because the boundary interferes with the weight changes. Forgetting due to the boundary at time (t) is equal to the probability that the weights "bump" into the boundary. This is equal to the expected value of the absolute weight change $(\eta_{ij} \underline{\Delta w})^1$ divided by the distance between the low and the high boundaries ($2b$). The probability that the boundary is not reached (α_{ij}) is then:

$$\alpha_{ij} = 1 - \text{Min}\left[\frac{\eta_{ij} \underline{\Delta w}}{2b}, 1\right] =$$
$$1 - \text{Min}\left[\frac{\eta_{ij} 2[a(1-a)]^2}{bN}, 1\right] \qquad (5)$$

where $0 < \alpha_{ij} < 1$. Let t represent the lag, or the encoded items between encoding and retrieval. Given a constant number of items encoded at each time period then t can be regarded as the time between encoding and retrieval. Performance over time for a single weight can be written as an exponential function of time. The performance over time ($d'(t)$) for the whole network can then be written as the average of the exponential functions with different decay parameters:

$$d'(t) = d'(0) \frac{1}{N^2} \sum_{i=1}^{N} \sum_{j=1}^{N} \alpha_{ij}^{t/2} =$$
$$d'(0) \frac{1}{N^2} \sum_{i=1}^{N} \sum_{j=1}^{N} e^{\ln(\alpha_{ij})t/2} \qquad (6)$$

where $d'(0)$ is the d' at time 0^2. Thus, it is predicted that bounded weights yield an exponential forgetting curve.

This network will show the slowest possible forgetting curve (completely flat) if the learning rate (in relation to

---

[1] The expected absolute weight change ($\underline{\Delta w}$) is the absolute weight change (abs(Δw_i)) times the probability for each weight change (p_i) summed over the four possible combinations of weight changes:

$$\underline{\Delta w} = \sum_{i=1}^{4} (\text{abs}(\Delta w_i) \, p_i) = \frac{1}{N} [\text{abs}((0-a)(0-a))(1-a)^2 + \text{abs}((0-a)(1-a))(1-a)a + \text{abs}((1-a)(0-a))a(1-a) + \text{abs}((1-a)(1-a))a^2]$$
$$= \frac{1}{N} [2a(1-a)]^2 \qquad (9)$$

[2] The factor one half in the exponent is included because the weight changes are dependent. The standard deviation of the dependent mean weight changes is equal to the square root of the expected value of the independent weight changes.

the boundary) is so slow that the boundary is never reached. The network can also show the fastest possible forgetting curve if the learning rate is so large that only the last item is stored in the weights. Intermediate fast forgetting curves can be found by using the learning rates that are in between the fastest and the slowest possible. It should therefore be possible to find a distribution of weight changes that shows a power function forgetting curve by combining slow and fast forgetting rates in a suitable way.

The question is what distribution of learning rates yields a power function forgetting curve for the sum of exponential. Mathematically, this is not an easy question. By using Laplace transformations, Newell and Rosenbloom (1981) argued that a rectangular distribution of exponential results in an aggregate power function. However, more recently Kahana (personal communication, 6 June 1998) argued that it can be shown mathematically that any smooth probability distribution of decay parameters (α_{ij}) in exponential functions yields an aggregated power function. This is also what is found in the simulations below.

SIMULATION

A simulation was run to study how forgetting curves depend on bounded weights and the distribution of η_{ij}. The following settings were used: the number of encoded patterns (p) 64, the number of nodes (N) 60, the activation level (a) 0.2, and the boundary (b) 0.00067. Initially all weights were set to a zero.

First, 64 to-be-encoded patterns and 64 lure patterns were created. Then each of the 64 patterns (p) was encoded once in a temporal order. All weights in the network were changed using the same learning rule (as specified earlier). The 1, 2, 4, 8, 16, 32, and 64 latest encoded patterns were retrieved. No learning occurred during retrieval. Each simulation was repeated 500 times.

The familiarity (μ) of a retrieved pattern was calculated by the dot product between the net input (net^t_i) and the activation of the encoded pattern scaled so that the expected value is zero ($\xi^t_i - a$) summed over the N number of nodes:

$$\mu = \sum_{i=1}^{N} net^t_i (\xi^t_i - a) \quad (7)$$

The results are presented as d' calculated from the familiarity of the targets (μ_t), the familiarity of the lure (μ_d) and the standard deviation of familiarity of the lure (σ_d):

$$d' = \frac{\mu_t - \mu_d}{\sigma_d} \quad (8)$$

The learning rate (η_{ij}) was varied as follows. Most prominent memory models use a constant learning rate, and several models have unbounded weights (e.g. CHARM, Metcalfe, 1991), whereas some are bounded (context to items association in Chappell and Humphreys' model, 1994). The effect of constant weight changes was simulated in Model 1A, 1B, and 1C. In Model 1A the weight change was set to a large value so only the last item can be recalled from the network (η_{ij} = 2). In Model 1C the weight change was set so slow that the boundaries can not be reached, i.e. the weight change was practically unbounded (η_{ij} = 0.008). In Model 1B the learning rate was set to an arbitrarily chosen intermediate level (η_{ij} = 0.04).

In Model 1D, 1E, and 1F the learning rates were different for each connection. The distribution was set to a linear distribution (Model 1D, $\eta_{ij} = \eta$), an exponential distribution [Model 1E, $\eta_{ij} = \exp(\eta)$], and a power function (Model 1F, $\eta_{ij} = \eta^{-1}$), where η is a random variable with a rectangular distribution, bounded so that η_{ij} falls between 1 and 0.008. The learning rates were updated for each subject. However, the learning rate has to be constant during the simulation of each subject to produce appropriate forgetting curves.

RESULTS

The results from the simulations are presented in Fig. 1a and 1b. It was predicted that the bounded weights should yield exponential forgetting curves, which is evident by a linear curve on log-linear plot. This was also found for Simulations 1A, 1B, and 1C (Fig. 1a). Model 1B used an intermediate boundary so that several items could be stored. The explained variance on exponential function is 1.000. The predicted slope according to Equation 6 was $\alpha = 0.94$, and the simulated slope was $\alpha = 0.93$, indicating a reasonably good fit between predicted and simulated slopes. The forgetting was faster than a power function. The explained variance R^2 on a power function was 0.78.

Model 1C, where the weights were unbounded (i.e. due to a very low learning rate) shows a flat "forgetting" curve independent of the time of learning. This forgetting curve is predicted from the Matrix Model (Humphreys, Bain, & Pike, 1989) and MINERVA II (Hintzman, 1987), among others. Model 1A with maximally bounded weights shows a forgetting curve where only the last encoded item can be retrieved (notice that the logarithmic curve is cut off so that very low d' are not displayed in the figure). Thus, the models with bounded weights and a constant learning rate show exponential forgetting curves.

In Model 1D to 1F, the learning rates were different for each weight and distributed as linear, exponential, and power functions. The results are shown in Fig. 1b. A good fit with a power function is in this graph represented by a linear curve with a negative slope. The results fit a linear relationship on the log-log scale well (Model 1D $R^2 = 0.993$, Model 1E $R^2 = 0.997$, Model 1F $R^2 = 0.993$). Thus, these models are consistent with power function forgetting curves often found empirically in long-term memory.

To summarize, power function forgetting curves were found using bounded weights and several different distributions of learning rates. Models with unbounded

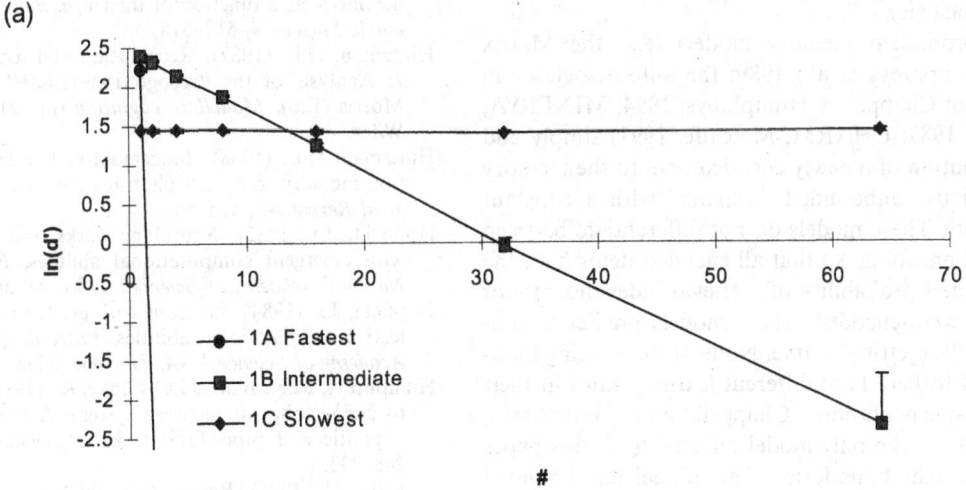

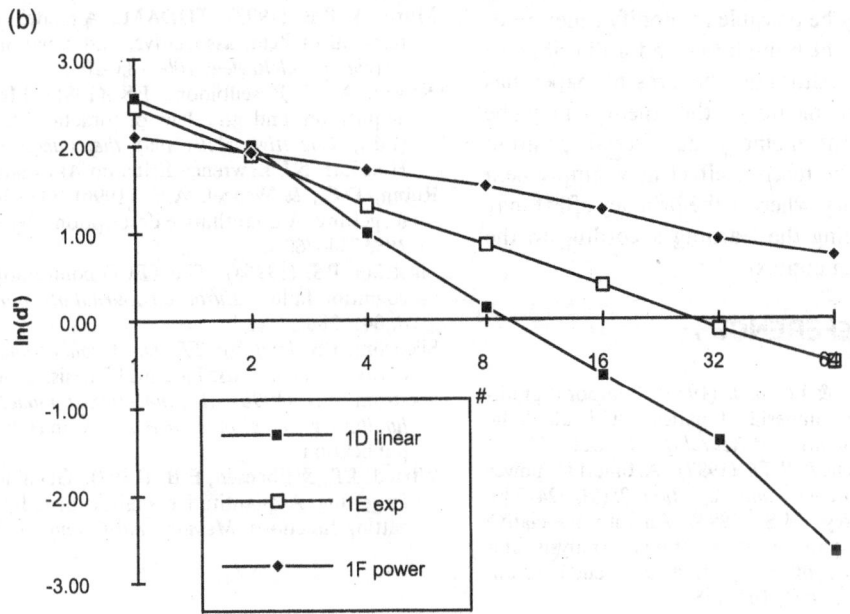

FIG. 1. (a) Simulated data for a constant distribution of learning rates: The y-axis shows the $\log_e$ (ln) of d' and the x-axis the number of items encoded before the item was retrieved on a linear scale (i.e. time). Model 1A shows the results for the fastest possible learning rate, Model 1B the results for an intermediate (i.e. $\eta_{ij} = 0.1$ learning rate, and Model 1C the results for the slowest possible learning rate. (b) Simulated data using three different distributions of learning rates: The y-axis shows the $\log_e$ of d' and the x-axis the number of items encoded before the item was retrieved (i.e. time) on a $\log_2$ scale. The distributions are linear (1D), exponential (1E), and power (1F).

weights or a constant learning rate did not show a power function forgetting curve.

DISCUSSION

A modified Hopfield model was proposed to account for the power function forgetting curves by assuming bounded weights and a distribution of learning rates. The bounded weights introduce exponential decays for individual weights. Summing exponential decays with different learning rates (or decay parameters) yields a power function forgetting curve consistent with empirical data.

An important aspect of the model is that the assumptions are biologically plausible. Weights may be conceived as synaptic plasticity. It is likely that synaptic plasticity in biological cells is bounded. The assumption of a positive distribution of learning rates in the present model is also a plausible assumption in neurological system. Since these assumptions are likely to be true in biological neural networks, it is also reasonable to conclude that a power function forgetting curve may be an emergent property of biological networks. However, neurological data showing unbounded synaptic plasticity, or no distribution of synaptic plasticity, may potentially falsify the present theory. The author is unaware of explicit neurological data on the distribution of time constants for synaptic plasticity, or boundaries for synaptic plasticity.

Most prominent memory models (e.g. the Matrix Model, Humphreys et al., 1989; the auto-associator in the model of Chappell & Humphreys, 1994; MINERVA, Hintzman, 1987; CHARM, Metcalfe, 1991) simply add the contribution of a newly encoded item to the memory vector and use unbounded "weights" with a constant learning rate. These models do not differentiate between the time of encoding, so that all encoded items have the same expected probability of retrieval independently of when they were encoded. These models predict a completely flat "forgetting" curve. None of the existing models referred to here have different learning rates in their current implementation. Chappell and Humphreys' (1994) model is the only model referred to in this paper that uses weight boundaries. This model has bounded weights in the connections from the representation of context to the items whereas the item to item connections are unbounded. It may be possible to modify other models by introducing weight boundaries and a distribution of the learning rates. Although the present paper has dealt with long-term memory, the theory may be extended to short-term memory and serial position effects. For example, the recency effect may simply be a special case of the theory, whereas the primacy effect may be modelled by changing the learning according to the novelty of the encoding context.

REFERENCES

Albert, M.S., Butters, N., & Levin, J. (1979). Temporal gradients in the retrograde amnesia of patients with alcoholic Korsakoff's disease. *Archives of Neurology, 36*, 211–216.

Anderson, R.B., & Tweney, R.D. (1997). Artifactual power curves in forgetting. *Memory and Cognition, 25*(5), 724–730.

Chappell, M., & Humphreys, M.S. (1994). An auto-associative neural network for sparse representations: Analysis and application to models of recognition and cued recall. *Psychological Review, 101*(1), 103–128.

Crovitz, H.F., & Schiffman, H. (1974). Frequency of episodic memories as a function of their age. *Bulletin of the Psychonomic Society, 4*, 517–518.

Hintzman, D.L. (1987). Recognition and recall in MINERVA 2: Analysis of the "recognition failure" paradigm. In P. Morris (Ed.), *Modelling cognition* (pp. 215–229). London: Wiley.

Hintzman, D.L. (1988). Judgement of frequency and recognition memory in a multiple trace memory model. *Psychological Review, 95*, 528–551.

Hopfield, J.J. (1982). Neural networks and physical systems with emergent computational abilities. *Proceeding of the National Academy of Sciences, USA, 81*, 3088–3092.

Hopfield, J.J. (1984). Neurons with graded responses have collective computational abilities. *Proceedings of the National Academy of Science USA, 81*, 3008–3092.

Humphreys, M.S., Bain, J.D., & Pike, R. (1989). Different way to cue a coherent memory system: A theory for episodic, semantic and procedural tasks. *Psychological Review, 96*, 208–233.

Metcalfe, J. (1991). Recognition failure and the composite memory trace in CHARM. *Psychological Review, 98*, 529–553.

Murdock, B.B. (1993). TODAM2: A model for the storage and retrieval of item, associative, and serial-order information. *Psychological Review, 100*, 183–203.

Newell, A., & Rosenbloom, P.S. (1981). Mechanism of skill acquisition and the law of practice. In J.R. Anderson (Ed.), *Cognitive skills and their acquisition* (pp. 1–55). Hillsdale, NJ: Lawrence Erlbaum Associates Inc.

Rubin, D.C., & Wenzel, A.E. (1996). One hundred years of forgetting: A quantitative description. *Psychological Review, 103*, 734–760.

Sikström, P.S. (1996a). The TECO connectionist theory of recognition failure. *European Journal of Cognitive Psychology, 8*, 341–380.

Sikström, P.S. (1996b). *TECO: A connectionist theory of successive episodic tests.* Doctoral Thesis, Umeå University.

Sikström, P.S. (1998). *A connectionist model for novelty and familiarity in episodic memory.* Manuscript submitted for publication.

Wixted, J.T., & Ebbesen, E.B. (1997). Genuine power curves in forgetting: A quantitative analysis of individual subject forgetting functions. *Memory and Cognition, 25*(5), 731–739

Subject Index

Aphasia, 339–346
Articulation rate and verbal span, 374, 375
Articulatory suppression, 306, 390, 412–413, 415, 416, 417
   during auditory localization, 318, 319
Associative information, 427
Attention
   differential, 428
   and duration estimation, 308, 314, 315
   and serial recall, 353–356
   and trace decay, 285
Auditory localization, 317–321
   articulatory suppression during, 318, 319
   and central executive, 321
   serial recall during, 318, 319, 320
Auditory scene analysis, 325
Autobiographical memory, 460

Babble speech, 324
Background sound, 322–327, 328–333, 412, 413, 415, 416, 417
BSB (brain-state-in-a-box) model, 437–445

Central executive
   assessment, 366, 367–368, 372
   and auditory localization, 321
   and long-term memory, 337
   and memory span, 359, 360, 363, 369
Changing-state hypothesis, 323, 324–325
Children
   expressive language skills, 365
   foreign language learning, 383–388
   language development, 364–373, 378–379, 383
   listening span, 365, 367
   memory span development, 353–358, 374–377
   phonological memory, 365
   phonological memory estimation, 366, 378–382, 384
   rehearsal by, 389–390
   serial recognition, 379, 380–382
   vocabulary knowledge, 365, 370, 380, 382, 386
Complex span task, 364–365, 371
Conceptual masking, 294
Concurrent articulation, 294, 295, 296, 298
Connectionist models, 400, 403–404, 437–445
Corsi Block Task, 341, 360, 367
Cues, 301–302, 306

Deep dysphasia, 346
Degradation, 292, 301, 447–450, 452
   and attention, 285
   rehearsal prevention, 285
Differential attention, 428
Differential forgetting, 427–428, 429
Digit span, 359, 361–362
   and learning, 344, 345
   pauses in recall, 356–357
Duration estimation, 308–316
   and attention, 308, 314, 315

Edge effect, 436–437
Episodic pointers, 323

Familiarity, 454
Feature adoption, 413, 417
Feature Model, 285, 292, 298, 332, 350, 403, 410–418
Foreign language learning, 383–388
Forgetting, 276–284, 285–292
   curves, 460–464
   differential, 427–428, 429
   interference, 277, 280, 283, 285, 286, 292
   output delays, 276–277, 280, 282–283
   trace decay, 285, 292
Frequency, judgement of, 428–429
Frontal lobe, 400

Hopfield network, 461

Immediate serial recall, *see* Serial recall headings
Inhibition, 365, 390
Inner speech, speed of, 294
Interference, 277, 283
    proactive, 285, 286, 288, 289–290, 291–292
    retroactive, 280, 282, 283, 285, 292
Interposition errors, 404
Inter-recall latencies, 421–424
Inter-word pauses, 356–357, 376, 390
Intrusions, 294–295
Irrelevant speech, 322–327, 412, 413, 415, 416, 417
Item information, 427

Judgement of frequency, 428–429
Judgement of primacy, 456, 457, 459
Judgement of recency, 456, 457, 459

Language comprehension/development, 364–373, 378–379, 383
    foreign language learning, 383–388
    and long-term knowledge, 383–384
Language comprehension scales, 368
Learning and memory, 339–346
Lexical effects, 298, 335, 336, 337, 353, 378, 450
List length effect, 354, 357
Listening span, 365, 367
Long-term memory
    and central executive, 337
    and language learning, 383–384
    and serial recall, 334–335, 337, 347–352
Long-term *versus* short-term store, evidence for 419–426

Masking, 294
Memory load, 313
Memory models, *see* Models
Memory span, 276–277, 282, 359–363, 451
    and central executive, 359, 360, 363, 369
    development, 353–358, 374–377
    and learning, 344–346
    and material type, 278–280
Mental rotation, 312–313
Modality of presentation, 285, 286, 288, 289, 329
Models, 277, 285–286, 329, 350–351, 429, 434–435, 464
    BSB (brain-state-in-a-box) model, 437–445
    connectionist, 400, 403–404, 437–445
    Feature Model, 285, 292, 298, 332, 350, 403, 410–418
    O-OER, 323–324
    OSCAR, 390–400, 403, 435, 437, 444
    oscillator-coding of relative position, 406–407, 408
    perturbation, 411
    Potter's two-stage, 298
    power function forgetting curves, 460–464
    Primacy Model, 403, 436, 445
    Start-End Model, 404, 406, 436, 437
    TODAM, 351, 430, 435, 444
    TODAM2, 430–431, 432–433, 435
Motor span, 360–361, 362
Multiple memory systems, 429

Noise, 322–327, 328–333

O-OER (Object-Oriented Episodic Record) model, 323–324
OSCAR (Oscillator-based Associative Recall), 390–400, 403, 435, 437, 444
Oscillator-coding of relative position model, 406–407, 408
Output delays, 276–277, 280, 282–283

Paced Visual Serial Addition test (PVSAT), 318, 319–320
Pauses during recall, 356–357, 376, 390
Peabody Picture Vocabulary Test, 342
Perturbation, 411–412, 415, 417
Phonological codes, 286, 289, 290–292, 293–294, 298, 306
Phonological loop, 293–294, 334, 335, 337, 353, 374, 383
Phonological memory
    capacity estimation, 366, 378–382, 384
    and central executive, 369
    in children, 365
    foreign language learning, 383–388
    and language comprehension, 365, 371
    and visuospatial memory, 369
    and vocabulary knowledge, 365, 380, 382, 386
Phonological similarity, 294–295, 296, 297–298, 301–307, 413, 450
Picture naming, 295–298
Position coding, 403–409, *see also* Serial position
Power function forgetting curves, 460–464
Pre-frontal cortex, 400
Presentation modality, 285, 286, 288, 289, 329
Presentation rate, 280, 293–300, 407–408
Primacy, judgement of, 456, 457, 459
Primacy effects, 296, 297, 329
Primacy Model, 403, 436, 445
Proactive interference, 285, 286, 288, 289–290, 291–292
Probability of recall, 451–452
Protrusion errors, 404, 405

Rapid serial visual presentation, 293–300
Reading span, 364–365, 371
Recall scoring, 301, 347–348
Recency, judgement of, 456, 457, 459
Recency effects, 296, 297, 329, 407, 436–437, 420
Redintegration, 434–446, 447–450, 452
Rehearsal, 293, 294, 298, 374, 389–390
    by children, 389–390
    prevention and trace decay, 285
Repetition blindness, 294
Response suppression, 436
Retroactive interference, 280, 282, 283, 285, 292
Rhyme, 301, 302, 304, 305, 306, 345

SART (sustained attention to response task), 366, 368
Segmentation, 324–325
Semantic representations, 334–338, 348–350
Sentence completion, 365, 367
Serial position, 280–282, 283, 296, 297, 359–360, 448–449
    coding, 403–409
Serial recall errors, 404–406

interpositions, 404
intrusions, 294–295
protrusions, 404, 405
Serial recall performance scoring, 301, 347–348
Serial recognition, 379, 380–382
Short-term *versus* long-term store, evidence for, 419–426
Signal detection theory, 454–459
Silent intervals during recall, 356–357, 376, 390
Sound localization, 317–321
   articulatory suppression during, 318, 319
   and central executive, 321
   serial recall during, 318, 319, 320
Span, *see* Memory span
Spatial memory, 374–377
   assessment, 341, 360, 367
   and phonological memory, 369
   span, 360, 362
Speech memory and noise, 328–333
Start-End Model, 404, 406, 436, 437
Storage mechanisms, distinctiveness of 419–426
Streaming, 325
Strength of items, 277–278, 454–459
Subvocal rehearsal, *see* Rehearsal
Suppression, 436
Sustained attention to response task (SART), 366, 368
Synthetic speech, 328

Temporal coding of position, 407–408
Temporal delays and forgetting, 276–277, 280, 282–283
Theory of Distributed Associative Memory, *see* TODAM; TODAM2
Time estimation, 308–316
   and attention, 308, 314, 315
TODAM, 351, 430, 435, 444
TODAM2, 430–431, 432–433, 435
Trace decay, 292, 301, 447–450, 452
   and attention, 285
   rehearsal prevention, 285
Transcortical sensory aphasia, 345–346

Verbal fluency, 367–368, 369, 371, 372–373
Very short-term conceptual memory, 293
Visual masking, 294
Visual pattern span, 367
Visual search, 310
Visuospatial memory, 374–377
   assessment, 341, 360, 367
   and phonological memory, 369
   span, 360, 362
Visuospatial sketchpad, 374
Vocabulary comprehension, 365, 370, 371, 380, 382, 386
   tests, 368, 385

Word class, 335, 336
Word frequency, 350, 448–449
Word length, 294, 295, 298, 412, 413, 415, 417, 449–450
Word span and learning, 344–345